Q&A
Family Law

Routledge Questions & Answers Series

Each Routledge Q&A contains questions on topics commonly found on exam papers, with comprehensive suggested answers. The titles are written by lecturers who are also examiners, so the student gains an important insight into exactly what examiners are looking for in an answer. This makes them excellent revision and practice guides.

Titles in the series:
Q&A Company Law
Q&A Commercial Law
Q&A Contract Law
Q&A Criminal Law
Q&A Employment Law
Q&A English Legal System
Q&A Equity and Trusts
Q&A European Union Law
Q&A Evidence
Q&A Family Law
Q&A Intellectual Property Law
Q&A Jurisprudence
Q&A Land Law
Q&A Medical Law
Q&A Public Law
Q&A Torts

For a full listing, visit www.routledge.com/cw/revision

Q&A
Family Law

Rachael Stretch

Routledge
Taylor & Francis Group
LONDON AND NEW YORK

Eighth edition published 2016
by Routledge
2 Park Square, Milton Park, Abingdon, Oxon OX14 4RN

and by Routledge
711 Third Avenue, New York, NY 10017

Routledge is an imprint of the Taylor & Francis Group, an informa business

© 2016 Rachael Stretch

The right of Rachael Stretch to be identified as author of this work has been asserted by her in accordance with sections 77 and 78 of the Copyright, Designs and Patents Act 1988.

All rights reserved. No part of this book may be reprinted or reproduced or utilised in any form or by any electronic, mechanical, or other means, now known or hereafter invented, including photocopying and recording, or in any information storage or retrieval system, without permission in writing from the publishers.

Trademark notice: Product or corporate names may be trademarks or registered trademarks, and are used only for identification and explanation without intent to infringe.

First edition published by Cavendish 1994
Seventh edition published by Routledge 2013

British Library Cataloguing in Publication Data
A catalogue record for this book is available from the British Library

Library of Congress Cataloging-in-Publication Data
Stretch, Rachael, author.
Family law / Rachael Stretch. – Eight edition.
  pages cm. – (Questions & answers)
  1. Domestic relations–England–Examinations, questions, etc. 2. Domestic relations–Wales–Examinations, questions, etc. I. Title.
  KD750.S77 2016
  346.4201'5076–dc23   2015020722

ISBN: 978-1-138-82958-9 (pbk)
ISBN: 978-1-315-73766-9 (ebk)

Typeset in TheSans
by Wearset Ltd, Boldon, Tyne and Wear
Printed in Great Britain by
Ashford Colour Press Ltd, Gosport, Hants

Contents

Table of Cases vii
Table of Legislation xiii
Guide to the Companion Website xix

Introduction 1

1 Nullity of Marriage 3
2 Divorce and Dissolution of Civil Partnerships 19
3 Financial Provision for Adult Partners 41
4 Maintenance for Children 67
5 Property Disputes 81
6 Domestic Violence and Occupation of the Home 99
7 Who is a Parent? Parental Responsibility and the Principles of the Children Act 1989 121
8 Private Law Disputes Relating to Children 127
9 Children and the Local Authority 151
10 Adoption 171

Index **195**

Table of Cases

A and B (Prohibited Steps Order at Dispute Resolution Appointment), Re [2015] EWFC B16   **127**
AD (A Minor), Re [1993] Fam Law 405   **130**
Adams v Adams [1984] FLR 768   **137, 139, 146, 161**
Ainsbury v Millington [1987] 1 WLR 379   **112**
Allington v Allington [1985] FLR 586   **139–140**
Archer v Archer [1999] 2 FCR 158   **27**
Asaad v Kurter [2013] EWHC 3852 (Fam)   **3**
Ashley v Blackman [1988] 3 WLR 222   **61**
Ash v Ash [1972] 2 WLR 347   **22, 25, 29, 30**
Attar v Attar (No 2) [1985] FLR 653   **57**
A v A (A Minor: Financial Provision) [1994] 1 FLR 657   **68, 73**
A v A (Minors) (Shared Residence Order) [1994] 1 FLR 669   **127**
A v A (Shared Residence) [2004] EWHC 142   **142**

B (A Child), Re [2009] EWCA Civ 545   **127, 147, 149**
B (A Child), Re [2012] EWCA Civ 737   **141**
B (A Minor) (Access), Re [1984] FLR 648   **146**
B (A Minor) (Access), Re [1992] 1 FLR 140   **136, 137**
B (Minors) (Sexual Abuse: Standard of Proof), Re [2008] UKHL 35   **152, 156, 191**
Banik v Banik [1973] 1 WLR 860   **31**
Barnes v Barnes [1972] 3 All ER 45   **61, 70, 76**

Barrett v Barrett [1988] 2 FLR 516   **76**
Bateman v Bateman [1979] 2 WLR 377   **71**
Bellinger v Bellinger [2003] UKHL 21; [2003] 2 AC 467   **16**
Bennett v Bennett [1969] 1 WLR 430   **34**
Berry v Berry [1986] 2 All ER 948   **76**
Besterman (Decd), Re [1984] 2 All ER 656   **93**
BN v MA [2013] EWHC 4250 (Fam)   **54, 56**
Borough of Poole v W and Another [2014] EWHC 1777 (Fam)   **172, 192**
Brixey v Lynas HL (1996) SLT 908, 1996 SC (HL) 1   **127**
Bryant v Bryant [1976] 120 Sol J 165   **62**
B-T v B-T [1990] FLR 654   **139**
Bullock v Bullock [1960] 2 All ER 307   **35**
Burns v Burns [1984] Ch 317   **81, 94, 97**
B v B (Occupation Order) [1999] 1 FLR 715   **99, 105**
B v S (Financial Remedy Matrimonial Property Regime) [2012] EWHC 235   **56**

C (A Minor) (Leave to Seek s 8 order), Re [1994] 1 FLR 26   **130**
C (Family Placement), Re [2009] EWCA Civ 72   **171**
C (Residence: Child's Application for Leave), Re [1995] 1 FLR 927   **131**
Calderbank v Calderbank [1975] 2 All ER 333   **43, 62**
Carson v Carson [1981] 1 All ER 478   **65**
CDM v CM, LM, DM (Children), Re [2003] 2 FLR 636   **127**

Table of Cases

Chapman v Chapman [1969] 3 A ER 476 **88**
Charman v Charman [2007] EWCA Civ 503 **41, 51, 53, 59**
Cleary v Cleary [1974] 1 WLR 73 **19, 21, 35**
Clutton v Clutton [1991] 1 All ER 340 **47, 61, 76**
Cooke v Head [1972] 1 WLR 518 **85**
Corbett v Corbett (otherwise Ashley) [1971] P 83 **3, 14, 15, 16, 17**
Cossey v UK (1990) 30 EHRR 622 **15, 16**
Cowan v Cowan [2001] EWCA Civ 679 **49, 50, 58**
Cowcher v Cowcher [1972] 1 WLR 425 **88**
Cox v Jones [2004] All ER (D) 281 **81**
Crossley v Crossley [2005] EWCA Civ 1581 **81**
Crowther v Crowther [1951] AC 723 **26**
CT, Re [1993] 2 FLR 2916 **133**
C v C (A Minor) [1991] 1 FLR 223 **145**
C v C (Non-Molestation Order) [1998] 1 FCR 11 **104**
C v C [1988] 2 FLR 2916 **132**

D (A Child), Re [2014] EWCA Civ 315 **121**
Daubney v Daubney [1976] 2 WLR 959 **61**
Dawson v Wearmouth [1997] 2 FLR 629 **128, 140, 150**
De Renville v De Renville [1948] 1 All ER 56 **7**
DL and ML v Newham LBC and Secretary of State for Education [2011] EWHC 1127 (Fam) **171**
Dolan v Corby [2011] EWCA Civ 1664 **110**
Dorrell v Dorell [1972] 3 All ER 343 **27**
Duxbury v Duxbury [1992] Fam 62 **62, 77**
D v A [1845] Rob Eccl 279 **5, 7, 10, 33**
D v D (Shared Residence Order) [2001] 1 FLR 495 **127**
D v D [1982] 12 Fam Law 101 **7**

El Gamal v Al Maktoum [2011] EWHC B27 (Fam) **3**
E-R (A Child), Re [2015] EWCA Civ 405 **127, 149**

Eves v Eves [1975] 3 All ER 768 **81, 85, 92, 94, 96**

Ferguson and Others v UK (2011) Application 8254/11 **3, 4**
Fisher v Fisher [1989] 1 FLR 423 **66**
Fowler v Barron [2008] EWCA Civ 377 **81**
Freeman v Swatridge [1984] FLR 762 **76**
Fuller v Fuller [1973] 1 WLR 730 **22**
F v F [2003] 1 FLR 847 127

G (Children) (Residence: Same-Sex Partner), Re [2006] 1 WLR 2305 **127, 146, 147, 148, 149**
Gallagher v Gallagher [1965] 2 All ER 967 **26**
Geary v Rankine [2012] EWCA Civ 555 **81, 94**
Gillick v West Norfolk and Wisbech Area Health Authority [1986] AC 112 **121, 123, 125, 129, 130, 133**
Gissing v Gissing [1971] AC 886 **86, 88, 89, 92**
Goodman v Gallant [1986] 1 All ER 311 **84, 88, 92**
Goodwin v UK 28957/95 [2002] 2 FLR 577 **15, 16**
Graham-York v York and Ors [2015] EWCA Civ 72 (10 February 2015) **81**
Grant v Edwards [1986] 3 WLR 114 **81, 94, 96**
Greer v Greer [1974] 4 Fam Law 187 **145**
Grigson v Grigson [1974] 1 All ER 478 **32**
Grubb v Grubb [2012] EWCA Civ 398 **99**
G v G (Occupation Order: Conduct) [2000] 2 FLR 36 **99**

H (A Minor), Re [1980] *The Times*, 20 July **139**
H (A Minor), Re [1990] 2 FLR 439 **145**
H (Minors) (Access), Re [1992] 1 FLR 148 **135, 140**
H (Minors) (Sexual Abuse: Standard of Proof), Re [1996] AC 563 **152**
H, Re [1993] 1 FLR 440 **124**
Hall v Hall [1960] 1 All ER 91 **26**
Hardy v Hardy [1981] 2 FLR 321 **61**

Harman v Glencross [1986] 1 All ER 545 **61**
Harrington v Gill (1983) 4 FLR 265 (CA) **94**
Hazell v Hazell [1972] 1 WLR 301 **92**
Hepburn v Hepburn [1989] 1 FLR 373 **66**
Herbert v Herbert [1819] 2 Hag Con 263 **9**
Hirani v Hirani [1982] 4 FLR 232 **3, 12, 13**
Horton v Horton [1947] 2 All ER 871 **7, 10, 33**
Hudson v Leigh [2009] EWHC 1306 (Fam) **3**
Humberside County Council v B [1993] 1 FLR 257 **110, 152**
Hussain v Hussain [1982] All ER 369 **6**
H v H (Financial Relief: Attempted Murder As Conduct) [2006] 1 FLR 990 **60**
H v H [1989] 1 FLR 212 **146**
Hyde v Hyde [1866] LRI P&D 130 **9, 54**
Hyman v Hyman [1929] AC 601 **54, 55**

J (a child: adopted child: contact), Re [2010] EWCA Civ 581 **172**
J (Care Proceedings: Past Possible Perpetrators in a New Family Unit), Re [2013] UKSC 9 **152**
J(HD) v J(AM) [1980] 1 All ER 156 **71**
JL v SL (No 2) [2014] EWHC 360 (Fam) **41**
Jones v Jones [1975] 2 All ER 12; [1975] 2 WLR 606 **61, 62, 71**
Jones v Kernott [2011] UKSC 53 **81, 89**
Jones v Maynard [1951] Ch 572 **82, 84**
J v C [1970] AC 668 **132**

K (Shared Residence Order), Re [2008] EWCA Civ s 26 **127**
K, Re [1988] 1 All ER 214 **146**
Katz v Katz [1972] 1 WLR 955 **19, 25, 30**
Kehoe v UK (ECtHR) (2009) 48 EHRR 2 **68**
Kilner v Kilner [1939] 3 All ER 957 **88**
Kingsnorth Finance Co Ltd v Tizard [1986] AC 54 **89**

L (A Child) (Contact: domestic violence), Re [2000] Fam 260 **127**

L (Children), Re [2006] EWCA Civ 1282 **152**
Lambert v Lambert [2002] EWCA Civ 1685 **41, 50, 53, 57, 58**
Lancashire County Council v B (A Child) (Care Orders: Significant Harm) [2000] 2 AC 147 **152, 168, 169**
Lang v Lang [1953] *The Times*, 7 July **26**
Lee v Lee [1984] FLR 243 **76**
Livingston-Stallard v Livingston-Stallard [1974] 3 WLR 302 **19, 22, 25, 30**
Lloyds Bank v Rosset [1991] 1 AC 107 **81, 85, 86, 89, 92, 94, 99**
London Borough of Tower Hamlets v M and Others [2015] EWHC 869 (Fam) **128**
Luckwell v Limata [2014] EWHC 502 (Fam) **41, 54, 59**
L v L [2011] EWHC 2207 (Fam) **99**
Lyons v Lyons [2010] EWCA Civ 177 **58**

M (a minor) (Care Order: Threshold Conditions), Re [1994] 2 AC 424, HL **152**
M (child's upbringing), Re [1996] 2 FCR 473 **127**
M (Medical Treatment: Consent), Re [1999] 2 FLR 1097 **123, 125, 133**
MA (Care: Threshold), Re [2009] EWCA Civ 853 **152**
Macey v Macey [1981] 11 Fam Law 248 **65**
MacLeod v MacLeod [2008] UKPC 64 **54, 59**
Marsh v Marsh [1977] 8 Fam Law 103 **139, 145**
Mathias v Mathias [1972] 3 All ER 136 **27, 31**
May v May [1986] 1 FLR 325 **132**
McFarlane v McFarlane [2006] UKHL 24 **41, 53**
McHardy & Sons v Warren [1994] *The Times*, 8 April **88**
Mehta v Mehta [1945] 2 All ER 690 **34**
Mesher v Mesher [1980] 1 All ER 126 **63**
MF v LB of Brent and Ors [2013] EWHC 1838 (Fam) **172**

Table of Cases

Midland Bank v Cooke [1995] 2 FLR 915; [1995] 4 All ER 562 **86, 89, 93**
Midland Bank v Dobson [1986] 1 FLR 171 **89**
Miller v Miller [2006] UKHL 24 **41, 51, 52, 53, 56, 57, 58**
Mills v McCartney [2008] EWHC 401 **52, 53, 59**
M-M (A Child), Re [2014] EWCA Civ 276 **68, 73**
Morgan v Morgan (1973) 117 SJ 223 **25**
Morgan v Morgan [1959] P 92 **10**
Morris v Morris [1985] FLR 1176 **47**
Mortgage Corp v Shaire [2000] 1 FLR 973; [2001] Ch 743 **90**
Mouncer v Mouncer [1972] 1 All ER 289 **19, 22, 29, 31**

N (A Child) (Adoption Order), Re [2014] EWFC 1491 **172**
Napier v Napier [1915] P 184 **7**
An NHS Trust v A B C and A Local Authority [2014] EWHC 1445 **121**
Nicolson (Decd), Re [1974] 2 All ER 386 **92–93**
N v F [2011] EWHC 586 (Fam) **41**

O (A Minor) (Care Order: Education: Procedure), Re [1992] 2 FLR 7 **155**
O (Care or Supervision Order), Re [1996] 2 FLR 755 **152**
O (Contact: Imposition of Conditions), Re [1995] 2 FLR 124 **127, 141**
O and N (Children) (Non-Accidental Injury), Re [2003] All ER (D) 64; [2003] UKHL 18 **152, 169**
O'Neil v O'Neil [1975] 3 All ER 289; [1972] Fam 135 **19**
Oxley v Hiscock [2004] EWCA Civ 546 **81**

P (A Child), Re [2005] EWCA Civ 1639 **127**
P (A Child), Re [2015] EWCA Civ 170 **127**
P (A Minor) (Education: Child's Wishes), Re [1992] 1 FLR 145 **131**
P (Contact: Discretion), Re [1998] 2 FLR 696 **127**
P (Placement Orders: Parental Consent), Re [2008] EWCA Civ 535 **172**
Parghi v Parghi [1973] 11 Sol J 582 **23, 31**
Parker v Parker [1972] 1 All ER 410 **23, 28, 31**
Parlour v Parlour [2004] EWCA 672 **47, 76**
Payne v Payne [2001] EWCA Civ 1 **128**
Peacock v Peacock [1991] 1 FLR 324 **65**
Perry v Perry [1963] 3 All ER 766 **26**
Pettit v Pettit [1962] 3 WLR 919; [1962] 3 All ER 37 **88, 89, 92**
Potter v Potter [1982] 3 All ER 321 **10**
Preston v Preston [1982] 1 All ER 41 **62, 76**
Pulford v Pulford [1923] P 18 **25**
Puttick v Attorney General [1980] Fam 1 **32, 34**

Q, Re (2011) EWCA Civ 1610 **178, 185**

R (Adoption: Contact), Re [2005] EWCA Civ 1128 **172**
R (child's upbringing), Re [1996] EWCA Civ 1320 **147**
R (Kehoe) v Secretary of State for Work and Pensions [2005] UKHL 48 **68**
R (on the application of G) (FC) v Southwark London Borough Council [2009] UKHL 26, [2009] All ER (D) 178 (May) **151**
Radmacher v Granatino [2009] EWCA Civ 649 **41, 52, 54, 55–56, 57, 59**
Reiterbund v Reiterbund [1975] 1 All ER 280 **27**
Richards v Richards [1972] 3 All ER 695 **29, 99, 100**
Rukat v Rukat [1975] Fam 63 **19, 49, 50**

S (Adoption Order or Special Guardianship Order), Re [2007] 1 FLR **181**
S (A Minor) (Parental Responsibility), Re [1995] 2FLR 648 **123**
S (Contact Dispute: Committal) [2005] 1 FLR 812 **141, 142**
S (Infants), Re [1967] 1 All ER 202 **132, 135, 139**

S and J [2004], Re [2004] EWCA Civ 18   **171**
S and J [2014], Re [2014] EWFC 4   **171**
SA v PA (Pre-marital agreement: Compensation) [2014] EWHC 392   **41**
Santos v Santos [1972] 2 All ER 246   **22, 27, 31**
S-B (Children), Re [2009] EWCA Civ 1048   **152**
Scott v Scott [1978] 5 All ER 65   **44, 71**
Scott v Scott [1986] 1 FLR 591   **135, 161**
Seaton v Seaton [1986] 2 FLR 398   **48**
Sekhon v Alissa [1989] 2 FLR 94   **88**
Sheffield City Council v E [2004] EWHC 2808 (Pam)   **32, 34**
Singh v Singh [1971] 2 All ER 828   **3, 12, 13**
Smith v Smith [1975] 2 All ER 19   **62**
Sottomayor v De Barros (No 1) (1877) 2 PD 81   **5, 9**
Stack v Dowden [2007] 2 AC 432   **81, 89**
Stephenson v Stephenson [1985] FLR 1140   **139, 146**
Stewart v Stewart (1973) 3 Fam Law 107   **132, 135, 139, 140, 145**
Stockford v Stockford [1982] 3 FLR 5874   **62, 70**
Suter v Suter and Jones [1987] Fam 111   **47, 61, 76**
S v AG (Financial Remedy: Lottery Prize) [2011] EWHC 2637 (Fam)   **41**
S v S [1962] All ER 816   **7**
S v S [1972] AC 24   **74**

T (A Minor)(Parental Responsibility: Contact), Re [1993] 2 FLR 450   **121**
Taczarnowski v Taczarnowski [1957] 2 All ER 563   **9**
Thomas v Fuller Brown [1988] 1 FLR 237   **94, 96**
Thurlow v Thurlow [1975] 2 All ER 979   **22, 25**
T v S (Financial Provision for Children) [1994] 2 FLR 883   **68, 73**

V v V (Contact: Implacable Hostility) [2004] 2 FLR 851   **142**
V v V [2011] EWHC 3230 (Fam)   **41, 54**

W (A Minor) [1983] 4 FLR 492162   **139, 145**
W (a minor) (Medical treatment: Court's jurisdiction), Re [1993] Fam 64   **123, 125**
W (Children), Re [2012] EWCA Civ 999   **127**
Wachtel v Wachtel [1973] 1 All ER 829   **62, 77**
Wagstaff v Wagstaff [1992] 1 All ER 275   **61**
Webster v Norfolk County Council and the Children (By their Children's Guardian) [2009] EWCA Civ 59   **172**
Whicker v Hume (1858) 10 HLC 124 1858   **5**
White v White [2000] UKHL 54   **41, 49, 50, 53, 57, 58, 62, 80**
Whiting v Whiting [1988] 1 WLR 565   **66**
Wilkinson v Kitzinger [2006] EWHC 2022 (Fam)   **4**
Williams & Glyn's Bank v Boland [1981] AC 487   **89**
Wolfenden v Wolfenden [1945] 2 All ER 539   **9**
W v A (1981) [1981] 1 All ER 100   **140**
W v W [1967] 1 WLR 65   **33**
W v W and C [1968] 1 WLR 1310   **145**
Wyatt v Vince [2015] UKSC 14   **41**

Young v Young [2013] EWHC 3637 (Fam)   **41**

Z-O'C (Children), Re [2014] EWCA Civ 1808   **152**
Z v Z (No 2) [2011] EWHC 2878   **41, 54, 56**

Table of Legislation

■ Statutes

Adoption Act 1976   175, 184
Adoption and Children Act 1989
   s 1(2)   173
Adoption and Children Act 2002   124
   s 1(1)   175, 185
   s 1(2)   171, 174, 176, 177, 181, 183, 184, 187, 190, 191, 192
   s 1(4)   171, 173, 174, 176, 177, 183, 184, 187, 190, 192
   s 1(4)(b)   174, 177, 185, 187, 188
   s 1(4)(c)   174, 187
   s 1(4)(e)   174, 177, 185, 192
   s 1(4)(f)   171, 177, 188
   s 1(5)   171
   s 1(6)   173, 175, 176, 183, 184, 190, 192
   s 19   171, 182, 183, 190, 191
   s 21   171, 182, 183, 190, 191
   s 21(2)   183
   s 21(2)(a)   183, 190, 191
   s 21(2)(b)   182, 183–184, 190
   s 21(2)(c)   183, 190, 191
   s 24   171
   s 25   171, 192
   s 25(2)   184
   s 25(3)   184
   s 26   171
   s 30   171, 192
   s 30(2)   184
   s 42   171, 174, 188
   s 42(2)   184
   s 42(2)(a)   190, 192
   s 42(2)(b)   182
   s 42(3)   173
   s 42(4)   186, 188
   s 42(5)   176, 177
   s 44   171, 173, 174, 176, 177, 186, 187
   s 46   185, 188
   s 46(1)   172, 180
   s 46(2)(a)   174
   s 47(2)   173, 178, 183, 186, 189, 190, 192
   s 47(9)   171, 173, 174, 177, 182, 186, 187, 190
   s 50   171, 177, 182, 184, 186, 187, 191
   s 51   171, 174, 191
   s 51(2)   173
   s 51A   172, 173, 188
   s 51A(3)(a)   187, 188
   s 51B   172
   s 52   172, 173, 175, 176, 185, 186, 189, 190, 191, 192
   s 52(1)   172
   s 114(4)   171
   s 144(3)   187
   s 144(4)(b)   186
Child Maintenance and Other Payments Act 2008   67, 77, 78, 79
   ss 20–30   68
Child Support Act 1991   67, 69, 72, 74, 75
Child Support Act 1995   67, 72
Children Act 1989   68, 103, 106, 112
   Part III   151
   Part IV   155
   s 1   136, 165
   s 1(1)   121, 122, 123, 124, 128, 129, 131, 134, 135, 136, 137, 138, 139, 140, 141, 142, 144, 145, 147, 148, 150, 151, 154, 155, 156, 158, 159, 161, 163, 167, 168, 179, 189
   s 1(2)   122, 128, 129, 131, 134, 135, 136, 137, 138, 139, 144, 145, 147, 154, 158, 163, 165, 167
   s 1(2A)   128, 134, 138, 140, 141

s 1(2B)   128, 136
s 1(3)   122, 128, 129, 131, 134, 135, 136, 137, 138, 139, 140, 144, 145, 147, 148, 154, 158, 159, 161, 163, 167, 168, 171
s 1(3)(a)   137
s 1(3)(b)   139, 149, 155, 156, 168
s 1(3)(c)   139, 149, 168
s 1(3)(e)   140, 149, 155, 156, 168
s 1(3)(f)   140, 149, 155, 168
s 1(4)   128, 179
s 1(5)   122, 128, 129, 131, 134, 135, 136, 137, 138, 144, 147, 148, 151, 154, 155, 156, 158, 162, 163, 165, 167, 179
s 2   162
s 2(1)   121, 130, 138, 140, 173, 176
s 2(2)   121, 123, 124, 125, 148, 149, 158, 163, 178, 183, 185, 186, 189, 190, 191, 192
s 2(5)   172
s 2(7)   172
s 3(1)   123, 125, 129–130, 138, 163, 180
s 3(5)   121
s 4   124
s 4(1)(a)   121, 124, 189
s 4(1)(b)   121, 124, 189
s 4(1)(c)   121, 123, 124, 186, 189
s 4A   122
s 4A(1)(a)   122
s 4A(1)(b)   122
s 8   122, 127, 128, 129, 130, 131, 133, 135, 136, 139, 140, 142, 144, 145, 148, 159, 161, 162, 173, 175, 176, 178, 181, 185, 187, 188, 190, 192
s 10   131
s 10(4)   128, 136, 139, 140, 144, 161, 175, 178, 185, 188
s 10(4)(a)   134, 137, 138, 144, 148, 150
s 10(5)   128, 136, 148, 161
s 10(5)(b)   147, 179
s 10(8)   128, 129, 130
s 10(9)   128, 134, 136, 148, 150, 158, 161
s 11   131, 135, 139, 141, 145
s 11(7)   128
s 11A   141, 143
ss 11A–11P   127
s 11H   143
s 11I   143
s 11J   141

s 11O   143
s 12   122, 127, 148, 149, 172, 175, 178, 185, 187, 188, 192
s 13(1)(a)   121, 128, 148, 149, 172
s 13(1)(b)   121, 128, 140, 172
s 14A(2)(a)   179
s 14A(5)   172
s 14A(5)(c)   179
s 14A(5)(e)   179
s 14C   172, 173, 175, 176, 178, 180, 185, 187, 188, 190, 192
s 14C(1)(a)   172
s 14C(1)(b)   172, 180
s 14C(3)(a)–(b)   172, 180
s 14C(4)   180
s 14C(20(b))   180
s 16   128
s 16(4A)   141
s 17   158
s 17(1)   158, 164
s 17(10)   151, 164
s 17(10)(a)   155, 162
s 17(11)   164
s 20   151, 158, 162, 164, 182, 185, 189
s 20(6)   164
s 20(8)   164
s 22   159
s 22(3)   165
s 22(4)   159
s 22(5)   165
s 31   152, 154, 155, 156, 157, 159, 160, 163, 166, 167, 169
s 31(2)   182, 184, 191
s 31(9)   152, 155, 156, 159, 167, 191
s 33   152, 154, 155, 157, 163, 169
s 33(1)   153
s 33(3)   152, 155, 156, 167
s 33(3)(a)   153
s 33(a)   122
s 34   152
s 34(6)   152
s 35   152, 154, 155, 163, 169
s 35(1)(b)   153
s 37   151
s 38   152, 156
s 38A   152
s 39(1)   161
s 43   154, 156, 162, 165

s 43(1)   151
s 43(5)(b)   153
s 43(7)   151
s 43(9)   165
s 44   154, 160, 162, 165
s 44(1)(a)   151, 160
s 44(1)(b)   151, 156
s 44(4)   151
s 44(4)(b)   156, 160
s 44(4)(c)   122, 151, 153, 156, 160
s 44A   151, 156
s 45(1)   153, 160
s 45(6)   165
s 45(8)   160, 166
s 45(11)   160, 166
s 46   151
s 46(1)   180
s 46(1)(a)   153
s 46(6)   153
s 47   151, 154, 155, 156, 164
Sch 1   73, 95, 97
Sch 2   78
Children and Adoption Act 2006   143
  s 3   127
  s 4   127
Children and Families Act 2014
  s 3   171
  s 9   172
  s 11   128, 134, 136, 138, 140, 141, 144
  s 12   127, 135, 148, 159
  s 18   19, 36, 40
Civil Partnership Act 2004   3, 4
  s 3   12
  s 41   12
  s 44   12
  s 44(1)   14
  s 44(5)   12, 14, 19
  s 44(5)(a)   12, 14
  s 49   3, 12
  s 50   3
  s 50(1)(a)   12, 13
  s 72   41
Cohabitation Bill 2008   82, 97
Cohabitation Rights Bill 2014   82, 97
Divorce Reform Act 1969   37
Domestic Proceedings and Magistrates' Court Act 1978   41, 68, 73, 78, 101
  s 1   43, 70

s 1(1)   69
s 2   42, 43, 44, 69, 70, 71, 72
s 3   42, 45, 70, 71
s 3(1)   43, 70
s 3(2)(a)   44
s 3(2)(b)   44
s 3(2)(e)   44
s 3(2)(f)   44
s 3(2)(g)   44
s 6   43, 45, 69–70, 71, 72
s 6(5)   45
s 7   43, 44, 70, 71, 72
s 7(3)(2)   71
s 7(4)   44, 71
s 25(1)   72
s 25(2)   72
s 25(3)   72
Domestic Violence and Matrimonial Proceedings Act 1976   101
Domestic Violence Crime and Victims Act 2004   103, 107
Education Act 1944   130
Equality Act 2010   81
Family Law Act 1996   38, 39, 40
  Part II   19, 20, 36
  Part IV   99, 108, 118
  s 30   99, 101, 108, 109, 116, 117
  s 30(2)   105, 109, 116
  s 30(3)   111
  s 30(7)   109
  s 30(9)   109
  s 33   99, 100, 105, 109, 112, 117
  s 33(1)   105, 108, 112
  s 33(3)   99, 105
  s 33(6)   99, 100, 101, 105, 108, 110, 113, 117, 118
  s 33(6)(a)   117
  s 33(6)(d)   117
  s 33(7)   99, 101, 105, 108, 110, 113, 117, 118
  s 33(10)   119
  s 35   99–100, 106, 107
  s 35(6)   100
  s 35(10)   100
  s 36   100, 106, 107, 112, 113
  s 36(6)   106, 109
  s 37   100, 107
  s 38   107

s 40   100, 108
s 40(1)   111, 119
s 40(2)   111, 119
s 41   107
s 42   111, 113, 115
s 42(1)   108
s 42(1)(a)   114
s 42(2)   111
s 42(5)   99, 101, 104, 108, 111, 114, 115
s 42(7)   104, 111
s 42A   99, 115
s 45   100, 112, 115
s 45(2)   114
s 46   104, 111
s 46(2)   104, 111
s 47   104, 112
s 60   104
s 62   99, 101, 102, 105, 108, 115
s 62(2)   103, 110, 111, 115
s 62(3)   111, 114, 118
s 62(3)(f)   114, 115
s 63   110, 117, 118
s 63(1)   99
Family Law Reform Act 1969
   s 20(1)   74
   s 25   121
   s 26   74
Gender Recognition Act 2004   3, 4, 15, 16, 17
Human Fertilisation and Embryology Act 2008
   s 4ZA   122
   s 33(1)   121
   s 35   121
   s 42(1)   121
   s 54(2)   122
Human Rights Act 1998   90
Inheritance (Provision for Family and Dependants) Act 1975   47–48, 91
   s 1(2)(a)   93
   s 3(1)–(2)   94
Land Registration Act 1925
   s 70   82, 87, 89
   s 70(1)(g)   89, 91, 93
Law of Property Act 1925
   s 52   91, 95, 114
   s 52(1)   81, 87
   s 53(1)(b)   81, 83, 87, 88, 91, 92

s 53(2)(b)   95, 114
Law of Property (Miscellaneous Provisions) Act 1989
   s 2   88, 92
Law Reform (Miscellaneous Provisions) Act 1970
   s 3   82, 83
Maintenance Enforcement Act 1991
   s 2   45
Marriage Act 1949
   Sch 1   7
Marriage (Prohibited Degrees) Act 1986   5, 7
Marriage (Same Sex Couples) Act 2013   4
   s 1(1)   3
Matrimonial and Family Proceedings Act 1984   46
Matrimonial Causes Act 1973   40, 46, 82, 92
   s 1   15
   s 1(1)   19, 20, 21, 24, 29, 36, 50, 53
   s 1(2)   19, 20, 21, 24, 25, 29, 33, 34, 36, 50
   s 1(2)(a)   19, 21, 25, 29, 34, 36, 53
   s 1(2)(b)   21, 25, 29, 30, 35, 36, 70
   s 1(2)(c)   19, 30–31
   s 1(2)(d)   19, 21, 22, 23, 26, 27, 28, 29, 31, 36, 37
   s 1(2)(e)   19, 21, 22, 23, 24, 26, 27, 28, 29, 31, 36, 37
   s 2   25
   s 2(3)   22
   s 2(6)   22, 27
   s 3(1)   19, 20, 21, 24, 25, 29
   s 5   19, 21, 23, 24, 27, 28, 29, 31, 49, 50, 51
   s 5(1)   23
   s 5(2)   23, 31
   s 5(3)   27, 31
   s 10   27, 28, 31
   s 10(2)   31
   s 10(3)   32
   s 11   3, 5, 9, 10, 15, 33
   s 11(a)(iii)   8
   s 11(b)   5, 6, 8, 10
   s 11(c)   15
   s 11(d)   5, 6, 10

s 12   3, 5, 7, 10, 17, 32, 33
s 12(1)   13
s 12(1)(b)   5
s 12(a)   5, 8, 15, 33
s 12(b)   8, 10, 15, 32, 33, 34
s 12(c)   25, 32, 34
s 12(d)   34
s 12(e)   34
s 12(f)   8, 10, 34
s 12(g)   17
s 12(h)   17
s 13   3
s 13(1)   34
s 13(2)   34
s 13(3)   10
s 13(3)(a)   8
s 18   33
s 18(1)   34
s 19   8, 9, 33, 35
s 19(1)   35
s 19(3)   35
s 23   61, 64, 74, 75, 79
s 24   61, 64, 74, 76, 79
s 24(1)(a)   41
s 24A   41, 65
s 24A(1)   41, 47
s 24A(2)   41, 47
s 24A(3)   47–48
s 25   9, 43, 45, 50, 51, 55, 58, 61, 64, 65, 70, 72, 74, 76, 78, 79, 95
s 25(1)   45, 48, 49, 50, 51, 53, 55, 56, 57, 58, 60, 63, 68, 73, 76
s 25(2)   45, 48, 49, 52, 53, 55, 56, 57, 58, 63, 73
s 25(2)(a)   49, 53, 60, 61
s 25(2)(b)   49, 51
s 25(2)(c)   76
s 25(2)(d)   53, 62
s 25(2)(e)   62
s 25(2)(f)   50, 57, 60, 62, 77
s 25(2)(g)   52, 54, 55, 57, 59, 62, 77
s 25(2)(h)   62
s 25(3)   74
s 25(3)(d)   75
s 25(4)   75
s 25A   49, 51, 52, 60, 73
s 25A(1)   45, 61, 76
s 25A(2)   46, 61, 76
s 25(e)   60
s 27   42, 45, 69, 72, 73
s 28   76
s 29   65
s 29(3)   65
s 31   64, 72, 76
s 31(2)   65
s 31(2)(f)   65
s 31(5)   65
s 31(7)   64, 65, 66
s 33A   79
s 52   74, 79
Matrimonial Homes Act 1983   101, 104
Matrimonial Proceedings and Property Act 1970
  s 37   80, 81, 85, 89, 90, 91, 93
Mental Health Act 1983   34
Pensions Act 1995   48
  s 166   27–28
Private International Law (Miscellaneous Provisions) Act 1995   5
  s 5   6
  s 6(1)–(2)   6
Protection from Harassment Act 1997   100, 103
Trusts of Land and Appointment of Trustees Act 1996
  s 14   90, 93
Welfare Reform Act 2012   67
Welfare Reform and Pensions Act 1999   28, 48

■ International Legislation

European Convention on Human Rights
  Art 8   90
  Art 12   16

Guide to the Companion Website

www.routledge.com/cw/revision

Visit the Law Revision website to discover a comprehensive range of resources designed to enhance your learning experience.

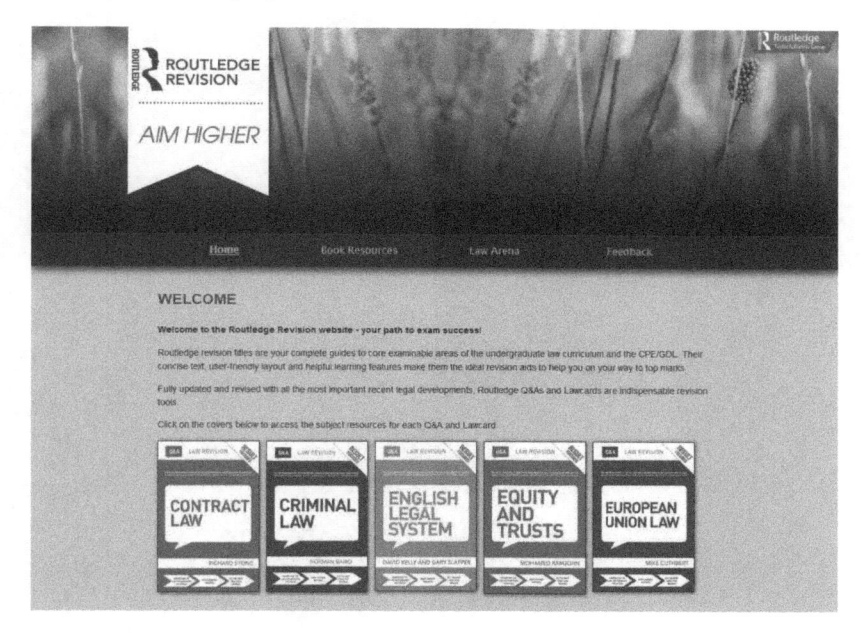

The Good, The Fair, & The Ugly
Good essays are the gateway to top marks. This interactive tutorial provides sample essays together with voice-over commentary and tips for successful exam essays, written by our Q&A authors themselves.

Multiple Choice Questions
Knowledge is the foundation of every good essay. Focusing on key examination themes, these MCQs have been written to test your knowledge and understanding of each subject in the book.

Bonus Q&As
Having studied our exam advice, put your revision into practice and test your essay writing skills with our additional online questions and answers.

Introduction

Family law is a fascinating and relevant topic. It covers human relationships and how the State views them. Family law changes as our understanding of what is family develops. This book includes those recent changes that have seen gay marriage legalised and important modifications to the treatment of parents and children. Like most family law courses, this book begins by looking at relationships between adults, especially those founded on marriage, before going on to consider how the law defines parenthood, how the law regulates parenthood and the powers and duties of the parent. Each chapter deals with a particular area of law. Each chapter contains a list of issues that the student should be able to understand and apply before then going on to set out practice questions and suggested answers where these issues and the relevant law are applied.

Statute law features strongly in family law, and you must be familiar with the statutory provisions that govern the various areas of the syllabus. Students frequently complain about the wealth of case law that they are exposed to; it may be comforting to remember that cases in the main merely illustrate how the statutory principles have operated in relation to a particular family. Since each family is different, cases should be regarded as providing guidance, rather than absolute rules and help to put those issues into perspective.

Family law can be an enjoyable and rewarding topic to study and I hope this book will be of use, not only in your revision and question-answering technique, but also in providing you with an enthusiasm for the subject.

Rachael Stretch
June 2015

1 Nullity of Marriage

INTRODUCTION

Many family law syllabuses begin by looking at the relationships between adults and in particular at the law surrounding marriage. This chapter will set out the law on who is able to marry and what makes a marriage void or voidable. This is an area that has undergone considerable change in recent years. Whereas once marriage was the preserve of the heterosexual couple, it is now possible for transsexuals to marry in their acquired gender (**Gender Recognition Act 2004**) and gay and lesbian marriages are now legally valid (**Marriage (Same Sex Couples) Act 2013 s 1(1)**).

Checklist

Students need to be familiar with the following areas:

- The effect of a marriage being declared void or voidable and the difference between a void marriage and a sham marriage (*El Gamal v Al Maktoum* (2011), *Assad v Kurter* (2013), *Hudson v Leigh* (2008)).
- The reasons why a marriage will be void under **Matrimonial Causes Act 1973 s 11**.
- *Corbett v Corbett* (1971), the subsequent case law on marriage and transsexuals and the effect of the **Gender Recognition Act 2004**.
- The legal recognition of homosexual and lesbian relationships through the **Civil Partnership Act 2004** and the **Marriage (Same Sex Couples) Act 2013**. The fact that civil partnerships are not available for heterosexual couples – *Ferguson and Others v UK* (2011).
- The effect of a marriage being voidable under the **Matrimonial Causes Act 1973 s 12** and the reasons why a marriage might be declared voidable including the development of **s 12** by the **Gender Recognition Act 2004**.
- The case law relating to duress and whether an objective or subjective test should be used (*Singh v Singh* (1971), *Hirani v Hirani* (1982)).
- **Matrimonial Causes Act 1973 s 13** and the bars on a claim under the **Matrimonial Causes Act 1973 s 12**.
- The reasons why a civil partnership will be void or voidable and how these compare to the nullity of marriage (**Civil Partnership Act 2004 s 49** and **s 50**).

Up for Debate

The nature of marriage and who is allowed to marry is a fertile area for debate. This usually focuses on the extent to which English law on marriage currently reflects, or should reflect, the traditional view that marriage is one man to one woman for life.

The following issues are likely therefore to be relevant:

- Was the **Marriage (Same Sex Couples) Act 2013** needed, or would the **Civil Partnership Act 2004** be sufficient? (*Wilkinson v Kitzinger* (2006))
- Is the law justified that the only way for a heterosexual couple to legalise their relationship is through marriage? (*Ferguson and Others v UK* (2011))
- Is the approach taken by the **Gender Recognition Act 2004** justified in not requiring medical treatment or surgery for gender recognition?
- In a pluralistic society, should there be greater legal recognition of actually polygamous marriages?

EXAM QUESTIONS

Exam questions on nullity are likely to take the form of either a problem question asking the student to identify whether a marriage can be ended because of nullity and if so under which ground, or an essay question exploring the role of nullity in today's society. Nullity can also be combined with divorce or with financial relief in problem questions.

QUESTION 1

Jane, an Englishwoman, went to Ruritania to work, and there she met and married Fred, a Ruritanian man with whom she had fallen in love. He told her that although the law of his country allowed him to take more than one wife, he felt that she was so special he would never do so. After a few months Jane tired of his adoring, but boring, company and decided to return home. She soon forgot about Fred and began to form a relationship with Tarzan, who had been briefly married to Jane's mother. Jane's mother had died two years previously and shortly after meeting, Jane and Tarzan married. However, after the ceremony Jane could not bring herself to have sexual intercourse with Tarzan, as she is tormented by the thought of his relationship with her mother.

▶ Advise Jane on the validity of her marriage.

How to Read this Question

The question is whether Jane's marriage to her latest husband, Tarzan, is valid. In order to determine this, it is crucial to decide whether she is married to Fred and therefore both Jane's marriages as well as the impact of the marriage between Jane's mother and Tarzan will need to be considered.

How to Answer this Question

Begin by examining the validity of the marriage to Fred before discussing whether Jane is validly married to Tarzan.

Applying the Law

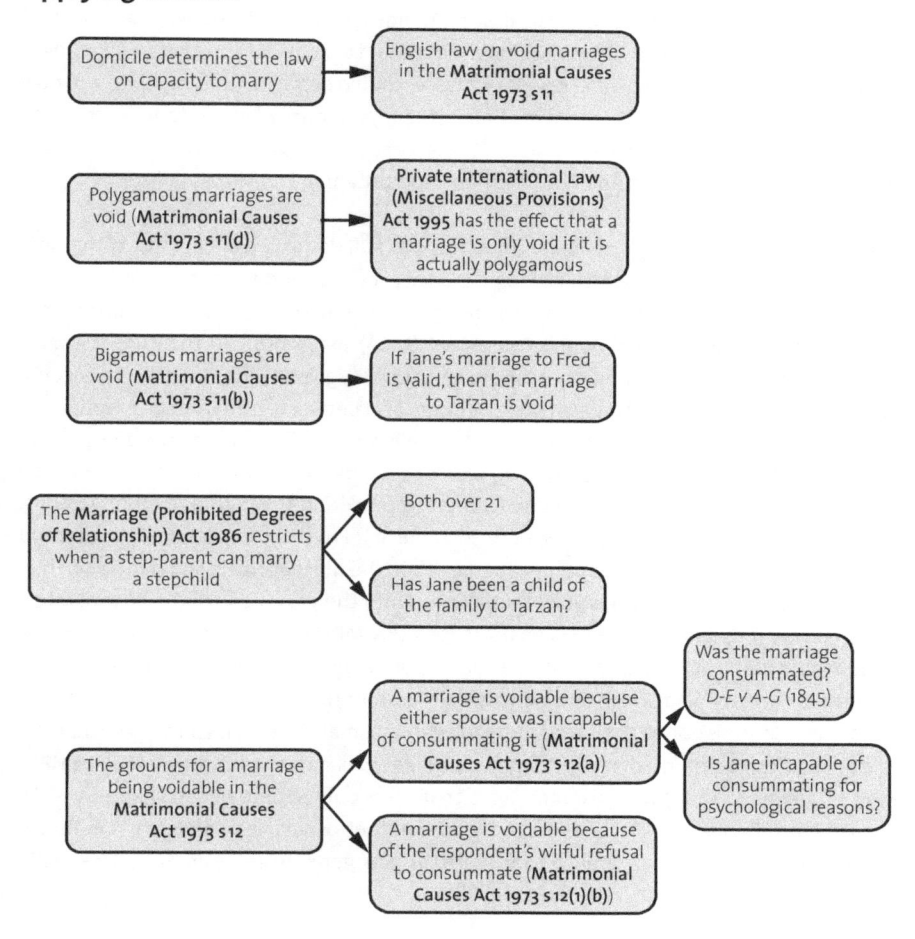

- Domicile determines the law on capacity to marry → English law on void marriages in the **Matrimonial Causes Act 1973 s 11**

- Polygamous marriages are void (**Matrimonial Causes Act 1973 s 11(d)**) → **Private International Law (Miscellaneous Provisions) Act 1995** has the effect that a marriage is only void if it is actually polygamous

- Bigamous marriages are void (**Matrimonial Causes Act 1973 s 11(b)**) → If Jane's marriage to Fred is valid, then her marriage to Tarzan is void

- The **Marriage (Prohibited Degrees of Relationship) Act 1986** restricts when a step-parent can marry a stepchild →
  - Both over 21
  - Has Jane been a child of the family to Tarzan?

- The grounds for a marriage being voidable in the **Matrimonial Causes Act 1973 s 12** →
  - A marriage is voidable because either spouse was incapable of consummating it (**Matrimonial Causes Act 1973 s 12(a)**) →
    - Was the marriage consummated? *D-E v A-G* (1845)
    - Is Jane incapable of consummating for psychological reasons?
  - A marriage is voidable because of the respondent's wilful refusal to consummate (**Matrimonial Causes Act 1973 s 12(1)(b)**)

ANSWER

In advising Jane on the validity of her marriages, it will be necessary to first examine the marriage to Fred, which took place in Ruritania. For this marriage to be valid, both parties must have had capacity to marry and the relevant formalities must have been complied with.

Capacity in English law is determined by the prospective spouses' ante-nuptial domicile – *Sottomayer v de Barros (No 1)* (1877). Fred was domiciled in Ruritania. Ruritania was clearly his permanent home: *Whicker v Hume* (1858). Thus Fred would seem to have capacity to marry Jane, although it is arguable whether Jane had capacity to marry Fred. She begins with an English domicile; however, when she goes to Ruritania to work, she may have obtained a Ruritanian domicile of choice. To establish this, it would be necessary for her to have made Ruritania her permanent home, that is, established a physical presence of a lasting nature, with an intention to make it her permanent home. In going to Ruritania to work, Jane's intentions are not clear. If she intended this as a temporary or transient measure, then there is insufficient determination to acquire a domicile of choice; however, if on meeting Fred, Jane decides that she should settle in Ruritania then she may have acquired a Ruritanian domicile of choice. If Jane is domiciled in Ruritania at the time of her marriage to Fred then she will also have capacity to marry, notwithstanding the potentially polygamous nature of the marriage, as Ruritanian law allows polygamy.

There is, however, a strong possibility that Jane was still domiciled in England at the time of her marriage to Fred, in which case her capacity must be judged according to English law. Crucially, the problem for the marriage between Fred and Jane is whether it is void for being polygamous (**Matrimonial Causes Act (MCA) 1973 s 11(d)**). In this case the marriage is not actually polygamous, but it has the potential, given Fred's domicile, to become polygamous. In *Hussain v Hussain* (1982) a marriage between a man and a woman in Pakistan which permitted polygamy was nevertheless held to be valid, as the woman had the Pakistani domicile and could not take a second husband, and the man had an English domicile and could not take a second wife, thereby rendering the marriage monogamous. This would not apply to the marriage between Jane and Fred, as the roles are reversed and Fred could still, in theory, take another spouse. Thus the marriage between Jane and Fred, whilst not actually polygamous, is potentially so. Until the provisions of the **Private International Law (Miscellaneous Provisions) Act 1995 (PIL(MP)A)** came into force in 1996, the **MCA 1973 s 11(d)** had the effect of making a potentially polygamous marriage by an English domiciliary void. This somewhat discriminatory rule was the subject of criticism by the Law Commission in their report on polygamous marriages, which thought that the rule as relating to potentially polygamous marriages was harsh. Accordingly the **PIL(MP)A 1995 s 5** amended **s 11(d)** to make marriages that were only potentially polygamous valid. The Act has retrospective effect, **s 6(1)**, but it does not retrospectively validate a potentially polygamous marriage if a party to that marriage has gone on to celebrate a later valid marriage, **s 6(2)**.[1]

Jane's marriage to Fred is, however, unhappy and she begins a relationship with Tarzan whom she later marries. The next issue therefore is what legal status, if any, this marriage to Tarzan has. First, if the marriage between Jane and Fred is valid, which it appears to be, then the marriage between Jane and Tarzan is void (**MCA 1973 s 11(b)**). Even though the marriage between Jane and Tarzan would be void as she is already validly married, this answer will consider whether there are any other issues which would make this marriage invalid.

One potential problem is that for a short while Tarzan was married to Jane's mother. There would be an absolute prohibition on Jane marrying Tarzan if he were her natural or adoptive father; likewise if she had at any stage been a child of the family whilst Tarzan

---

[1] Good answers will not merely state that a marriage cannot be polygamous under English Law but will apply this rule to the facts and explain what this means. In particular, it is important that the student is aware of the potentially discriminatory effect of **s 11(d)** and therefore can understand and explain the reason for the **PIL(MP)A 1995**.

was married to her mother: **Marriage Act 1949 Sched 1**. However, if Jane had never been treated by Tarzan as a child of the family and Tarzan's relationship with Jane's mother had occurred when Jane was no longer living at home, then provided that Tarzan and Jane are both over 21 they will be able to marry: **Marriage (Prohibited Degrees) Act 1996**.[2]

There are possible grounds for arguing that the marriage between Jane and Tarzan is voidable for one of the reasons in the **MCA s 12**. It does not seem that the marriage has been consummated. Jane's attitude has ensured that there has been no complete and regular intercourse (*D v A* (1845)) once the marriage has taken place. Premarital intercourse does not suffice for consummation. It is then necessary to consider whether this is due to incapacity to consummate or wilful refusal.

Either party can petition on the basis that there is some physical or psychological reason preventing consummation (*D v D* (1982)). Here it would seem that Jane has psychological problems that are preventing intercourse. In order for the decree to be granted these reasons must exist at the date of the petition and the date of the hearing (*Napier v Napier* (1915)), but there must also be no practical possibility of intercourse (*S v S* (1962)). In this case it is not clear what, if anything at all, can be done to help Jane; neither is it apparent whether she wishes to be helped to overcome the problem. If it is felt that there is a possibility of intercourse should Jane accept help which would not expose her to too great a risk, then Jane's refusal to seek such assistance may amount to a wilful refusal to consummate. This would be a settled and definite decision without just cause (*Horton v Horton* (1947)), and would give Tarzan the opportunity to petition for nullity.[3]

A voidable marriage is valid unless and until it is dissolved by way of nullity decree (*De Renville v De Renville* (1948)), unlike the void marriage. Therefore, Jane should seek a nullity decree in respect of her marriage to Tarzan.

QUESTION 2

Kate was a journalist covering a civil war in the depths of Africa. There she met a fellow English journalist, Leo, with whom she fell instantly and madly in love. They wanted to marry but were in the midst of heavy fighting and were unable to make the journey to the nearest city. They exchanged marriage vows in front of Mike, a missionary who was hoping to become a priest. Both Kate and Leo were captured by rival factions in the civil war, and Kate assumed Leo had been killed when she did not hear from him again. Kate met another journalist, Nick, in the prisoner of war camp within which she was held and, finding she was pregnant by Leo, agreed to marry Nick so that her child would have a father. The marriage was intended by both as a companionship only relationship, as

---

2 The concern with step-parent/stepchild relationships is that the step-parent might have groomed the stepchild and the relationship might be abusive. This explains why the ban on step-parent/stepchild relationships only applies if the step-parent has been in a parental position to the stepchild.

3 A spouse can petition for non-consummation on the basis of their own incapacity to consummate, but not on the basis of their own refusal to consummate.

neither wished to have intercourse with the other. After Kate's baby was born, Nick found he looked on Kate with increasing affection, and wanted her to be more than his housekeeper. However, Kate refused to have intercourse with him, and Nick has now met Olive, with whom he hopes to have a proper marriage.

▶ Advise Nick.

How to Read this Question

Nick's ability to marry Olive is dependent on whether he is validly married to Kate. The marriage between Kate and Nick in turn is only valid if the marriage between Kate and Leo is not. There are therefore three marriages to consider.

Answer Structure

The question should be answered chronologically, looking first at the marriage between Kate and Leo, then at the marriage between Kate and Nick before considering how this impacts on Nick's relationship with Olive.

Applying the Law

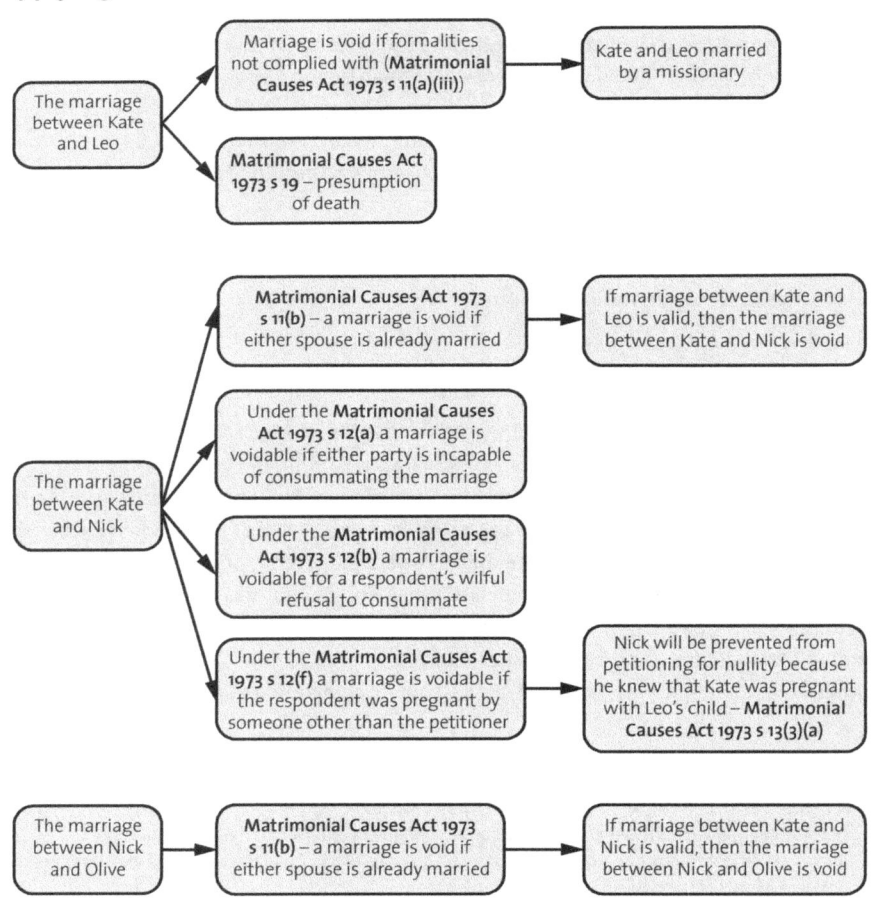

```
The marriage between Kate and Leo
  → Marriage is void if formalities not complied with (Matrimonial Causes Act 1973 s 11(a)(iii))
    → Kate and Leo married by a missionary
  → Matrimonial Causes Act 1973 s 19 – presumption of death

The marriage between Kate and Nick
  → Matrimonial Causes Act 1973 s 11(b) – a marriage is void if either spouse is already married
    → If marriage between Kate and Leo is valid, then the marriage between Kate and Nick is void
  → Under the Matrimonial Causes Act 1973 s 12(a) a marriage is voidable if either party is incapable of consummating the marriage
  → Under the Matrimonial Causes Act 1973 s 12(b) a marriage is voidable for a respondent's wilful refusal to consummate
  → Under the Matrimonial Causes Act 1973 s 12(f) a marriage is voidable if the respondent was pregnant by someone other than the petitioner
    → Nick will be prevented from petitioning for nullity because he knew that Kate was pregnant with Leo's child – Matrimonial Causes Act 1973 s 13(3)(a)

The marriage between Nick and Olive
  → Matrimonial Causes Act 1973 s 11(b) – a marriage is void if either spouse is already married
    → If marriage between Nick and Kate is valid, then the marriage between Nick and Olive is void
```

Nullity of Marriage

ANSWER

In advising Nick on his ability to marry Olive it will be necessary to examine the validity of his marriage to Kate, which in turn is affected by the validity of the marriage between Kate and Leo. It is proposed that the first marriage to be discussed will be that of Kate and Leo.

The capacity of Kate and Leo to contract a valid marriage is to be judged by the law of their ante-nuptial domicile: *Sottomayer v de Barros (No 1)* (1877). Both Kate and Leo have English domicile and do not appear to have acquired a domicile of choice in Africa. The English law rules on capacity are based on Lord Penzance's definition of marriage as 'the voluntary union for life of a man and a woman to the exclusion of all others': *Hyde v Hyde* (1866). Thus the **Matrimonial Causes Act (MCA) 1973 s 11** requires the parties to be over 16, of opposite sex, not within the prohibited degrees, and not already married. It would therefore seem that Kate and Leo have capacity to marry.

It is also necessary that a valid marriage complies with the formal requirements of the *lex loci*, the location where the marriage is taking place: *Herbert v Herbert* (1819). Unfortunately, in the instant case, Kate and Leo do not appear to have complied with any formalities prescribed by local law. Indeed, in a civil war situation, it may be virtually impossible for them to do so. The English law will nevertheless recognise such marriages if it is not possible to comply with local law because of insurmountable difficulties, provided that the English common law formalities have been complied with: *Taczanowski v Taczanowski* (1957). This requires the parties to declare that they take each other as husband and wife to the exclusion of all others and these vows must usually be exchanged before an ordained minister. This concept has been criticised as artificial, especially where the parties have no connection with England, but it might operate to make the ceremony between Kate and Leo a valid marriage. However, Mike is not an ordained minister, and this may mean that the marriage is invalid unless it can be argued that, in the circumstances, this missionary was the best person available to lend an air of formality as in *Wolfenden v Wolfenden* (1945).

If the marriage is void through lack of compliance with the formalities, then there is no need to seek a nullity decree unless financial provision is sought under the **MCA s 25**. If, however, the marriage is valid, then it may have been possible for Kate to seek dissolution of her marriage by seeking to rely on the presumption of death. This would enable her to apply if she could show that no one who should have heard from Leo has done so in the past seven years and if the period exceeds seven years then the presumption that Leo is dead will operate, thereby entitling Kate to a dissolution of her marriage: **MCA 1973 s 19**.

If the marriage between Kate and Leo was void or had been dissolved before the marriage to Nick, then it would appear that both Kate and Nick would have capacity to marry according to the law of their domiciles. English law would be applied, since their capture and detention in prisoner of war camps could not result in them acquiring a domicile of choice. The **MCA 1973 s 11** would require them to both be over the age of 16, of opposite sex, not within the prohibited degrees and not already validly married. Even if they had capacity to marry, they must comply with the formalities required by the place where the marriage took place, the *lex loci*. It is not clear where the marriage took place and it is therefore assumed that either the necessary formalities were complied with or it was a situation where the doctrine of the English common law marriage would provide validity.

If, however, Kate's marriage to Leo was still valid then the subsequent marriage to Nick is void since **s 11(b)** requires neither party to be lawfully married. Likewise **s 11(d)** prevents an English domiciliary from entering into a polygamous union anywhere in the world, even if the local law permits polygamy.[4]

If the marriage to Nick is valid then it may still be voidable by reference to the provisions of the **MCA 1973 s 12**. It would seem that the marriage has not been consummated; there has been no complete and regular sexual intercourse (*D v A* (1845)). However, there does not appear to be any incapacity, just an initial decision that the relationship would be platonic, followed by Kate refusing to alter the status quo. This may be evidence of a wilful refusal to consummate the marriage, thereby rendering the marriage voidable under the **MCA 1973 s 12(b)**. In *Horton v Horton* (1948) it was held that there needed to be a settled and definite decision by the respondent reached without just cause. Initially there was a mutual understanding, and the status quo cannot be regarded as a refusal by either party: *Potter v Potter* (1982). However, when Nick tries to alter the situation and Kate refuses, this may give the necessary definite decision on Kate's part, although it would still be necessary to examine whether her refusal was without just cause. They had agreed at the outset that theirs was to be a platonic relationship: would it be unreasonable for her to refuse to alter the nature of the relationship? Much might depend on how old the couple were; with a young couple, the courts are more likely to hold a refusal unreasonable, whereas *obiter* comments suggest that in the case of elderly couples a companionship arrangement might not be voidable: *Morgan v Morgan* (1959). Since Kate has had a child she cannot be too old and it is likely that her refusal is unreasonable.[5]

Kate was also pregnant by another man at the time of her marriage to Nick, and this can be the basis for a petition under **s 12(f)** – pregnancy *per alium*. However, **s 13(3)** provides a bar to petitioning if Nick was aware of this fact at the time of the marriage. This seems likely given that he did not want intercourse with Kate initially, and so the petition would only succeed on the basis of non-consummation.

---

4 This paragraph explains the link between the validity of the marriage between Kate and Leo and the validity of the marriage between Kate and Nick. It is impossible for them both to validly exist at the same time.

5 A marriage can be voidable for non-consummation either because of wilful refusal, or because of incapacity. Nick is potentially able to rely on Kate's refusal to consummate depending on whether that refusal was wilful and that means that whether she had a just excuse needs to be discussed.

In conclusion, if Nick's marriage to Kate is void, then he is free to marry Olive. A void marriage is treated as if it never existed and no nullity decree is required. If, however, the marriage to Kate is merely voidable, then Nick must ensure that he obtains a nullity decree before marrying Olive.

QUESTION 3

Matthew is 22. He has always had a poor relationship with his parents and two years ago things got so bad that he was told to move out. Matthew moved to London and he began leading a very expensive lifestyle filled with designer clothes, fast cars and foreign holidays. Sadly, Matthew could only get poorly paid work and he soon fell into debt. Having used up his credit cards and after being refused a loan by his bank, Matthew borrowed £25,000 from a backstreet lender. Nine months ago, Matthew realised that he would not be able to pay this loan back and he became very worried.

One of Matthew's friends, Luke, is gay. He suggested to Matthew that they become civil partners. Luke has a well-paid job and would be able to help Matthew financially. Luke knew that Matthew was not gay and accepted that they would not have a sexual relationship but he had fallen in love with Matthew and wanted to help him. Five months ago, Luke and Matthew went though a civil partnership ceremony. Sadly, the partnership has not been happy. Matthew now says that he finds Luke repulsive. He brings women back to their home which Luke finds very upsetting. Luke has now met Keith and would like to be free to begin a relationship with Keith.

▶ Advise Luke on ending his civil partnership with Matthew.

How to Read this Question

This question is more open than the previous two. Answers should look at the ways that Luke can end his civil partnership with Matthew and should therefore look at dissolution as well as nullity. Moreover, whilst there are many similarities between nullity and civil partnerships and nullity and marriage, there remain some important differences and the answer should recognise this.

How to Answer this Question

Focus on how Luke's civil partnership with Matthew can be ended and look first at nullity before considering the alternative of dissolution. Answers should explain the effect of both nullity and dissolution for Luke.

Answer Structure

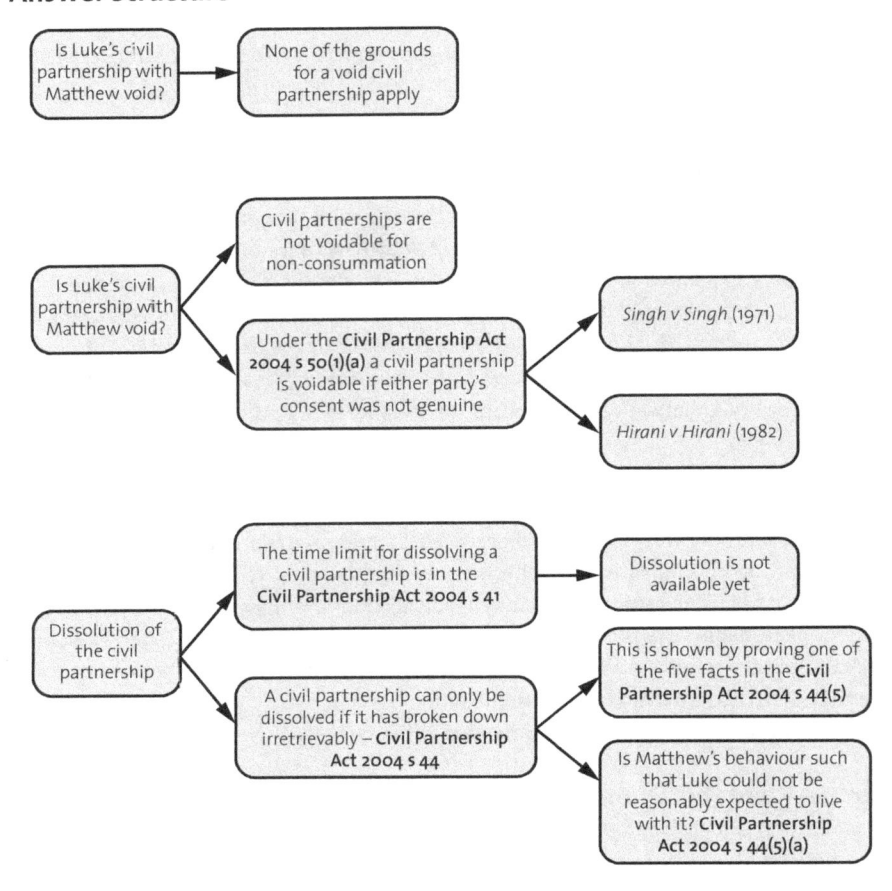

```
Is Luke's civil partnership with Matthew void? → None of the grounds for a void civil partnership apply
```

```
Is Luke's civil partnership with Matthew void?
├── Civil partnerships are not voidable for non-consummation
└── Under the Civil Partnership Act 2004 s 50(1)(a) a civil partnership is voidable if either party's consent was not genuine
    ├── Singh v Singh (1971)
    └── Hirani v Hirani (1982)
```

```
Dissolution of the civil partnership
├── The time limit for dissolving a civil partnership is in the Civil Partnership Act 2004 s 41 → Dissolution is not available yet
└── A civil partnership can only be dissolved if it has broken down irretrievably – Civil Partnership Act 2004 s 44
    ├── This is shown by proving one of the five facts in the Civil Partnership Act 2004 s 44(5)
    └── Is Matthew's behaviour such that Luke could not be reasonably expected to live with it? Civil Partnership Act 2004 s 44(5)(a)
```

ANSWER

Matthew and Luke went through a seemingly valid civil partnership ceremony five months ago. Sadly, the partnership has not proved happy and Luke now seeks to end it. The two ways of doing this would be through nullity, or through dissolution. As the partnership is not yet a year old, dissolution is not immediately available, and therefore nullity will first be considered. From the facts it seems that this is not a void civil partnership. Matthew and Luke are eligible to become civil partners – they are both men, seemingly both over 16, not related and not already married or in a civil partnership (**Civil Partnership Act 2004 s 3**) and the formalities for a valid civil partnership have been complied with (**Civil Partnership Act 2004 s 49**); instead, the question is whether this civil partnership is voidable.[6]

---

6 Students should always make sure they read the question carefully, and answer what has been set as fully as possible. Here, they are invited to consider all ways of ending the relationship and therefore dissolution should be considered as well as nullity. Note though that nullity has the advantage of being available in the first year.

The relationship between Matthew and Luke has never been sexual. Marriage is closely linked to sexual intercourse, and non-consummation, either because of wilful refusal or because of incapacity, is a ground for a voidable marriage (**Matrimonial Causes Act 1973 s 12(1)**). The same does not apply to civil partnerships. The fact that civil partners have never had a sexual relationship does not make their partnership voidable. This is because the legal definition of consummation requires penetration of the vagina by the penis, which means that all civil partnerships by their very nature cannot be consummated.

Another argument that Luke could use is that Matthew did not validly consent to the civil partnership – his financial problems meant that he was forced to agree to the partnership and therefore it is voidable because of duress (**Civil Partnership Act 2004 s 50(1)(a)**). Although it was not Luke himself who was the victim of the duress, the Act is clear that either party can use the duress. The issue of what constitutes duress has been discussed in relation to whether a marriage is voidable under the **Matrimonial Causes Act 1973** and there have been two different judicial approaches. The first, hardline approach is characterised by the decision in *Singh v Singh* (1971). In this case, the court determined that an arranged marriage was not voidable because of duress as the wife had not feared for her life, limb or liberty. In *Hirani v Hirani* (1982), the court took a more sympathetic approach and recognised that in a close-knit family, it would be very difficult for a young girl to choose family dishonour and to be disowned by disobeying her parents. The court in *Hirani* said that the crucial question was whether the spouse in reality was free to make a decision. More recent cases seem to prefer the *Hirani* approach.

Applying these tests, is the partnership between Luke and Matthew voidable because of duress? If the *Singh* test is applied Matthew would have to argue that if he did not become Luke's civil partner he faced severe physical harm or homelessness. The facts state that Matthew had borrowed money from a backstreet lender and whilst it might be imagined that he possibly faced some threats if he did not repay, the nature of these threats is not explicit. Moreover, even if Matthew risked physical harm were he not to repay the loan or risked losing his home, it is far from clear that becoming Luke's civil partner was the only solution. On the other hand, Matthew is reasonably young and the fact that he is estranged from his parents may make him more vulnerable and would mean that he could not go to them for financial assistance. In fact, recent precedent suggests that the *Hirani* approach is likely to be preferred and whilst this will be more sympathetic towards Matthew, it is still far from clear that the civil partnership will be held voidable because of duress. The facts state that Matthew was worried about not being able to repay the loan; this, however, is not the same as Matthew's will being overridden and him being forced into the civil partnership.[7]

---

7 The answer has correctly identified that either spouse can use duress as a grounds for nullity, not just the 'victim' of the duress. The case law on duress is interesting as there is a conflict between the stricter, older cases such as *Singh* and more recent case law which is more subjective. As of yet, there are no leading cases where duress is claimed in a civil partnership, and it is probable that a similar approach to that used in *Hirani* would be used.

Another option is for Luke to wait until the partnership is a year old and then apply for the partnership to be dissolved. Although it is clear that the partnership has broken down irretrievably (**Civil Partnership Act s 44(1)**), it can only be dissolved if one of the facts in **s 44(5)** exists. Matthew has clearly been having relationships with women whilst in a civil partnership with Luke. Although adultery is one of the divorce facts in the **Matrimonial Causes Act 1973**, it is not a fact under the **Civil Partnership Act 2004**; however, it is very probable that Matthew's relationships with women would constitute behaviour under **s 44(5)(a)**. In addition, Matthew states that he finds Luke repulsive and living with these insults would constitute behaviour under **s 44(5)(a)**. Therefore Luke could apply for the partnership to be dissolved once it has lasted a year.[8]

Finally, Luke seems to be better off financially than Matthew and Luke should also be aware that Matthew will be entitled to claim financial relief from him. The fact that the civil partnership has been very brief, and that Matthew is a young man, means that this is likely not to be a significant amount.

> ### Aim Higher
> * Good answers will demonstrate a clear understanding of the relevant legislative provisions and case law.
> * A good student will develop this by exploring how case law on duress which was decided against a background of parental pressure and arranged marriage can be applied to a civil partnership.

QUESTION 4

'[T]he biological sexual constitution of an individual is fixed at birth (at the latest), and cannot be changed, either by the natural development of organs of the opposite sex, or by medical or surgical means. The respondent's operation, therefore, cannot affect her true sex.' (Per Omrod J *Corbett v Corbett* (1971) P 83)

▶ Critically examine whether this is still an accurate description of English law.

How to Read this Question

In *Corbett*, the court decided that the marriage between a male to female transsexual and a man was void as despite extensive sex change treatment she remained male. Answers need to consider *Corbett* itself as well as how the law has developed since.

---

8 Although there is a great deal of similarity between marriage and civil partnerships, there are some important differences. Notably there is not the same connection between a civil partnership and a sexual relationship as there is between marriage and a civil partnership. One reason for this is that a civil partnership would not be able to satisfy the legal definition of consummation.

Applying the Law

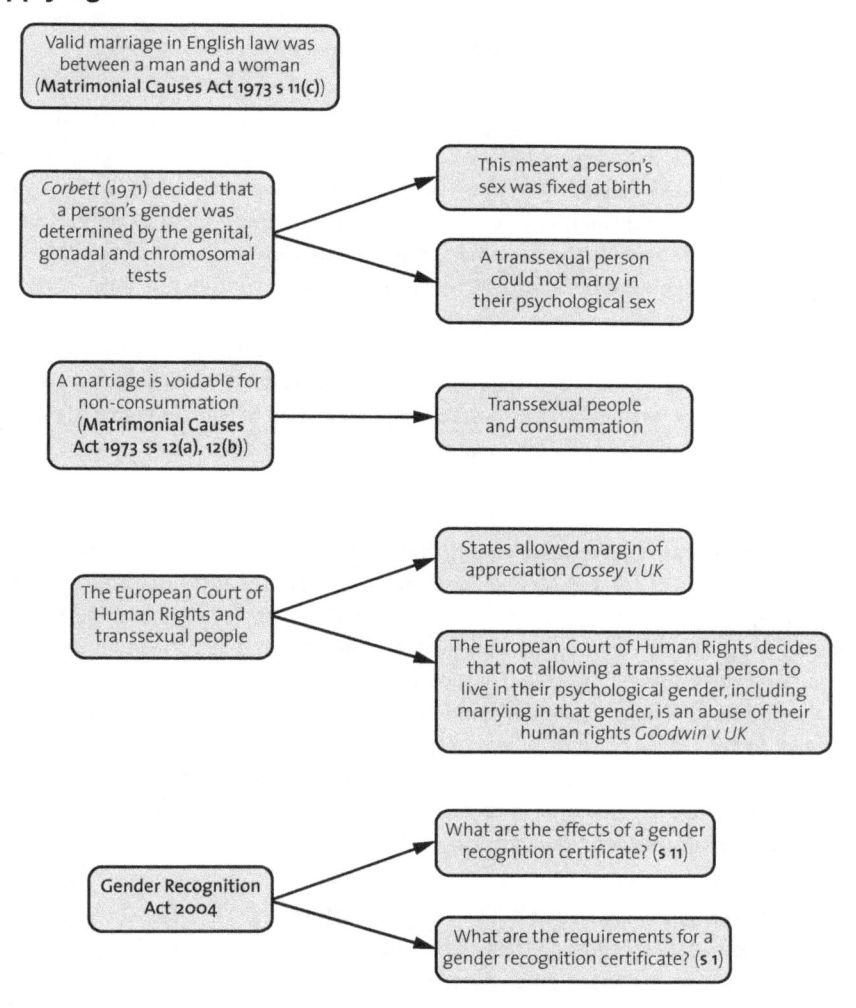

```
┌─────────────────────────────────┐
│ Valid marriage in English law was│
│ between a man and a woman        │
│ (Matrimonial Causes Act 1973 s 11(c))│
└─────────────────────────────────┘

┌─────────────────────────┐         ┌─────────────────────────┐
│ Corbett (1971) decided that│──────▶│ This meant a person's    │
│ a person's gender was   │         │ sex was fixed at birth   │
│ determined by the genital,│        └─────────────────────────┘
│ gonadal and chromosomal │         ┌─────────────────────────┐
│ tests                   │──────▶│ A transsexual person     │
└─────────────────────────┘         │ could not marry in       │
                                    │ their psychological sex  │
                                    └─────────────────────────┘

┌─────────────────────────┐         ┌─────────────────────────┐
│ A marriage is voidable for│        │                         │
│ non-consummation         │──────▶│ Transsexual people       │
│ (Matrimonial Causes     │         │ and consummation        │
│ Act 1973 ss 12(a), 12(b))│        └─────────────────────────┘
└─────────────────────────┘

                                    ┌─────────────────────────┐
┌─────────────────────────┐         │ States allowed margin of │
│ The European Court of   │──────▶│ appreciation Cossey v UK │
│ Human Rights and        │         └─────────────────────────┘
│ transsexual people      │         ┌──────────────────────────────────────┐
└─────────────────────────┘──────▶│ The European Court of Human Rights decides│
                                    │ that not allowing a transsexual person to │
                                    │ live in their psychological gender, including│
                                    │ marrying in that gender, is an abuse of their│
                                    │ human rights Goodwin v UK            │
                                    └──────────────────────────────────────┘

                                    ┌─────────────────────────┐
┌─────────────────────────┐         │ What are the effects of a gender│
│ Gender Recognition      │──────▶│ recognition certificate? (s 11)│
│ Act 2004                │         └─────────────────────────┘
└─────────────────────────┘         ┌─────────────────────────┐
                           ──────▶│ What are the requirements for a│
                                    │ gender recognition certificate? (s 1)│
                                    └─────────────────────────┘
```

ANSWER

According to the **Matrimonial Causes Act 1973 s 11(c)**, parties to a marriage should be male and female. This requirement has caused problems for transsexuals because unless a transsexual can marry in her acquired gender, her options for marriage are likely to be significantly limited. The leading case for a long time has been that of *Corbett v Corbett* (1971) which is quoted in the question. In this case the petitioner was seeking nullity from his marriage to a male-to-female transsexual. The High Court agreed that the marriage was void. It stated that a person's gender was determined by their biology, that is by the chromosomal, the gonadal and the genital tests, and because by these tests the respondent was a man, her marriage was void. The court in *Corbett* also stated that, in any case, a marriage involving a male-to-female transsexual would be voidable because she would be unable to consummate her marriage as a woman. Whether transsexuals can consummate in their new gender is a less significant argument though as, in any case, consummation is merely a grounds for a voidable marriage.[9]

The approach in *Corbett* was for a long time upheld by both the English and the European courts. For example, in *Cossey v UK* (1990) Caroline Cossey's claim to be recognised in her new gender and to be able to marry was rejected and the approach of the English courts was upheld by the European Court. For a long time, the European Court of Human Rights viewed the extent to which the acquired gender of transsexuals was recognised to be a matter for national appreciation, allowing individual countries to take different approaches to reflect the different degrees to which transsexualism was accepted by their population. For English law, this changed with the European Court's decision in *Goodwin v UK* (2002). In this case, the European Court decided that denying transsexuals the right to marry was a breach of the **European Convention of Human Rights Art 12**, and that it was no longer appropriate for a person's gender to be determined purely by reference to biological conditions present at their birth.

While the European Court was deciding the *Goodwin* case, the English courts were hearing the claims of Mr and Mrs Bellinger for their marriage to be declared valid. The Court of Appeal in *Bellinger* (2002) was sympathetic to Mrs Bellinger but the majority upheld the decision in *Corbett* that a person's gender was fixed at birth. In his dissenting judgment, Thorpe argued that the law should be changed to take account of changes in social attitudes towards transsexuals and developing medical knowledge. Mrs Bellinger appealed to the House of Lords where despite the decision in *Goodwin* she was unsuccessful. The House of Lords decided that the issue was too important to be decided by a court and that reform would have to come from Parliament. This has now happened through the **Gender Recognition Act 2004**.

The **Gender Recognition Act 2004** enables transsexuals to apply to a Gender Recognition Panel for a certificate recognising their change of gender. This certificate will enable them to marry in their new gender. Perhaps controversially, the Act does not require a transsexual to have undergone surgery before (s)he can obtain a certificate. The reason for this is that if surgery were needed for a gender recognition certificate, an individual who, for medical reasons, was unable to have a full sex change would, perhaps unfairly, be prevented from being recognised in their new gender. Instead a person must show that they have lived for two years in their acquired gender and intend to live in that gender for the rest of their life. If a person is married in their original sex, they can only obtain an interim gender recognition certificate. This interim certificate will make the marriage voidable and once the marriage is dissolved, it can be converted to a full certificate. The Act will not

....

9 *Corbett* is still valid case law and a transsexual would still be defined as their sex at birth using the genital, gonadal and chromosomal tests. The *Corbett* test would not, however, apply to an intersexual as in their case the genital, gonadal and chromosomal tests would not give a clear, unambiguous answer, allowing an intersexual to use the psychological test to choose their gender.

apply retrospectively and individuals like Mrs Bellinger will still find that their existing marriages are void.[10]

The UK approach is interesting because it does not base a person's gender on their biology. It will be possible for an individual to have the sexual characteristics of a man, but be registered by the Gender Recognition Panel as a woman. Furthermore, the fact that a person has to intend to live in their acquired sex does suggest that gender recognition is based, at least in part, on a person's psychological commitment to their new sex. This is a significant development from the approach adopted in *Corbett*.

Aim Higher

Good answers will be able to explain the contrast between the approach in *Corbett* which based gender on the physical (genital, gonadal and chromosomal) and discounted the psychological and the approach of the **Gender Recognition Act** which allows a changed gender based on an intention to live in the acquired gender and therefore which favours the psychological over the physical. Good answers will evaluate the effectiveness and fairness of these approaches and will consider whether the Gender Recognition Act has taken the approach it has because it is concerned with gender identity rather than sex identity.

---

10 The **GRA 2004** amended the **MCA 1973 s12** and a marriage will now be voidable either because one of the spouses acquires a new gender under the **GRA 2004** after the marriage (**MCA 1973 s12(g)**) or because a spouse has only acquired their gender thanks to the **GRA 2004** (**MCA 1973 s12(h)**). The later provision would enable a person who inadvertently marries a transsexual to end their marriage.

2 Divorce and Dissolution of Civil Partnerships

INTRODUCTION

Divorce questions frequently feature on examination papers, either as a whole question or linked with other issues. Divorce is increasingly common, with recent statistics showing that around one in three marriages ends in divorce. The law on divorce is set out in the **Matrimonial Causes Act 1973**. The grounds for divorce and divorce procedure were to be reformed in the **Family Law Act 1996 Part II**. The **Children and Families Act 2014 s18** has repealed this.

Checklist

Students need to understand and be able to apply the following:

- the time limits on the availability of divorce – **Matrimonial Causes Act 1973 s 3(1)**;
- that the ground for divorce in the **Matrimonial Causes Act 1973 s 1(1)** is irretrievable breakdown;
- how a petitioner shows irretrievable breakdown by proving one of the five facts in the **Matrimonial Causes Act 1973 s 1(2)**;
- to establish the adultery fact (**Matrimonial Causes Act 1973 s 1(2)(a)**) the petitioner has to show that the respondent has committed adultery and that the petitioner finds it intolerable to live with him (*Cleary* (1974));
- what is meant by behaviour that the petitioner cannot reasonably be expected to live with (*O'Neil v O'Neil* (1975), *Katz v Katz* (1972), *Livingstone-Stallard v Livingstone-Stallard* (1974));
- what has to be shown to establish desertion and how long the desertion has to be for (**Matrimonial Causes Act 1973 s 1(2)(c)**); why this fact is rarely used;
- what is meant by living apart (**Matrimonial Causes Act 1973 ss 1(2)(d), 1(2)(e)**). Can spouses be living apart if they share the same address (*Mouncer v Mouncer* (1971))?
- **Matrimonial Causes Act 1973 s 5** means that a divorce can be prevented if it would mean grave financial (*K v K (Financial Provision)* (1996)) or other (*Rukat v Rukat* (1975)) hardship;
- the criticisms of divorce procedure in the **Matrimonial Causes Act 1973** and attempts to reform the law on divorce in the **Family Law Act 1996 Part II**;
- why the **Family Law Act 1996 Part II** has not been implemented and will not now be implemented (**Children and Families Act 2014 s 18**);
- the impact of the special procedure on divorce law;
- divorce procedure and mediation;
- the dissolution of civil partnerships under the **Civil Partnership Act 2004 s 44(5)**.

Up for Debate

Whilst there is unlikely to be a debate about the availability of divorce, the issue is more likely to be when divorce should be allowed and what the procedure should be. This might include the conflict between basing divorce on fault and basing it on consent.

- Should English law introduce divorce by consent?
- Should a petitioner have to show that the respondent has been at fault in order to obtain a divorce?
- Is it appropriate that the **Family Law Act 1996 Part II** has been abandoned?
- Is mediation appropriate in divorce procedure and if so how should it be used?

EXAM QUESTIONS

Divorce is a popular topic for exams, either on its own, or with financial relief, or, where appropriate, domestic violence. Problem questions require the student to advise a spouse whilst essay questions require a critical view of procedure.

QUESTION 5

Fred and Wilma married 10 years ago, and were initially very happy; however, Fred started to go out with his friends every Saturday night, leaving Wilma at home with their daughter, Pebbles. Fred frequently returned home drunk, waking Wilma and Pebbles with his raucous singing. One Saturday, Fred crashed his car, returning home after a night in the pub, and was severely injured and left with permanent paraplegia. Wilma visited Fred every day whilst he was in hospital, but when he returned home she realised that the marriage was effectively at an end. Wilma continued to cook for Fred, and she would help bathe and dress him. She did not tell Fred of her feelings, but she began to have an affair with a neighbour, Barney. Wilma told Barney that she would never leave Fred whilst he still needed her, but five years after the accident Wilma moved out of the matrimonial home, to live with Barney, taking Pebbles with her. Wilma said that Fred's depression and irritability had proved too much for her, and she could no longer cope with the strain of looking after him. Fred has refused to consider divorce, saying that he needs Wilma to look after him and that he misses Pebbles.

▶ Advise Wilma as to whether she has any basis for divorce.

How to Read this Question

The question is only looking at the availability of divorce and not what the consequences of that divorce would be.

Answer Structure

Answers need to be clear that divorce is not available until the couple have been married a year (**Matrimonial Causes Act 1973 s 3(1)**), that it is not available unless the marriage has irretrievably broken down (**Matrimonial Causes Act 1973 s 1(1)**) and that one of the five facts in the **Matrimonial Causes Act 1973 s 1(2)** will have to be shown.

Divorce and Dissolution of Civil Partnerships

Applying the Law

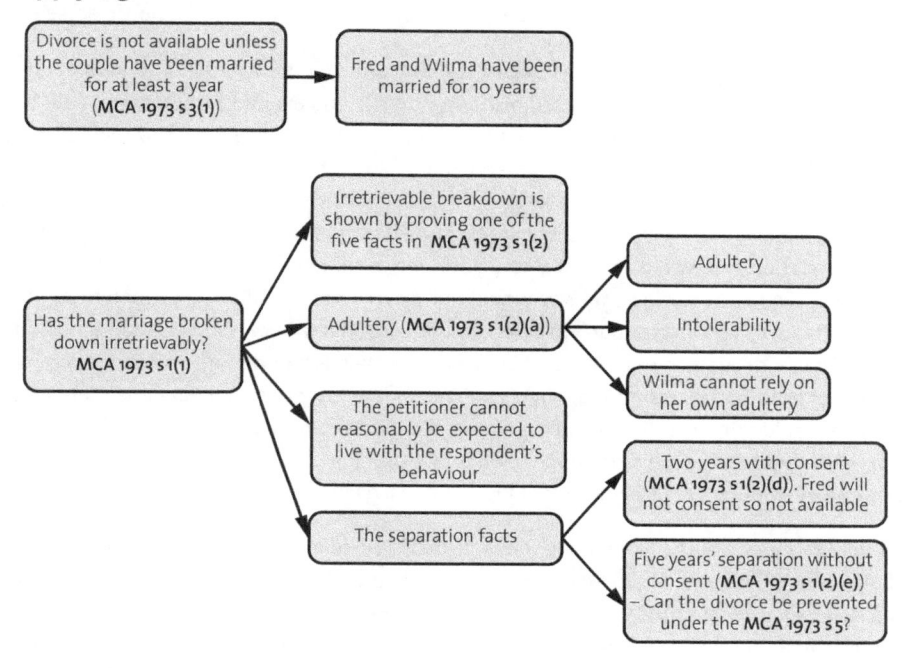

- Divorce is not available unless the couple have been married for at least a year (**MCA 1973 s 3(1)**) → Fred and Wilma have been married for 10 years

- Has the marriage broken down irretrievably? **MCA 1973 s 1(1)**
  - Irretrievable breakdown is shown by proving one of the five facts in **MCA 1973 s 1(2)**
  - Adultery (**MCA 1973 s 1(2)(a)**)
    - Adultery
    - Intolerability
    - Wilma cannot rely on her own adultery
  - The petitioner cannot reasonably be expected to live with the respondent's behaviour
  - The separation facts
    - Two years with consent (**MCA 1973 s 1(2)(d)**). Fred will not consent so not available
    - Five years' separation without consent (**MCA 1973 s 1(2)(e)**) – Can the divorce be prevented under the **MCA 1973 s 5**?

ANSWER

Wilma is able to petition for divorce as she has been married to Fred for over a year (**Matrimonial Causes Act (MCA) 1973 s 3(1)**). At present, there is one ground for divorce, namely that the marriage between Fred and Wilma has broken down irretrievably: **MCA 1973 s 1(1)**. However, in order to establish irretrievable breakdown, Wilma must establish one of the five facts in the **MCA 1973 s 1(2)**.

Adultery is not a relevant fact. Although it is quite clear that Wilma has had voluntary sexual intercourse with Barney, she cannot petition on the basis of her own adultery. Instead this may be relied on by Fred if he were to cross-petition, with the additional requirement of intolerability having to be satisfied.[1]

A more realistic option for Wilma is to use the fact in the **MCA 1973 s 1(2)(b)** that the respondent has behaved in such a way that the petitioner cannot reasonably be expected to live with the respondent. Although Fred's drunkenness might come within the definition of behaviour that a respondent could not be expected to live with, Wilma will not be able to rely on this as the drunkenness is at least five years in the past. This leaves Wilma with having to show that Fred's behaviour since the accident is such that she cannot reasonably be expected to live with it. Although Wilma will not be precluded from using

---

1 A spouse cannot rely on their own adultery to petition for divorce. Also note that as well as the sexual relationship with a third party (the adultery), the petitioner must also prove that it was intolerable; however, the intolerability does not have to be because of the adultery (*Cleary* (1974)).

behaviour that is the result of the accident and therefore arguably not Fred's fault (*Thurlow v Thurlow*), she will not be able just to rely on the fact that Fred is now disabled.

Once some kind of behaviour has been established, it is then necessary to look at the character of the individual concerned (*Ash v Ash* (1972)), and examine whether it would be reasonable to expect them to continue to live together: *Livingstone-Stallard v Livingstone-Stallard* (1974). Applying that to Wilma and Fred, it could be contended that the strain of looking after Fred, who has been severely incapacitated through his own negligence, is too much for Wilma. Against this it could be argued that Wilma has been having an adulterous relationship with Barney, she has continued to share the same house with Fred for a number of years, stating that she would not leave him, and, although cohabitation of more than six months is not an absolute bar under **s 2(3)** to a successful petition based on behaviour, it does seem that her unwillingness to remain is based more on her developing romance with Barney rather than Fred's behaviour. Nevertheless, in reality it is likely that Wilma would bring her divorce petition using the special procedure. This would mean she would be unlikely to face much opposition or questioning and there would be little examination of whether Fred's behaviour really justified a divorce.[2]

It may be more realistic to examine the facts based on separation, namely **s1(2)(d)** and **(e)**. Both require the petitioner to establish separation in that the parties have lived apart. Living apart is explained in **s2(6)** by reference to whether the husband and wife live with each other in the same household. If they do, then they are not living apart. In Fred and Wilma's case, they have been living in two households once Wilma left to live with Barney. However, there is still the possibility that they lived apart prior to this, whilst in the same house. Although it will not suffice to show merely that there was no intercourse between them (*Mouncer v Mouncer* (1972)), if it can be shown that they did not share any married life, then they may be treated as living apart (*Fuller v Fuller* (1973)). From the facts, it is clear that Fred and Wilma did have some shared life, but Wilma could try to argue that her case is like *Fuller v Fuller* in that this shared life was in a different capacity of nursemaid/patient and not husband/wife. However, this case is distinguishable from *Fuller*, in that in *Fuller* the wife's boyfriend lived in the same household and it was clearly recognised by all parties that the marriage was at an end. Unfortunately for Wilma, no third party was present in the household apart from Pebbles, and Fred did not realise that Wilma no longer cared for him as a spouse.[3]

In addition to living apart, the petitioner must show that at least one of the parties recognised that the marriage was at an end, even though this does not need to be communicated: *Santos v Santos* (1972). Clearly this could not have existed until Fred returned home from the hospital, but Wilma may have difficulty establishing this if Fred contests the petition. She did not inform anyone of that conclusion, although, when she told Barney of her unwillingness to leave Fred, she may have communicated the conclusion that the marriage was at an end.

---

2   Most divorce petitions use the behaviour fact. Thanks to special procedure, few divorces are defended and it is in reality quite easy to establish the behaviour fact. Despite this, it is important that answers do refer to and apply the relevant case law and that they note whether, if this case law were to be applied, the behaviour fact would be made out.

3   Although it is possible to live apart whilst sharing a house, *Mouncer* shows that this is difficult to do. This may in part explain why the separation facts are rarely used.

To petition under **s1(2)(d)**, Wilma needs to show two years living apart, and that the respondent consents to the granting of the decree. Given Fred's attitude, it is unlikely that Wilma will be able to provide the court with Fred's positive consent to the granting of the divorce.

Therefore, the only other option open to Wilma would seem to be the fact of five years' separation in **s1(2)(e)**. As discussed earlier, there needs to be the fact of five years living apart, coupled with Wilma's recognition that the marriage was at an end. This necessitates the finding that Fred and Wilma were living apart whilst still in the same house, something that is not without difficulty. If this were to fail, Wilma would need to wait for five years after leaving Fred before she petitioned.

Regardless of when her petition based on **s1(2)(e)** is presented, Fred may oppose the granting of the decree if the dissolution of the marriage would cause him grave financial or other hardship, and in all the circumstances it would be unjust to dissolve the marriage: **MCA s 5(1)**.

Fred's argument would be based on the loss of Wilma's care and the fact that he misses Pebbles. The court is required to look at all of the circumstances of the case, including the conduct of the parties, their interests and the interests of any children or other persons: **s 5(2)**. It is unlikely that the court would dismiss the petition as Fred's hardship arises from the breakdown of the relationship with Wilma, not the granting of a divorce: *Parghi v Parghi* (1973). Even if there is no divorce, he will still not have Wilma's care, as she is now having a relationship with Barney. Since both Fred and Wilma seem to be young, and Wilma is involved in another relationship, the court might consider that justice demands the divorce be granted to give Wilma the freedom to start a new life, as in *Parker v Parker* (1972). There is no evidence that Fred would suffer grave financial hardship on divorce, and therefore he is unlikely to succeed in his use of **s 5**.[4]

Common Pitfalls

In a problem question on the availability of divorce, it is important to focus on the most relevant facts rather than wasting time discussing each of the five facts.

Aim Higher

Extra marks will be gained for demonstrating good understanding of the relevant case law and analysing how the controls on the availability of the facts in the case law contrast with the reality of easily available divorce due to the special procedure.

---

4   Only rarely will a respondent be able to succeed under **s 5**. Most hardships will often be due to the relationship breaking down and the petitioner moving out rather than due to the legal recognition of this through a divorce.

QUESTION 6

X and Y were married seven years ago, when they were both 50, but, unknown to Y, X's hobby was the keeping of reptiles, including a snake. Y was terrified of the snake and threatened to leave if X did not get rid of it. X was very fond of his snake, and felt Y was being unreasonable in forcing him to choose between her and his snake. X refused to get rid of the snake, offering instead to confine it to the spare room, but six months later Y stormed out of the matrimonial home. X did not hear from Y for several months, and only heard of her whereabouts when he was contacted by a mental hospital where Y was a patient. X visited Y frequently in hospital, but Y was suffering from insane delusions about snakes. After six months in hospital, Y was discharged to be cared for in the community but refused to return home to X whilst he had the snake.

X and Y have not lived in the same house for the past six-and-a-half years, and X now wishes to divorce Y. Y is opposed to the divorce as she is concerned about her financial situation should she lose her widow's pension on X's death.
▶ Advise X who wants a divorce.

How to Read this Question
The fact that Y is concerned about her financial situation clearly points towards a possible claim under **s 5** of the **Matrimonial Causes Act (MCA) 1973** if X uses five years' separation without consent as the basis for the divorce.

Applying the Law

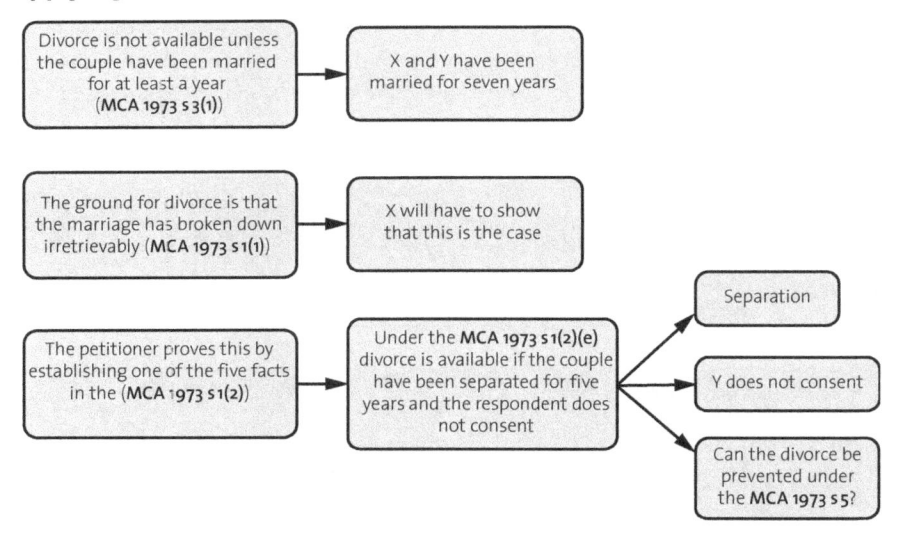

- Divorce is not available unless the couple have been married for at least a year (**MCA 1973 s 3(1)**) → X and Y have been married for seven years
- The ground for divorce is that the marriage has broken down irretrievably (**MCA 1973 s 1(1)**) → X will have to show that this is the case
- The petitioner proves this by establishing one of the five facts in the (**MCA 1973 s 1(2)**) → Under the **MCA 1973 s 1(2)(e)** divorce is available if the couple have been separated for five years and the respondent does not consent
  - → Separation
  - → Y does not consent
  - → Can the divorce be prevented under the **MCA 1973 s 5**?

ANSWER

If X wishes to petition for divorce now, he must establish the one ground for divorce in the **MCA 1973 s 1(1)**: that the marriage has broken down irretrievably. Since his marriage to

Divorce and Dissolution of Civil Partnerships

Y has lasted longer than one year, he is not prevented from presenting his petition by the bar in the **MCA 1973 s 3(1)**. However, the petition must do more than allege irretrievable breakdown; it must also specify one of the five facts in the **MCA 1973 s 1(2)**.

There is no evidence that either party to the marriage has committed adultery and so it is unnecessary to consider the application of the **MCA 1973 s 1(2)(a)**. The next fact, contained in **s 1(2)(b)**, is that the respondent has behaved in such a way that the petitioner cannot reasonably be expected to live with her. X will need to point to some behaviour by Y, and there may be difficulty in doing this. The first thing mentioned in the question is Y's insistence that X removes his snake from the house. Whilst X's distress at losing his pet is understandable, a snake is not something that many people would feel easy living with. Much might depend on the kind of snake, how large it is and the way in which it is confined. Y's simple desertion cannot be evidence of behaviour (*Morgan v Morgan* (1973)) and there would also be problems if X were to try to rely on Y's illness or mental condition. Behaviour needs to be some action or conduct by one spouse that affects the other and is referable to the marriage: *Katz v Katz* (1972). The development of a mental illness by Y, after she left the matrimonial home, is somewhat problematic, especially since the nature of the illness may suggest that it was precipitated by X and his snake. The courts often take the view that marriage involves a certain amount of give and take and understanding for a spouse's illness (*Thurlow v Thurlow* (1975)), and X would probably need to refer to stressful incidents committed by Y in her illness, rather than just her unhappy condition. If her delusions resulted in violence, as in *Thurlow*, or caused him considerable distress as in *Katz*, then he might succeed, but this is doubtful. The nature of Y's behaviour must be such that, taking into account the issues and personalities of the parties (*Ash v Ash* (1972)), it is not reasonable to expect X to live with Y (*Livingstone-Stallard v Livingstone-Stallard* (1974)). It could be argued that a snake-loving husband cannot reasonably be expected to live with a snake-hating wife! It would be open to Y to defend X's petition based on behaviour, and she could always cross-petition on the basis of X's behaviour. He has constantly failed to assuage her fears of the snake, and indeed, it could be argued that his love for and relationship with the snake have been destructive and his deliberate refusal to give the snake away despite his wife's genuine fear is behaviour that makes it unreasonable to expect her to live with him. From the facts, Y does not want a divorce, but, if one appears to be inevitable, it may be that she will seek one on the basis of X's behaviour.

Another possibility available to X is to petition on the basis of Y's desertion of him for a period of two years prior to the presenting of the petition under the **MCA 1973 s 12(c)**. This fact is very rarely relied on in practice and has a number of technical requirements. First, X must establish that there has been factual separation in that there has been a withdrawal from married life: *Pulford v Pulford* (1923). When Y left X, she withdrew from married life, and they have not cohabited together since. X's visits to the hospital probably do not count as periods of living a married life, since they were out of his concern for Y, and there is no evidence that she was in any way responding to him. If, however, there were brief resumptions of married life during these visits, the reconciliation provisions in the **MCA 1973 s 2** provide that such periods totalling six months or less shall be disregarded.

It is then necessary to establish that Y had the intention to desert. At the time she left X, it seems that Y, although distressed, was not insane and her mental illness developed later. If this is so, then she had the intention permanently to desert X, unless she just intended to storm out to teach X a lesson and force him to remove the snake. Subsequently, Y has become mentally ill, and at common law her desertion would cease when she developed the incapacity: *Crowther v Crowther* (1951). This has been affected by the **MCA 1973 s 2(4)**, which provides that the court can treat the period of desertion as continuing through the period of mental incapacity; if the evidence is such that had Y not been incapable, the court would infer that her desertion continued. From the facts, there is no evidence that Y had changed her mind, and so the likelihood is that she would still have the intention to desert even during her period in hospital. It is quite clear that on her discharge, she has no intention of returning to X whilst the snake remains in the house, and so she would continue in desertion.

If, however, at the time of leaving X, Y was suffering from delusions about the snake, then her capacity to form the intention to desert is questionable. In *Perry v Perry* (1964) it was suggested that the respondent be judged on the basis that the delusions were true, and therefore if she has delusions that her husband and the snake would harm her, then she may not be held to have formed the intention to desert. In such a case, X will need to establish at what point Y ceases to suffer from the delusions and is capable of forming the intention to desert.

X must then establish that he did not consent to the desertion; if he did then it is more appropriate to use **s 1(2)(d)** (two years living apart and consent), or **s 1(2)(e)** (five years living apart). The problem X faces here is that Y left only after he refused her ultimatum for staying. A petitioner who refuses a respondent's reasonable offer of reconciliation cannot rely on desertion: *Gallagher v Gallagher* (1965). Much will depend on whether Y's offer of staying with the snake removed was reasonable, in which case she is not in desertion, as in *Slawson v Slawson* (1942). It is by no means clear that X can establish that Y is in desertion; indeed, it may be that if he has refused her reasonable offer of reconciliation, he will be in desertion (*Hall v Hall* (1960)).

If X can show that he did not consent to Y's desertion, then he must finally establish that Y deserted without just cause. The same problem concerning X's relationship with the snake and the fear it caused Y is encountered. Indeed, if it could be said that X's behaviour in refusing to remove the snake, despite the terror it caused his wife, is grave and weighty (*Lang v Lang* (1953)), and has caused Y to leave, this would thereby place X in constructive desertion.

If desertion can be established, it must be for a continuous period of at least two years immediately prior to the presenting of the petition. In X and Y's case, they separated shortly after their marriage seven years ago, and have not really resumed married life since. It seems likely that the two-year period is satisfied, notwithstanding what was said previously regarding the period of Y's mental illness. It is clear from the facts of the case that the couple have been living apart for a considerable time. There have been two separate households (**MCA 1973 s 2(6)**), but it will be necessary to show that one party formed the conclusion that the marriage was at an end, even though this was not communicated to the other: *Santos v Santos* (1972). Looking at X, it is not clear when, if at all, he reached this conclusion. Initially, he offers to confine the snake to ensure Y does not leave; he also visits Y whilst she is in hospital. It may be that on Y's discharge, it becomes clear to X that the marriage has ended, but there is no evidence of this. X did not mention it to anyone, make a note, nor is there evidence of a relationship with anyone else. If Y were to defend this case, she might well contend that X never recognised the marriage was at an end, and this could cause X difficulty in establishing that he did to the court's satisfaction. If living apart can be established, it seems clear that X and Y have lived apart for at least two years. However, Y seems unlikely to consent to the granting of the divorce as required in **s 1(2)(d)**. This would necessitate X relying on the fact of five years living apart in **s 1(2)(e)**. It seems that the couple have lived apart since shortly after their marriage, which is longer than five years, but again the problem of recognition of the ending of the marriage (*Santos*) may mean that the five-year period is not yet established. If it is, then X does not need Y's consent to the divorce, although she may be able to prevent or postpone the divorce through the use of **ss 5** or **10** of the **MCA 1973**.[5]

The **MCA 1973 s 5** provides that a respondent may oppose the granting of a divorce on the grounds of grave financial or other hardship, and that, in all the circumstances of the case, it would be wrong to dissolve the marriage. Y has expressed concern about her financial situation if the divorce were to be granted. Hardship is defined to include the loss of the chance of acquiring any benefit (**s 5(3)**), and here Y is concerned at the possible loss of a widow's pension. At present, on divorce, the ex-wife would lose her entitlement to a widow's pension. This would not cause grave financial hardship if only the state widow's pension were lost, as this would be replaced by income support or a retirement pension: *Reiterbund v Reiterbund* (1975). However, if on X's death his widow would be provided with an occupational pension, then this might cause grave financial hardship if it were lost. Much will depend upon Y's personal financial position, since if she has independent means or wealth she is unlikely to be prejudiced. In *Archer v Archer* (1999), the 53-year-old wife risked losing £18,000 per annum on her 55-year-old husband's death if the divorce were granted. However, she had a house valued at £200,000 and her own investments of £300,000, and therefore would not suffer grave hardship through the divorce. If, however, she is in difficult financial circumstances, then grave hardship may be established: *Dorrell v Dorrell* (1972). She is now in her late 50s and is the kind of wife that **s 5** was designed to protect, in that a widow's pension is not a remote possibility, but something that might realistically accrue to her if married, but be denied to her on divorce: *Mathias v Mathias* (1972).

Under the **Pensions Act 1995 s 166**, part of one partner's private pension can be earmarked for the benefit of the other partner. However, this would only be of benefit on the

---

5   Desertion is rarely relied on as a fact. It is easier to use behaviour rather than waiting two years, or for the petitioner to consent to the living apart and use **s 1(2)(d)**. There is no advantage to the petitioner in being the wronged party and using desertion rather than living apart.

retirement of the partner with the pension. The more radical option of splitting X's pension fund between him and Y has been made possible by the pension-sharing provisions of the **Welfare Reform and Pensions Act 1999**. This would arguably remove any argument that the divorce would cause grave hardship. If such a defence is raised, then X may be able to obtain his divorce if he can put forward reasonable proposals that would compensate Y for the loss of pension, such as the provision of an annuity or insurance policy (*Parker v Parker* (1972)). In the circumstances, if X cannot adequately compensate Y, then the court may consider, in all the circumstances, including the conduct of X, that it would be wrong to dissolve the marriage.[6]

Even if Y does not seek to rely on **s 5**, she may seek to postpone the granting of the decree based on either **s 1(2)(d)** or **(e)** until the court has considered her financial position. The **MCA 1973 s 10** provides that on such an application the court must look at all of the circumstances of the case, including the age, health, conduct, needs and resources of the parties. The decree will not be made absolute until the court is satisfied that either no financial provision for Y will be made, or that the financial provision made by X is reasonable and fair or the best that can be made in the circumstances. Therefore, it is important for X to be prepared to outline his proposals for financial provision for Y, if any can be made.

QUESTION 7

H and W have been married for 30 years, and are now both aged 60. H is a successful businessman and has, for many years, been involved in Freemasonry. H and W have become increasingly estranged over the years, especially since their daughter, J, grew up and left home. When J left home, W joined some adult education classes and has become increasingly involved in women's rights and radical politics. H finds this embarrassing and has had to endure many taunts from his friends about his wife getting 'out of control'. W has become increasingly assertive and will not cook H's meals or wash and iron his clothes, arguing that she is no longer his slave.

W frequently makes jokes about H's involvement with the Freemasons and has refused to accompany H to the annual Freemasons' social event, 'Ladies' Night', saying that it is derogatory to women. This is too much for H who told her to 'shape up or get out'. W responded by changing the locks on the doors to the matrimonial home, whilst H was out at work, to teach him a lesson. W made H wait on the doorstep for two hours before throwing him the new keys. H moved back in, but W refuses to cook and clean for him, and H now wishes to divorce W. W is unwilling to consider divorce as she does not wish to upset her elderly mother, C, who is a staunch Catholic and vehemently opposed to divorce. C has threatened to disinherit any of her children who divorce.

▶ Advise H on whether he can obtain a divorce.

---

[6] In this case, one concern is that Y might lose her pension entitlement were she and X to divorce. Because this is a factor, the answer is right in explaining how pensions can now be dealt with as part of ancillary relief and how, therefore, concern about pensions is unlikely to lead to a successful **s 5** application.

Divorce and Dissolution of Civil Partnerships

How to Read this Question

The question is solely about whether H could obtain a divorce, not what the consequences of that divorce would be.

Applying the Law

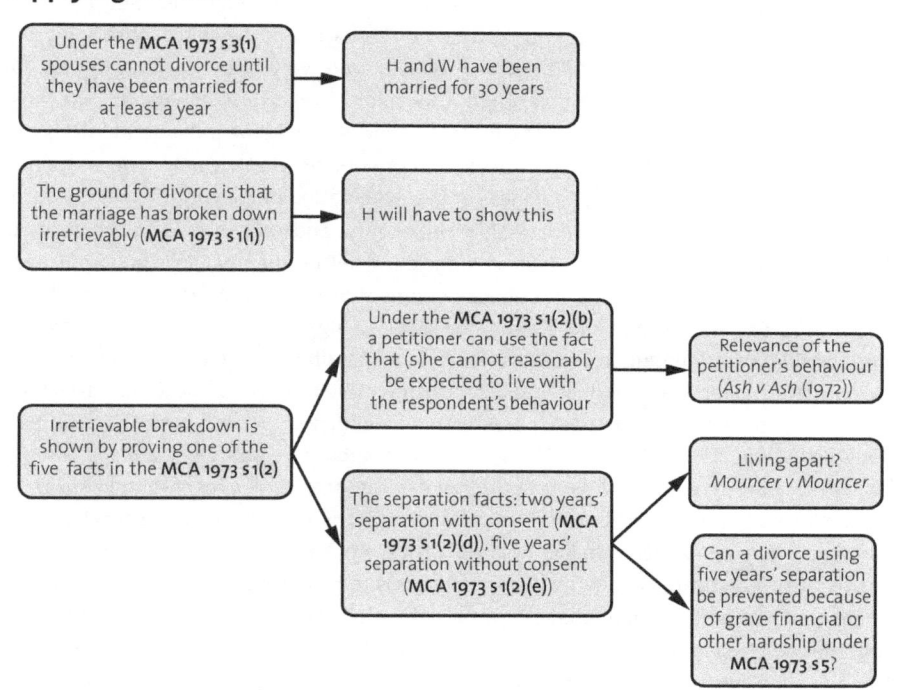

- Under the **MCA 1973 s 3(1)** spouses cannot divorce until they have been married for at least a year → H and W have been married for 30 years

- The ground for divorce is that the marriage has broken down irretrievably (**MCA 1973 s 1(1)**) → H will have to show this

- Irretrievable breakdown is shown by proving one of the five facts in the **MCA 1973 s 1(2)**
  - Under the **MCA 1973 s 1(2)(b)** a petitioner can use the fact that (s)he cannot reasonably be expected to live with the respondent's behaviour → Relevance of the petitioner's behaviour (*Ash v Ash* (1972))
  - The separation facts: two years' separation with consent (**MCA 1973 s 1(2)(d)**), five years' separation without consent (**MCA 1973 s 1(2)(e)**)
    → Living apart? *Mouncer v Mouncer*
    → Can a divorce using five years' separation be prevented because of grave financial or other hardship under **MCA 1973 s 5**?

ANSWER

H can petition for divorce if he can show that his marriage has broken down irretrievably: **Matrimonial Causes Act (MCA) 1973 s 1(1)**. This must be evidenced by one of the five facts in **s 1(2)** (*Richards v Richards* (1972)), since irretrievable breakdown in isolation is insufficient to obtain a divorce. The marriage between H and W has obviously encountered difficulties; however, the facts must be such that one of the five facts in **s 1(2)** can be established. The marriage is of a lengthy nature, and so the bar on presenting petitions within one year of marriage contained in the **MCA 1973 s 3(1)** does not apply. There is no evidence in this case of either H or W committing adultery, and therefore **s 1(2)(a)** is inapplicable. However, there is a need to consider **s 1(2)(b)** whereby a petition may be presented on the basis that the respondent has behaved in such a way that the petitioner cannot reasonably be expected to live with them.[7]

---

[7] The only ground for divorce under the **MCA 1973** is irretrievable breakdown but that has to be shown by proving one of the five facts in **s 1(2)**. When writing an answer to a divorce question make sure that the answer is clear that the ground is irretrievable breakdown rather than suggesting that one of the facts is itself the ground for the divorce.

Initially, H will need to specify exactly what constitutes behaviour on W's part. In *Katz v Katz* (1972), behaviour was defined in terms of action or conduct by one spouse that affects the other and is referable to the marriage. It seems that H has been upset by W's new-found interests, and by the jokes made by his friends. It seems harsh to argue that W's desire to gain new interests has somehow constituted behaviour towards H. Many women find the need for new horizons as they grow older and their children leave home. The fact that H feels threatened or embarrassed by this cannot fairly be attributable to W. If, however, W's new interests were very extreme, causing her to completely isolate herself from H, then this might constitute behaviour. She has refused to do any cooking or cleaning for H, and this seems to be a deliberate decision by her. It is not apparent whether both she and H work, or whether only H does; such a factor will determine the reasonableness of the expectation of contribution. W has also begun to ridicule H's involvement with Freemasonry, and has refused to accompany him on one particular occasion. Again, it is unclear whether the ridicule is good-natured joking in private or cruel jibing in public. It seems that W has not withdrawn from all social activities with H, but merely the one 'Ladies' Night' that her conscience found unpalatable. W's changing of the locks was behaviour, albeit of a joking nature, but it is by no means clear that H will succeed on this fact. Then it will be necessary to show that, given the individual parties' characters and conduct (*Ash v Ash* (1972)), it is unreasonable to expect H to live with W. This is a partly subjective approach, and, according to Bagnall J in *Ash v Ash*: 'a violent petitioner can reasonably be expected to live with a violent respondent... and if each is equally bad, at any rate in sinister respects, each can reasonably be expected to live with the other.' Applying this to the present case, H seems to be a dedicated chauvinist whilst W seems to be an equally trenchant feminist. There could be an argument that these two extremes could never be expected to live together. The reasonableness of the expectation of contribution is judged objectively, the so-called 'jury test' in *Livingstone-Stallard v Livingstone-Stallard* (1974). Here the parties have had a long marriage, and the readjustment that naturally occurs as the parties adapt in later years will cause problems in most marriages. The disagreements in this case may not be so extreme that it is not reasonable to expect H to live with W. The changing of the locks was to teach H a lesson after his ultimatum, not a vindictive exclusion of a blameless spouse. Incidents can have a cumulative effect (*Livingstone-Stallard v Livingstone-Stallard* (1974)), but seen in totality it seems that H will have difficulty in establishing behaviour. It seems to be the classic case of 'six of one, half a dozen of the other'.[8]

The fact of desertion in **s1(2)(c)** will be difficult to establish for H. W has refused to cook or clean for H, but seems willing to talk to him and share aspects of family life. The fact that H and W are not truly living apart as two households will also make any petition under **s1(2)(d)** or **(e)** unlikely to succeed. The fact that the relationship is strained is

---

8 This illustrates the subjective nature of the behaviour fact. The question is not whether the behaviour complained of is objectively unreasonable, but whether it would be reasonable to expect that particular petitioner with their personality, character and habits to put up with the respondent's behaviour.

insufficient to show the parties are maintaining two households: *Mouncer v Mouncer* (1972). However, if H were to move out or cease to share any common life, then he could petition for divorce after two years with W's consent. This does not seem likely to be forthcoming, in which case H would need to establish five years living apart, in terms of physical living apart coupled with his recognition that the marriage was at an end: *Santos v Santos* (1972).

In such a situation, W may seek to prevent the divorce by relying on the **MCA 1973 s 5**. It could be argued that the granting of the divorce would cause her grave financial or other hardship, and that in all the circumstances it would be wrong to grant the petition. W wishes to avoid upsetting her elderly mother who, for religious reasons, is opposed to divorce. There is no evidence to show whether W herself is opposed to divorce for religious reasons and, in any case, the court will look for strong evidence of social ostracism before refusing the petition, as in *Banik v Banik* (1973). The mere fact that divorce is frowned upon would be insufficiently grave to justify opposing the divorce: *Parghi v Parghi* (1973).

However, W can also argue that divorce would cause her grave financial hardship. This could include the loss of any benefit that the respondent might acquire if the marriage were not dissolved: **MCA 1973 s 5(3)**. This was designed to cover the possible loss of widow's pensions, etc., which could be a severe hardship for a woman of W's age: *Mathias v Mathias* (1972). It is not clear whether this covers the potential loss of inheritance from a third party. The section is widely drafted and could potentially cover it, but it would seem harsh to H to deny him a divorce because of the possible reaction of his elderly mother-in-law. The court is instructed to look at all of the circumstances of the case, including the conduct of the parties and their interests and those of any children or other persons: **MCA 1973 s 5(2)**. If H can make some sort of attempt to mitigate any possible financial hardship for W, then he may be allowed his divorce (*Parker v Parker* (1972)), and since he is a successful businessman it seems likely that he could purchase some kind of annuity or set aside some lump sum to offset the loss of any widow's pension, and possibly any inheritance if that is a valid consideration.[9]

Even if W does not invoke **s 5**, then she may well use the provisions in the **MCA 1973 s 10** to postpone the divorce being made absolute. Where petitions are presented on facts in **s 1(2)(d)** or **(e)**, the respondent can apply to the court for consideration of her financial position: **s 10(2)**. In such a situation, the court will not award a decree absolute unless no financial provision is to be made, which is unlikely in this case, or unless the financial provision is reasonable and fair or the best that can be made in the circumstances: **MCA 1973 s 10(3)**. After such a long marriage, and given H's standing as a businessman,

---

9   Claims by the respondent that a divorce would lead to grave financial or other hardship under **MCA 1973 s 5** are rarely successful. The hardship has to be due to the divorce, rather than to the breakdown of the relationship and the couple living separately. Moreover, in relation to financial hardship, this can be mitigated by the financial relief awarded on the divorce.

W is likely to be entitled to financial provision. Therefore H should be prepared to present a clear explanation to the court of the financial provision he is proposing: *Grigson v Grigson* (1974).

QUESTION 8

Kathy was a devout Christian, and devoted a great deal of her time to charitable works, including prison visits. On one visit to the prison she met John, who had been convicted of rape and attempted murder. John impressed Kathy with his charm and repentance, and soon she fell in love with him. They were married whilst John was still in jail some eight years ago, but with Kathy's help John was released early five years ago. Immediately on his release, John's personality changed and he shouted obscenities at Kathy, forcing her to perform degrading acts, but stopping short of actual intercourse. He then hit Kathy, who has been too frightened to tell anyone of what happened. John disappeared and since then there have been numerous reports linking John with rapes throughout the country, but nothing has been heard of him since an incident three years ago, when the victim shot her attacker, who fitted John's description. The attacker had been badly wounded, as much blood was found at the scene and nearby. DNA tests reveal that the blood is almost definitely John's. Kathy does not want to divorce John, for religious reasons, but is most anxious to know what can be done to end her marital obligations to him.

▶ Advise Kathy.

How to Read this Question

This question is about ending a marriage without using divorce. In this case nullity, presumption of death and judicial separation may all be relevant.

Applying the Law

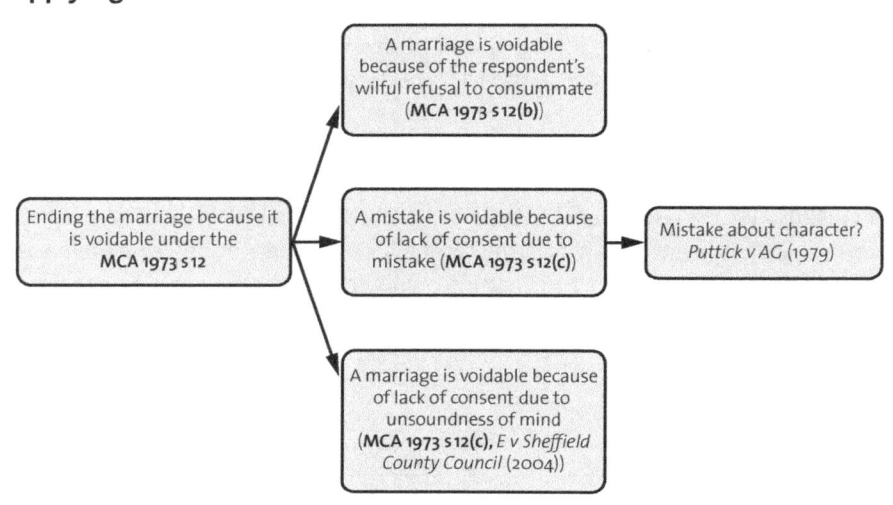

```
                              ┌──────────────────────────┐
                              │ A marriage is voidable   │
                              │ because of the respondent's│
                              │ wilful refusal to consummate│
                              │     (MCA 1973 s 12(b))   │
                              └──────────────────────────┘
                                          ▲
┌──────────────────────────┐   ┌──────────────────────────┐   ┌──────────────────────────┐
│ Ending the marriage because it│→│ A mistake is voidable because│→│ Mistake about character? │
│   is voidable under the  │   │  of lack of consent due to│   │    Puttick v AG (1979)   │
│      MCA 1973 s 12       │   │  mistake (MCA 1973 s 12(c))│   │                          │
└──────────────────────────┘   └──────────────────────────┘   └──────────────────────────┘
                                          ▼
                              ┌──────────────────────────┐
                              │ A marriage is voidable because│
                              │  of lack of consent due to│
                              │    unsoundness of mind   │
                              │ (MCA 1973 s 12(c), E v Sheffield│
                              │    County Council (2004))│
                              └──────────────────────────┘
```

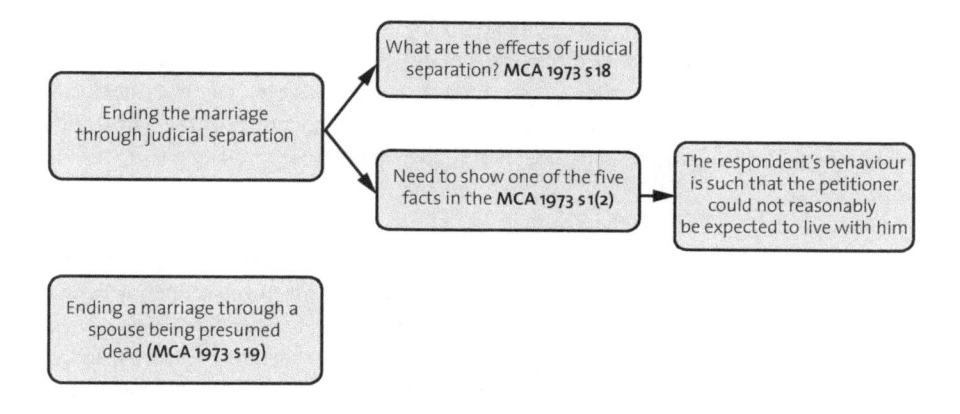

Divorce and Dissolution of Civil Partnerships | 33

- Ending the marriage through judicial separation
  - What are the effects of judicial separation? **MCA 1973 s 18**
  - Need to show one of the five facts in the **MCA 1973 s 1(2)**
    - The respondent's behaviour is such that the petitioner could not reasonably be expected to live with him

- Ending a marriage through a spouse being presumed dead (**MCA 1973 s 19**)

ANSWER

Since Kathy is adamantly opposed to the idea of divorcing John, it is necessary to consider the other options available to her if she wishes to end her marital obligations towards John. There are three possibilities, namely nullity, judicial separation and presumption of death and dissolution of marriage.

Nullity proceedings are available in respect of void marriages by reference to the grounds in the **Matrimonial Causes Act (MCA) 1973 s 11** and in respect of voidable marriages by reference to the grounds in the **MCA 1973 s 12**. None of the grounds for a void marriage appear to be present in this scenario and therefore the question is whether this would be a voidable marriage under **s 12** of the **MCA 1973**. A voidable marriage is treated as valid unless and until it is voided. This means that a nullity decree is a necessity in order to end Kathy's obligations, but it is only possible for her to petition for nullity during John's lifetime.

The first two grounds in **s 12(a)** and **(b)** require the marriage not to have been consummated. Consummation is one act of complete and regular intercourse after the marriage: *D v A* (1845). It is unclear whether Kathy and John had the opportunity to have sexual intercourse whilst John was in prison. If they did not do so, then the incident after John's release does not amount to consummation. There must be full penetration of the vagina by the penis; sexual activities other than this do not suffice (*W v W* (1967)). If the marriage has not been consummated, then the reason for this must be examined. **Section 12(a)** requires incapacity to consummate on the part of the petitioner or the respondent. There is no evidence that either Kathy or John is incapable of consummating the relationship; rather it seems that John has deliberately chosen not to. This may be evidence of wilful refusal to consummate by John, thereby enabling Kathy to petition. In *Horton v Horton* (1947), it was necessary to show 'a settled and definite decision come to without just cause', and such a situation would seem to be indicated here by John's treatment of Kathy and his immediate departure.[10]

---

10 Note that Kathy would not be able to rely on the fact that the marriage was not consummated during John's prison sentence as at that time John would have had a 'just cause' for not consummating the relationship.

The **MCA 1973 s12(c)** makes a marriage voidable through lack of consent through mistake, duress, unsoundness of mind, or otherwise. In Kathy's case, she could try to argue that she had made a mistake about John's reformed character. However, mistake must be as to the nature of the ceremony (*Mehta v Mehta* (1945)) or the identity of the party, but a mistake as to a quality of the party does not render the marriage voidable (*Puttick v AG* (1979)).

The facts seem to indicate that John's mind is unbalanced, to say the least, but in order for the marriage to be invalid it must be shown that at the time of the ceremony he was suffering from such an unsoundness of mind that he could not understand the nature of the ceremony (*Sheffield City Council v E and Another* (2004)). This rarely succeeds, and, in the present case, John seems to have exploited the prospects that marriage brings in terms of early release, and, therefore was unlikely to have satisfied the test of unsoundness of mind.

There is no evidence of duress or any other factor to vitiate consent, and there is no evidence of the grounds in **s12(e)** (venereal disease) or **s12(f)** (pregnancy *per alium*). The only other option available to Kathy is to rely on **s12(d)** and argue that although John was capable of consenting to the marriage, he was suffering at the time from a mental disorder, within the meaning of the **Mental Health Act 1983**, of such a kind or extent as to be unfit for marriage. The test is whether the party was capable of carrying out the ordinary duties and obligations of marriage (*Bennett v Bennett* (1968)), and, despite his criminal tendencies, it would seem that John was not suffering from some such disorder.

If the petition is presented on the basis of non-consummation, then the possible bars to the granting of the decree need to be considered. Kathy has not behaved in any way to lead John to believe that she would not annul the marriage and so statutory approbation does not apply: **MCA 1973 s13(1)**. There are no time bars to petitions based on non-consummation, although a petition based on any other ground must be presented within three years of the marriage: **MCA s13(2)**. The only possible waiver of this time limit is a discretionary one if at any time the petitioner has been suffering from a mental disorder. Kathy's wedding took place eight years ago, and since she has never suffered such a defect, she could not petition on any basis other than **s12(b)** (wilful refusal to consummate).

If the marriage has been consummated, then Kathy's other option is to seek a decree of judicial separation. The decree does not end the marriage, but it does end the duty to cohabit: **MCA 1973 s18(1)**. There is no need to establish that the marriage has irretrievably broken down, but the petitioner must establish one of the five facts in the **MCA s1(2)**. John has committed rape, and this will amount to adultery since he has voluntarily had sexual intercourse with a woman whilst he was married to Kathy. **Section 1(2)(a)** further requires the petitioner to show that she finds it intolerable to live with the respondent, and there is little doubt, given what has happened, that this subjective test can be satisfied. The intolerability need not arise from the adultery (*Cleary v Cleary* (1974)), and therefore John's treatment of Kathy will help satisfy the fact in **s1(2)(b)**. In addition, there is little doubt also that John has behaved in such a way that it is not reasonable to expect Kathy to continue to live with him: **MCA s1(2)(b)**. Therefore Kathy will be able to obtain a decree of judicial separation.

There is the additional possibility here that John may be dead. The forensic and identification evidence seems to indicate that he was shot and badly wounded, and as nothing has been heard of him by friends or relatives, or victims of his crimes, it may be possible to apply to the court for a decree of presumption of death and dissolution of marriage: **s19 MCA**. **Section 19(1)** provides that any married person who has reasonable grounds for supposing that his or her spouse is dead may present a petition to the court to have the spouse presumed dead and the marriage dissolved. **Section 19(3)** provides a presumption that a person is dead if he or she has been absent for seven years or more, but this does not apply to John. Therefore, Kathy will need to provide the court with details as to why she believes John to be dead. She seems to have made enquiries about him (*Bullock v Bullock* (1960)), and despite a huge police search for him, he has not been found. His last known appearance was in circumstances to suggest he had been fatally wounded and so Kathy could succeed in her application under **s19**. If she does, and John reappears, then the decree nisi will be rescinded, but if the decree has been made absolute, the marriage remains ended.

Therefore, it can be seen that despite her unwillingness to divorce, Kathy has several options available to her to end her obligations towards John.

QUESTION 9

The present procedures for ending a marriage fail both the parties and society generally. Something radical must be done.
- Discuss.

How to Read this Question

The question claims that current divorce law is not working and that significant reform is needed. Answers need to examine divorce procedure to see whether it is effective and whether it does support families, and if not, whether and how it should be reformed.

Applying the Law

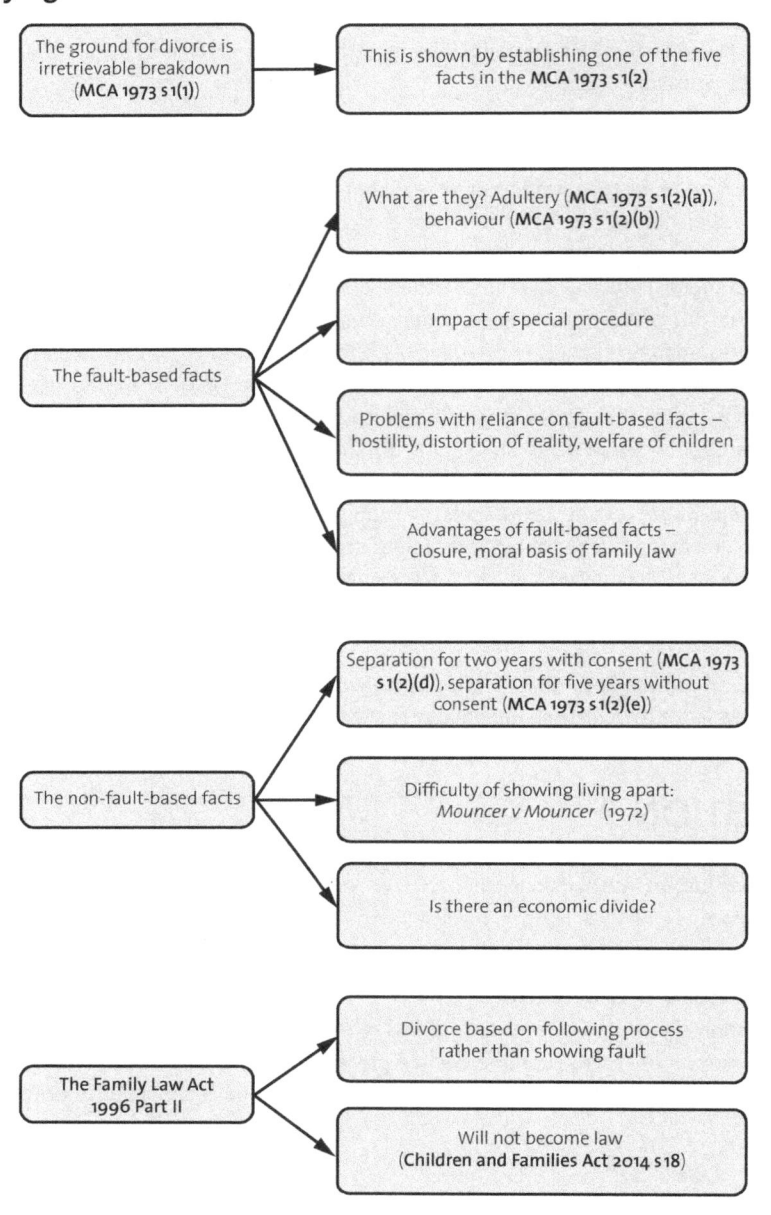

- The ground for divorce is irretrievable breakdown (**MCA 1973 s 1(1)**) → This is shown by establishing one of the five facts in the **MCA 1973 s 1(2)**

The fault-based facts
- What are they? Adultery (**MCA 1973 s 1(2)(a)**), behaviour (**MCA 1973 s 1(2)(b)**)
- Impact of special procedure
- Problems with reliance on fault-based facts – hostility, distortion of reality, welfare of children
- Advantages of fault-based facts – closure, moral basis of family law

The non-fault-based facts
- Separation for two years with consent (**MCA 1973 s 1(2)(d)**), separation for five years without consent (**MCA 1973 s 1(2)(e)**)
- Difficulty of showing living apart: *Mouncer v Mouncer* (1972)
- Is there an economic divide?

The Family Law Act 1996 Part II
- Divorce based on following process rather than showing fault
- Will not become law (**Children and Families Act 2014 s 18**)

ANSWER

A marriage may end in divorce if one of the parties successfully presents a petition alleging that the marriage has irretrievably broken down (**Matrimonial Causes Act (MCA) 1973 s 1(1)**), and proves this by establishing one of the five facts in the **MCA 1973 s 1(2)**. Very few petitions are contested (less than 1 per cent), and the vast majority of divorces are granted by way of the special procedure whereby the petition is read and approved without oral hearing. However, for many couples, divorce is a bitter process, and does not end their problems, but merely leads to further dispute and antagonism. It is therefore necessary to examine the current divorce procedures and see how far, if at all, they serve the parties' and society's interests.

Historically, marriage has been regarded as an institution that should be firmly supported and not undermined by the State. However, increasing numbers have found their marriages intolerable and have sought an end to their marital obligations. Initially, it was only possible to divorce a partner who could be shown to be at fault. This inevitably leads to bitter accusations about past indiscretions and conduct and is hardly conducive to civilised conduct after the divorce. This bitterness can have repercussions on the welfare of any children as well as the parties' willingness to cooperate in other matters, such as financial agreements.[11]

Despite much opposition, especially from vocal clergy, the **Divorce Reform Act 1969** introduced the concept of a no-fault divorce. This is now to be found in the **MCA 1973** s 1(2)(d) and **(e)**, namely divorce after two years' separation with the respondent's consent to the granting of the petition, and five years' separation if there is no such consent. The idea behind a no-fault divorce is that it would reduce bitterness and antagonism and improve the ongoing relationship between the parties and their children. However, the provisions of **s 1(2)(e)** have been objected to by those who opposed the idea of an 'innocent' spouse being divorced against his or her wishes.

The **MCA 1973** does not provide for a completely no-fault divorce system, and it retains fault-based facts of adultery, behaviour and desertion. Despite the availability of no-fault divorce, more than 80 per cent of petitions allege adultery or behaviour, which enables immediate divorce and obviates the need to live apart for a lengthy period. Thus, in reality, no-fault divorce exists in less than one-fifth of cases, and the requirement of physical separation is often difficult to achieve for families on low incomes. Presently, therefore, most divorces do involve the petitioner alleging fault on the part of the respondent. This encourages petitioners to rake over incidents in the past, often exaggerating them, in order to obtain a speedy divorce. This can increase the respondent's resentment, lead to cross-petitions, antagonism and lasting conflict that can be very damaging to the welfare of the children.

Once it is recognised that divorce is inevitable in many cases, good divorce law should ensure that it provides an effective method of ending marriages that have not worked with the minimum of bitterness, leaving the parties in a position where future cooperation in financial matters and the upbringing of the children can be achieved. The present law does not do that because of the tendency for most divorces to be fault-based. In 1985, the Booth Committee on Matrimonial Causes Procedures recommended that all

---

11 There is, however, a contrary argument that an 'innocent' spouse may feel bitter if (s)he is not able to cite the other spouse's fault in claiming a divorce.

divorce should be fault-free, since the fault element increases bitterness and stops sensible discussion about crucial future issues. The only basis of divorce should, according to the Committee, be irretrievable breakdown of marriage without specifying any further facts. This has been criticised, but in reality the lack of investigation in the special procedure adopted by the courts for most divorces means that this could be happening already if the parties agree not to contest the petition. There is little evidence that fault-based divorce reduces the divorce rate or saves marriages from failure and, from society's point of view, the bitterness of fault-based divorce spills over into ancillary matters and children issues, which are costly in terms of legal aid and human misery.

The Law Commission reported in 1990 (The Ground for Divorce) and agreed that the way forward lay in no-fault divorce. Its report suggested that irretrievable breakdown without any further fact should be the basis of divorce. Once a person felt that their marriage had broken down, they should be able to lodge a sworn statement in court to that effect. The Law Commission thought that a joint application could also be made, and that once this had happened, the parties should be given an information pack outlining what should happen next and the need to sort out financial arrangements and arrangements for the children. Mediation would be available to assist the parties to reach agreement on these matters, and then after 11 months it would be open to either party to apply for a divorce stating that the marriage had in fact irretrievably broken down. Thus, the important practical issues would be sorted out before the divorce was granted, and hopefully the no-fault nature of proceedings would ensure the minimum of bitterness. The Law Commission wanted the court to retain the power to refuse divorce on the basis of grave financial or other hardship. Critics argued that this would further undermine the institution of marriage, make divorce easier to obtain and could lead to parties instigating proceedings as a threat, thereby setting the process in motion. There would also be no method of ending a marriage sooner than 12 months, and the statistics presently show that many petitioners prefer not to wait once they have decided the marriage is at an end.

The Lord Chancellor published a Green Paper on divorce reform at the end of 1993, which mirrored the Law Commission's view that the way ahead might well be no-fault divorce on the basis of irretrievable breakdown. A period of reflection once the initial application was made was considered a good idea. There has been considerable public debate on this matter, with opinion divided upon whether the proposals would make divorce too easy and undermine marriage. Most commentators felt, however, that reform was long overdue and hoped that the provisions of the **Family Law Act 1996** were going to address the problems of the past.

Further criticism of the present system concerns the enormous financial cost of protracted litigation for the public purse, and there are those who have suggested that legal aid should be withdrawn in contested divorce cases and ancillary relief applications. Others suggest that it should only be available if the parties agree to conciliation.

Mediation is a process whereby an impartial and trained individual meets with the parties and encourages them to reach an agreement on areas of dispute such as financial provision and arrangements for the children. This hopefully reduces bitterness, saves costs and has an important role in making divorce less traumatic and adversarial. Mediation may take place in court, and in 1971 a Practice Direction allowed courts to refer cases to the court's welfare officer if it was thought he could help with the process. Initially, pilot schemes were established, but they have spread throughout the country and allow emotional and possibly confrontational issues to be handled in a constructive manner. Criticisms have been made, in that the parties often feel under pressure to reach an agreement in a short time, and it is very important that the parties are legally represented and kept fully informed. The Law Commission and the Green Paper did not suggest making mediation compulsory in all divorces, as it is its voluntary nature that ensures cooperation and a willingness to reach agreement.

Out-of-court mediation schemes also exist whereby trained personnel offer assistance to parties to reach agreement independently of the court system. Some people believe that these schemes are more successful since they are not so involved in the legal process and can be used before the parties' positions become too entrenched. However, there has been concern that such schemes can be dominated by the more forceful partner and that information may be withheld.

The **Family Law Act 1996** tried in statutory format to provide a mechanism which recognised that divorce was a social reality, but at the same time tried to get the couple concerned to properly consider whether their relationship was at an end. The no-fault concept attempted to reduce bitterness if divorce was to occur, but the information meetings and period for reflection and consideration were designed to encourage parties to think about reconciliation. Assistance was provided to parties by giving information about organisations helping resolve difficulties, as well as funding for conciliation services and marriage support services.

The Act also sought to reduce bitterness and encourage future cooperation by requiring the couples to seek to negotiate their own arrangements regarding finance and their children where possible. The option of mediation was available in the hope that expensive adversarial litigation could be avoided. However, the pilot schemes have shown that the Government's expectations for mediation have not been met. Fewer than one in 10 couples were prepared to mediate rather than litigate, and the vast majority felt better protected by lawyers. Mediation can be expensive and time-consuming, and requires a certain willingness on the part of those involved. Mediation can often be thwarted by the attitude and actions of one of the parties. In addition, the Government failed to fund and train sufficient mediators to provide a nationwide service.

The most serious flaw shown by the pilot schemes is that it is a mistake to think that legislation can control human emotions at such a traumatic time. The information meetings were badly thought out, and whilst objective information is desirable, the compulsory nature of the meetings antagonised and humiliated some participants. The nature of these meetings was also not properly thought through, and it is unrealistic to think that parties really do spend the period for reflection and consideration doing these two things.

The complex statutory provisions, far from reducing conflict, actually increased the potential for an obstructive party to delay the divorce and obstruct resolution of issues regarding the children and finances. Whilst the current law is far from ideal, and although the **Family Law Act 1996** had many laudable aims, the practical experience of the pilot schemes has led to the conclusion that the law would be 'jumping from the frying pan into the fire'. Consequently, the Government abandoned plans to implement the far-reaching provisions of the **Family Law Act 1996** relating to divorce, and decided to stick with 'the devil we know', the **Matrimonial Causes Act 1973**. This was further confirmed by **Children and Families Act 2014 s 18** which stated that **Family Law Act 1996 Part II** would not be implemented.

In conclusion, therefore, it does appear that the present system and procedures for obtaining divorce fail the parties, their children and society generally. Whilst no reform seems perfect, a move towards no-fault divorce in the **Family Law Act 1996**, with an emphasis on conciliation, would go some way to ensuring that failed marriages end with the minimum of animosity and that future relationships between family members are not irrevocably soured. However, a completely no-fault scheme may leave those who have been grievously upset by the behaviour of their spouses feeling badly treated. Whatever reform is made, there will always be those who feel let down at the ending of their relationship.

Common Pitfalls

You will never be given an essay question that invites you to, for instance, tell the examiner everything that you can remember about divorce, so please do not do it! Here the question clearly asks you to identify the problems with current divorce law for the spouses *and* for society as a whole *and* to discuss whether something radical needs to be done. Your answer should consider all these points.

Aim Higher

Good answers that show critical thought will be backed up by good knowledge of the statute and case law.

3 Financial Provision for Adult Partners

INTRODUCTION

The following two chapters consider financial provision. This chapter looks at financial relief for adult partners both during the relationship and when the relationship has ended, and Chapter 4 considers financial support for children. Whilst spouses can claim financial support from each other, both during and after the marriage, adult partners who have not married have no right to maintenance.

Checklist

Students should know and be able to apply the law surrounding:

- financial relief for spouses during the marriage under the **Matrimonial Causes Act 1973** and the **Domestic Proceedings and Magistrates' Courts Act 1978** and should be able to explain which provision is more suitable for a particular spouse;
- the powers available to the court to make orders for financial relief following a divorce;
- when these powers can be used (*Wyatt v Vince* (2015));
- how the family home can be allotted following a divorce: **MCA 1973 s 24A, MCA 1973 s 24(1)(a)**, Mesher orders, Martin orders;
- the courts' powers to order pensions following divorce;
- the requirement to consider a clean break; be able to refer to and apply relevant case law: **MCA 1973 s 25A(1)**. Should the periodical payments be limited for a term? **MCA 1973 s 25A(2)**, *Mcfarlane v Mcfarlane* (2006);
- how the law on pre-nuptial settlements has developed and how these are currently viewed by the courts (*Granatino v Radmacher* (2010), *Z v Z (No 2)* (2011), *V v V* (2011), *Luckwell v Limata* (2014), *SA v PA (Pre-marital agreement: compensation)* (2014));
- understand that the aim of the court in dividing marital assets is fairness and be able to discuss whether this means that there is a presumption in favour of an equal split (*White v White* (2001), *Miller v Miller* (2006), *Lambert v Lambert* (2003));
- what property will come within the assets to be apportioned by the court (*Miller v Miller* (2006), *Charman v Charman* (2007), *N v F* (2011), *S v AG Financial Remedy Lottery Prize* (2011), *JL v SL (No 2)* (2015)) and the difficulty sometimes of determining what assets a spouse has (*Young v Young* (2013));
- financial relief and whether it is aimed at compensating spouses for their loss (*Mcfarlane v Mcfarlane* (2006));
- financial relief for civil partners under the **Civil Partnership Act 2004 s 72**.

Up for Debate

- What should be the law's approach to pre-marital contracts?
- Should there be a time limit on when financial relief can be claimed and how long for?
- How should the court discover and assess the marital assets?
- Is equal division of marital assets fair?

EXAM QUESTIONS

This is a popular topic. It may be combined with a divorce, child maintenance or property. Problem questions focus on advising individual spouses whilst essay questions may look at recent judicial developments.

QUESTION 10

Abigail and Ben have been married for eight years. They have no children, and both of them have worked throughout the marriage. Abigail has had a successful career as a solicitor, but recently lost her job when the firm she worked with closed their local office. However, she was offered a job in an office with an associated firm of solicitors, some 250 miles away, and as the job situation was bleak, Abigail accepted the position. She rented a small flat near her new job, and returned home to Ben each weekend. However, her visits became more infrequent, and now she hardly ever returns home.

When Abigail and Ben married, Ben was a schoolteacher with a passion for composing music. With Abigail's encouragement, he gave up his job and has concentrated on composing. However, not many pieces attracted the music companies' approval, and his earnings have averaged £4,000 per annum. Abigail's earnings are in the region of £50,000 per annum, but she only sends money to Ben occasionally. Ben does not want to get a divorce, but needs money to cover the mortgage and other bills.

▶ Advise Ben.

How to Read this Question

Ben does not want to divorce but is struggling financially. This question is therefore focused on maintenance for spouses within a marriage.

Applying the Law

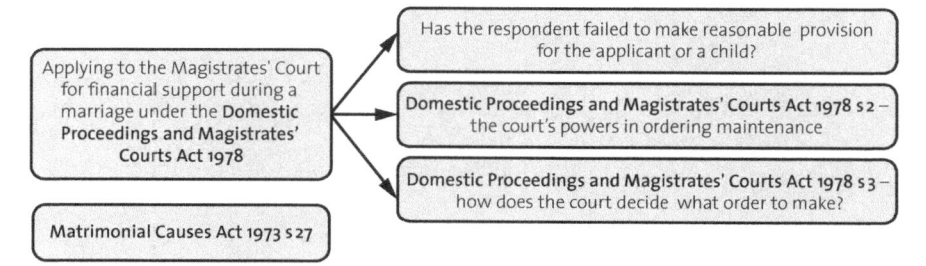

- Applying to the Magistrates' Court for financial support during a marriage under the **Domestic Proceedings and Magistrates' Courts Act 1978**
  - Has the respondent failed to make reasonable provision for the applicant or a child?
  - Domestic Proceedings and Magistrates' Courts Act 1978 s2 – the court's powers in ordering maintenance
  - Domestic Proceedings and Magistrates' Courts Act 1978 s3 – how does the court decide what order to make?

- Matrimonial Causes Act 1973 s 27

ANSWER

The parties in this case do not wish to divorce, and therefore the wide powers available for ancillary relief applications are inapplicable. Ben is experiencing financial difficulty in maintaining his lifestyle and the former matrimonial home in the absence of regular financial support from Abigail. In order to remedy this situation, Ben must either seek a court order requiring Abigail to provide him with financial assistance, or negotiate some kind of separation or maintenance agreement with Abigail. The present case is somewhat unusual in that the wife is in the dominant financial position, but the courts treat applications by husbands and wives on property and financial matters on the 'basis of complete equality': *Calderbank v Calderbank* (1975). Therefore it is possible for Ben to apply either to the Magistrates' Court under the **Domestic Proceedings and Magistrates' Courts Act (DPMCA) 1978** or to the County Court under the **Matrimonial Causes Act (MCA) 1973**.

Most applications are made to the Magistrates' Court since it is a quicker and cheaper process. Often spouses who rely on legal aid will only receive legal aid for proceedings in the Magistrates' Court. The **DPMCA 1978** only provides financial relief for spouses, and this may be available by virtue of **ss 2, 6** or **7** of the Act.

In order to apply under **s 2**, the applicant, Ben, must establish one of the grounds in **s 1**, namely that the respondent has failed to provide reasonable maintenance for the applicant, or failed to provide or make proper contribution to the maintenance of a child of the family, or has behaved in such a way that the applicant cannot reasonably be expected to live with them, or has deserted the applicant. It is certainly arguable that, on the facts, Abigail has failed to make reasonable provision for Ben. Whether Abigail has been making reasonable provision for Ben will be determined by the Magistrates' Court. They will first consider what level of maintenance they would have ordered and this is compared with what Abigail is in fact paying. If, as seems likely in this case, Abigail is paying less than the court would have ordered, the ground of failure to maintain will be established. There is no need to show that Abigail was deliberately depriving Ben of support; she may genuinely have thought he was managing, yet still find the **s 1** ground established.

There are no children of the family and behaviour does not seem an issue. Desertion is a complex concept, and although there is no requirement for a specific time it could be difficult to establish that Abigail is in desertion. Whilst there is physical separation, it would seem that the job situation would give just cause for the initial separation, and so, consequently, Ben would be best advised to use the failure to maintain ground. **Section 2** gives the court the power to make periodical payment orders, and to award lump sums up to a maximum of £1,000 per application. The lump sum can be awarded to cover debts or expenses already incurred by the applicant, so if Ben has incurred such expenditure he could seek a lump sum. The periodical payments will be unsecured, and in determining Ben's entitlement, the court will have regard to the factors in **subs 3(1)** of the Act. These factors are similar to those contained in the **MCA 1973 s 25**, and the court will look at all the circumstances of the case.

First consideration is given to the welfare of any children of the family, but there is none in this case. The court will then look at the income, earning capacity and financial resources of the parties: **DPMCA 1978 s 3(2)(a)**. Abigail's income is considerably greater than Ben's, but he may be earning at a lower level than his earning capacity. Consideration must be given to whether Ben can reasonably be expected to take steps to increase his earning. Ben is a qualified teacher, who would normally earn in excess of £6,000 per annum. His composing was undertaken with Abigail's encouragement, and so it is likely that the court would agree that he needs financial assistance for the immediate future. However, the policy of encouraging spousal self-sufficiency would mean that Ben would not be able to expect support to continue indefinitely.

By examining the needs and obligations of the parties (**DPMCA 1978 s 3(2)(b)**), it is obvious that Ben's resources will not stretch to maintaining himself and the mortgage on the matrimonial home, whereas Abigail's needs can easily be met by her resources. It seems likely therefore that Abigail will be ordered to pay some kind of periodical payment to Ben. The court will try, where possible, to have regard to the standard of living enjoyed by the couple previously, and ensure that any drop in standard does not fall inequitably on one party: *Scott v Scott* (1978). At present, Ben seems to be struggling to live frugally, whilst Abigail's income is enabling her to enjoy a much higher standard of living. The age of the parties is unknown, but there is no indication that they are particularly old, and the marriage has lasted eight years, so cannot be regarded as short. There are no known disabilities (**DPMCA 1978 s 3(2)(e)**), and so the only other relevant factors are the parties' contributions (**s 3(2)(f)**) and conduct (**s 3(2)(g)**). Each party seems to have contributed in his/her own way to the marriage; each has worked and there is no evidence of any conduct that it would be inequitable to disregard. This seems to be a case where the couple have unfortunately drifted apart, without any blame to be attached.

Consequently, it seems apparent that a periodical payment order would be made. The court could also award Ben a lump sum up to a maximum of £1,000, and since Abigail has been away for some time, it is likely that he could have accumulated debts and a lump sum payment would enable him to pay off the debts. However, the order ends if the parties cohabit for more than six months.

It is also possible to make an application under the **DPMCA 1978 s 7** where the parties have been separated for a continuous period of more than three months, with neither being in desertion. This would seem to be the case here and so if Ben can show that Abigail has been making payments to him, albeit sporadically and of differing sums, he can apply for an order placing those payments on a permanent and compulsory basis. However, he must specify to the court the total or aggregate amount of these payments in the three months prior to the application. The court is then limited to making a periodical payment order that does not exceed the aggregate amount. This may not help Ben, as it seems that Abigail's contributions over the past three months have been inadequate for his needs, and so the court will not make an order if it does not provide reasonable maintenance, and will treat the application as if it had been made under **s 2: s 7(4)**. **Section 7** also does not provide for lump sums, so would be inappropriate where Ben needs help to repay debts, etc.

Financial Provision for Adult Partners | 45

If Ben and Abigail can agree a level of financial provision, then such an agreement can be embodied in a court order by virtue of the **DPMCA 1978 s 6**. The court would still need to be satisfied that the level of provision is adequate and fair, and can refuse the order if the parties refuse to agree to amendments required by the court: **DPMCA 1978 s 6(5)**.

If a periodical payment order is made, it can be payable weekly or monthly, and the **Maintenance Enforcement Act 1991 s 2** enables the Magistrates to specify how the payments should be made: for example, standing orders or attachment of earnings orders. The order would end on the death of either party or if they cohabit for more than six months: **DPMCA 1978 s 25(1)**.

The other possibility available to Ben is to make an application to the County Court under the **MCA 1973 s 27**. The ground for applying is that Abigail has failed to provide reasonable maintenance for Ben. This is established in the same way as the Magistrates' Court would, and reference is made to the factors in the **MCA 1973 s 25** in determining the level of maintenance. These factors mirror those already discussed in relation to the **DPMCA 1978 s 3**. Although application to the County Court is more costly, its powers are somewhat wider than those of the Magistrates' Court are in that it can order both secured and unsecured periodical payments, and lump sums of unlimited amounts.

QUESTION 11

The clean break – fact or fiction? Discuss with reference to the concept of a clean break and how the **Matrimonial Causes Act 1973** achieves it.

How to Read this Question

The question requires an explanation of what is meant by a clean break in divorce and an exploration of how the **Matrimonial Causes Act 1973** has promoted clean break and the extent to which this has been successful. It would also be appropriate in this answer to consider whether there are any provisions in the **MCA** that are contrary to the idea of a clean break.

Applying the Law

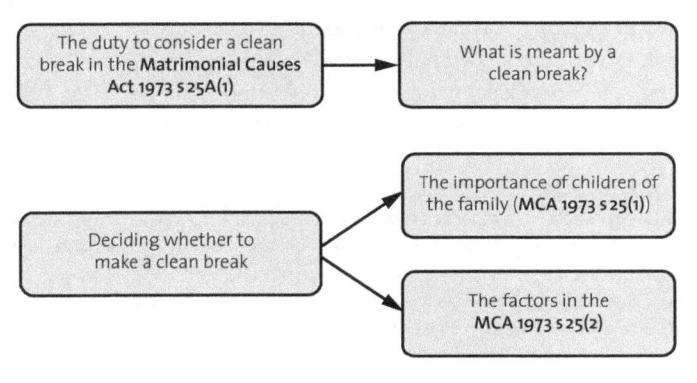

- The duty to consider a clean break in the **Matrimonial Causes Act 1973 s 25A(1)** → What is meant by a clean break?

- Deciding whether to make a clean break →
  - The importance of children of the family (**MCA 1973 s 25(1)**)
  - The factors in the **MCA 1973 s 25(2)**

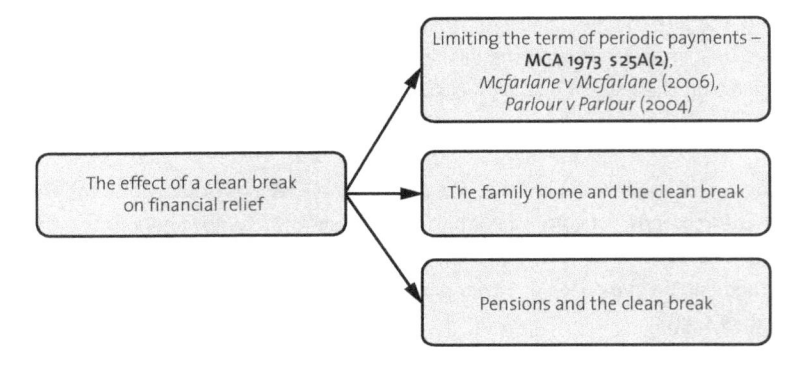

```
┌─────────────────────────────┐      ┌──────────────────────────────────┐
│                             │ ───► │ Limiting the term of periodic payments – │
│                             │      │         MCA 1973 s 25A(2),       │
│                             │      │     Mcfarlane v Mcfarlane (2006),│
│                             │      │       Parlour v Parlour (2004)   │
│  The effect of a clean break│      └──────────────────────────────────┘
│     on financial relief     │ ───► ┌──────────────────────────────────┐
│                             │      │ The family home and the clean break │
│                             │      └──────────────────────────────────┘
│                             │ ───► ┌──────────────────────────────────┐
└─────────────────────────────┘      │   Pensions and the clean break   │
                                     └──────────────────────────────────┘
```

ANSWER

The **Matrimonial and Family Proceedings Act 1984** amended the **Matrimonial Causes Act 1973** in a number of respects designed to encourage greater spousal self-sufficiency on divorce. It would be a mistake, however, to assume that these provisions make a clean break a routine result in ancillary relief proceedings. This was never the intention of the legislation and, in an economically uncertain climate, it is an unrealistic expectation in most cases.[1]

The Law Commission issued a discussion paper in 1980 to seek views on the financial consequences of divorce and as a result in 1981 they issued a report proposing change. It was felt that the change in the basis of divorce from fault-based divorce to that based on irretrievable breakdown meant that it was no longer appropriate to provide continuing lifelong maintenance for an ex-spouse. There had also been a dramatic increase in the number of divorces over the years, and so many divorced people go on to remarry and incur new financial commitments. There was considerable pressure from so-called second families to be relieved of the financial pressures caused by the first family. Many women also worked or had the opportunity to do so, and the concept of man as a lifelong provider for his ex-wife was the subject of much criticism.[2]

The Law Commission did not, however, feel able to recommend a radical alteration to financial provision on divorce and a complete shift to total spousal self-sufficiency in all cases was ruled out. In many families this would not be possible. Women frequently are disadvantaged in employment matters, as they often give up work, or take less demanding work to fit in with family commitments. Where there are children, it is usually the woman who gives up or adapts her career to look after them, and after a divorce most children continue to live with their mother. The demands of child care, and the difficulty

---

1 As with all essay questions, it is important to answer the question set, rather than just spewing out everything remembered about clean breaks. Here the issues are the statutory basis for clean breaks and how likely and how effective they are in reality.
2 This introduction explains how changes in society have led to legal changes designed to encourage clean break divorces. In an essay question where the student is called to evaluate the reasons behind a provision or how effective it is, it is often useful to discuss the context within which the provision works.

of finding flexible employment, provide considerable handicaps to a woman's earning capacity. Many women could only work during school hours or must pay considerable costs for child care, and it is unrealistic to expect her to be able to support herself in such circumstances.[3]

Likewise, a woman who has been married for a considerable time and who has been absent from the workplace would find it difficult to be self-supporting. There is considerable age discrimination and an elderly or middle-aged woman would experience difficulty in acquiring a job or retraining and acquiring relevant skills. Nevertheless, there are spouses who could readjust quickly on the termination of marriage and support themselves, and the lack of continuing support obligations may help reduce animosity. The young, childless wife could arguably adjust without hardship, as could a spouse whose family resources are considerable and can be divided and invested to provide an income. Consequently, it was felt desirable that in appropriate cases self-sufficiency should be encouraged.

The desirability of a clean break is highlighted in **s 25A(1)** where the court is given a duty to consider whether it would be appropriate to order that the financial obligations of the parties towards each other be terminated as soon as is just and equitable. This is a duty to consider a clean break, not to impose it routinely (*Clutton v Clutton* (1991)), where the Court of Appeal recognised that a clean break is often inappropriate and unfair. It was thought initially that the presence of children would make a clean break impossible (*Suter v Suter and Jones* (1987)), and this has been highlighted by the controversy surrounding the **Child Support Act 1991**, whereby any arrangements made, including generous clean break provisions, were disregarded in assessing the father's financial liability for his children.

If the court decides to provide maintenance for a spouse, then it is given an additional duty under **s 25A(2)** to consider whether it would be appropriate to award maintenance for a limited period only (*Parlour v Parlour* (2004)). This would then in theory allow the spouse to adjust without undue financial hardship. In practice, however, there are still many women who could not readjust with any degree of certainty because, for example, they are too old (*Morris v Morris* (1985)), or because there are very young children (*Suter v Suter and Jones* (1987)). It is arguably dangerous to make a limited order in respect of a woman with no job, and for whom the future is uncertain. However, a limited order might be advantageous to a man, who could then plan his own future, and possibly a second family, with more certainty. Thus a limited order might be desirable where the woman has reasonable prospects of readjusting, but with the safety net of applying for a variation by way of an extension if her plans do not work out.

The final power that the court has is under **s 25A(3)**, which is to completely end all further financial obligations of the spouses to one another, including applications under the

---

3   The first consideration in financial relief is the welfare of children of the family and therefore a clean break would not be ordered if it was detrimental to their welfare.

Inheritance (Provision for Family and Dependants) Act 1975. This power could be used where it is considered desirable to remove the possibility of a spouse claiming increased provision in the future. It will be exercised rarely, for instance, in cases where a generous financial solution has already been agreed or in special cases, such as *Seaton v Seaton* (1986), where the severe disability of one spouse and the inability of the other to improve his quality of life led to a termination of obligations.

The law also encourages a clean break by its introduction of the concept of pension splitting, which will divide up pension assets at the time, rather than earmarking provisions as contained in the **Pensions Act 1995**, which will still link the parties to one another. This has been enacted in the **Welfare Reform and Pensions Act 1999**, but the complex procedures and the financial reality of pension splitting mean this is only worthwhile where the pension holder has built up a sizeable pension fund.

Emotionally, most divorcing couples would prefer a clean break. Nevertheless, it will not always be practical or possible. The first consideration of the court in determining financial relief is the welfare of children of the family (**Matrimonial Causes Act 1973 s 25(1)**), in many families it will not be possible to provide for the future well-being of the children of the family within the context of a clean break. This is further exacerbated by economic uncertainty. Another issue if that for many divorcing couples the main asset is the family home. The welfare of the children, as well as other considerations in s 25(2), mean that this will sometimes be dealt with through a Mesher order or a Martin order delaying the final resolution of the couple's financial affairs. In short, whatever the benefits of a clean break, for many divorcing couples it will be unattainable.

QUESTION 12

Ursula and Vincent have been married for 32 years. Six years ago Vincent began a relationship with his secretary, Wendy, and after six months he moved in with her. Vincent and Wendy now have two children, Yvonne and Zachery, aged four and two. Vincent has decided that he would like to divorce Ursula and marry Wendy. Ursula is opposed to the divorce. She is Roman Catholic and feels that divorce is wrong. She also believes that eventually Vincent will tire of Wendy and return to her.

When Ursula and Vincent got married, she was a primary schoolteacher and he worked as a photographer. Vincent wanted to set up on his own and the couple rented a small shop. At weekends and during the evenings, Ursula would help him as his assistant and she would drive him to assignments. After two years, Vincent decided to enter some of his photographs in a national competition. He won and suddenly became a very sought-after and fashionable photographer. He was able to move to better premises in a more exclusive area and to take on staff. About this time, the couple also had the first of their six children. Ursula decided to leave her job and become a full-time housewife and mother. She was often on her own as Vincent spent a lot of time abroad on fashion shoots. The couple's youngest child, currently aged eight, has Down's syndrome.

Financial Provision for Adult Partners

Over the years, Vincent's career has gone from strength to strength. He not only makes a lot of money from photography but he is now in demand as a celebrity himself. In all, his income per annum is £450,000. Fifteen years ago, Vincent bought a penthouse flat in London, which is now worth £2.5 million. Ursula and the children still live in the family home, which has been valued at £3.5 million.

▶ **Advise Ursula on the divorce and the ancillary relief for her.**

How to Read this Question

As Ursula is opposed to the divorce, you need to first consider whether she can prevent the divorce before looking at what maintenance she would be entitled to under the **Causes Act 1973**.

Applying the Law

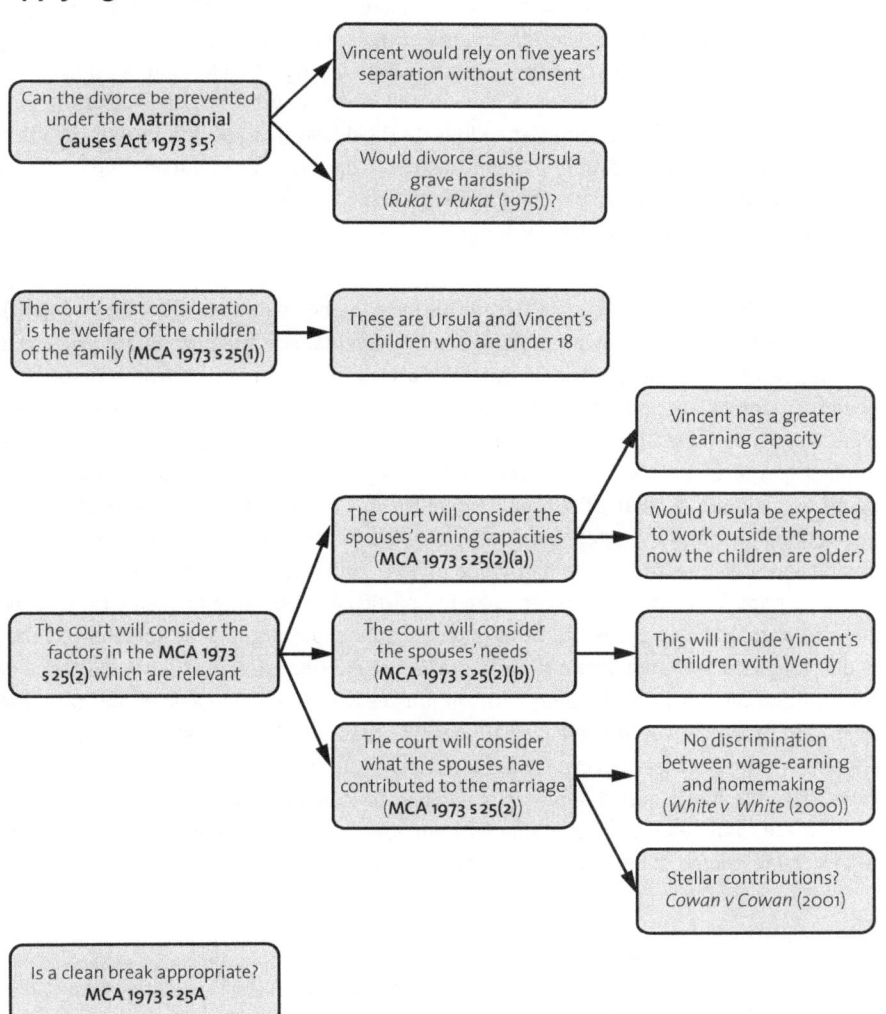

- Can the divorce be prevented under the **Matrimonial Causes Act 1973 s 5**?
  - Vincent would rely on five years' separation without consent
  - Would divorce cause Ursula grave hardship (*Rukat v Rukat* (1975))?

- The court's first consideration is the welfare of the children of the family (**MCA 1973 s 25(1)**)
  - These are Ursula and Vincent's children who are under 18

- The court will consider the factors in the **MCA 1973 s 25(2)** which are relevant
  - The court will consider the spouses' earning capacities (**MCA 1973 s 25(2)(a)**)
    - Vincent has a greater earning capacity
    - Would Ursula be expected to work outside the home now the children are older?
  - The court will consider the spouses' needs (**MCA 1973 s 25(2)(b)**)
    - This will include Vincent's children with Wendy
  - The court will consider what the spouses have contributed to the marriage (**MCA 1973 s 25(2)**)
    - No discrimination between wage-earning and homemaking (*White v White* (2000))
    - Stellar contributions? *Cowan v Cowan* (2001)

- Is a clean break appropriate? **MCA 1973 s 25A**

ANSWER

In order to obtain a divorce, Vincent will have to prove that his marriage to Ursula has broken down irretrievably (**Matrimonial Causes Act (MCA) 1973 s1(1)**) and that one of the five facts in the **MCA 1973 s1(2)** is satisfied. On the facts it seems that Vincent has been living with Wendy for five-and-a-half years, and therefore he could use five years' separation without consent. However, Ursula may try to prevent the divorce under the **MCA 1973 s5** claiming that, as a Roman Catholic, it would cause her grave hardship to be divorced. It is unlikely, though, that her claim would be successful. Cases such as *Rukat v Rukat* (1975) suggest that claims under **s5** are rarely successful. It is probable that the court would allow the divorce and therefore the next issue to discuss is financial relief.[4]

The court will use the **MCA 1973 s25** to determine financial relief. According to **s25(1)**, the court's first consideration is the welfare of the children. Given that the couple have been married for over 30 years it is likely that some of their children are now adults and would no longer be a consideration for the court, but their youngest child (and possibly some others) are still minors and therefore they would be the court's first consideration. Furthermore, the fact that the youngest child is disabled is likely to be significant. Having a disabled child may make it more difficult for Ursula to obtain work outside the home. In addition, it might be that Ursula could argue that she and her children need the stability of being able to remain in the family home.

The court will look at the couple's contributions to the marriage: **MCA 1973 s25(2)(f)**. Vincent has been the breadwinner. Thanks to his hugely successful photography business he has been able to provide the couple with a very high standard of living. Ursula has been the homemaker and mother. In the leading case of *White* (2000), the House of Lords were clear that there should be no distinction between the two types of contribution. Applied to the facts this would mean that Ursula's contribution could be assessed as being as valuable as that of Vincent. However, in *Cowan* (2001) the Court of Appeal allowed the husband a greater share of the couple's wealth because his business acumen and design skills meant that he had made an extraordinary contribution. Applied to the facts, perhaps Vincent could argue that his particular skills should mean that he be allowed a greater share. On the other hand, Ursula could argue that she showed particular talent as a homemaker during the times when Vincent was absent, and that her contribution also included helping with the business in the early days. In any case, the later case of *Lambert v Lambert* (2002) suggests that contributions should be assessed equally in part because looking for a special contribution is unfair on the spouse who looks after the home and children as it is more difficult to show a special contribution doing these than being an entrepreneur or employed. It is also worth noting that Ursula will not be restricted to her reasonable requirements.

---

4 Watch out for **s5** of the **MCA 1973** in divorce and financial relief questions. Although a **s5** application is rarely successful, in reality it is important to consider whether it does apply in cases where the petitioner is relying on five years' separation without consent.

The facts state that Vincent now has two children with Wendy. Although these children will not be the court's main consideration under **s 25(1)**, under **s 25(2)(b)** the court will take account of Vincent's need to maintain these children. Another important factor is the earning capacity of Vincent and Ursula. Thanks to his talent and high profile, Vincent looks to enjoy continued professional success. Ursula, on the other hand, has had her more modest career interrupted, and it is likely that it would prove more difficult for her to find financially rewarding employment that would fit around the demands of caring for a disabled child. The court would take into account the fact that this has been a long marriage. The court may also consider whether Ursula should be compensated for the end of the marriage (*Charman v Charman No 4* (2007)). Although Ursula has not given up a lucrative career, she would be less well off because the marriage has ended.[5]

Having identified relevant factors in the **MCA 1973 s 25**, it is now possible to suggest how a court might deal with ancillary relief in this question. The facts state that Ursula and the children are currently living in the family home. It would be appropriate to transfer this home outright to Ursula. This provides the children with security and it is not unduly harsh on Vincent as he could keep the penthouse.

Under the **MCA 1973 s 25A**, the court would also have to consider whether a clean break would be appropriate. In this case, it is unlikely that a clean break would be appropriate because the marriage has lasted a long time and because the couple still have children who need care. As a clean break is not appropriate, it is likely that the court would also award Ursula periodic payments.

Common Pitfalls

- Before discussing financial relief, answers should consider whether the **MCA 1973 s 5** is relevant.
- There are a lot of considerations in financial relief. Keep a logical structure and refer to the legislation so as not to get muddled or confused.

Aim Higher

- Case law shows how courts have applied the **s 25** criteria. Use recent case law to illustrate how fair division is interpreted.

---

5 The principle of compensation was discussed in both *Miller* and *Charman*. The idea is that a spouse may need to be compensated by financial relief either because they took decisions during the marriage which have benefited the family as a whole but have cost them personally, for example giving up work to care for children, or because they would lose out by the marriage ending, for example due to loss of a pension.

QUESTION 13

Quentin is 45 and has been married to Polly, aged 35, for three years. Quentin is a very successful businessman. He started his company when he was 20 and it is now worth £25 million. When Quentin met Polly she was a technical translator and earned £35,000 per annum. One year after they were married, Polly gave up her job. Polly had to work abroad a lot and Quentin persuaded her that this was making it more difficult for them to settle into married life. Polly also wanted to start a family and believed this would be easier without the stress of a busy job. Sadly, this has not proved successful. The couple have drifted apart and Polly has become very unhappy. She had a short affair with a friend from university and Quentin has found out about this and decided to divorce her. Before the couple married, Quentin's solicitor drew up an agreement which restricted any claim that Polly might have if the marriage were to end to £500,000. Polly signed this as she was afraid that otherwise Quentin would pull out of the marriage.

▶ Advise Quentin on the financial consequences of ending his marriage to Polly.

How to Read this Question

Quentin only wants to know about financial consequences of the divorce so you do not need to discuss whether divorce would be available. The main issue here is whether the pre-nuptial agreement would be applied and if not how maintenance would be determined given the shortness of the marriage.

Applying the Law

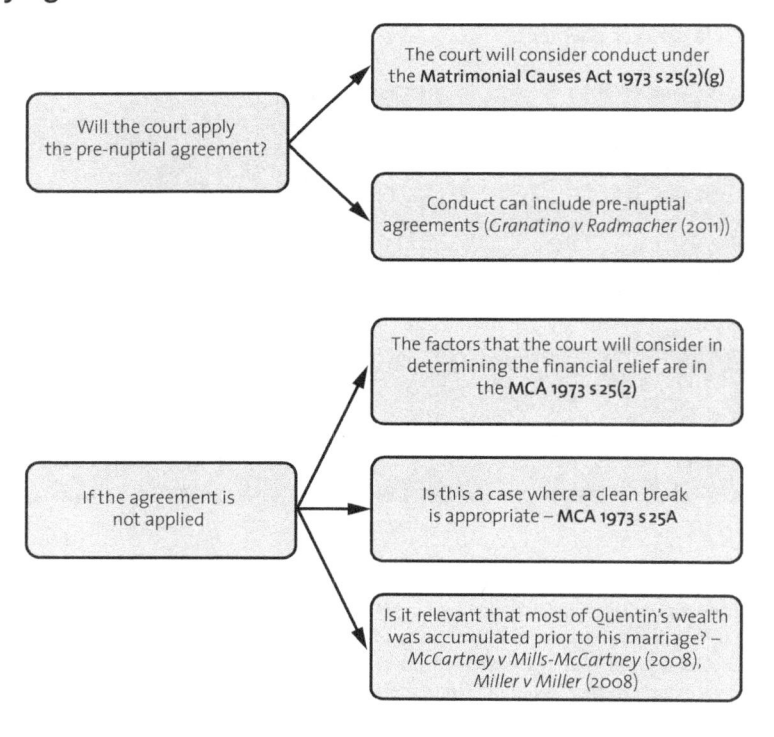

- Will the court apply the pre-nuptial agreement?
  - The court will consider conduct under the **Matrimonial Causes Act 1973 s 25(2)(g)**
  - Conduct can include pre-nuptial agreements (*Granatino v Radmacher* (2011))

- If the agreement is not applied
  - The factors that the court will consider in determining the financial relief are in the **MCA 1973 s 25(2)**
  - Is this a case where a clean break is appropriate – **MCA 1973 s 25A**
  - Is it relevant that most of Quentin's wealth was accumulated prior to his marriage? – *McCartney v Mills-McCartney* (2008), *Miller v Miller* (2008)

ANSWER

Quentin will claim that his marriage to Polly has irretrievably broken down (**Matrimonial Causes (MCA) 1973 s 1(1)**) and will rely on the fact of her adultery in order to obtain a divorce (**MCA s 1(2)(a)**). As there are no children of the family, **s 25(1)** of the **MCA 1973** does not apply, therefore the division of property will be based on the factors in **s 25(2)**. It is also important to remember that when dividing the property the aim of the court will be to be fair (*White v White* (2000)). Furthermore, the courts are likely to view an equal division of the property as the starting point, only to be departed from if there are good reasons for doing so (*Miller* (2006), *Charman* (2008)).

Quentin is a very wealthy man. At one time, claims by very wealthy spouses were restricted to their reasonable needs. In *White v White*, the Court of Appeal and House of Lords recognised that this approach was unfair. It gave insufficient recognition to the contribution of a spouse whose role had been as homemaker and led to a very unequal division of wealth. In *White* itself the wife did not receive a half share of the couple's wealth, but this was because some of the investment had originally come from the husband's family and therefore an equal split would not have been fair. This approach was followed in *Lambert v Lambert* (2002) where the wife of a wealthy and successful businessman was entitled to half the assets. Quentin and Polly's case is, however, distinguishable. Unlike the spouses in *White* and *Lambert*, Polly and Quentin's marriage is a short one and under **s 25(2)(d)** of the **MCA 1973** this will be relevant and will reduce her award.

Furthermore, Quentin may well argue that any award that Polly receives should be limited to funds from matrimonial assets. He would argue that although the business is valued at £25 million, most of this wealth was accumulated before he was married to Polly and therefore it would not be fair for her to benefit from this. This was the approach taken in *Miller v Miller* (2006) and *Mills v McCartney* (2009). In both these cases, very wealthy men were able to restrict the claims of their wives by arguing that the greater portion of their wealth should not be included as a matrimonial asset as it had been earned before the marriage.

One of the factors in **s 25(2)** is each spouse's earning capacity (**s 25(2)(a)**). Quentin would seem to have a very large earning capacity, whilst Polly's is far smaller. She did have a career as a technical translator, but she gave that up. Fortunately for Polly she has only been out of work for a couple of years and therefore it is unlikely that her skills will have grown out of date; nevertheless, she is currently out of work and has lost a couple of years of career development. Recent cases such as *McFarlane* (2004) and *Charman* (2008) have recognised that a spouse may need to be compensated for the loss (s)he has incurred both because of the marriage through giving up work and because the marriage has not lasted and therefore she has not benefited as she might expect to.

Whatever settlement the court orders, their aim will be to be fair. However, the court may find its discretion fettered if it decides to follow the pre-nuptial agreement between Quentin and Polly. Although courts used to refuse to follow pre-nuptial agreements, recent decisions have shown that they may be taken into account under s 25(2)(g). This was seen as favouring the parties' autonomy and their ability to determine for themselves how best to order their finances. In the leading case of *Radmacher v Granatino* (2010), the Supreme Court decided that the court would normally apply a pre-nuptial agreement if the couple had received proper independent legal advice. This approach has since been followed in *V v V* (2011) and *Z v Z (No 2)* (2011). There is little information here on the circumstances in which the agreement was signed and whether Polly was properly legally advised. There is, however, a good chance that the pre-nuptial will be binding.

On balance, therefore, whilst Polly will certainly be entitled to financial relief, her award is likely to be limited to a small part of Quentin's wealth. Much of his wealth will be excluded as not part of the matrimonial wealth and it is possible that the pre-nuptial agreement will be applied.

QUESTION 14

Discuss the extent to which English law upholds pre-nuptial agreements.

How to Read this Question

Need to explain what pre-nuptial agreements are and how English law on financial relief has developed from completely rejecting them to enforcing them in certain situations.

Applying the Law

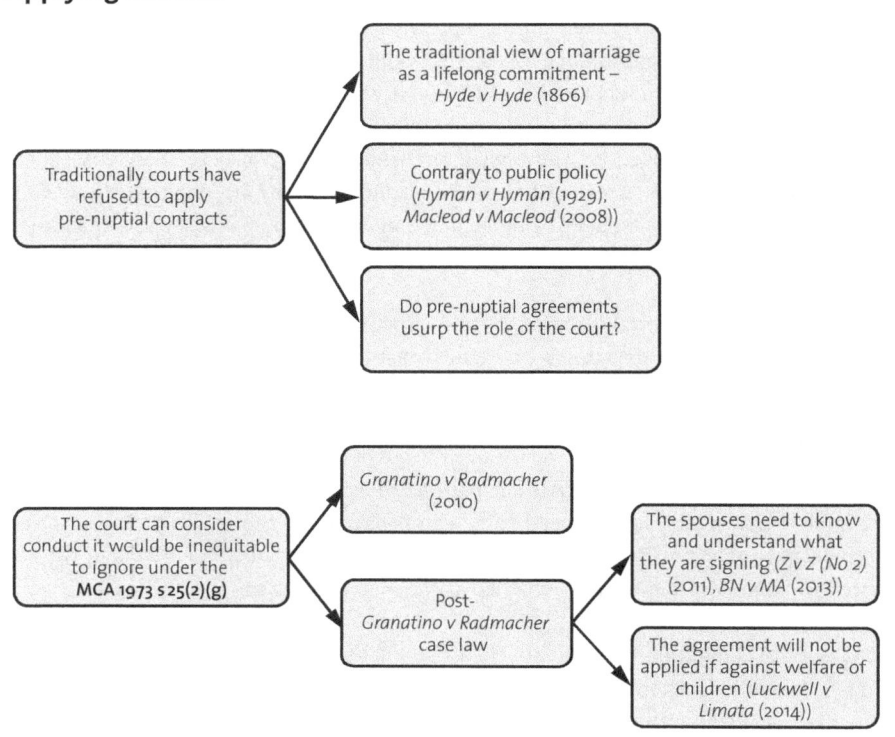

Traditionally courts have refused to apply pre-nuptial contracts
- The traditional view of marriage as a lifelong commitment – *Hyde v Hyde* (1866)
- Contrary to public policy (*Hyman v Hyman* (1929), *Macleod v Macleod* (2008))
- Do pre-nuptial agreements usurp the role of the court?

The court can consider conduct it would be inequitable to ignore under the MCA 1973 s 25(2)(g)
- *Granatino v Radmacher* (2010)
- Post-*Granatino v Radmacher* case law
  - The spouses need to know and understand what they are signing (*Z v Z (No 2)* (2011), *BN v MA* (2013))
  - The agreement will not be applied if against welfare of children (*Luckwell v Limata* (2014))

ANSWER

As their name suggests, pre-nuptial agreements are contracts agreed between the future husband and wife setting out how they want their property to be divided in the event of a divorce. Until recently, these agreements were of very limited effectiveness in English law. The traditional view of the English judges had been to reject them as immoral and contrary to public policy. It was seen as immoral to contemplate and plan for the end of the marriage before it had even been celebrated and against the very character of marriage as a lifelong commitment (*Hyman v Hyman* (1929)). Furthermore the **Matrimonial Causes Act (MCA) 1973** is clear that the awarding of financial relief is a matter for judicial discretion and sets out in **s 25** the factors that need to be carefully weighed and balanced in determining it. A pre-nuptial agreement will not always consider these factors and in any case would restrict the judges in the exercise of their discretion.[6]

This view that pre-nuptial agreements could not determine the settlement awarded persisted to *Macleod v Macleod* (2008) where the Privy Court were keen to distinguish a post-marriage agreement which could determine the settlement and a pre-nuptial agreement which following existing precedent could not.

Despite this history, the argument that a pre-nuptial agreement is immoral because it discusses the possible ending of the marriage in divorce is not wholly convincing. The reality is that a significant minority of marriages will end in divorce and especially for people celebrating a second or even third marriage discussing a pre-nuptial agreement will not be seen as shocking or immoral but sensible and realistic. Certainly it is arguable that pre-nuptial agreements are a result of increasing marriage fragility rather than the cause. As for judicial discretion, it should perhaps be noted that there is an increasing willingness and indeed encouragement to couples to settle their own affairs. Mediation must at least be considered and will, unless there are compelling factors, for example domestic violence, be used, with the result that divorcing couples are deciding their own financial arrangements which are then ratified by the courts. Consequently, the idea that pre-nuptial agreements are a unique strike against complete judicial discretion is perhaps far-fetched.

In more recent years, the traditional total rejection of pre-nuptial agreements has softened. The fact that a spouse has signed a pre-nuptial agreement has, provided that they have been properly advised, been viewed as conduct that should be considered when deciding on financial relief under **s 25(2)(g)** of the **MCA 1973**. This increasing judicial willingness to apply pre-nuptial agreements was confirmed by the Supreme Court in the leading case of *Radmacher v Granatino* (2010). In *Radmacher*, a husband was unsuccessful in arguing that his award should not be limited by the pre-nuptial agreement. In particular he argued that the pre-nuptial agreement was irrelevant as it had made no allowance for children to be born and had been signed without proper legal advice. Despite

---

6 **MCA 1973 s 25(1)** states that the welfare of the children of the family is the court's first consideration in determining the financial relief. **Section 25(2)** sets out the other factors to be considered.

these factors both the Court of Appeal and the Supreme Court decided that the pre-nuptial agreement should be followed and that a pre-nuptial agreement that was entered into freely would be applied unless, in all the circumstances of the case, it would be unfair to apply the agreement. In *Radmacher* itself, it was fair to use the agreement to limit the husband's award because his wife's considerable wealth had been gained prior to the marriage and therefore he had not contributed towards it, he did not need to be compensated for having given up his career in order to support the family and his needs were adequately met by the terms of the pre-nuptial agreement.[7]

Following on from *Radmacher v Granatino* courts have been prepared apply the pre-nuptial agreement even if it leads to different results than the division of assets under the **MCA 1973 s 25(1) and s 25(2)** would usually do. The argument is that this promotes both certainty and autonomy. Courts have been clear that it is important that the parties make their decision to enter the pre-nuptial agreement freely and that they are independently advised and properly informed (*Z v Z (No 2)* (2011), *BN v MA* (2013), *B v S (financial remedy matrimonial property regime)* (2012)). This is unsurprising given that the justification for following pre-nuptial agreements is that it promotes autonomy.

The idea that a pre-nuptial agreement will be followed unless it would not be fair to do so has been applied in the post-*Radmacher* case law. It is helpful therefore to consider what circumstances might make it unfair to apply a pre-nuptial agreement. One possibility is that the needs of children of the family might overrule the pre-nuptial agreement. This seems a reasonable interpretation given that under **s 25(1)** of the **MCA 1973**, the needs of children of the family are the first consideration in determining financial relief. This was the case in *Luckwell v Limata* (2014) where the court decided not to apply a pre-nuptial agreement that would have left the husband without a home. The welfare of the children was the first consideration (**MCA 1973 s 25(1)**) and this demanded both parents having somewhere to live. On the other hand, it is worth remembering that in *Radmacher* itself, the couple had children but this did not prevent the agreement being applied. On the other hand, in *Radmacher*, applying the agreement did not disadvantage the children as they were to spend the majority of their time with their mother.

Another possibility is that an agreement will not be binding if the spouse does not have competent and independent legal advice. This would make sense as the justification for upholding pre-nuptial agreements is that it would support autonomy, but this rationale is undermined if the spouse is not properly informed. Furthermore, in *B v S (financial remedy matrimonial property regime)* (2012) the fact that the wife had not received independent legal advice meant that the court did not follow the pre-nuptial agreement. Again though, it is possible that even without legal advice, a pre-nuptial agreement might still be applied. One of the husband's arguments against applying the agreement in *Radmacher* was that he had not been properly legally advised. In his case, however, this

---

[7] It is interesting to read *Radmacher* alongside cases such as *Miller* where issues such as compensation and what is matrimonial property for the purposes of financial relief are discussed.

argument was rejected, in part because he was expected, due to his nationality, to be more aware of the purpose and the effects of a pre-nuptial agreement.

The issue of pre-nuptial agreements has been considered by the Law Commission. Unsurprisingly their discussions have reflected the issues in the recent cases, namely whether and to what extent pre-nuptial agreements should be enforceable and in particular what legal advice should be necessary and what effect children should have on the enforceability of the pre-nuptial agreement.

QUESTION 15

Discuss the extent to which English law promotes the equal division of property on divorce.

How to Read this Question

The question is about how property is divided on divorce both by the courts and through private ordering and the extent to which this is based on equal division. Because the court's aim in dividing property is to be fair (*White v White* (2000)) this will also mean examining whether equal division is fair and whether it promotes the welfare of children of the family.

Applying the Law

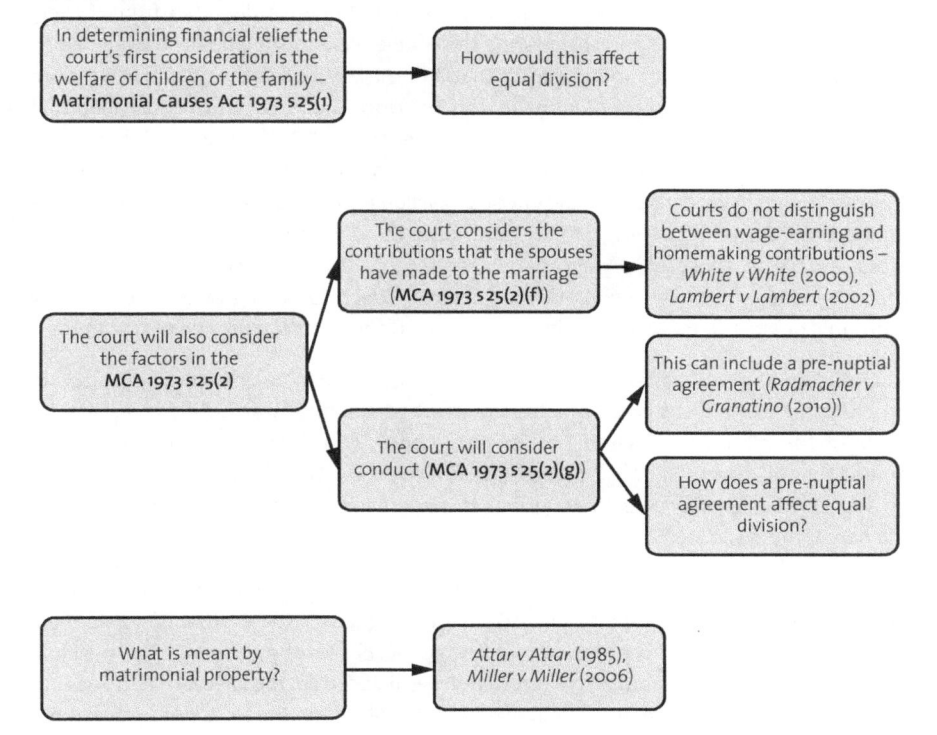

- In determining financial relief the court's first consideration is the welfare of children of the family – **Matrimonial Causes Act 1973 s 25(1)** → How would this affect equal division?

- The court will also consider the factors in the **MCA 1973 s 25(2)**
  - The court considers the contributions that the spouses have made to the marriage (**MCA 1973 s 25(2)(f)**) → Courts do not distinguish between wage-earning and homemaking contributions – *White v White* (2000), *Lambert v Lambert* (2002)
  - The court will consider conduct (**MCA 1973 s 25(2)(g)**)
    - This can include a pre-nuptial agreement (*Radmacher v Granatino* (2010))
    - How does a pre-nuptial agreement affect equal division?

- What is meant by matrimonial property? → *Attar v Attar* (1985), *Miller v Miller* (2006)

ANSWER

Upon the breakdown of a marriage, the couple's property needs to be divided and potentially one spouse will be claiming maintenance from the other. The statutory rules for how this division should be achieved are set out in the **Matrimonial Causes Act (MCA) 1973 s 25**. It seems from case law (*White v White* (2000)) that the main aim of the division is to be fair to both spouses and therefore the question is whether fairness has been, and is being, interpreted as an equal division.

Looking first at the statute, this does not seem to support an equal division. The starting point for a couple with minor children is that the needs of those minor children are the court's first consideration (**MCA 1973 s 25(1)**). For many couples, the most important asset will be the family home and this provision will often mean that the spouse who has care of the child after the divorce will either get a greater share of this family home, or be able to stay in it. In reality, therefore, economic pressures mean that for many divorcing couples an equal split is not an option (*Lyons v Lyons* (2010)). It will arguably only be in the big money cases where there are sufficient resources to enable the needs of the children to be met with property left over so that an equal division may be possible. After **subs 25(1)**, **subs 25(2)** sets out a list of factors which should direct the division of property. Whilst these will not be relevant in every case, when applied they could mean that depending on the facts and the history of the marriage, one spouse gets a greater share.

Although there is clearly no statutory presumption in favour of an equal division and there are factors in **s 25** which argue against equality, in the leading case of *White v White* (2000), the House of Lords stated that equality should only be departed from if there were compelling reasons to do so. In *White* the couple were millionaires and were divorcing after over 30 years of marriage. At that time, the wife's claim would have been restricted by her reasonable requirements to £800,000. The House of Lords decided that this was unfair and did not adequately recognise her contribution to the marriage and her award was significantly increased. Although *White* is a hugely important decision, it is very questionable whether it did favour equal division for most divorcing couples. There is a difference between equality, i.e. the contributions of a housewife and mother being rated equally to those of a wage earner, and equal division, which means that the couple's property has to be equally divided. Second, *White* was a big money case involving multi-millionaires. In more modest households, a different division may be necessary.

Notwithstanding this, post-*White* courts have discussed when an equal division is appropriate. Initially, the focus was on determining when a spouse was entitled to a greater share of the matrimonial assets. In *Cowan v Cowan* (2001), the husband successfully argued that his contribution exceeded that of his wife and therefore he was entitled to a greater share. In *Lambert v Lambert* (2002), this approach was rejected as being unfair to the non-earning spouse.

More recently the issue has changed and the discussion has instead centred on what is meant by matrimonial property. In *Miller v Miller* (2006), the House of Lords were concerned with a very short marriage involving a very wealthy husband. The husband argued that some of his property should not be included in the division as it was his personal property rather than matrimonial property. Although the House of Lords did not accept the husband's definition of matrimonial property, they did agree that equal division could only apply to the matrimonial property and therefore not all the husband's assets were included. Similarly in *McCartney v Mills* (2008), the wife received significantly less than 50 per cent as most of the husband's fortune had been accumulated before the marriage. *Miller* was a very short marriage and in *Charman v Charman* (2007) the court decided that a similarly restrictive definition of matrimonial property was not appropriate in a longer marriage. The court in *Charman v Charman* (2007) also determined that financial relief could be used to compensate a spouse for giving up his or her career, or for the cost of ending the marriage.

Another factor which may restrict the equal division of property on divorce is private ordering either through a post-marital agreement or through pre-nuptial agreements. Courts have long recognised the ability of spouses to determine and agree their own financial affairs on divorce. A couple that decides the division for itself might be more happy with the division than spouses whose affairs are court-imposed. Furthermore, the couple themselves will understand the subtleties and complexities of their financial needs and assets. The disadvantage of the couple negotiating their financial affairs is that it may advantage the more confident, more financially aware spouse and this may mean either unequal division where the court may have tended towards parity, or an equal division where other factors, for example children's welfare, might have tended the court towards an unequal split. As for pre-nuptial agreements, these were once ignored by the court as contrary to public policy (*Macleod v Macleod* (2008)), but courts can now apply them under the **MCA 1973 s 25(2)(g)** (*Radmacher v Granatino* (2010)). Whilst courts are not constrained to apply pre-nuptial agreements, and will not do so if a spouse has not been properly advised, or where the agreement works against the welfare of the children of the family (*Luckwell v Limata* (2014)), it is clear that ignoring the pre-nuptial agreement cannot be based solely on the fact that it does not institute an equal division.

QUESTION 16

Edward and Fiona met whilst at university 15 years ago. They lived together for a while, but then married after the birth of their child, George, now aged 12. Subsequently, two daughters were born, Isobel, aged six, and Jessica, aged two. Unfortunately, Jessica was born severely disabled and requires constant care and attention. The strain on the couple has been enormous, and there have been several rows. Fiona, in desperation, had a brief affair with Jessica's physiotherapist, Kevin, but felt so guilty about it that she confessed to Edward and begged forgiveness. Edward reacted violently at the news and seriously injured Fiona, leaving her also severely disabled.

Fiona had worked as a teacher throughout the marriage, taking maternity leave when she had the children. Since Jessica's birth, she had found it increasingly difficult to work and care for Jessica, and since Edward attacked her she has been unable to work.

Fiona is divorcing Edward, citing his behaviour, and it seems that Edward will not contest the petition. However, it is proving difficult to get agreement about the financial aspects of divorce. The former matrimonial home is valued at £250,000 with an outstanding mortgage of £50,000. Edward earns £40,000 per year as a manager of a small supermarket and the couple have no other assets, save for a small car, valued at £2,000, that Edward uses to go to work, and £3,000 in a building society account.

- Advise Fiona on her prospects of obtaining ancillary relief.

How to Read this Question

The focus of this question is on the financial relief for Fiona and her children through the provisions of the **Matrimonial Causes Act (MCA) 1973**.

Applying the Law

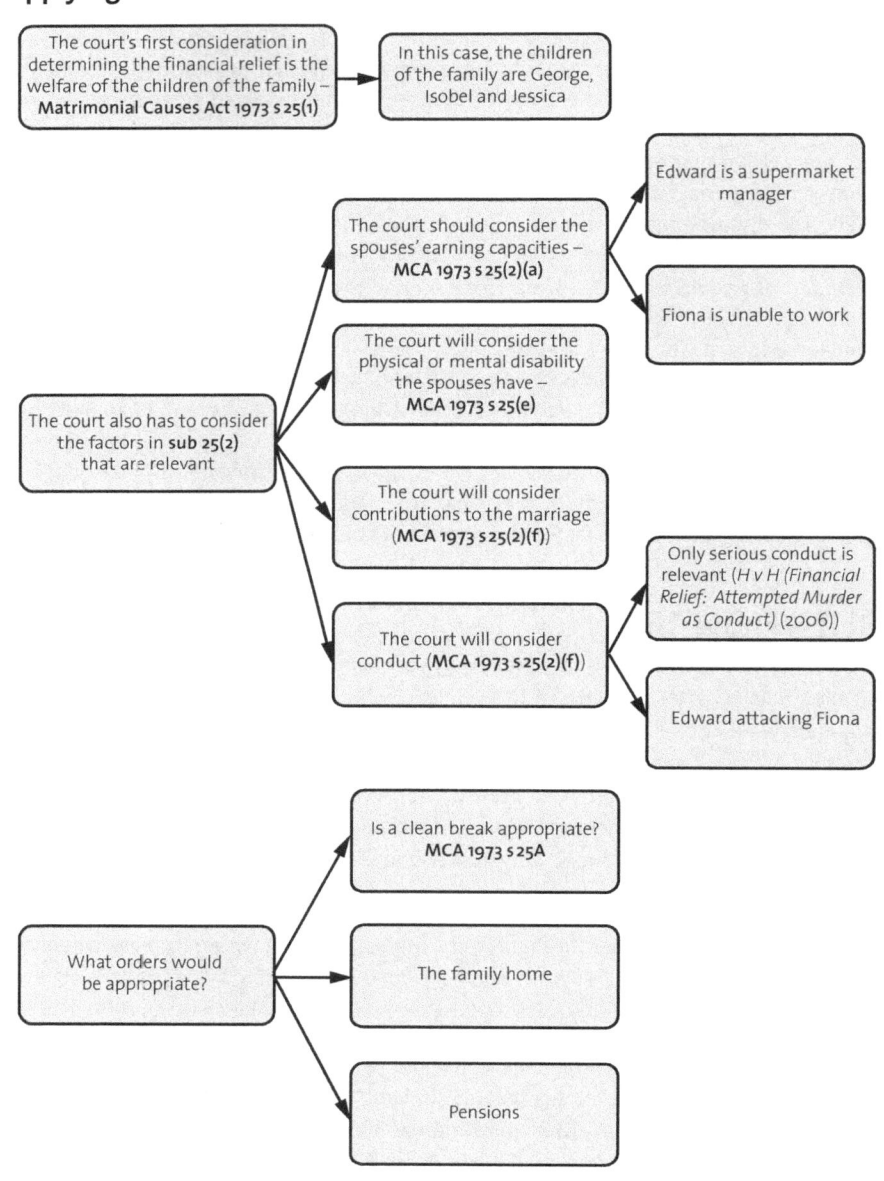

- The court's first consideration in determining the financial relief is the welfare of the children of the family – **Matrimonial Causes Act 1973 s 25(1)**
  - In this case, the children of the family are George, Isobel and Jessica

- The court also has to consider the factors in **sub 25(2)** that are relevant
  - The court should consider the spouses' earning capacities – **MCA 1973 s 25(2)(a)**
    - Edward is a supermarket manager
    - Fiona is unable to work
  - The court will consider the physical or mental disability the spouses have – **MCA 1973 s 25(e)**
  - The court will consider contributions to the marriage (**MCA 1973 s 25(2)(f)**)
  - The court will consider conduct (**MCA 1973 s 25(2)(f)**)
    - Only serious conduct is relevant (*H v H (Financial Relief: Attempted Murder as Conduct)* (2006))
    - Edward attacking Fiona

- What orders would be appropriate?
  - Is a clean break appropriate? **MCA 1973 s 25A**
  - The family home
  - Pensions

ANSWER

If Edward and Fiona divorce, then the court has wide powers to achieve a just and reasonable financial settlement. The **MCA 1973 s 23** permits awards of secured or unsecured periodical payments as well as lump sum orders, whereas **s 24** permits property orders, including sale, transfer and settlement of property. These powers are exercised with reference to the guiding principles in the **MCA 1973 s 25**, and allow for provision for spouses.

When the court determines the financial relief first consideration will be the welfare of any children of the family under the age of 18. The three children here will need secure accommodation with their mother, and it is important to ensure that, whatever financial arrangements are reached, the children have a roof over their heads: *Harman v Glencross* (1986).

The court must then bear in mind the desirability of a clean break and the policy of encouraging spouses' self-sufficiency: **MCA 1973 ss 25A(1) and 25A(2)**. However, it is clear on these facts that, because of Fiona's disability which was inflicted by Edward, a clean break is unlikely. The obligation is for the court to consider, not necessarily impose, a clean break (*Clutton v Clutton* (1991)) and, consequently, in a case such as this where the presence of the children and other factors make a clean break unsatisfactory, it will not be imposed (*Suter v Suter and Jones* (1987)).

First, the court will examine the income, earning capacity and other resources of the parties: **s 25(2)(a)**. Edward earns an average income of £40,000 per annum, and there is no evidence that he could reasonably be expected to earn more. He is not deliberately underearning: *Hardy v Hardy* (1981). There are few assets here; only the house which is in joint names, one car and modest savings. Fiona, on the other hand, has no financial resources beyond these assets. She has no income, and her earning capacity as a teacher has been destroyed by her disability. Although the facts disclose that she was having difficulty coping with the demands of Jessica, she did have income and now she can earn nothing. It is unclear what would happen if she were to receive compensation for her injuries, for example from the Criminal Injuries Compensation Scheme, or from an insurance policy. Traditionally, damages for pain and suffering were not included as a spouse's assets (*Daubney v Daubney* (1976)), and this case is similar to that of *Jones v Jones* (1975) where the husband could not include damages as part of his wife's assets when he himself had been responsible for inflicting the injury. However, this policy has been criticised in *Wagstaff v Wagstaff* (1992) and it is possible that if Fiona were receiving substantial income from an insurance policy, for example, it might be taken into account.

From the facts, it seems obvious that whilst Edward's means are reasonable, Fiona has no means of supporting herself. There is a safety net of State benefits, but generally the courts are unwilling to take this into account, as it enables a husband to avoid his obligation to his wife by having the State maintain her: *Barnes v Barnes* (1972). The courts try to protect public funds by refusing to take such benefits into account (*Ashley v Blackman* (1988)), unless the husband's means were so limited that any order would take him below subsistence level (*Stockford v Stockford* (1981)). In the present case, Edward's means are such that he would be expected to support his wife without her recourse to State benefits.

It is then necessary to examine the financial needs and obligations of the parties. Edward clearly needs to be able to house himself, and provide accommodation for his children when they visit him: *Calderbank v Calderbank* (1975). However, Fiona needs to provide the children with a permanent home, and Fiona's disability and Jessica's disability are special considerations that increase her needs: *Smith v Smith* (1975). Fiona would have difficulty in housing herself and it seems likely that she will need to remain in the former matrimonial house.

The standard of living enjoyed before the breakdown of the marriage is not often maintained on divorce, but the court will be concerned to ensure that the drop in standard is not borne unequally: *Preston v Preston* (1982). The parties are not particularly old, nor has the marriage been particularly short (**s 25(2)(d)**), but clearly Fiona's disability is a relevant factor under **s 25(2)(e)**: *Jones v Jones* (1975).

In terms of contributions made by the parties or likely to be made in the future (**s 25(2)(f)**), both parties have worked to support the family, and Fiona has been a wife and mother. *White v White* (2000) suggests there should be no discrimination between the contribution of the wage earner and the contribution of the homemaker. Looking at future contributions, Fiona will have day-to-day care of the children, which will involve her in added responsibility, in that she will have to supervise the children and obtain physical assistance for tasks she and they cannot perform.

The court will also consider conduct if it would be inequitable to disregard it: **s 25(2)(g)**. Usually conduct is irrelevant (*Wachtel v Wachtel* (1973)), and ordinary adultery is irrelevant (*Duxbury v Duxbury* (1987)). However, Edward's extremely violent response is likely to count against him (*Jones v Jones* (1975)) since it has effectively destroyed Fiona's financial prospects.

The facts do not disclose whether Fiona will lose any benefit because of the divorce: **s 25(2)(h)**. Consequently, it seems that the facts require some kind of financial provision for Fiona, as well as her being allowed to remain in the matrimonial home. The home in this case is jointly owned, but if it were sold there would be inadequate proceeds to rehouse the parties. It is relatively easier for a single person to obtain accommodation than for a disabled woman with three children, and so Fiona would be able to remain in the home. It could be argued that whilst it is not usually desirable to deprive a husband of his equity in the home, it may be sensible to do so in instances of extremely bad conduct (*Bryant v Bryant* (1976)) or where there may be problems enforcing maintenance. Here it may be desirable to order Edward to transfer his interest in the home to Fiona, but this may cause difficulty, given the outstanding mortgage. Fiona would then need to receive sufficient financial provision from Edward to enable her to pay the mortgage.

Financial Provision for Adult Partners 63

Another option is to allow Fiona to remain in the matrimonial home until her death or remarriage. Since both she and Jessica have disabilities, any shorter period is inappropriate. This is a variation on the Mesher order (*Mesher v Mesher* (1980)), which postpones sale indefinitely, but which will not necessarily deprive Edward of his capital interest in the home. It is also possible for Edward to pay the mortgage, by making an undertaking.

The extent to which English law favours an equal division is going to be largely influenced by the wishes of the spouses themselves. Much financial relief is determined not by the courts, but by the couples themselves, either through agreements during the process of the divorce or through premarital agreements. Noticeably courts have increasingly been prepared to follow an agreement where the spouse was advised and where it does not significantly disadvantage children of the family even if it leads to an unequal division and even if a spouse receives less than they would have done.

Common Pitfalls

❖ As the question is about financial relief, focus on this. Weaker answers will get distracted by discussing the fault during the marriage and whether and why a divorce is available.

❖ Because there are a lot of things to consider under the **MCA 1973 ss 25(1), 25(2)** it is easy to get confused and muddled and/or be repetitive. Try to avoid this with a logical structure and by planning your answer first.

Aim Higher

As always, knowing the legislation is essential, but better answers will be able to discuss and apply the relevant case law in order to reach a credible and well-argued conclusion as to what the court would be likely to do in this case.

QUESTION 17

Peter and Wendy were divorced eight years ago, when they were both aged 36. Peter was ordered to pay periodical payments of £200 per month for Wendy and £100 per month for each of the couple's two children, Michael, then aged eight, and John, aged six. The former matrimonial home was jointly owned, and an order was made permitting Wendy to remain there until John, the youngest child, was 17. At that point, the house was to be sold and the proceeds divided equally between Peter and Wendy.

At the time of the divorce, Wendy worked part-time, earning £18,000 per year, but one year later Peter was made redundant, and Wendy was forced to work full-time to make ends meet. Peter applied to the court for variation of the order, and the court substituted a nominal order for Wendy and reduced the payments for the children to £50 per month each. Peter worked only occasionally for the following five years and did not obtain employment until he met and married Belle, a wealthy widow. Peter now lives with Belle, and earns £70,000 per year in a job Belle got for him with her father's company. Wendy earns £25,000 per year and has now applied to the court for the last order to be varied so as to obtain substantial periodical payments from Peter. Wendy is also reluctant to sell the matrimonial home, which is worth £280,000 with a £20,000 mortgage.

Peter is annoyed at the prospect of having to continue to support Wendy, and seeks advice as to whether he can be free of future obligations to her.

▶ Advise Peter.

How to Read this Question

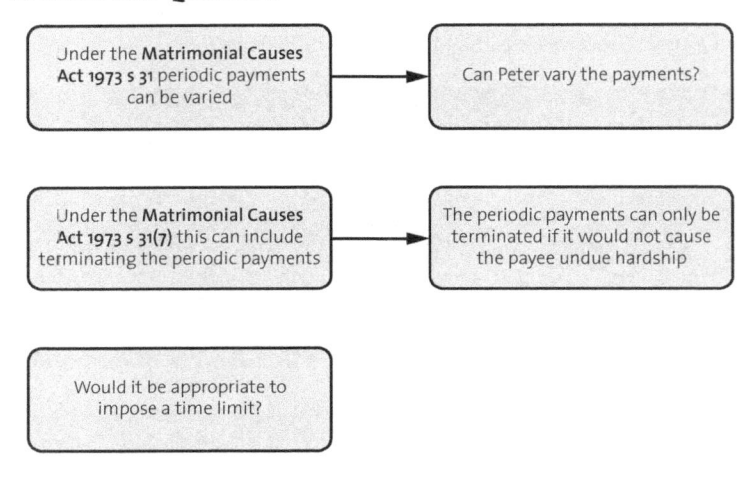

- Under the **Matrimonial Causes Act 1973 s 31** periodic payments can be varied → Can Peter vary the payments?
- Under the **Matrimonial Causes Act 1973 s 31(7)** this can include terminating the periodic payments → The periodic payments can only be terminated if it would not cause the payee undue hardship
- Would it be appropriate to impose a time limit?

ANSWER

This question requires an analysis of the powers of the courts to vary orders that have been made for ancillary relief. The original order, made on divorce, provided for periodical payments for Wendy and the children under the **Matrimonial Causes Act (MCA) 1973 s 23**, and a settlement of property order, the so-called Mesher order, under the **MCA 1973 s 24**.[8]

These orders would have been made after a consideration of the factors in the **MCA 1973 s 25** and have already been varied once when Peter became redundant. In order to alter arrangements once more, Wendy has made an application for variation under the **MCA 1973 s 31**. The court has power under **s 31** to vary periodical payments for a spouse or children of the family, and this may involve increasing or reducing the amount payable. The court must also consider under **s 31(7)** whether to impose a fixed term for which the order will be paid, thereby enabling the payee to readjust before terminating the payer's obligations. It is also possible on variation that the court will terminate the order.

---

8 The advantage of variation is that it enables an order to be changed if circumstances alter and therefore could be seen as fairer. The disadvantage is that it is against the clean break principle.

The court cannot order that periodical payments be replaced by a lump sum order for a spouse, although this is possible for a child: **s 31(5)**. This means that the court cannot force Peter to pay a lump sum to Wendy in lieu of periodical payments, although he could, if he wished, negotiate this with Wendy, and their agreement could then be conveyed to the court, who would terminate the periodical payment order after the lump sum is paid, as in *Peacock v Peacock* (1991). There is no power to vary what are seen by the courts as one-off final settlements, such as lump sums (**s 31(2)**), unless to vary the instalments, or property transfer orders. An order for sale of any property can, however, be varied: **ss 24(A) (1) and 31(2)(f)**. In this case, there were no lump sum orders, and the property was dealt with by way of a Mesher order. Therefore, as there is no power to vary this, both Peter and Wendy will have to wait until John reaches 17 for the house to be sold and proceeds divided. There is no way that the court can order the sale to be postponed or for Wendy's share in the proceeds to be increased: *Carson v Carson* (1981). Nor can the court order the sale to be brought forward. It would seem that the only variation here would be by consent of both parties.

Consequently, the only aspect of the order that can be varied is the periodical payment part. It seems clear that Wendy wishes to increase this, whereas Peter would like to reduce, and hopefully extinguish, his obligation. The periodical payments for children usually do not extend beyond their seventeenth birthday: **MCA 1973 s 29**. Michael is now aged 16 and John aged 14, therefore the order in relation to Michael will end shortly. If Michael is working and supporting himself, then Peter could ask the court to end the order earlier than Michael's seventeenth birthday. This increase in his son's income and financial resources would satisfy the change in circumstances normally required for variation: **s 31(7)**. However, if Michael has remained in full-time education, it may be that Peter's liability to maintain him will be extended up to 18, or beyond: **s 29(3)**. The amount payable in respect of Michael and John may also be increased. The court will examine any change in circumstances (**s 31(7)**), taking into account any change in the **MCA 1973 s 25** factors.

Since the last order was made, Peter has obtained a job, and therefore his income and financial resources have increased. In addition, he has married Belle, who is wealthy in her own right. Although a court will not make a periodical payment order that would have to be paid by a second spouse (*Macey v Macey* (1981)), the second spouse's resources are relevant in that they free up Peter's income to meet the needs of his first family. Thus, it seems likely that the court would take the view that Peter could afford to increase the periodical payments for his sons who, as they have grown older, have increased needs and costs.

Insofar as Peter's obligations to Wendy are concerned, again his income and resources have improved since the last order. In addition, during the period of his redundancy, Wendy has had to make increased contributions to the welfare of the family by looking after both boys, working full-time and trying to make ends meet in difficult financial circumstances. The court might well feel that, now Peter's prospects have improved, he should do something to mitigate the drop in Wendy's standard of living.

Peter's main argument would lie in the fact that Wendy is now working full-time and that since the children are older, she can support herself. The court must consider the desirability of limiting periodical payments to a fixed period of time (**s 31(7)**), to enable the payee, Wendy, to adjust without undue hardship. In the circumstances, it would be harsh to immediately terminate Wendy's order and, in *Whiting v Whiting* (1988), the Court of Appeal said that a wife's order could be her guarantee against ill health or redundancy in the future. Given that she has shouldered responsibility for financially maintaining the family for the five years of Peter's redundancy, it would not be equitable to allow him to terminate her order now that he has improved his financial position. Even the imposition of a fixed term may not occur, as the courts have shown a marked reluctance to do this: *Hepburn v Hepburn* (1989); *Fisher v Fisher* (1989).

In conclusion, it would seem that there is no prospect of varying the Mesher order, but the periodical payments may well be varied. Peter's chances of terminating his obligations seem to be slim.

4 Maintenance for Children

This chapter looks at maintenance for children. A person can be liable for a child either because he or she is their birth parent or adoptive parent, or because they have married the child's parent and have assumed responsibility for them.

Checklist

Student should understand and be able to apply the law on:

- the role of private ordering and child maintenance and the fact that parents are encouraged to agree child maintenance: **Child Maintenance and Other Payments Act 2008**;
- the development of child maintenance based on a biological or adoptive relationship with the child: **Child Support Act 1991, Child Support Act 1995, Child Maintenance and Other Payments Act 2008, Welfare Reform Act 2012**;
- who can claim maintenance under the **Child Maintenance and Other Payments Act 2008** and for which children?
- who is liable under the **Child Maintenance and Other Payments Act 2008**? What is meant by a non-resident parent?
- what happens if the alleged father denies paternity? When does the law presume that he is the father?
- the three different formulae that can be used to calculate child maintenance:
    - cases after 25 November 2013 are child maintenance schemes and will use the formula in the **Child Maintenance and Other Payments Act 2008**
    - cases from 1 March 2003 but before November 2013 are 1993 scheme cases
    - cases before 1 March 1993 will use the 1991 Act formula;
- how maintenance is assessed under the **Child Maintenance and Other Payments Act 2008**:
    - this is based on gross income. If the non-resident parent's gross income is between £200 and £800 per week (s)he will pay: 12 per cent for one child, 16 per cent for two children and 19 per cent for three or more children
    - for any gross income over £800 per week, the non-resident parent will pay 9 per cent for one child, 12 per cent for two children and 15 per cent for three children;

- how maintenance is collected under the **Child Maintenance Acts** and difficulties with collecting it and enforcing payments: *R (On the application of Kehoe) v Secretary of State for Work and Pensions* (2005), *Kehoe v UK* (2008);
- how the law tries to encourage payment and how it responds to non-payers: **Child Maintenance and Other Payments Act 2008 ss 20–30**;
- the justifications for basing child maintenance on a biological or adoptive relationship and any problems with this;
- justifications for using the non-resident parent's income as the basis for the child maintenance and any problems with this;
- child maintenance and divorce: **Matrimonial Causes Act 1973 s 25(1)**;
- child maintenance for a child or children of the family where there has been a marriage under **Matrimonial Causes Act 1973** or **Domestic Proceedings and Magistrates' Courts Act 1973**;
- who can claim child maintenance under the **Children Act 1989** and how the maintenance is calculated;
- that maintenance under the **Children Act 1989** is for the benefit of the children and not to provide financial support for an unmarried adult partner (*T v S (Financial Provision for Children)* (1994), *A v A (A minor: Financial Provision)* (1994), *Re M-M (a child)* (2014)).

Up for Debate

❖ The relationship between state assistance and child maintenance. Should benefits be reduced if child maintenance is not claimed? Should a parent's benefits be reduced if they receive child maintenance?

❖ The relationship between child maintenance and parental responsibility.

QUESTION 18

Philip and Rosy married six years ago, and have two children, Holly and Molly, aged four and two respectively. After the birth of the children, Rosy suffered from severe post-natal depression and, much to Philip's concern, she began to neglect the children. He frequently came home to find the children locked in the house, and Rosy nowhere to be seen. Matters came to a head three months ago when the couple had a heated argument, during which Philip slapped Rosy once after she made unfounded allegations that he had abused the children. Rosy stormed out of the house and since then has not visited Philip or the children. Philip has sent Rosy money on occasions, but he has found it very difficult to meet the bills and pay for child care from his modest income. Philip has now received a letter from Rosy threatening to take him to court unless he sends her £100 each week. Philip says he cannot afford to pay anything like this sum, as he earns £120 per week, out of which he must pay child care costs of £60 as well as other household bills.

▸ Advise Philip.

Maintenance for Children 69

How to Read this Question
The question asks for advice for Philip. It is crucial therefore to determine what the issues are and what concerns and aims Philip has. Here the problem seems to be the level of maintenance Rosy expects Philip to pay and whether he can claim any child maintenance.

Applying the Law

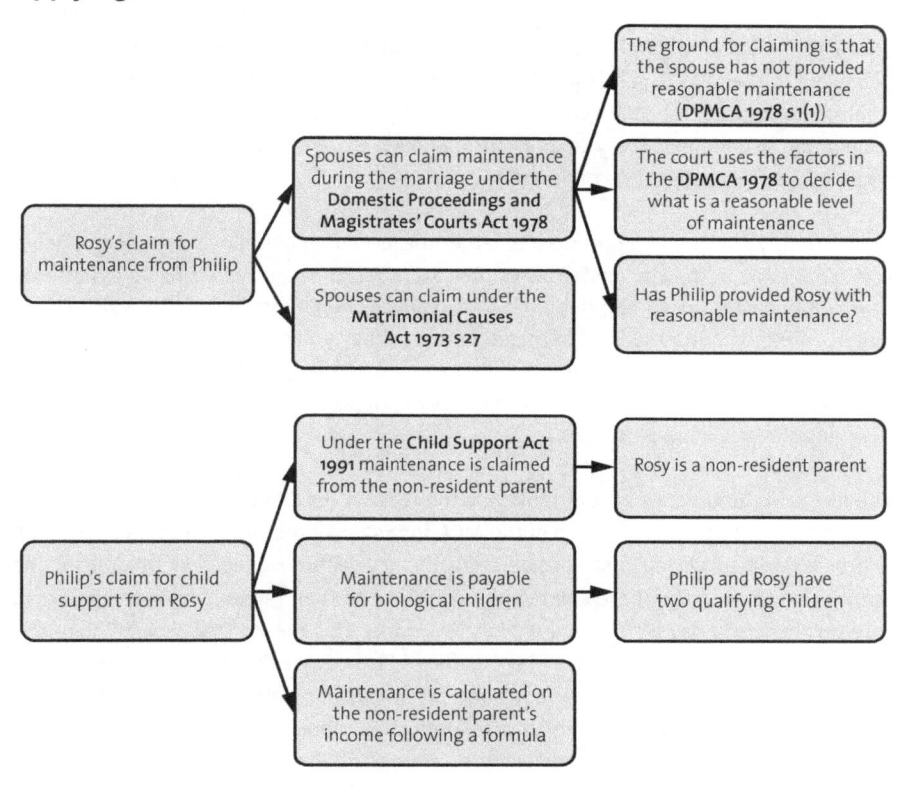

```
Rosy's claim for maintenance from Philip
├── Spouses can claim maintenance during the marriage under the Domestic Proceedings and Magistrates' Courts Act 1978
│   ├── The ground for claiming is that the spouse has not provided reasonable maintenance (DPMCA 1978 s 1(1))
│   └── The court uses the factors in the DPMCA 1978 to decide what is a reasonable level of maintenance
└── Spouses can claim under the Matrimonial Causes Act 1973 s 27
    └── Has Philip provided Rosy with reasonable maintenance?

Philip's claim for child support from Rosy
├── Under the Child Support Act 1991 maintenance is claimed from the non-resident parent
│   └── Rosy is a non-resident parent
├── Maintenance is payable for biological children
│   └── Philip and Rosy have two qualifying children
└── Maintenance is calculated on the non-resident parent's income following a formula
```

ANSWER

The courts have wide powers to order ancillary relief if the parties divorce, but it seems in this case that the issue of financial provision must be resolved without recourse to such powers. If, in the future, Philip and Rosy are unable to reconcile, then financial provision can be reorganised on divorce. In the meantime, there is the possibility that Rosy could seek financial provision from Philip by applying to either the Magistrates' Court or the County Court. Since Philip is caring for the children, she will be seeking maintenance for herself only.

An application may be made to the Magistrates' Court under the **Domestic Proceedings and Magistrates' Courts Act (DPMCA) 1978**, and this is a somewhat cheaper and quicker process than an application to the County Court under the **Matrimonial Causes Act (MCA) 1973**. Only spouses may use the Magistrates' Court, and Rosy may seek relief under **s 2**, or possibly **ss 6** or 7. If she applies for an order under **s2** for periodical payments and/or a lump sum, then Rosy must establish one of the grounds in **s1**. **Section 1** provides jurisdiction for the court to make a **s2** order if the respondent has failed to provide reasonable maintenance for the applicant or a child of the family, or has behaved in such a way that the applicant cannot reasonably be expected to live with him, or has deserted the applicant.[1]

The most likely ground is that the respondent has failed to provide reasonable maintenance. The behaviour ground may be difficult to establish for Rosy, as it mirrors the test for behaviour in the **MCA 1973 s1(2)(b)**. The only behaviour by Philip was when he struck Rosy after her accusations of child abuse. This is an isolated act of violence, and whilst violence should not be condoned, Rosy's behaviour had been extremely provocative. There is also no substance to an allegation of desertion.

Consequently, the court will consider whether the level of maintenance provided by Philip was reasonable in the circumstances of the case. First, the court will consider what level of maintenance it would be minded to award, given the factors in **DPMCA 1978 s3**. This will be compared with the level of maintenance paid by Philip, and if Philip is paying less than the court would have awarded, the **s1** ground will be established. It is immaterial whether Philip was deliberately depriving Rosy of support, or whether he was innocently believing she was managing.

The level of maintenance is determined by the facts in the **DPMCA 1978 s3(1)**, which are broadly similar to those contained in the **MCA 1973 s25**. All the circumstances of the case will be examined, giving first consideration to the welfare of the two children of the family, Holly and Molly. These children are staying with their father, who is struggling to care for them and pay for child care whilst he works. This means that whilst Philip may have financial resources in terms of his income of £120 per week, he has considerable financial obligations of child care and housing as well as feeding and clothing the children. It is not clear, on the facts, whether Rosy is earning any money; if she does have income it would seem that she only has herself to support on it. Even if she has no income, the court is required to consider any earning capacity she has or can reasonably be expected to acquire. Whilst she may not have worked when the children were so small, now that she no longer cares for them, she should be able to seek work.

Usually, the court will not take into account the availability of State benefits as a resource for the applicant. However, this family does not appear to have sufficient resources for Philip to be able to support the children himself and still send money to Rosy. The net-effect method (*Stockford v Stockford* (1981)) whereby the court looks at what each party has, rather than the one-third rule, would be appropriate here, but it is unlikely that the court would want to make any order that would take Philip below subsistence level (*Barnes v Barnes* (1972)).

---

1 It is important to decide which Act to apply under as both have advantages. The Magistrates' Court is quicker and cheaper. On the other hand, the **Matrimonial Causes Act 1973** offers a wider range of remedies and larger awards.

Maintenance for Children

The court will also look at the other factors in s 3, namely the standard of living enjoyed by the family, the age of the parties and the duration of the marriage. Any drop in the standard of living should be equally borne if possible: *Scott v Scott* (1978). Physical and mental disability also requires consideration and here Rosy is suffering from severe post-natal depression. This may affect her ability to support herself.

In terms of contributions made by the parties, initially both contributed, one by working, the other by looking after the home and children. However, as Rosy has deteriorated in health, so Philip's contribution to the welfare of the family has increased, with him ultimately bearing responsibility for child care. This further contribution must be taken into account, thereby, possibly, reducing his obligation to maintain Rosy. Conduct will also be taken into account if it would be inequitable to disregard it. Philip has been violent towards Rosy on one occasion; however, the violence was not extreme, nor was it repeated (*Bateman v Bateman* (1979)), nor did it affect Rosy's earning capacity (*Jones v Jones* (1975)).

Indeed the violence was provoked by Rosy's unfounded suggestion of abuse, and by her chronic neglect of the children. It may be that this could amount to conduct on her part, but if it is involuntary and caused by mental illness, as in *J (HD) v J (AM)* (1980), then it may not result in an immediate ending of Philip's obligations to Rosy.

In conclusion, it would seem that there are very few resources in this family, and if Rosy is well enough to work, it is unlikely she would receive much, if anything, by way of financial support from Philip. However, if she is too ill to work, it may be pointless making anything more than a nominal order, because to do otherwise would reduce Philip and the children to below subsistence level. Instead, Rosy would need to claim State benefits. Given the unavailability of resources, it would not be possible to order Philip to pay any lump sum to Rosy either.

An application could be made by Rosy under the **DPMCA 1978 s 7**, if the parties have been separated for a continuous period exceeding three months, with neither in desertion. Rosy would need to show that Philip has been making payments to her, and this is so, even though the payments have been made irregularly and infrequently. However, the court only has power to make a periodical payment order that does not exceed the aggregate value of payments made by Philip over the previous three months: **s 7(3)(2)**. If the court considers that this is insufficient for Rosy's reasonable maintenance needs, it can treat the application under **s 7** as an application for a **s 2** order: **s 7(4)**. Given the relatively small sums Philip has paid to Rosy, it is unlikely that a **s 7** order would be sought or ordered.

If Philip and Rosy could come to some reasonable arrangement about financial provision, then this arrangement can be formalised by court order under the **DPMCA 1978 s 6**. Again, the court would need to be satisfied that the level of maintenance was fair, and, given the circumstances, a **s 6** order does not seem likely. Rosy could also make an application to the County Court for financial provision. The County Court has powers to make secured or unsecured periodical payments for the applicant and/or a child of the family, and lump sum orders of unlimited amounts. The basis for financial provision in the **MCA s 27** is that the respondent has failed to provide reasonable maintenance for the applicant and/or a child of the family. This would be determined in much the same way as in the Magistrates' Courts, with reference being made to the factors in **s 25**. Again, the County Court is unlikely to make any order that would reduce Philip to below subsistence level.

If Rosy were in employment there is the possibility that Philip could seek financial assistance in the upkeep of the children under the **Child Support Act 1991**. Rosy would be a 'non-resident parent' within the meaning of the Act, and both Holly and Molly would be 'qualifying children'. Philip is a 'person with care' and therefore a maintenance requirement would be established. That maintenance requirement would then need to be discharged in part by Rosy and in part by Philip's income.[2]

If Rosy moves back to live with Philip, then any **s 2** or **s 6** order that had been made would terminate after six months' cohabitation: **DPMCA ss 25(1)** and **(2)**. A **s 7** order would terminate on resumption of cohabitation: **DPMCA 1978 s 25(3)**. A County Court order is not affected automatically by a resumption of cohabitation, although this would be a change in circumstances that would entitle the respondent to apply for variation or discharge of the order: **MCA 1973 s 31**.

In conclusion, it would seem that whilst Rosy may apply to the courts for financial provision, the precarious financial position the family are in may make it unlikely that she will receive any, or any substantial, financial provision from Philip.

QUESTION 19

Angela, aged 25, has four children: Bobby, aged eight; Cindy, aged six; Darren, aged four; and Elzine, aged two. Bobby and Cindy are children from her relationship with Frank, whom she never married. Darren and Elzine were born during her marriage to Greg. Greg does not think Elzine is his daughter, as her colouring is totally different from either his or Angela's. Greg has petitioned for divorce on the basis of Angela's adultery, and Angela does not intend to defend this divorce. However, she is concerned about the financial consequences of this for herself and her children. She is living, at present, in the former matrimonial home, a council flat, and Greg is quite happy for her to remain there.

▶ Advise Angela.

How to Read this Question

Angela wants to know about the financial consequences of the divorce for herself and for her children. Answers therefore need to explore financial relief on divorce and maintenance for children under the **Child Support Acts** and under the **Matrimonial Causes Act (MCA) 1973**.

---

2 The **Child Support Act 1991** originally used the term 'absent parent'. Non-resident parent replaced this as being more neutral.

Maintenance for Children

Applying the Law

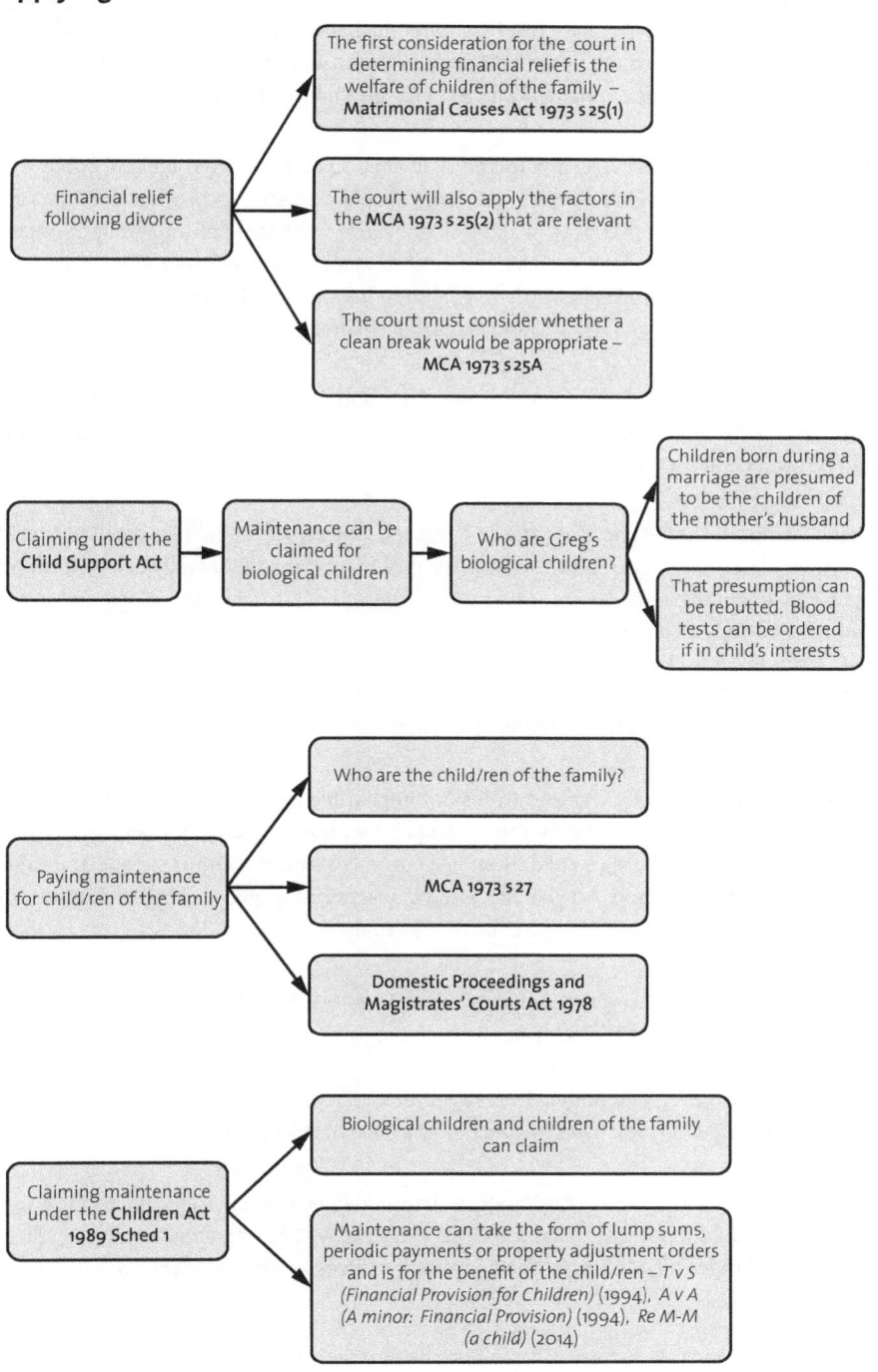

Financial relief following divorce
- The first consideration for the court in determining financial relief is the welfare of children of the family – **Matrimonial Causes Act 1973 s 25(1)**
- The court will also apply the factors in the **MCA 1973 s 25(2)** that are relevant
- The court must consider whether a clean break would be appropriate – **MCA 1973 s 25A**

Claiming under the Child Support Act → **Maintenance can be claimed for biological children** → **Who are Greg's biological children?**
- Children born during a marriage are presumed to be the children of the mother's husband
- That presumption can be rebutted. Blood tests can be ordered if in child's interests

Paying maintenance for child/ren of the family
- Who are the child/ren of the family?
- MCA 1973 s 27
- **Domestic Proceedings and Magistrates' Courts Act 1978**

Claiming maintenance under the Children Act 1989 Sched 1
- Biological children and children of the family can claim
- Maintenance can take the form of lump sums, periodic payments or property adjustment orders and is for the benefit of the child/ren – *T v S (Financial Provision for Children)* (1994), *A v A (A minor: Financial Provision)* (1994), *Re M-M (a child)* (2014)

ANSWER

Angela's entitlement to ancillary relief from her husband Greg will be determined by reference to the court's powers in the **MCA 1973 ss 23** and **24** and the guidelines in the **MCA s 25**. However, the issues of financial provision for the children are complex.

There are four children involved here and they need to be considered in turn. Bobby and Cindy are the natural children of Frank, who would be liable to provide maintenance under the **Child Support Act 1991**. In addition, they may be children of the family of Angela and Greg if they have been treated by Angela and Greg as such: **MCA s 52**. Greg could then incur financial responsibility towards the children under the **MCA 1973**. There is no **Child Support Act** liability since they are not his natural children.[3]

Darren is the natural child of Angela and Greg and therefore Greg could incur **Child Support Act** liability towards Darren. The other possibility is that the **Child Support Act** can be avoided at present by the making of a consent order.

Elzine was born during the marriage of Greg and Angela and there is a presumption of legitimacy, which may be rebutted on the balance of probabilities: **Family Law Reform Act 1969 s 26**. It will therefore be presumed that Elzine is the natural child of Greg unless this can be rebutted. A confession of adultery does not necessarily establish that the child is not Greg's but it is likely that DNA testing, which can be directed by the court (**Family Law Reform Act 1969 s 20(1)**), would establish Elzine's parentage. It is usually in the child's interests for such testing to be ordered: *S v S* (1972).

If Elzine is Greg's natural child, and this is not impossible even though her colouring may differ, then Greg's liability to maintain will again be under the **Child Support Act 1991**. If, however, Elzine is not Greg's child, then her natural father, if identifiable and traceable, would have **Child Support Act** liability. Greg's obligations would be incurred under the **MCA 1973**, if he had treated her as a child of the family.

It is unclear whether Greg and Angela continued to live together after Elzine's birth. If they separated shortly afterwards because of Greg's suspicions, then he may be able to show that he never treated Elzine as a child of the family. However, if there was a shared family life, when Greg and Angela lived together and acted as Elzine's parents, then Greg, despite his misgivings, will have treated her as a child of the family.

Liability to maintain a child of the family is determined by the provisions of the **MCA 1973 s 25(3)**, if the child is not Greg's natural child. Thus Bobby, Cindy and possibly Elzine will be provided for under the **MCA 1973**. The financial resources and needs of the parties and the

---

3   Liability for children can be based either on being their natural parent or on assuming responsibility for them through marriage. Sometimes a child will qualify for maintenance both through blood and through marriage.

children will be considered, together with any disability the child may have. This does not seem to be an issue here, nor is there evidence that the parties were educating children privately, or intended to do so: **s 25(3)(d)**. Thus it will essentially be a question of considering Greg's available resources.

Since the children are not Greg's own children, it is necessary (**s 25(4)**) to consider whether he assumed responsibility for them, and on what basis. The extent of his liability and whether he did so knowing that they were not his children, must be examined, as must the liability of anyone else to maintain the children. From the facts, it is clear that he knew Bobby and Cindy were not his children, but it is unclear what, if any, liability for their maintenance is being borne by their natural father, Frank. If the Child Support Agency can track him down and succeed in obtaining child support from him, then this could reduce Greg's liability. It does seem, however, that Greg has borne some financial responsibility for both children, and so some periodical payments for their benefit will be ordered. If Elzine is not his natural child, then his liability towards her as a child of the family will be determined as above. Essentially, much will depend on how he behaved after her birth and on the possible liability of her as yet unnamed father.

Angela can also seek financial provision from the natural father of her children under the **Child Support Act 1991**. If Angela is in receipt of State benefits, she will have no choice; the Agency is automatically involved in benefit cases. A parent receiving benefit is required to provide information identifying the father of her child and authorise the Child Support Agency to pursue him for child support. Thus, Frank, Greg and the as yet unnamed father of Elzine could all be pursued by the Agency. If Angela is not in receipt of benefits, Greg could agree a consent order with Angela regarding financial provision for his natural child or children, but would be advised to ensure that the level of maintenance is equivalent to that which would be ordered under the **Child Support Act**.

The Child Support Agency will impose liability on an absent parent, that is, a natural parent not living in the same household as his or her children. The children all have their home with Angela, the caring parent, and since each child is under 16 with one parent absent, they are all qualifying children. Each child's natural father will have his liability assessed by reference to the statutory formula for calculating the maintenance requirement. This formula is applied automatically and without discretion, giving rise to considerable criticism. Frank, who may have played little role until now in his children's lives, will find that he will incur financial liability.

Angela's income would be ignored and there are no allowances for Frank's housing costs and so on. However, this figure may be adjusted downwards, if Frank acquires a second family, or if the children spend time living with him.

This calculation would also be made in respect of the other biological fathers of Angela's children. However, only Greg, the man she married, could incur any direct financial obligations to Angela herself. This obligation could possibly be by way of periodical payments, either secured or unsecured, a lump sum order (**s 23**), or property transfer, or variations under **s 24**. The factors in the **MCA s 25** must be considered, including the welfare of any children of the family as a first consideration (**s 25(1)**). Here there are a number of children of the family and their welfare requires them to be adequately housed. There does not seem to be any controversy over what should happen to the former matrimonial home, as Greg is happy for Angela to remain there with the children. The court has power to order the transfer of council house tenancies and although the local authority has no right to prevent this, they are entitled to be present and to voice their opinion, as in *Lee v Lee* (1984).

In relation to financial provision, the court must consider the desirability of a clean break between the parties (**s 25A(1)**), but is under no obligation to impose one (*Clutton v Clutton* (1991)). Clearly, it is difficult to have a clean break if there are young children (*Suter v Suter and Jones* (1987)), or if the wife has been out to work for some time. However, the court may consider that whilst Angela may need immediate support, it could be desirable to limit maintenance for a fixed period: **s 25A(2)**, *Parlour v Parlour* (2004). This could give Angela time to adjust without undue hardship, but it might not be appropriate if her future is too uncertain, as in *Suter v Suter and Jones* (1987). Only if the future is sufficiently predictable should limited maintenance be imposed: *Barrett v Barrett* (1988).[4]

It seems likely that if maintenance is awarded by way of periodical payments, they will not be limited but will terminate on Angela's death or remarriage (**MCA s 28**) or if Greg successfully applies to vary or terminate his obligations (**MCA s 31**).

The amount of maintenance will be determined by reference to the financial resources, income and earning capacity of the parties. It is not clear how much Greg earns, if at all. If Greg is in receipt of State benefits himself, he will not usually be ordered to pay substantial sums to Angela, although an order may still nevertheless be made (*Freeman v Swatridge* (1984)); usually, however, it is a nominal order (*Berry v Berry* (1986)). If Greg does have earnings, it is likely that he will have to pay something to Angela. She is not earning at present, and with young children it may be difficult for her to realise or acquire earning capacity. Nevertheless, she should be advised that the court will not countenance a 'meal ticket for life' and, since she seems to be young, she will need to take steps towards self-sufficiency in the future. No order will usually be made that would take Greg below subsistence level (*Barnes v Barnes* (1972)), and to that extent the court will take into account the safety net of welfare benefits available to Angela.

The drop in standard of living (**s 25(2)(c)**) should be equally borne (*Preston v Preston* (1982)), but the fact that this seems to be a relatively short marriage is offset by the fact that two more children were born, and that there were two other children for whom Greg assumed responsibility. In those circumstances, Angela would find it impossible to adjust

---

4 Courts have a duty to consider whether a clean break is appropriate; however, the fact that the welfare of children of the family is the court's first consideration means that in the case of minor children a clean break will not often be appropriate.

immediately to her changed circumstances. The parties are not particularly old, nor are they disabled, and they both appear to have contributed to the marriage and welfare of the family: **s 25(2)(f)**. The only other factor that may have a relevance is conduct under **s 25(2)(g)**. This is not routinely a consideration (*Wachtel v Wachtel* (1973)), and should only be used if it would be inequitable to disregard it. Generally speaking, adultery is not conduct (*Duxbury v Duxbury* (1987)), and it does not appear that there are any additional factors that make Angela's behaviour repugnant and indefensible.

Consequently, it seems likely that some financial provision will be awarded to Angela. The exact amount depends upon Greg's resources and will be affected by his obligations to maintain the various children of the family. In addition, Angela may seek child support from the natural fathers of her children.

Common Pitfalls

In a question such as this with a number of children all needing maintenance it is important to be clear which children are claiming as natural children and which as children of the family and therefore what the relevant statutes are. Remember too that there have been recent changes in this area through the **Child Maintenance and Other Payments Act 2008**.

Aim Higher

Extra marks could be gained through explaining any difficulties with using these Acts.

QUESTION 20

Henry and Wanda married five years ago, after the death of Henry's first wife, Bronwen. Henry and Bronwen had two children, Scott, now aged 14, and Charlene, now aged 12. Henry and Wanda have one child, Jimmy, aged three. Henry owns the matrimonial home, which is a large four-bedroomed executive house, valued at £650,000 with a mortgage of £50,000 outstanding. When Jimmy was born, Wanda used her entire savings of £40,000 to build an extension to the house, which included a playroom and 'den' for the children. Wanda has no further savings, and has not worked since before Jimmy was born. Henry earns £60,000 per annum. The marriage has encountered difficulties, and both parties agree that a divorce is the best option for them. Scott and Charlene will remain with their father, and Wanda will care for Jimmy. Wanda wishes to obtain periodical payments for herself and Jimmy, and a lump sum to enable her to buy a new home. Wanda is legally aided and has heard horror stories about what can happen if the dispute drags on. Henry is being quite reasonable and his lawyer has indicated to Wanda that he feels a compromise can be negotiated and agreed by way of a consent order.

▶ Advise Wanda on the financial settlement for her and the children.

How to Read this Question

As Wanda is considering a consent order the answer needs to explain whether this would be enforceable. In this case Scott and Charlene are planning to stay with Henry, whilst Jimmy will be living with his mother, therefore Wanda is likely to have obligations to pay child maintenance as well as a right to claim child maintenance.

Applying the Law

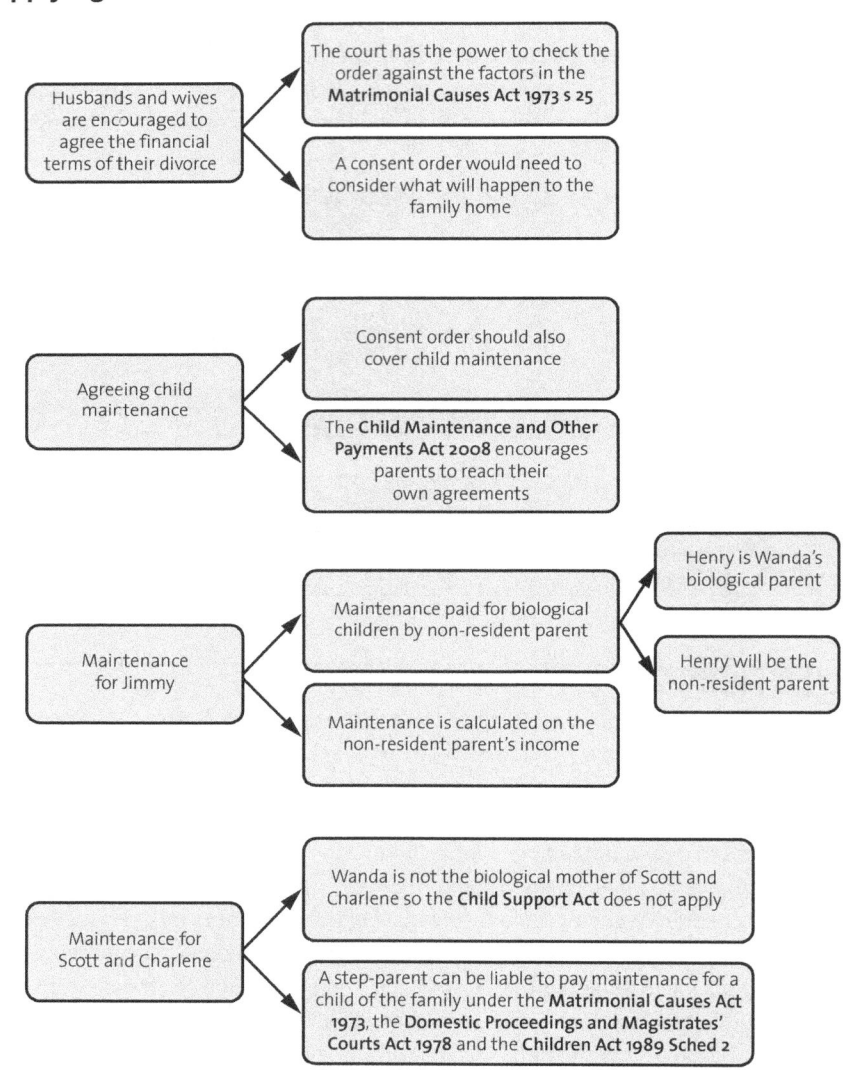

Husbands and wives are encouraged to agree the financial terms of their divorce
- The court has the power to check the order against the factors in the **Matrimonial Causes Act 1973 s 25**
- A consent order would need to consider what will happen to the family home

Agreeing child maintenance
- Consent order should also cover child maintenance
- The **Child Maintenance and Other Payments Act 2008** encourages parents to reach their own agreements

Maintenance for Jimmy
- Maintenance paid for biological children by non-resident parent
  - Henry is Wanda's biological parent
  - Henry will be the non-resident parent
- Maintenance is calculated on the non-resident parent's income

Maintenance for Scott and Charlene
- Wanda is not the biological mother of Scott and Charlene so the **Child Support Act** does not apply
- A step-parent can be liable to pay maintenance for a child of the family under the **Matrimonial Causes Act 1973**, the **Domestic Proceedings and Magistrates' Courts Act 1978** and the **Children Act 1989 Sched 2**

ANSWER

If the parties divorce, then the court has wide powers to order ancillary relief in the form of secured or unsecured periodical payments or lump sum orders (**Matrimonial Causes**

Act (MCA) 1973 s 23), and property orders under the MCA s 24, which will be determined by reference to the factors in the MCA s 25. However, this case is one of the few relatively amicable 'divorces' and the parties are keen to agree the level of ancillary relief rather than have it imposed on them by the courts. If the parties are able to reach agreement then the various aspects of the agreement are embodied in a consent order. This order is then formally presented to the court which can approve it under the MCA 1973 s 33A. The order will then be as enforceable as any other order. The parties are often influenced in reaching agreement by the realisation of what a court is likely to order on the s 25 guidelines.[5]

It is necessary to ensure that a consent order embodies all aspects of ancillary relief, as such an order is usually regarded as full and final, and consequently difficult to vary or appeal against. Wanda should therefore ensure that the consent order properly reflects any agreed financial provision for Jimmy, herself and any lump sum that Henry is agreeable to paying. In terms of financial provision for Jimmy, he is the natural child of both Henry and Wanda. If agreement is not reached, then Henry as the non-resident parent would be liable to pay maintenance for Jimmy; however, it is worth noting that the **Child Maintenance and Other Payments 2008** encourages parents to agree maintenance before turning to child support claims.

The two children of Henry's former marriage, Scott and Charlene, may well qualify as children of the family (MCA 1973 s 52), as they have been treated by both Henry and Wanda as such, even though they are not Wanda's natural children. Wanda will have no **Child Support Act** liability towards them as they are not her natural children, but she could potentially have to contribute to their maintenance under the MCA 1973. However, she has no job or obvious resources and it would seem inappropriate for her to have to support them. Therefore the consent order should reflect this.

In terms of periodical payments for Wanda, it is clear that she will at least initially require them. She has no job, nor any savings, and would find it difficult to get work given the young age of her child and the fact that she has not worked for a number of years. Consequently, she will need to look to Henry for such support but as she is relatively young, she cannot expect this to continue indefinitely. Assuming that substantial sums can be agreed upon, it will then be necessary to agree the period during which these will be paid. An immediate clean break would be unfair to Wanda; even if the clean break were to be deferred, as it would not be possible to predict her future accurately, therefore, it might be best to agree that the order can be varied or discharged later in relation to periodical payments for Wanda.

Wanda also needs a home for herself and Jimmy and it does not seem unreasonable to suggest that, whilst Henry can remain in the matrimonial home with his two children, he

---

5 Consent orders are encouraged as the couple are more likely to understand what will best suit their circumstances and are more likely to follow the terms of an agreement that they have reached.

should raise a lump sum to enable Wanda to buy a small home for herself. Although the home is owned absolutely by Henry, Wanda has contributed during the marriage by paying for the extension, looking after the house and children, and it is right that she should have some share of the family assets. It is also in Henry's interest that his son, Jimmy, should be properly and securely housed. In *White v White* (2000) the House of Lords suggested that any financial resolution considered by the judge should be measured against the yardstick of equality and that equal division should only be departed from if there were good reason, which should be explained by the judge. This should enable her to buy a modest home and is within the range of what Henry could borrow by way of mortgage on his home. However, this increase in Henry's borrowing may mean he is less able to make periodical payments at the level suggested earlier, and so Wanda must be prepared to make some sort of compromise here. It should be pointed out to Henry that by paying for the extension, Wanda could acquire an interest in the house by virtue of her contribution, under the **Matrimonial Proceedings and Property Act 1970 s 37**.

5

Property Disputes

INTRODUCTION

Although the **Matrimonial Causes Act 1973** covers financial relief after divorce and spouses' duty to maintain each other during the marriage (see Chapter 3), there is still a role for general property law in regulating property ownership between individuals who are in a familial relationship.

Checklist

Students should be able to understand and apply the rules on the following:

- that legal ownership of land is established by conveyance (**Law of Property Act 1925 s 52(1)**);
- that beneficial ownership can be established by either express or implied trust;
- that an express trust has to be in writing: **Law of Property Act 1925 s 53(1)(b)**;
- how an implied trust can be established: by a resulting trust, by a constructive trust and by proprietary estoppel;
- that a resulting trust requires a direct contribution to the purchase price and that the presumption of advancement has been abolished by the **Equality Act 2010**;
- that a constructive trust requires a common intention to share the property that a person has relied on to their detriment;
- how a common intention to share the property can be shown: *Eves v Eves* (1975), *Grant v Edwards* (1987);
- what will constitute detrimental reliance: *Lloyds Bank v Rosset* (1991), *Eves v Eves*, *Crossley v Crossley* (2005);
- what is needed to establish proprietary estoppel: the person claiming has to show that he reasonably believed that he was going to have an interest in the land, that he acted in reliance on this belief, that it must be fair to give them an interest in land;
- how the **Matrimonial Property and Proceedings Act 1970 s 37** gives a spouse a beneficial interest following a contribution to an improvement on property;
- understand and be able to explain the rules on how ownership of land is quantified (*Oxley v Hiscock* (2004), *Cox v Jones* (2004), *Stack v Dowden* (2007), *Fowler v Barron* (2008), *Jones v Kernott* (2011), *Graham-York v York* (2015));
- students should also be able to critically examine the land law rules and how they can lead to seemingly unfair results: *Burns v Burns* (1984), *Geary v Rankine* (2012);

- how the **Land Registration Act 1925 s 70** protects a beneficial interest against third parties;
- students should be able to discuss whether cohabitants should be entitled to greater protection and attempts at reforming the law in the **Cohabitation Bill 2008** and the **Cohabitation Rights Bill 2014**;
- how the law views gifts between engaged couples: **Law Reform (Miscellaneous Provisions) Act 1970 s 3**;
- how the law views joint bank accounts and property purchased with money from a joint account: *Jones v Maynard* (1951).

Up for Debate

- Does the law give sufficient protection to cohabitants?
- Should cohabitation lead to an automatic beneficial interest and if so when?
- Should cohabitants be able to claim financial relief at the end of their relationship and if so how should that financial relief be assessed?

QUESTION 21

The marriage between Michael and Sarah has encountered difficulties, and the couple have decided to part amicably. They are both keen to go their separate ways with no financial responsibilities towards each other, and so they propose to divide their assets according to their beneficial entitlements in property law. They do not want the court to impose an arrangement under the **MCA 1973**.

Advise Michael and Sarah on their beneficial entitlement to the following:

(a) an antique diamond ring, worth £5,000, that belonged to Michael's grandmother, given by him to Sarah on their engagement;
(b) £20,000 invested in a building society savings account, which is held in joint names;
(c) shares to the value of £6,000 registered in Michael's name, but paid for with a cheque drawn on the couple's joint bank account;
(d) the matrimonial home, registered in Sarah's name. The initial deposit of £20,000 was paid by Sarah with money from an inheritance, but the mortgage instalments have been met from the joint bank account. Michael spent every weekend for a whole year renovating the property and carrying out all the interior design. The house was purchased for £100,000 five years ago, and is now worth £150,000. The outstanding mortgage is £20,000.

How to Read this Question

The question is clear that the **Matrimonial Causes Act 1973** is to be ignored and basic property laws are to be used instead. The question has four parts. Where this is a mark scheme, students should spend their time on the part that carries the greatest proportion

Property Disputes 83

of marks. Here, where there is no mark scheme, it is part (d), dealing with the disposal of the matrimonial home, which is the most complex and on which students should spend the bulk of the time.

Applying the Law

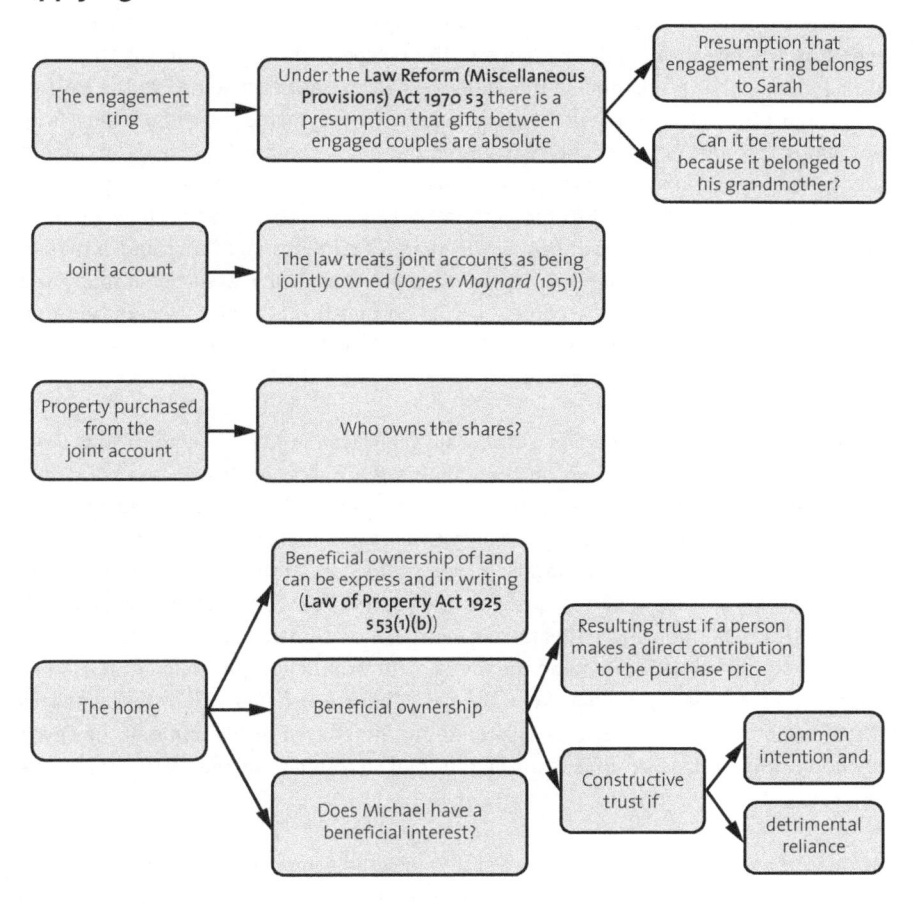

```
The engagement ring  →  Under the Law Reform (Miscellaneous Provisions) Act 1970 s 3 there is a presumption that gifts between engaged couples are absolute
    →  Presumption that engagement ring belongs to Sarah
    →  Can it be rebutted because it belonged to his grandmother?

Joint account  →  The law treats joint accounts as being jointly owned (Jones v Maynard (1951))

Property purchased from the joint account  →  Who owns the shares?

The home  →  Beneficial ownership
                →  Beneficial ownership of land can be express and in writing (Law of Property Act 1925 s 53(1)(b))
                →  Resulting trust if a person makes a direct contribution to the purchase price
            →  Does Michael have a beneficial interest?
                →  Constructive trust if
                    →  common intention and
                    →  detrimental reliance
```

ANSWER

(a) The position of engagement rings is often determined by reference to the **Law Reform (Miscellaneous Provisions) Act 1970 s 3**. This section provides that the gift of an engagement ring should be assumed to be an absolute gift but the presumption may be rebutted by proving that the ring was given on the implied condition that it should be returned if the marriage did not take place for any reason. In the instant case Michael and Sarah have gone on to marry. However, the presumption that a man has given a woman a gift in such a situation would be very strong. The diamond ring, however, is quite valuable and has been a family heirloom; so in order for it to belong to Michael rather than Sarah it would be necessary for Michael to show that the presumption of advancement has been rebutted by a contrary intention. This contrary intention needs to be that he only intended the ring to be a conditional gift upon the marriage subsisting. It is easier to show in the case of a valuable family heirloom but, nonetheless, the presumption that this is a gift appears to be quite strong and on balance it would seem that Sarah is entitled to keep the ring.[1]

(b) Money invested in a joint savings account may cause difficulty in that it will often depend on the intention of the parties and their respective contributions as to who is entitled and in what proportion. In this case, the parties have contributed to the savings account but little is known about what arrangements they made for withdrawing from the savings account. Where money is invested in a joint account there is an argument that the money should be regarded as jointly owned. In *Jones v Maynard* (1951) both husband and wife contributed to the account just as Michael and Sarah have done. In that case, as in the present, both paid in their various earnings and funds and, although the husband paid in more than the wife, it did seem that they viewed the account as a common savings account. The argument would be that this is a joint account and that they are therefore both equally entitled since they viewed it as a common pool. There is no evidence that they merely intended the shares to reflect their contributions.

(c) The shares purchased for £6,000 which are registered in Michael's name only were purchased with a cheque drawn on the couple's joint account. If the case of *Jones v Maynard* (1951) were to be followed then the shares would be jointly owned since the investments could be regarded as joint investments and merely a continuance of their arrangements for the joint account. However, there is an argument that if both were entitled to draw on the account to purchase whatever they wished to by way of investments or chattels, then each separate investment or chattel should be regarded as belonging to the person who made the investment or purchase of the chattel as in *Re Bishop (Deceased)* (1965). If that were the case then the shares would be owned by Michael absolutely since they are registered and purchased in his name. If, however, they could regard it as an extension of the joint account then the shares would be jointly owned.

(d) The former matrimonial home is registered in Sarah's name only. This declaration of legal title in the conveyance would conclusively establish that Sarah is the sole legal owner unless it can be established that there is fraud or mistake (*Goodman v Gallant* (1986)). There is no evidence that there has been any separate declaration of a beneficial entitlement in favour of Michael and an interest under a trust must be created and evidenced in writing. However, it is possible that Michael may have an interest in the home by way of some resulting implied or constructive trust. The initial deposit of £20,000 was paid by Sarah and the mortgage instalments have been met from the joint account. Michael has renovated the property and carried out interior design. It is necessary to examine to what extent, if any, Michael has acquired or enlarged his interest in the home.

---

1   When a question is divided into parts, it makes sense to also clearly divide your answer. This way both you and the examiner can be sure that you have dealt with all the issues.

To acquire an interest under a resulting, implied or constructive trust it will be necessary to show that there is a common intention between the parties that, although Sarah has the legal entitlement, Michael has a beneficial interest in the home. It will also be necessary to show that Michael, as the owner of the beneficial interest, has acted to his detriment based on this common intention. Michael has not made any direct contribution towards the deposit; however, it is arguable that he has made contributions towards the mortgage instalments. The couple have had a joint bank account which they have regarded as a common pool; both have paid their salaries into the account and both have made various drawings on the account. This would seem to provide evidence of a direct contribution as required in *Lloyds Bank v Rosset* (1991), which would thereby establish an interest on behalf of Michael. His contributions do appear to be substantial in terms of meeting the mortgage requirements and it seems that the £80,000 mortgage that was initially required has reduced to some £20,000 outstanding now. Therefore, if one could argue that there is a joint contribution to the mortgage instalments then Michael will acquire some kind of interest in the home. There is the further possibility that this interest may have been enlarged by his efforts each weekend, renovating and designing the interior of the home.[2]

According to *Lloyds Bank v Rosset* (1991) the only way that this contribution would suffice would be if it were to be substantial in money or money's worth to the improvement of the property. In *Lloyds Bank* itself the wife's decorating and supervision of workmen was insufficient to give rise to an interest. In Michael's case, much would depend upon the extent of the renovations that he carried out. The interior design really would be superfluous. However, the renovation and the amount of impact that is made on the transformation of the property would determine whether this would give or enlarge any interest in the home. Following *Lloyds Bank v Rosset* (1991), caution must be exercised in trying to give an interest under this head. The cases of *Cooke v Head* (1972) and *Eves v Eves* (1975) illustrate just how substantial the work must be in order to qualify under this head. However, there is the possibility that if Michael does not acquire an interest under a trust by virtue of this work he may nevertheless enlarge his interest in the home by reference to the **Matrimonial Proceedings and Property Act 1970 s 37**. This section provides that where a husband or wife contributes in money or money's worth to the improvement of property in which, or in the proceeds of sale of which, either or both of them have the beneficial interest, the person who contributes shall, if the contribution is of a substantial nature and not subject to any agreement to the contrary, be treated as having acquired by virtue of his contribution a share or an enlarged share. The extent of such a share is the extent that the court considers just and equitable.

Here it could be argued that Michael has contributed to the improvement of the property. His work can be measured in money or money's worth; he has spent every weekend for a substantial period of time; and it does seem to be the sort of work that would normally be

---

2 It is easier to establish a beneficial entitlement if there has been a direct financial contribution to the ownership of the property and therefore this is what is considered first. In this case Michael would get a beneficial entitlement because of his contributions towards the mortgage. It is more doubtful whether his work on the house by itself would be enough to gain him a beneficial interest.

paid for if done by someone else. The question is, then, whether the work is of a substantial nature. Ordinary everyday do-it-yourself and common repairs to property should not suffice to enlarge Michael's interest. However, if the work has been substantial and has improved the house then he ought to be entitled to enlarge his share. The enlarged share must not be negated by any agreement by the spouses and the court has a discretion in deciding to what extent Michael's share will be increased.

In conclusion, therefore, the house is now valued at £150,000 with a mortgage outstanding of £20,000; this leaves equity of £130,000 in the house. The initial deposit of £20,000 by Sarah represents one-fifth of the original value of the home; the remaining four-fifths was contributed to by both parties in paying the mortgage and since their intention appears to have been that they should require a joint interest by so doing, the mortgage contributions will be split two-fifths to Michael, two-fifths to Sarah. This would give Michael a two-fifths share in the equity and Sarah three-fifths share in the equity. However, some adjustment may need to be made for the improvement effected by Michael's renovations and, on balance, it would seem that the couple would more or less be jointly entitled to any proceeds of sale.

In *Midland Bank v Cooke* (1995) it was stressed that it is important to establish an interest under a constructive trust by reference to the strict rules in *Gissing v Gissing* (1971) and *Lloyds Bank v Rosset* (1991). However, once the common intention to share can be shown by reference to those rules, as it can in this case, then, in quantifying the shares of the parties, the court can take into account the whole history of the relationship, including behaviour and contributions that would not suffice in themselves to create the interest in the first place. Thus, whilst Michael's renovations would not suffice as evidence of a common intention giving rise to a constructive trust, they can be referred to so as to determine the size of the shares the parties intended. This arguably reinforces the argument that the parties should have more or less equal shares here.[3]

QUESTION 22

Arthur and Guinevere married 16 years ago, and they have three children, aged 12, 10 and 8, respectively. The matrimonial home, Camelot, was bought when they married, with a deposit of £10,000 provided by Arthur's parents as a wedding present, and the remaining cost paid by mortgage. The house was registered in Arthur's name only. Guinevere worked briefly before the children were born, and has worked as a teacher since the youngest child started school. The mortgage instalments were paid from a joint bank account into which both Arthur and Guinevere paid their salaries. Two years ago, Guinevere used £15,000 she won in a competition to redecorate and recarpet the house.

---

3 Although this question is divided into four parts, the answer does not give the same consideration to all the parts. Far more discussion is spent on the issue of who owns the house. This is unsurprising. It is likely to be the most important issue for the couple themselves and it is the one where there is the most legislation and case law to apply. Sometimes a student will be faced with a question which is divided into parts where the examiner sets out the marks available for each part. In this case, the student should allocate her time and words in answering the question proportionally according to the marks available.

Property Disputes 87

The mortgage on the house was virtually paid off when Arthur decided to go into business on his own. He borrowed £50,000 from the Westland Bank and secured the loan on the home, without Guinevere's knowledge. The business failed; Arthur defaulted on the mortgage, and has left Guinevere.

The Westland Bank is seeking to evict Guinevere from Camelot, and she does not wish to leave.
▶ **Advise Guinevere on:**
   (a) her property rights, if any, in Camelot;
   (b) whether the bank will be successful in evicting her.

Applying the Law
The question is about Guinevere's property entitlement under land law rules and whether they can be enforced against a third party (the bank).

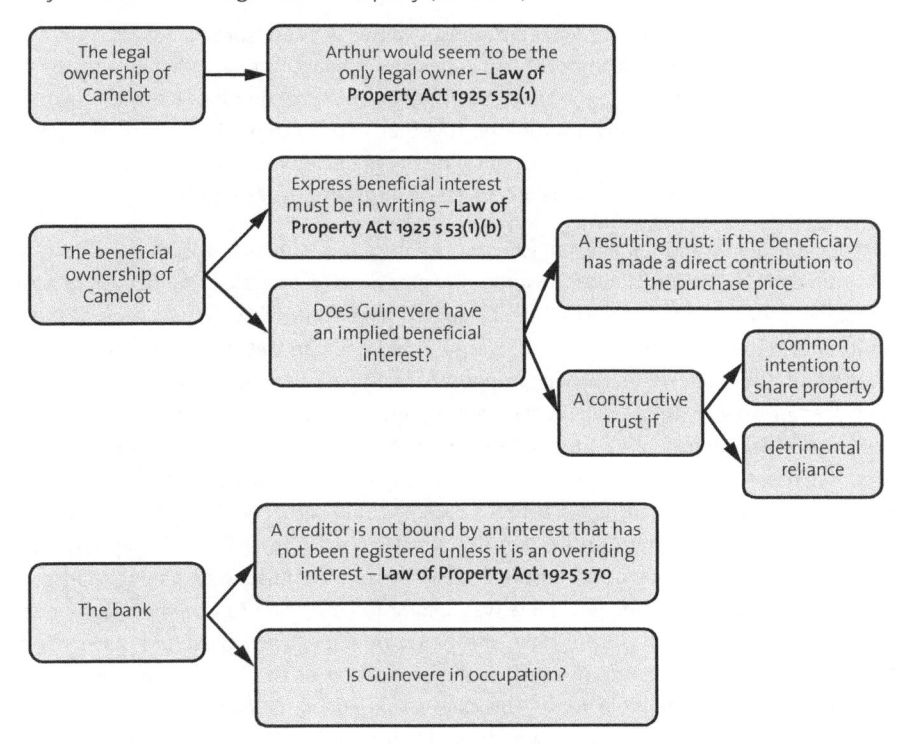

- The legal ownership of Camelot → Arthur would seem to be the only legal owner – **Law of Property Act 1925 s 52(1)**
- The beneficial ownership of Camelot
  - Express beneficial interest must be in writing – **Law of Property Act 1925 s 53(1)(b)**
  - Does Guinevere have an implied beneficial interest?
    - A resulting trust: if the beneficiary has made a direct contribution to the purchase price
    - A constructive trust if
      - common intention to share property
      - detrimental reliance
- The bank
  - A creditor is not bound by an interest that has not been registered unless it is an overriding interest – **Law of Property Act 1925 s 70**
  - Is Guinevere in occupation?

ANSWER
(a) Guinevere is seeking advice on her property rights, if any, in Camelot, the matrimonial home. Normally, on the breakdown of a marriage, a spouse would be better served by seeking a financial settlement under the wide powers of the **Matrimonial Causes Act 1973**. However, in this case, these powers could only resolve the financial situation between Arthur and Guinevere on divorce. Guinevere's most immediate problem concerns her

possible eviction by the bank who are her husband's creditors. Her best chance of avoiding or postponing this is if she can show that she has an entitlement in property law to the home. This may then possibly be enforceable against the bank.

Any such interest must be determined according to strict rules of property law (*Pettitt v Pettitt* (1970)), with no room for the court to order what seems fair in the circumstances. On the facts, it is clear that Guinevere has no legal interest in the property which is registered in Arthur's name only. The original conveyance will be conclusive unless it can be shown that there was fraud or mistake: *Goodman v Gallant* (1986). Consequently, there is no legal or beneficial entitlement evidenced in the conveyance. There does not appear to be any subsequent declaration of trust either, since that must be in writing (**Law of Property Act 1925 s 53(1)(b)**; **Law of Property (Miscellaneous Provisions) Act 1989 s 2**). Therefore, any beneficial entitlement on Guinevere's part must be by way of implied, resulting or constructive trust, which does not need to comply with formalities.

Although technically there are legal differences between these three kinds of trust, the courts frequently make no attempt to distinguish (*Gissing v Gissing* (1971)), since the basic requirements of the trusts are the same. Such trusts require evidence of a common intention to share an interest in the property, together with detrimental acts by the party seeking the beneficial interest. The technical distinctions between the trusts arise in how such a common intention is established, or deemed to exist, by the courts.

Often a common intention is established by pointing to a direct contribution made by a party towards the acquisition of the home. This may be the provision of a deposit or part of a deposit, or by paying some of the mortgage. Such a contribution would tend to show an intention to share, unless it could be argued to be a loan: *Sekhon v Alissa* (1989). The amount of the share is usually in proportion to the parties' respective contributions (*Cowcher v Cowcher* (1972)), unless the contrary intention can be shown. In the present case, the initial deposit came from Arthur's parents as a wedding present to the couple. Wedding presents do not always belong to the couple jointly; it depends on the intention of the donor (*Kilner v Kilner* (1939)). Arthur's parents could arguably be said to be providing a gift for them both to share. In *McHardy & Sons v Warren* (1994) the Court of Appeal held, in a case such as Arthur's and Guinevere's, that where the husband's parents had provided a deposit as a wedding gift, there was a common intention to give the wife a beneficial interest. Somewhat surprisingly, the Court of Appeal held that this gave her a half-share with her husband, not just in the proportion of the home that the deposit represented, but in the whole home. This case would benefit Guinevere enormously, but has been subject to criticism since it would enable the wife to defeat a creditor's claim.

In addition to the deposit, it seems that the mortgage instalments have been paid from a joint bank account, into which both parties paid their salaries. Although there was a period during which Guinevere did not work, it can be argued that by their behaviour the parties have provided evidence of a joint enterprise. They both placed all their income into this account for their joint use and benefit, and neither has reserved any individual interest (*Chapman v Chapman* (1969)). This would reinforce the argument that they have equal joint interests.

Guinevere has made the further investment of her £3,000 competition prize to redecorate the house and buy new carpets. This would be an indirect contribution, and likely, following *Lloyds Bank v Rosset* (1991), to be inadequate since it is not substantial. Minor redecoration and the buying of household goods does not acquire or enlarge an interest at common law: *Pettitt v Pettitt* (1970). Neither will her contribution as wife and mother assist her: *Burns v Burns* (1984).[4]

The only other way in which Guinevere may increase her interest is by way of the **Matrimonial Proceedings and Property Act 1970 s 37**. This is available to spouses only and she must show that she has made a substantial contribution in money or money's worth to the improvement of the home. On the facts, although £3,000 is a lot of money, it will not have added much, if anything, to the value of the property, since it was used to pay for things that improve the quality of life for the occupier, rather than increase the value of the property. Only if the property had been very run-down or possibly derelict would she succeed.

It therefore seems likely that Guinevere would be able to establish a beneficial interest in the property, possibly in equal share with Arthur. Applying the principle in *Midland Bank v Cooke* (1995) the whole history of the relationship and the parties' conduct and contributions can be looked at to determine the size of shares intended. Thus, once Guinevere establishes an interest under a trust according to the strict rules in *Gissing v Gissing* (1971) and *Lloyds Bank v Rosset* (1991), she could argue that there was an intention that they should have equal shares. However, she should be advised that the courts will scrutinise carefully any such claim which would have the effect of depriving a third party creditor of his rights: *Midland Bank v Dobson* (1986).[5]

(b) It seems that Guinevere has a beneficial interest in the home; however, the Westland Bank have made a mortgage advance to Arthur which they now wish to recover. This depends on whether the bank are bound by Guinevere's interest. In the case of registered land, the bank take free of interests that are not registered, unless the interest is an overriding interest: **LRA 1925 s 70**. Guinevere's interest may be overriding because of her occupation of the home (**LRA s 70(1)(g)**), and will bind the bank unless they made enquiry which did not disclose her interest (*Williams & Glyn's Bank v Boland* (1981)). She and the children were clearly in occupation, which does not necessarily need to be continuous or exclusive: *Kingsnorth Finance v Tizard* (1986). Any bank lending to a man should make enquiries of the existence of a spouse and be alerted to the possibility of her having an interest.

Thus, it would seem that the bank are bound by her interest. It is then necessary to see if the bank could force a sale of the property. The bank have a charge on the property, but

---

4 The above cases illustrate that only rarely will work done or money given to improve the home environment lead to a beneficial interest.
5 See *Stack v Downton* (2007) and *Jones v Kernott* (2011) on how beneficial shares in property should be quantified. The latter determined that although an equal division would be the starting point, this could be rebutted depending on the facts.

have not, as yet, declared Arthur bankrupt. The appropriate provision is the **Trusts of Land and Appointment of Trustees Act 1996 s 14** and the court will make such order as it feels is just and reasonable in the circumstances of the case. The court will look at the interests of the creditors, and the conduct of the spouse, Guinevere, in contributing to the situation. In the present case, the bank have behaved somewhat rashly by granting a mortgage to Arthur without seeking Guinevere's consent and Guinevere has not contributed to the bankruptcy situation. She clearly needs a roof over her head and those of the children, and does not appear to have any substantial resources that would enable her to rehouse herself. The children are still young and need a stable home and this is a genuine case of Guinevere having a real interest, not just a sham arrangement to defeat creditors. In the present case, Guinevere should be able to resist the order for sale, at least whilst the children are still young. However, the courts do not lightly entertain **s 14** applications that will leave genuine creditors without recourse. Therefore, it is still possible that a court, depending on the value of the home, might order a sale, since Guinevere's half-share might be sufficient for her to rehouse herself.

In *Mortgage Corp v Shaire* (2000) the judge thought that **s 14** had altered the law in favour of the family vis-à-vis the creditor. It was stated that a distinction could be drawn between orders for sale in favour of a creditor in bankruptcy situations, where the creditor was likely to succeed, and orders for sale in favour of a bank or building society which has a charge over the property, and is protected in the long term, where the family might have a greater chance. This greater flexibility may be necessary to enable the courts to comply with the **Human Rights Act 1998. Article 8** of the **European Convention** confers the right to respect for family and private life, and by automatically ordering a sale of the home against the wishes of a blameless spouse there may be a violation.

QUESTION 23

Eric and Elsie were married 40 years ago, and lived in a house purchased by Eric with a deposit of £300, the remaining mortgage of £3,000 being paid by Eric over the following 25 years. The house is now valued at £350,000 and is registered in Eric's sole name. Elsie worked for the first eight years of the marriage, using her earnings to pay all the household expenses, which Eric could not otherwise have afforded. She did not work while the two children of the marriage were small, but has worked for the past 20 years. Elsie's earnings have been used by the couple for household expenses, to install central heating and recently to add a conservatory to the back of the house.

Eric has just died, leaving all his property to Freda, his secret mistress.

▶ **Advise Elsie on what her beneficial entitlement is, if any, to the matrimonial home, and how, if at all, her position may be improved.**

How to Read this Question

The question involves a discussion of Elsie's property law entitlement to a share in the home. She will again need to rely on trust principles and/or the **Matrimonial Proceedings and Property Act 1970 s 37**.

Applying the Law

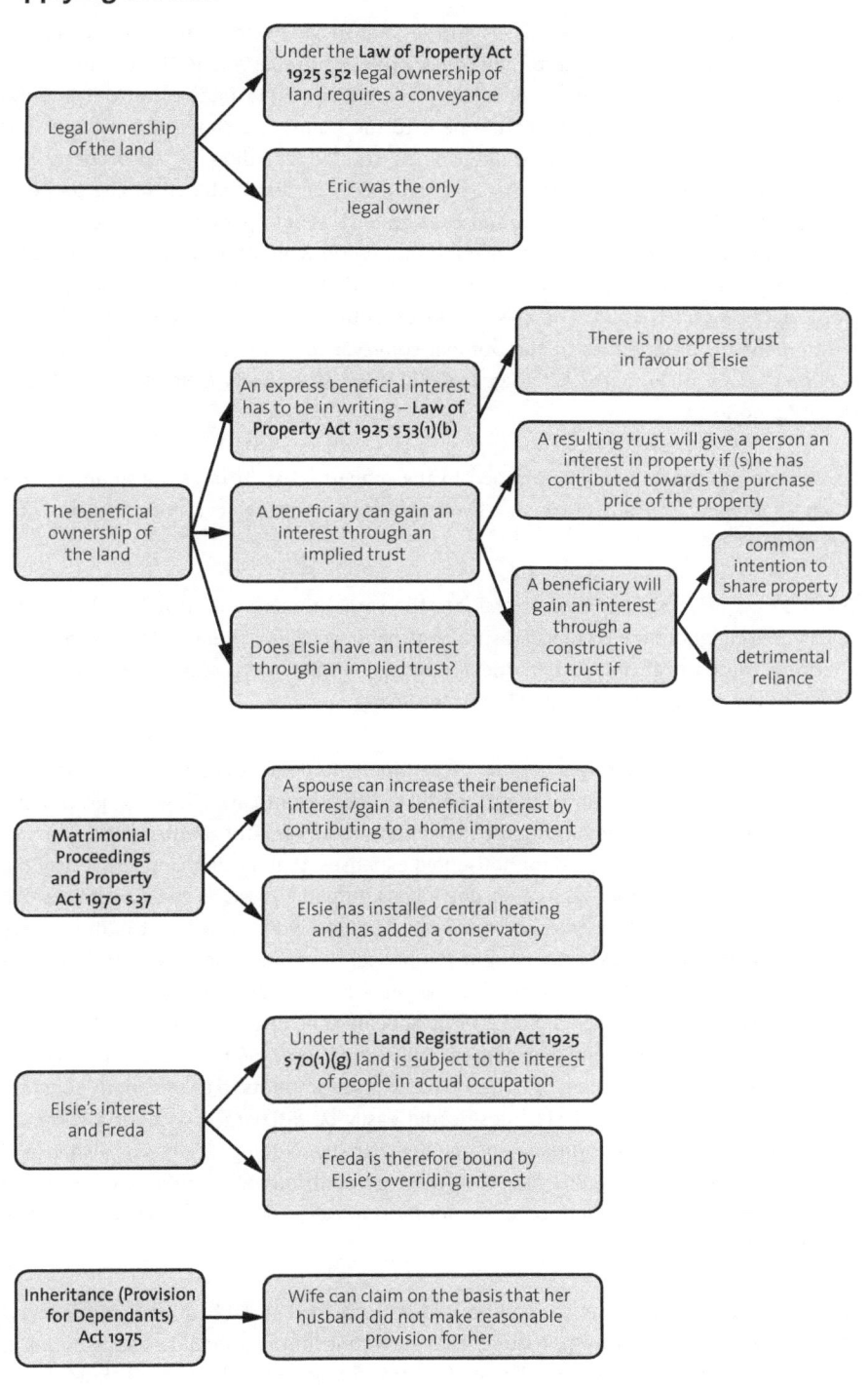

Legal ownership of the land
- Under the **Law of Property Act 1925 s 52** legal ownership of land requires a conveyance
- Eric was the only legal owner

The beneficial ownership of the land
- An express beneficial interest has to be in writing – **Law of Property Act 1925 s 53(1)(b)**
  - There is no express trust in favour of Elsie
- A beneficiary can gain an interest through an implied trust
  - A resulting trust will give a person an interest in property if (s)he has contributed towards the purchase price of the property
  - A beneficiary will gain an interest through a constructive trust if
    - common intention to share property
    - detrimental reliance
- Does Elsie have an interest through an implied trust?

Matrimonial Proceedings and Property Act 1970 s 37
- A spouse can increase their beneficial interest/gain a beneficial interest by contributing to a home improvement
- Elsie has installed central heating and has added a conservatory

Elsie's interest and Freda
- Under the **Land Registration Act 1925 s 70(1)(g)** land is subject to the interest of people in actual occupation
- Freda is therefore bound by Elsie's overriding interest

Inheritance (Provision for Dependants) Act 1975
- Wife can claim on the basis that her husband did not make reasonable provision for her

ANSWER

In this case, since Eric has died, Elsie's entitlement in the matrimonial home will need to be determined by reference to the ordinary rules of property law. There is no power for the court to order what it considers just and equitable under the **Matrimonial Causes Act 1973**. Instead, Elsie's entitlement to the home or a share of it vis-à-vis her husband's mistress, Freda, will be determined strictly according to the property law entitlement of both women: *Pettitt v Pettitt* (1970). The legal interest in the property was registered in Eric's name only, and consequently would pass on his death according to his will. The original conveyance in Eric's name would be conclusive as to legal entitlement in the absence of fraud (*Goodman v Gallant* (1986)), and this would pass to Freda if Eric's will is valid. There is no documentary evidence of legal or beneficial entitlement for Elsie, either in the original conveyance or in any subsequent written document: **Law of Property Act 1925 s 53(1)(b); Law of Property (Miscellaneous Provisions) Act 1989 s 2**.

Consequently, Elsie will only be entitled to the property if she can establish an interest under an implied, resulting or constructive trust, since no formal requirements are necessary in such cases.

The basic requirements of these trusts are the same (*Gissing v Gissing* (1971)), and the courts tend to ignore the technical distinctions between them. There must be a common intention to share an interest in the property, and the party seeking the beneficial interest, Elsie, must show she acted to her detriment.

The usual method of sharing a common intention is to point to a direct contribution to the purchase and acquisition of the property. In the present case, Elsie did not pay the deposit, nor did she pay any mortgage instalments. However, for the first eight years of the marriage, her earnings paid for household expenses, thereby enabling Eric to pay the mortgage, which he otherwise could not have afforded. This is arguably sufficient to show a common intention (*Hazell v Hazell* (1972)), since, without her contribution, there was no way that Eric could have bought the house. However, Elsie only contributed for eight years initially, and then for the last 20 years of the marriage she paid household expenses. For the last 20 years, however, it appears that Eric could manage financially without her paying household expenses. Following *Lloyds Bank v Rosset* (1991), it is unlikely that the mere payment of household expenses amounts to a sufficiently substantial indirect contribution by Elsie. These could easily be discharged without a common intention that she should acquire or enlarge her share by so doing. There is no evidence of any express agreement by Eric and Elsie that her contributions would acquire her an interest (*Eves v Eves* (1975)), and so, consequently, the second period of contribution will be disregarded.

Elsie may also argue that she has contributed by installing central heating and a conservatory. *Lloyds Bank v Rosset* (1991) requires that such contributions should be substantial. In *Re Nicolson (Decd)* (1974), the installation of central heating was felt to be substantial, and a conservatory may make a substantial contribution to the improvement of the property. Thus, it should be possible to evidence the common intention to share by reference to Elsie's first eight years' contributions, the central heating and conservatory.

Clearly these show that Elsie acted to her detriment, and so she should have a beneficial entitlement to a share in the home. In assessing the size of the share, *Midland Bank v Cooke* (1995) suggests that the whole history of the relationship can be examined to determine what size share the parties intended. This may mean that other aspects of Elsie's behaviour which were insufficient to create an interest may, nevertheless, be referred to at this second stage to give her a larger share of the home, possibly as much as one-half.

There is the further possibility of relying on the **Matrimonial Proceedings and Property Act 1970 s 37** to argue that the central heating and conservatory amount to a substantial contribution in money or money's worth to the improvement of the home. This would enlarge her original interest from her eight years' contributions.

Once Elsie establishes an interest in the home, this will bind Freda. Elsie is in actual occupation of the home and by virtue of the **LRA 1925 s 70(1)(g)** she has an overriding interest which would bind any subsequent purchaser. There will be no possibility of Freda arguing she was unaware of Elsie's existence, and since Freda is not a bona fide purchaser she will inherit the property subject to Elsie's interest.

Technically, they would both have interests under a trust for sale, and Freda might apply to the court for an order for sale under the **Trusts of Land and Appointment of Trustees Act 1996 s 14**. The court can make such order as it sees fit in the circumstances of the case. An examination of Elsie's interests and the purpose of the trust, which had been to provide a home for Elsie and Eric, will be made, and the court will need to consider whether to order a sale and divide the proceeds between the two women.

If Elsie considers that her share under property law is inadequate, she may consider an application to the court under the **Inheritance (Provision for Family and Dependants) Act 1975**. The wife of the deceased may apply and must show that her husband's will failed to provide reasonable financial provision for her. This is an objective determination, and does not depend upon what her husband Eric wished or thought reasonable. **Section 1(2)(a)** provides that the court must consider whether the financial provision made is reasonable in the circumstances, whether or not the provision is required for the spouse's maintenance. In this case, no provision has been made for Elsie and even though she may be working, and capable of supporting herself, it seems likely that no reasonable provision has been made.

The general view of the provisions of the Act is that they are designed to ensure that the spouse of the deceased is in a similar position on death as she would have been on divorce: *Re Besterman (Decd)* (1984).

Section 3(1) provides for a number of factors to be considered, including the resources of the applicant and other beneficiaries, the size and nature of the estate, and any other relevant matter, including the conduct of the applicant. Little is known of Freda's position and financial dependence on Eric, but Elsie appears to have been a devoted and supportive wife for 40 years, and entitled to some provision from Eric's estate. For a spouse, the length of the marriage as well as the age of the spouse and their contribution to the marriage should also be examined: **s3(2)**. Elsie has for many years worked and looked after the home and children, and this would ensure she receives the provision she deserves. This would mean that she could obtain an order giving her a larger share in the home, or even allowing her to remain there until her death (*Harrington v Gill* (1983)). Little is known about whether Eric had any other financial assets that could be used to provide periodical payments for Elsie, but at least she can use the Act to ensure that her position is improved.

QUESTION 24

Should unmarried couples gain an automatic beneficial interest in the home they share after long-term cohabitation?

How to Read this Question

Answers will need to explain how cohabitees can currently gain an interest in property and whether there are any problems with this approach. The desirability and practicality of giving cohabitees an automatic right should also be examined.

Applying the Law

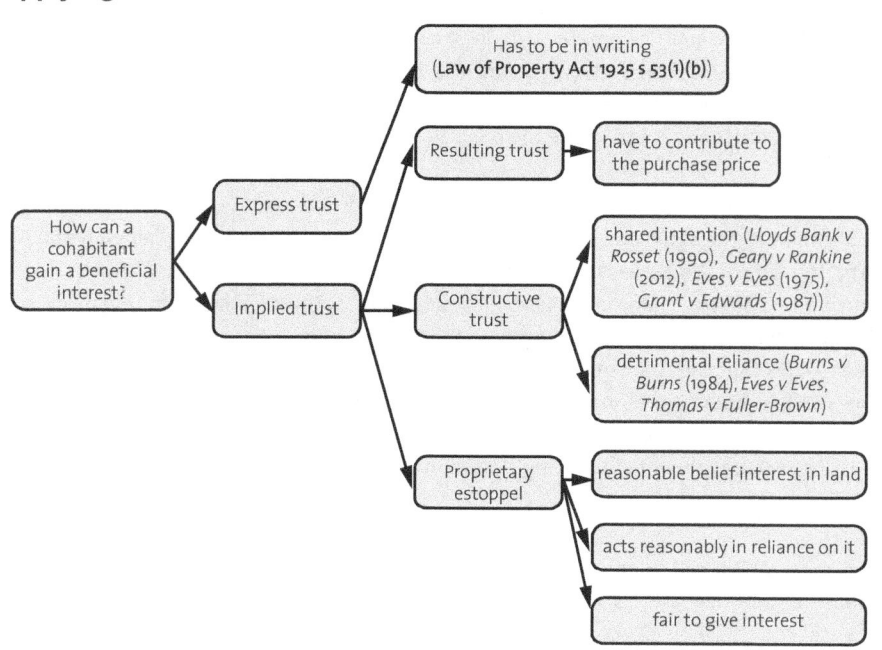

```
How can a                Express trust ──► Has to be in writing
cohabitant                                  (Law of Property Act 1925 s 53(1)(b))
gain a beneficial
interest?                                  Resulting trust ──► have to contribute to
                                                                the purchase price
                         Implied trust ──►
                                           Constructive ──► shared intention (Lloyds Bank v
                                           trust             Rosset (1990), Geary v Rankine
                                                             (2012), Eves v Eves (1975),
                                                             Grant v Edwards (1987))

                                                          ──► detrimental reliance (Burns v
                                                              Burns (1984), Eves v Eves,
                                                              Thomas v Fuller-Brown)

                         Proprietary ──► reasonable belief interest in land
                         estoppel
                                      ──► acts reasonably in reliance on it

                                      ──► fair to give interest
```

Property Disputes 95

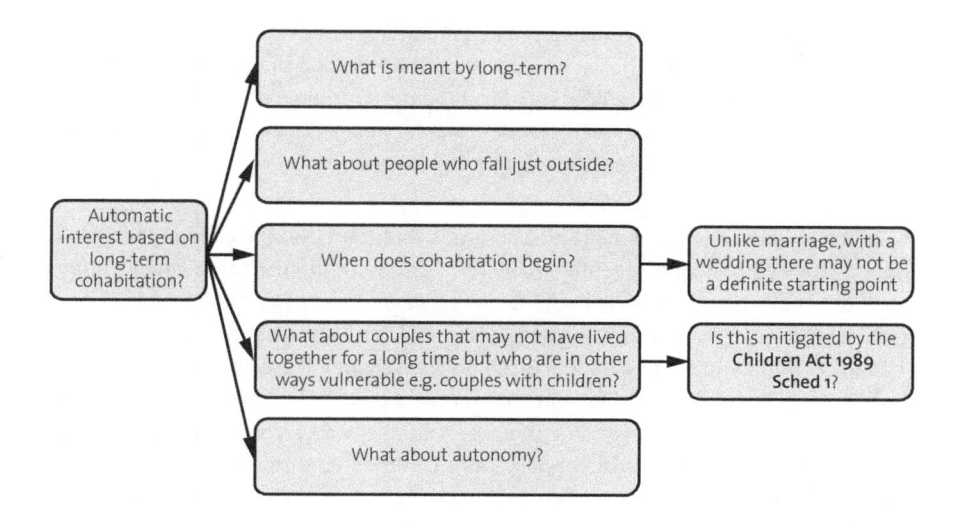

- Automatic interest based on long-term cohabitation?
  - What is meant by long-term?
  - What about people who fall just outside?
  - When does cohabitation begin? → Unlike marriage, with a wedding there may not be a definite starting point
  - What about couples that may not have lived together for a long time but who are in other ways vulnerable e.g. couples with children? → Is this mitigated by the **Children Act 1989 Sched 1**?
  - What about autonomy?

ANSWER

When a married couple divorce, the court has the power to allocate their property in a way that recognises the history of the couple and attempts to respond to their future needs (**Matrimonial Causes Act 1973 s 25**), there is no corresponding right for unmarried couples. Their right to ownership of land is dealt with using general land law principles and the fact that they are, or were once, in a family relationship is irrelevant. This means that a person can only be a legal owner of land via a conveyance (**Law of Property Act 1925 s 52**) and it also means that the legal owner might hold the property for the benefit of the beneficial owners.

One way for a person to have a beneficial interest in land is for that to be created expressly; under **Law of Property Act 1925 s 53(2)(b)** that has to be in writing. If a couple purchase a house together, they will get legal advice and the legal and beneficial ownership of the land will be discussed and decided on. In this scenario both the legal and beneficial ownership of the land will be clearly set out. In contrast, if the situation is one where an individual moves in with his/her partner to a property which that partner already owns and occupies, it is less likely that legal advice will have been sought and far less likely that any beneficial interest for the relocating partner will be set out in writing.

This then leaves the implied beneficial interests and a person can have an implied beneficial interest in property via a resulting trust, a constructive trust or proprietary estoppel. Under a resulting trust, an individual gains a beneficial interest in land if (s)he contributes towards the purchase price. It is arguable that it is unlikely that this will help the individual who moves in with his/her partner into that partner's existing home. In this case, the property will already be purchased, or if there is a mortgage, it will already be set up and be being paid from the current occupier's bank account. One possibility is that the cohabitant paying living expenses will make it easier for the existing occupier to pay the mortgage but it is not clear whether this would be enough to give the cohabitant a beneficial interest under a resulting trust.

Under a constructive trust a cohabitant can gain an interest if there has been a shared agreement that the cohabitant has an interest in the land and the cohabitant has acted to his/her detriment in reliance of that understanding. Both the requirement for a shared understanding and the requirement for detrimental reliance make it difficult for some cohabitants to establish an interest using this framework.

The problem with the requirement for a common intention that the cohabitant have an interest in property is that in reality many couples do not discuss their legal positions, and those that do may very well seek legal advice and have the nature of their legal rights set out clearly in writing, negating the need for a constructive trust. The issue of what the common intention was will often only arise when there are difficulties in the couple's relationship and at this point the recollections of the parties are likely to be very different. Furthermore, the law requires that there be a common intention that ownership be shared; this is not the same as a common intention that the occupation of the property be shared, any discussions or agreements are likely to relate to occupation rather than ownership. The difficulty of establishing a common intention is shown by the case law. In *Eves v Eves* and *Grant v Edwards* the court held that there were common intentions that the ownership of the property should be shared despite the male partners in these cases lying to their female partners as to why the female partners could not be legal owners. Although the results in *Eves v Eves* and *Grant v Edwards* seem fair, it is not really credible to say that there was a common intention that the ownership of the property should be shared when this was something that the male partners were trying dishonestly to avoid.

Even if there is a common intention to share the ownership of the property, a person only has a beneficial interest under a constructive trust if (s)he can show that he has acted in a way in reliance on that which has caused him/her detriment. The problem here is what sorts of behaviour are sufficient to count as detrimental reliance. The court takes the view that many acts are the norm and due to a person's occupation of the property rather than being because of their reliance that they had an interest in the land. One problem with this is that the approach of the courts can seem discriminatory. If a cohabitant improves the property by carrying out his/her traditional gender role – perhaps cleaning for a woman, or decorating for a man, the court is likely to dismiss this as something normal that would always happen due to their occupation of the property and not an example of detrimental reliance. If, however, an individual adds to the property in a way that is different from his/her traditional gender role, the court is more willing to see this as an example of detrimental reliance. This can be seen if the cases of *Eves v Eves* and *Thomas v Fuller-Brown* are contrasted.

Under proprietary estoppel a cohabitant can gain an interest if (s)he reasonably believes that (s)he has an interest in the land, (s)he acts in reliance of that belief and the court considers it just and fair to give him/her an interest in the land. This is very similar to the requirements for a constructive trust and many of the problems with using a constructive trust to gain a beneficial interest will also apply here.

There are clearly, therefore, difficulties with the current legal position. Strictly applied, it can mean that a person can have no rights to a property that they have occupied for nearly 20 years and where they have paid bills and which they have helped decorate (*Burns v Burns* (1984)); would the alternative, that they gain an interest after long-term cohabitation, be fairer?

One problem with this proposal is that it is too vague. What is meant by long-term cohabitation? The **Cohabitation Bill 2008** would have given couples rights after two years' cohabitation. Similarly, the **Cohabitation Rights Bill 2014–2015** if successful will give some cohabitants who have lived together for at least two years the right to apply for a financial order. Is two years sufficiently lengthy to count as long-term cohabitation? What about five years' cohabitation? Furthermore, even if the length of time can be agreed on, it can still sometimes be difficult to determine how long a couple have actually lived together. If the couple buy a house together, it can be fairly easy, but in that scenario the legal and beneficial ownership of the property is also likely to be clear. What may be more difficult is the situation where one partner moves in with another. It might sometimes be difficult to determine when staying over is replaced by moving in. Moreover, even if the length of time and starting point can be agreed on, it still leaves the question of what share of beneficial ownership a cohabitant should have.

Furthermore, it could be argued that if the aim is to protect cohabitants, basing that protection on the length of time a couple has lived together is not the fairest or most effective way. Both the **Cohabitation Bill 2008** and the **Cohabitation Rights Bill 2014–2015** would extend protection to cohabitants with children even if they did not satisfy the time requirement. Alternatively, it could be argued that the **Children Act 1989 Sched 1** already provides flexibility in providing maintenance for children of cohabiting parents and therefore this issue is to some extent addressed.

One problem with reforming the law is that under the current situation a person's beneficial ownership can already be protected if certain measures are taken. The informed couple who have actively decided how they wish to hold their property can see this reflected in their legal and beneficial ownership. It is arguable that a rule that a person who has lived as a cohabitant for a long time would automatically gain an interest would undermine this and be harmful to some couples' autonomy. Perhaps rather than reform the answer is that people ought to be better informed and use the existing mechanisms.

In conclusion, whilst the existing rules on beneficial ownership are ill-fitted to the reality of many cohabiting couples' lives, a rule that a long-term cohabitant would automatically gain an interest is vague and unworkable.

6 Domestic Violence and Occupation of the Home

INTRODUCTION

When a relationship deteriorates, it will often be necessary to examine what protection from personal violence is available. There is also the issue of who should occupy the former home. These areas of law have, in the past, been criticised as a 'hotchpotch of enactments' per Lord Scarman in *Richards v Richards* (1984), and have undergone reform and rationalisation in the **Family Law Act 1996 Part IV**.

Checklist

Students should be able to:

- understand and be able to apply the definition of associated person in the **Family Law Act 1996 s 62**;
- understand how courts define molestation (*G v G (Occupation Order: Conduct)* (2000));
- understand the effects of a non-molestation order: **Family Law Act 1996 s 42(5)**;
- understand how the criminal law can be used to enforce non-molestation orders: **Family Law Act 1996 s 42A**;
- apply the definition of an entitled applicant: **Family Law Act 1996 s 33**;
- understand who has matrimonial home rights (**Family Law Act 1996 s 30**) and when a cohabitee will have a beneficial interest (*Lloyds Bank v Rosset* (1990));
- understand how the **Family Law Act 1996 s 33(7)** works to create a presumption in favour of an occupation order being made if the applicant can show that (s)he or a relevant child is suffering or is at risk of suffering significant harm (**Family Law Act 1996 s 63(1)**) if an occupation order is not made and in what circumstances this presumption would be rebutted (*B v B* (1999));
- understand when the factors in the **Family Law Act 1996 s 33(6)** will be applied to see if an occupation order should be made in favour of an entitled applicant (*L v L* (2012), *Grubb v Grubb* (2012));
- understand what the effects of an occupation order in favour of an entitled applicant can be and how long these orders last (**Family Law Act 1996 s 33(3)**);
- understand how applications from ex-spouses and ex-civil partners with no right to occupy under the **Family Law Act 1996 s 35** differ from applications by entitled applicants under **s 33** in respect of the factors to be considered by the court

(Family Law Act 1996 s 35(6)) and how long the order can last (**Family Law Act 1996 s 35(10)**);
- identify which cohabitants would apply for an occupation order under the **Family Law Act 1996 s 36**; apply and discuss the factors that the court would use to determine whether to make an occupation order (**Family Law Act 1996 s 33(6)**) including those factors that distinguish applications under **s 36** from those under **s 33**; understand how long an occupation order under **s 36** can last;
- understand when the **Family Law Act 1996 s 37** will be used and how the court would determine whether to grant an occupation order under this section;
- understand what extra provisions can be added to an occupation order under the **Family Law Act 1996 s 40**;
- explain when it will be appropriate for an applicant to apply for an occupation order or a non-molestation order *ex parte* (**Family Law Act 1996 s 45**);
- explain when a person will be able to obtain an injunction under the **Protection from Harassment Act 1997**.

Up for Debate

- Whether the distinction between entitled and non-entitled applicants in respect of occupation orders is justified.
- What is meant by domestic violence and does the law respond appropriately to new forms of harm?

EXAM QUESTIONS

Problem questions involve advising the victim or perpetrator of domestic violence and may be combined with divorce, maintenance or property issues. Essay questions would be evaluating the orders available under the **Family Law Act 1996**.

QUESTION 25

'The sooner the range, scope and effect of these powers are rationalised into a coherent and comprehensive body of statute law, the better.' Per Lord Scarman in *Richards v Richards* (1984).

Do you consider that the **Family Law Act 1996** provisions relating to domestic violence and occupation of the home address Lord Scarman's concerns and will result in improved protection for the vulnerable and those at risk?

How to Read this Question

This question requires a discussion of the effectiveness of the domestic violence provisions in the **Family Law Act 1996**. The student needs to see whether they address the concerns of Lord Scarman and whether they have led to increased protection for the vulnerable.

Applying the Law

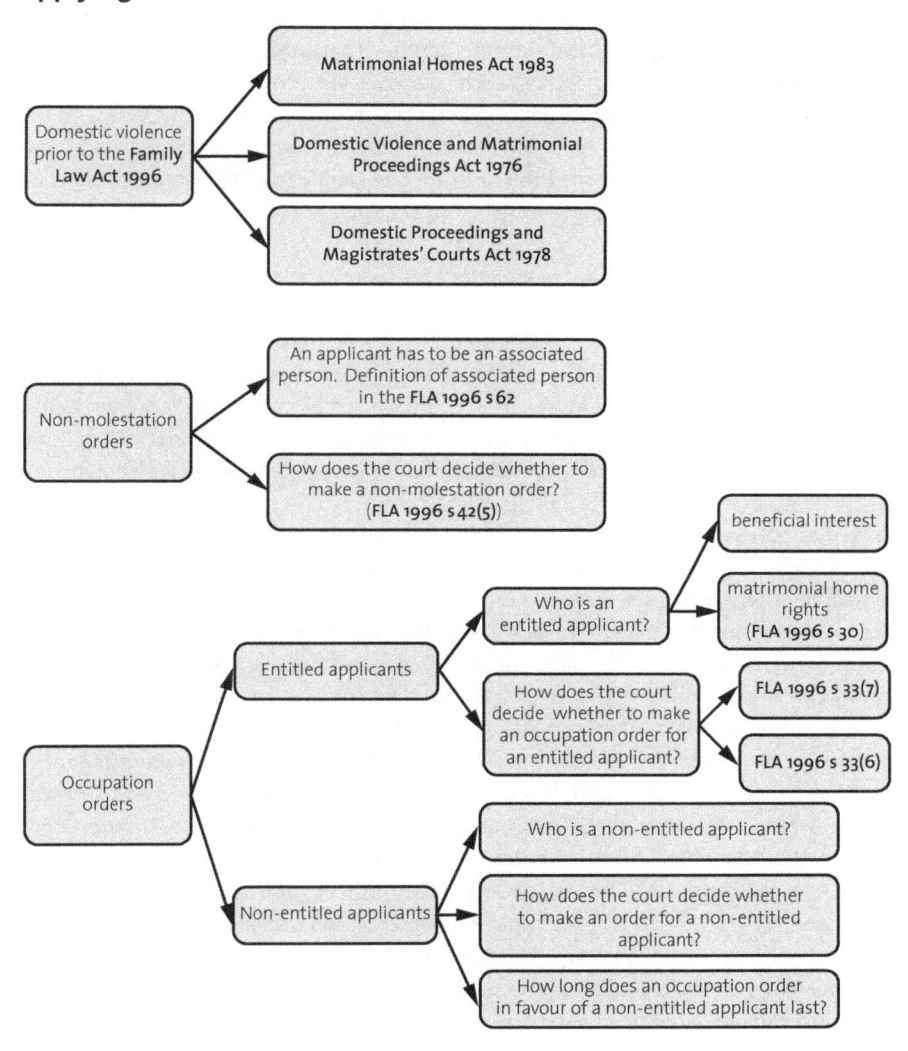

```
Domestic violence prior to the Family Law Act 1996
    ├── Matrimonial Homes Act 1983
    ├── Domestic Violence and Matrimonial Proceedings Act 1976
    └── Domestic Proceedings and Magistrates' Courts Act 1978

Non-molestation orders
    ├── An applicant has to be an associated person. Definition of associated person in the FLA 1996 s 62
    └── How does the court decide whether to make a non-molestation order? (FLA 1996 s 42(5))

Occupation orders
    ├── Entitled applicants
    │   ├── Who is an entitled applicant?
    │   │   ├── beneficial interest
    │   │   └── matrimonial home rights (FLA 1996 s 30)
    │   └── How does the court decide whether to make an occupation order for an entitled applicant?
    │       ├── FLA 1996 s 33(7)
    │       └── FLA 1996 s 33(6)
    └── Non-entitled applicants
        ├── Who is a non-entitled applicant?
        ├── How does the court decide whether to make an order for a non-entitled applicant?
        └── How long does an occupation order in favour of a non-entitled applicant last?
```

ANSWER

The criticisms made by Lord Scarman were directed at law that had developed on a piecemeal basis, and consisted of a variety of enactments and inherent powers that varied from court to court. The 'hotchpotch of enactments' consisted of the **Matrimonial Homes Act 1983**, the **Domestic Violence and Matrimonial Proceedings Act 1976** and the **Domestic Proceedings and Magistrates' Courts Act 1978**. All these statutes contained various methods of seeking occupation of a home, and some gave a measure of protection from personal violence. However, the procedures varied from court to court, the principles to be applied also varied, and some measures were available only to spouses whereas others were available to cohabitants. Little wonder that this confusing and anomalous situation led the Law Commission in its report in 1992 on Domestic Violence and Occupation of the Family Home to recommend abolition of this variety of enactments and their replacement with a single, comprehensive statutory formula that would apply to all courts. This would obviate the need to gamble on which court was likely to give the most favourable response, and would encourage a uniform and consistent approach by the courts to the issues of violence and occupation of the home. The Law Commission included a draft bill, and it is this bill that has provided the basis for the **Family Law Act 1996** provisions on domestic violence, which came into force in October 1997.

The previous law provided a number of options for spouses, and more limited avenues for cohabitants, but left others at risk to depend upon the inherent jurisdiction of the court. With the increasing incidence of cohabitation as a long-term way of life for many couples, that position could not be justified, and for those who were not in the standard heterosexual relationships, the law offered little in the way of protection from domestic violence. The Law Commission proposed a radical shake-up in the categories of applicant who would be able to use the new legislation, and the proposals have been accepted.[1]

As well as spouses and those who are living together as husband and wife, applications can be made by ex-spouses and ex-cohabitants. This recognises that, on the breakdown of such relationships, problems may occur and the threat of violence can continue long after a relationship has ended. Similarly, those who have been parties to an agreement to marry are qualified to make applications. These qualifications are recognised in the **Family Law Act 1996** by the concept of 'associated persons', to be found in **s 62**. However, the concept of associated person is wider than the above categories, and includes those who live or have lived in the same household, provided this is not a landlord/tenant or employer/employee relationship. It also includes close relatives of a person or his/her spouse, whether by blood, marriage or adoption. This list includes mother, stepmother, grandmother, daughter, granddaughter, aunt, sister, niece, father, stepfather, grandfather, son, grandson, uncle, brother and nephew. This recognises that such relationships can frequently give rise to issues of domestic violence and occupation of family homes. Those who are parents of the same child, or who have or had parental responsibility for the same child, are also associated persons, as are those who are parties to the same family proceedings, since these situations can often lead to tension and conflict.[2]

The Law Commission also proposed extending the categories to include those who have had a sexual relationship with each other. Many such relationships turn sour and expose a party to the threat of violence or molestation. This would have been a controversial extension of the law and could have caused difficulty in practice if the sexual nature of the relationship was disputed, or would have been embarrassing. The Act does not

---

1 Note how this question refers to the societal context within which changes to domestic violence legislation were enacted. This is useful as providing a background against which their effectiveness can be examined.
2 Although wide, the definition of associated person does not cover all individuals who might be affected by molestation. It does not, for instance, cover an ex-partner's new partner.

contain such a provision, and so only those with a sexual relationship and who have lived together were initially associated persons. The **Domestic Violence Crime and Victims Act 2004** has extended the definition to include couples who have had an intimate relationship but have not actually lived together.

The Act follows the Law Commission's recommendations and does not limit relief to heterosexual cohabitants. Provided the couple lived together, it does not matter whether their relationship was homosexual, heterosexual or not sexual at all. This led to considerable criticism in some sections of the press as indicating an undermining of marriage and an encouragement of cohabitation and homosexuality. The Government responded by pointing out that the Act does seek to promote marriage, and does, in some respects, give more favourable treatment to those who are married. However, there are those who argue that the Act did not go far enough, and that the concept of associated persons is an unnecessary limitation on those who can seek assistance.

The Act also introduces the concept of 'relevant child' in **s 62(2)**. This is a child who is living with a party to proceedings or might reasonably be expected to live with a party, any child in relation to which an application under an adoption order or the **Children Act 1989** is in question in the proceedings, and any other child whose interests the court considers relevant.

It may be that those persons falling outside the categories recognised in the **Family Law Act 1996** can be given some protection by the **Protection from Harassment Act 1997**, or by the seeking of an injunction under the inherent powers of the court.

Under the old law, applicants seeking personal protection faced different criteria in different courts. In the Magistrates' Court it was necessary to show actual violence or the threat of it before an order could be made, whereas in the County Court relief was available to prevent molestation. This meant that spouses who had been the victims of harassment and pestering that stopped short of violence could get no assistance in the Magistrates' Court, yet their lives could still be made extremely unpleasant by such behaviour. The Law Commission recommended that the County Court approach be adopted in all courts, so that there would be no need to wait until the situation had escalated into violence before assistance could be sought.

The Act prefers the Law Commission approach, and provides for non-molestation orders in **s 42**. Such orders are available to protect an applicant who is an associated person and/or any relevant child. The application may be made in conjunction with other family proceedings or may be made on its own, or it is possible for the court to make an order without an application being made if it is hearing other family proceedings and considers the order should be made. This power for the court to make an order of its own accord is an advance on the old law, and is to be welcomed in that it gives the court the power to respond to damaging situations that arise as other proceedings unfold.

The court will consider all the circumstances of the case in determining whether to make an order, including the need to ensure the safety, well-being and health of the applicant and relevant child (**s 42(5)**). Thus, there is a change in emphasis away from the old law that concentrated on the nature of the respondent's violent conduct to the new consideration of the effect on the applicant and child. The term molestation is not defined in the Act but would include conduct other than violence. Consequently, harassment and pestering, violence and threats would all be restrained by the order, which can be made for a limited time or until further order (**s 42(7)**). Molestation was defined in *C v C (Non-Molestation Order)* (1998) as deliberate conduct involving a high degree of harassment, and did not cover an ex-wife giving embarrassing information about her ex-husband to the newspapers.[3]

It is possible for the court to accept an undertaking from respondents instead of making an occupation order or non-molestation order (**s 46**), but no power of arrest can be attached to an undertaking (**s 46(2)**). This means that a court cannot accept an undertaking from a respondent if it would otherwise have had the grounds for attaching a power of arrest to the non-molestation or occupation order. By virtue of **s 47**, if the court makes a non-molestation order and the respondent has used or threatened violence against the applicant or child, then a power of arrest must be attached, unless the court is satisfied that in all the circumstances the applicant and child will be adequately protected without one. This makes it much more likely that a power of arrest will be attached than under the old law, and gives a greater measure of protection to applicants.

The Law Commission recommended that non-molestation orders should be capable of lasting for indefinite periods of time, and the Act provides that such an order may be made for a specific period or until a further order is made (**s 42(7)**).

Under the old law, a victim of domestic violence was often placed in the difficult position of having to instigate proceedings against a former loved one about whom there might still be mixed feelings. In addition, there was the extra fear that the commencement of proceedings might provoke further violence. In many cases, the police would be involved in attending incidents of violence, but, with the victim often unwilling to pursue a criminal complaint, little effective protection could be given. The Law Commission made the radical proposal of allowing the police to apply for civil protection on behalf of the victim of domestic violence. This could well encourage victims to seek police help, and stop them feeling responsible for commencing actions against the respondent. In **s 60** provision is made for rules of court to be drawn up allowing certain prescribed persons or representatives to act and bring proceedings for the protection of victims of domestic violence.

In cases involving occupation of the home, the old law varied in the principles to be applied in determining applications and the powers available. The **Family Law Act 1996** renames the rights of occupation in the **Matrimonial Homes Act 1983** and calls them 'matrimonial home rights'. Such rights are still only given to spouses, and matrimonial

---

3 The non-molestation order is a civil power aimed at protecting the victim, not at punishing the person responsible for the molestation. It makes sense therefore that the focus is on the impact on the victim rather than on the nature of the violent conduct.

home rights are defined in **s 30(2)** as the right not to be evicted or excluded from the home unless by court order, and the right if not in occupation to enter and occupy with a court order. They exist in relation to dwelling houses that are, or have been, or were intended to be, the joint home of the parties. The Act takes up the Law Commission's recommendation that such rights should exist in relation to a house that, whilst never actually the home of the parties, had been intended by them to be so. Matrimonial home rights exist if one spouse has an entitlement to occupy the dwelling house by virtue of a beneficial estate, contract or other enactment, and the other spouse has no such entitlement, or has an equitable right only.

Such rights are important in relation to occupation of the home because they will almost inevitably mean that an applicant for an occupation order, who is a spouse, qualifies as an entitled applicant within **s 33**. The Act draws a distinction between entitled applicants and non-entitled applicants for occupation orders, but simplifies the old law by creating a single occupation order. However, the criteria to be applied in deciding whether to make the order, whilst contained in one Act, vary according to the nature of the applicant and respondent. There is concern that time may be wasted with argument as to the exact nature of the applicant's status before the appropriate criteria can be selected.

The Law Commission thought it appropriate to retain some distinction between those seeking occupation of a home in respect of which they had some rights, and those seeking to occupy a home in respect of which they had no such rights. Those who have an interest have traditionally always stood a better chance of achieving occupation than those who do not, and this will certainly continue under the Act. Applicants with a beneficial entitlement, or a contractual entitlement, or entitlement to occupy by virtue of any enactment, or matrimonial home rights, will be deemed 'entitled applicants' (**s 33(1)**). The court can make an order in respect of a dwelling house that is, or was, intended to be the home of the applicant and a person with whom the applicant is associated. This concept of associated person is widely defined in **s 62** and does not limit the making of occupation orders to married couples or those who are cohabiting heterosexuals.

The order can contain a number of provisions (**s 33(3)**), including requiring the respondent to allow the applicant to enter and remain in the house or part of it, and restricting or terminating the respondent's right to occupy the house or part of it, and excluding the respondent from the area where the home is situated.

The starting point for deciding whether an occupation order should be made is the balance of harm test in **s 33(7)**. If the court are satisfied that the applicant, or a relevant child, will suffer significant harm if the occupation order is not made, then there is a presumption in favour of the order being made. The defendant will only be able to prevent the order being made if (s)he is able to show that making the order would cause him greater harm than not making the order would cause the applicant or relevant child (*B v B* (1999)). If the court is not satisfied that the applicant or a relevant child would suffer significant harm if the order is not made, the court will look at the factors in **s 33(6)** to determine whether to make the order.

Entitled applicants can thus seek an order against a wide range of respondents, provided the respondent is an associated person, and there is no maximum period for which an occupation order will be granted. This is to be contrasted with the position of the non-entitled applicant, where orders can last for a six-month initial period, which can then be renewed for an additional six-month period.

The non-entitled applicant can seek an order but only against a spouse, former spouse, cohabitants or former cohabitants. Thus, the category of respondent is more severely limited. If the respondent is entitled to occupy the house, and is a spouse or former spouse, application should be made under **s 35**, whereas if the respondent is entitled, but is a cohabitant or former cohabitant, application should be made under **s 36**.[4]

This would require the court to first consider the making of an occupation rights order, giving the right to occupy the home, and then to make a regulatory order excluding the other party. Under **s 35**, in making an occupation rights order, the court will take all the circumstances of the case into account, including the housing needs and resources of the parties and any relevant child; the financial resources of the parties; the likely effect on the health, safety and well-being of the parties and any relevant child of any order or no order being made; the conduct of the parties in relation to each other and otherwise; the length of time that has passed since the parties lived together; the length of time since the marriage was dissolved; and the existence of any proceedings between the parties under the **Children Act 1989** or in relation to ownership of property.

If the parties were not married but had cohabited, **s 36** requires the court to consider the housing needs and resources of the parties; their financial resources; the likely effect on the health, safety and well-being of the parties and any relevant child of any order or no order being made; the conduct of the parties in relation to each other and otherwise; the nature of the relationship, specifically that they have not given the same level of commitment as a marriage; the length of time they have lived together as husband and wife; whether there are any children; the time that has passed since they lived together; and the existence of any proceedings between the parties under the **Children Act 1989** or in relation to ownership of property (**s 36(6)**).

Thus, it can be seen that the cohabiting nature of the relationship does not carry the same weight as a marriage would, and specific regard is had to the length and nature of the cohabiting relationship.

If an occupation order is made, then the court can make a regulatory order excluding the respondent from the home or restricting his occupation. The factors influencing the court in determining whether to make such an order are the housing needs and resources of

---

4   There is a tension between domestic violence powers and property rights and this is particularly marked when a non-entitled applicant is applying for an occupation order against someone who has an interest in the property.

the parties; their financial resources; the effect of any order or failure to make an order on the health, safety or well-being of the parties or relevant child; the conduct of the parties in relation to each other and otherwise; the likelihood of significant harm to the applicant or relevant child if no order is made; and the likelihood of significant harm to the respondent if an order is made. With non-entitled applicants, unlike the position with entitled applicants, there is no compulsion to make an order on the basis of a risk of significant harm. This puts cohabitants at a disadvantage compared to spouses, since spouses will usually be entitled applicants by virtue of their matrimonial home rights. However, the **Domestic Violence Crime and Victims Act 2004** arguably improved the position of cohabitants by removing s 41.

If neither the applicant nor the respondent is entitled to occupy, and this is only likely to be so in the rare cases of squatters and bare licensees, then orders can be sought under s 37 if the parties are spouses or former spouses, and s 38 if they are cohabitants or former cohabitants. The s 37 factors mirror those in s 35, and contain the statutory presumption in favour of making an order for a spouse if there is the risk of significant harm to the spouse or relevant child. **Section 38** contains the same factors as in s 36 but there is, again, no statutory presumption in favour of an order where there is the risk of significant harm to a non-entitled cohabitant.

In conclusion, the new law goes a long way to answering Lord Scarman's criticisms of the old law. To find the law relating to occupation orders and non-molestation orders in one statute is helpful, but the provisions are nonetheless complex, and will involve categorising applicants before entitlement can be examined according to the correct section of the statute. In addition, there are those who argue that the statute goes too far in offering protection to those beyond the traditional married relationship, whereas there will be others for whom the distinction between those who are married and those who are not cannot be justified.

QUESTION 26

Heidi and Ian, both aged 19, began to live together because Heidi was pregnant. When the baby was born, Ian suspected that he was not the baby's father as the baby's appearance was totally different from his and Heidi's. The couple share a small one-bedroomed flat, and have had numerous arguments. Ian has a short temper and has frequently smashed household objects in his anger at Heidi's burnt cooking. One day the couple were out shopping when they met a friend who made a joke about the fact that the baby looked nothing like Ian. Ian exploded with rage and pushed the trolley full of groceries at Heidi, badly bruising her legs. He then pushed the pram over in his haste to leave the supermarket. Although the baby was unhurt, Heidi was too scared to go to their home, and has been staying with her mother. Ian, full of remorse, keeps telephoning to speak to Heidi, who will have nothing to do with him. These telephone calls are occurring with increasing frequency, and the last one included a comment by Ian that his family would not stand by and let Heidi make a fool of him.

Heidi wishes to return to her flat with the baby, but does not feel she would be safe there with Ian.

- Advise Heidi on her options under Part IV of the Family Law Act 1996.
- Advise Heidi, on the assumption that:
  (a) she and Ian are married;
  (b) she and Ian are not married.

How to Read this Question

Heidi wants to return to the flat and she is worried about her safety. The question therefore involves considering whether Heidi would be able to obtain an occupation order and a non-molestation order. Because the question is in two parts, (a) and (b), it is clear that the position of Heidi as an entitled and as a non-entitled applicant should be considered.

Applying the Law

HEIDI AND IAN ARE MARRIED

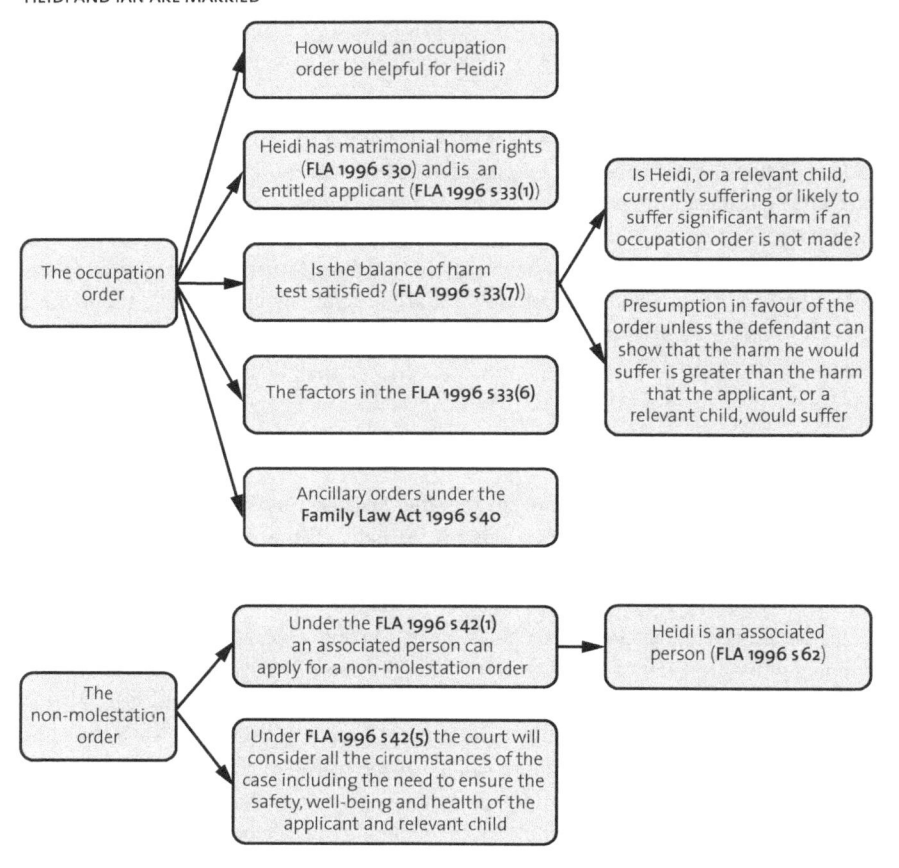

- The occupation order
  - How would an occupation order be helpful for Heidi?
  - Heidi has matrimonial home rights (**FLA 1996 s 30**) and is an entitled applicant (**FLA 1996 s 33(1)**)
  - Is the balance of harm test satisfied? (**FLA 1996 s 33(7)**)
    - Is Heidi, or a relevant child, currently suffering or likely to suffer significant harm if an occupation order is not made?
    - Presumption in favour of the order unless the defendant can show that the harm he would suffer is greater than the harm that the applicant, or a relevant child, would suffer
  - The factors in the **FLA 1996 s 33(6)**
  - Ancillary orders under the **Family Law Act 1996 s 40**

- The non-molestation order
  - Under the **FLA 1996 s 42(1)** an associated person can apply for a non-molestation order → Heidi is an associated person (**FLA 1996 s 62**)
  - Under **FLA 1996 s 42(5)** the court will consider all the circumstances of the case including the need to ensure the safety, well-being and health of the applicant and relevant child

HEIDI AND IAN ARE NOT MARRIED

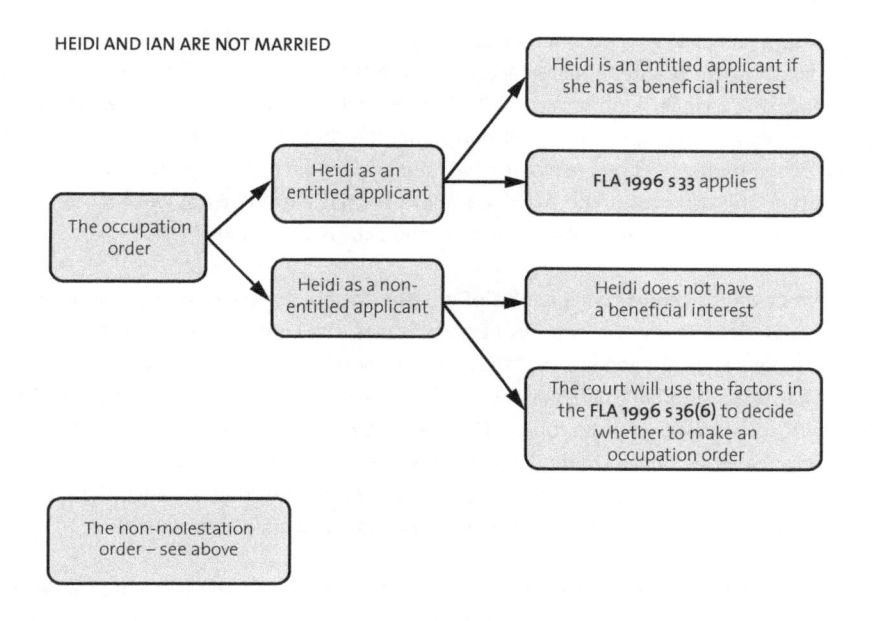

```
The occupation order
├── Heidi as an entitled applicant
│   ├── Heidi is an entitled applicant if she has a beneficial interest
│   └── FLA 1996 s 33 applies
└── Heidi as a non-entitled applicant
    ├── Heidi does not have a beneficial interest
    └── The court will use the factors in the FLA 1996 s 36(6) to decide whether to make an occupation order

The non-molestation order – see above
```

ANSWER

(a) Heidi needs to obtain protection from domestic violence, and occupation of the flat that has functioned as a matrimonial home. If Heidi is married to Ian, she may have matrimonial home rights in relation to the flat, since it has been the matrimonial home (**Family Law Act 1996 s 30(7)**). It is not clear from the facts whether it is only Ian who is entitled to occupy the flat. If Ian is the sole tenant, then Heidi, as the non-entitled spouse, is given matrimonial home rights by **s 30**, which are defined in **s 30(2)** as the right not to be evicted or excluded from the home unless by court order, and the right, if not in occupation, to enter and occupy with a court order. If they are both joint tenants, then **s 30(9)** gives Heidi the same rights. Heidi can therefore return to the flat, but would rightly be concerned about the safety of this course of action. Consequently, she will need to see whether or not Ian can be excluded, and this will only be possible by way of a court order under **s 33**.[5]

Heidi is an entitled applicant under **s 33**; she is entitled to occupy the home because she has matrimonial home rights. The occupation order can require Ian to allow Heidi to enter and occupy the flat, and can prohibit Ian or restrict him from exercising his right to occupy the flat, or the area in which it is situated. Since the flat is so small, it is not feasible to expect Heidi to occupy part of the flat, with Ian occupying the rest.

---

5   The **FLA 1996** provides two orders – the non-molestation order which protects the beneficiary from molestation, and the occupation order which controls occupation of the family home. In answering a domestic violence question, the first step is to determine what the victim wants and therefore which is the more appropriate order. If the occupation order is the most suitable order, the question then is whether the victim is applying as an entitled or a non-entitled applicant.

The factors in **s 33(6)** govern whether an order will be made and the type of regulatory order that will be granted. These factors require the court to consider all the circumstances of the case, including the housing needs and resources of the parties; the likely effect of any order or non-exercise of powers by the court on the health, safety or well-being of the parties and any relevant child; and the conduct of the parties in relation to each other and otherwise. The baby is a relevant child within **s 62(2)** since it lives with either party, and this is regardless of whether the baby is Ian's child or not.

In some cases, the court has a choice of whether or not to make an occupation order, whereas in other cases, the 'significant harm' cases, the court is compelled to make an order. Under **s 33(7)**, if it appears that the applicant or relevant child is likely to suffer significant harm attributable to the conduct of the respondent if the order is not made, then the court must make an order, unless the respondent or relevant child is likely to suffer equal or greater significant harm if the order is made. This requires the court to first consider whether there is the likelihood of significant harm, and then balance the harm of making an order with the harm of not making an order (*Dolan v Corby* (2011).[6]

Harm is defined in **s 63** to mean ill-treatment or impairment of mental or physical health, with the additional criterion of impairment of development for a child. Ill-treatment includes both physical and sexual abuse in relation to a child, and development is widely defined to include physical, emotional, intellectual, social or behavioural development. The concept of 'significant' is likely to mean considerable or important, if guidance in earlier cases on the meaning of such wording in other statutes is followed: *Humberside County Council v B* (1993).

Ian has behaved very badly towards Heidi and the baby. Even though he may be upset and suspicious, this does not justify his explosive and violent temper. Throwing and breaking objects, just because his dinner is burnt, is excessive and the incident in the supermarket certainly gives cause for concern about the safety of both Heidi and her baby. The persistent telephone calls and possible threats would all strengthen Heidi's argument that she and the baby run the likely risk of significant harm if no order is made.

Little is known about the living conditions at Heidi's mother's home, but it is not good for the development of the child to be living in cramped conditions. Heidi would seem to have nowhere else to go, yet returning to the flat is not a realistic option whilst Ian remains there. Ian, on the other hand, has behaved in a reprehensible way towards Heidi and the baby and could well find alternative accommodation. His violence does not appear to be isolated and the facts seem to indicate the likelihood of significant harm. This would mean that the court must make an order unless Ian would be likely to suffer equal or greater significant harm if the order were made. The consequences of the order

---

6   If the court determines that the applicant or a relevant child is suffering or would be likely to suffer significant harm this creates a presumption in favour of the order. The court will then only not make an order if the respondent shows that (s)he would be at greater risk of harm if an order were to be made than the applicant or relevant child would be if an order were not to be made.

for Ian would be that he would need to find alternative living accommodation. There is no evidence to suggest that he would find this impossible, nor is there evidence to suggest that he would suffer any other kind of harm. Consequently, it seems that the court will make an order allowing Heidi to occupy the flat and excluding Ian from the flat. It may be that, given the nature of Ian's behaviour and the threats he has made, the court will go further and exclude him from the general area where the flat is situated. If an order is made, it can be for a specified period, or until an event takes place, or until a further court order. In this case it appears that the flat is rented, and the order may well be of greater duration than if the flat was owned by Ian.

If the court makes an occupation order in respect of the flat, it has power to make ancillary orders under **s 40(1)**, to order either party to pay rent, mortgage, repairs or outgoings on the property. It does not seem appropriate here for an order to be made compensating Ian for the loss of his right to occupy. Whether any order is made depends on all the circumstances of the case, including the financial needs, resources and obligations of the parties (**s 40(2)**). On the facts, little is known about the resources of the parties and whether Heidi can pay anything towards the rent, or whether Ian should contribute. Clearly, an order could be made requiring Heidi to take care of the contents of the flat, and, since she has matrimonial home rights, any payment by her in respect of the rent will be treated as if made by Ian; the landlord will be bound to accept her payment (**s 30(3)**).

It would also be sensible for Heidi to apply for a non-molestation order under **s 42**. This order would prohibit the respondent from molesting the applicant if the applicant is an associated person with the respondent and/or any relevant child. As explained earlier, Heidi and Ian are associated persons by virtue of their marriage (**s 62(3)**), and the baby is a relevant child (**s 62(2)**). Such an application can be made with the application for the occupation order, or can be made regardless of whether or not an occupation order is sought (**s 42(2)**). Consequently, if Heidi remains at her mother's home and does not seek an order in relation to the flat, it would nonetheless be advisable to seek the non-molestation order.

The court will consider all the circumstances of the case including the need to ensure the safety, well-being and health of the applicant and relevant child (**s 42(5)**). Thus, there is a change in emphasis from the old law's concentration on the nature of the respondent's violent conduct, to the new consideration of the effect on the applicant and child. The term molestation is not defined in the Act but would include conduct other than violence. Ian's harassment, pestering, violence and threats would all be restrained by the order, which can be made for a limited time or until further order (**s 42(7)**). It is possible for the court to accept an undertaking from respondents instead of making an occupation order or non-molestation order (**s 46**) and it may be that sometimes, when a respondent is brought to court, he sees the error of his ways and is prepared to give such an undertaking rather than have an order made against him. No power of arrest can be attached to an undertaking (**s 46(2)**), and so a court cannot accept an undertaking from a respondent if it would otherwise have had the grounds for attaching a power of arrest to the non-molestation or occupation order. By virtue of **s 47**, if the court makes such an order and the respondent has used or threatened violence against the applicant or child, then a power of arrest must be attached, unless the court is satisfied that in all the circumstances the applicant and child will be adequately protected without one. This makes it much more likely that a power of arrest will be attached than under the old law, and the facts in the present case seem to indicate that a power of arrest is likely to be attached, given the violence and continuing threats.

It is unlikely that the facts of this case justify the draconian measure of applying for the orders *ex parte*, and it does not seem likely that the **s 45** criteria will be met unless there is the threat of immediate harm to Heidi and the baby. This will mean that Ian will have notice of Heidi's applications, and be able to make his own representations as to why an order should not be made.

(b) If Heidi and Ian are not married, then Heidi cannot have matrimonial home rights in relation to the flat, and she would only be entitled to occupy the flat if she too were a tenant. Even then, she would have no right to exclude a joint tenant: *Ainsbury v Millington* (1987). Consequently, Heidi would need to use the provisions of the **Family Law Act 1996** to seek an occupation order in relation to the flat, and a non-molestation order in relation to her and the baby. Heidi and Ian are still associated persons by virtue of being persons who are or who have been living together as husband and wife, and the baby is still a relevant child.

To apply for an occupation order, it would be necessary to see if Heidi and Ian are 'entitled' persons. Clearly, Ian as the tenant is an entitled respondent, but it is not clear whether Heidi is an entitled applicant. If she is also the tenant then she would be entitled within **s 33(1)** and the earlier discussion on the occupation order under **s 33** would apply. However, if Heidi is not entitled to occupy the flat by virtue of a beneficial estate, interest or contract, or any enactment giving her the right to remain in occupation, then **s 33** will not apply.

Instead, she will only be allowed to apply for an occupation order against a respondent who is or was a spouse or cohabitant. Ian falls into this category, and so the application will be made under **s 36** since Ian and Heidi were cohabitants rather than spouses. The order, if granted, will not only allow her to occupy, but will expressly grant her the right to occupy, which she otherwise would not have.

In making an occupation rights order, the court will take all the circumstances of the case into account, including the housing needs and resources of the parties and any relevant child; the financial resources of the parties; the likely effect on the health, safety and well-being of the parties and relevant child of any order or no order being made; the conduct of the parties in relation to each other and otherwise; the nature of the relationship; the length of time they have lived together as husband and wife; whether there are any children; the time that has passed since they lived together; and the existence of any proceedings between the parties under the **Children Act 1989** or in relation to ownership of property.

In this case Heidi and Ian have cohabited, but as both are still only 19, this will not have been for a particularly lengthy period. They have a child, and Ian has been violent and threatening. Clearly, both Ian and Heidi need a home, and as Heidi is staying in what appears to be unsatisfactory living accommodation with her mother, it seems likely that the court would be prepared to grant her occupation rights in respect of the rented flat.[7]

In addition, the court can make a regulatory order in respect of the flat whereby Ian's occupation right will be restricted or suspended, or he may be required to leave the flat or area in which it is situated. The factors influencing the court in determining whether to make such an order are the housing needs and resources of the parties; their financial resources; the effect of any order or failure to make an order on the health, safety or well-being of the parties or relevant child; the conduct of the parties in relation to each other and otherwise; the likelihood of significant harm to the applicant or child if no order is made; and the likelihood of significant harm to the respondent if an order is made.

On the facts, the needs of Heidi and the baby would seem to take priority, as they will suffer significant harm if Ian is allowed to remain in the flat, whereas Ian will suffer the inconvenience of having to rehouse himself if an order is made. Consequently, an order is likely to be made, but the order is limited to six months' duration, and can only be extended once further in the case of cohabitants. Thus, this would provide some interim protection for Heidi and the baby, but would not give a longer period of protection which she might have obtained had she been married.

The same provisions in **s 42** regarding non-molestation orders would apply to Heidi as a cohabitant in the same way as it did if Heidi were married to Ian. The two would still be associated persons by virtue of having lived together as husband and wife, and the baby would still be a relevant child. Thus, there is no distinction in relation to protection from molestation between spouses and cohabitants, but it can be seen that a cohabitant can be at a disadvantage when seeking occupation of the home.

Common Pitfalls

- As this is a problem question, avoid a general discussion of occupation orders or molestation orders and instead explain how the order will help the claimant in the question and whether one would be available on the facts.
- When advising an entitled applicant, do not confuse the **Family Law Act 1996 s 33(6)** and the **Family Law Act 1996 s 33(7)**.

Aim Higher

- Use relevant case law to explain how the court decides whether to make an occupation or molestation order.
- Be critical of the effectiveness of the orders and evaluate how effectively English law reconciles protection from domestic violence and property rights.

---

7 There is no equivalent provision to **s 33(7)** in **s 36** and therefore nothing that might potentially create a presumption in favour of an order.

QUESTION 27

Julie has been living with Darren for the past year in a house owned by Darren. Julie has just given birth to a baby boy, Billy, and she has a daughter, Gemma, by a previous partner, Rick. Rick was violent to Julie and Gemma and has written several threatening letters to Julie from jail. Rick is due to be released from jail presently.

(a) What, if anything, can Julie do to try to protect herself and her family from Rick?
(b) Julie has been told by her friend that as she is Darren's common law wife, there is no need for her to get married in order to be able to stay in the home. Is this correct?

How to Read this Question

The first part of the question is about what domestic violence remedies can be used to protect Julie and the second part is about Julie's rights as an unmarried partner.

Applying the Law

WHAT, IF ANYTHING, CAN JULIE DO TO TRY TO PROTECT HERSELF AND HER FAMILY FROM RICK?

- A non-molestation order is used to stop the defendant's molestation of the claimant (**FLA 1996 s 42(1)(a)**) → Rick is writing threatening letters to Julie and therefore a non-molestation order would be helpful

- Associated persons can apply for non-molestation orders → Definition is in **FLA 1996 s 62(3)** → Rick and Julie are parents of the same child and therefore she is an associated person (**FLA 1996 s 62(3)(f)**)

- *Ex parte* applications → Applications for non-molestation orders can be heard *ex parte* if there is otherwise a risk of significant harm to the applicant or a relevant child (**Family Law Act 1996 s 45(2)**)

- Deciding whether to make a non-molestation order – **FLA 1996 s 42(5)** → Need to secure the health, safety and well-being of the applicant

COMMON LAW WIFE?

- The legal and equitable ownership of Darren's flat will be dealt with according to general land law principles
  - Legal ownership
    - Law of Property Act 1935 s 52
    - Darren is the legal owner
  - Equitable ownership
    - Express trust (**Law of Property Act 1925 s 53(2)(b)**)
    - Implied trust
      - resulting trust
      - constructive trust

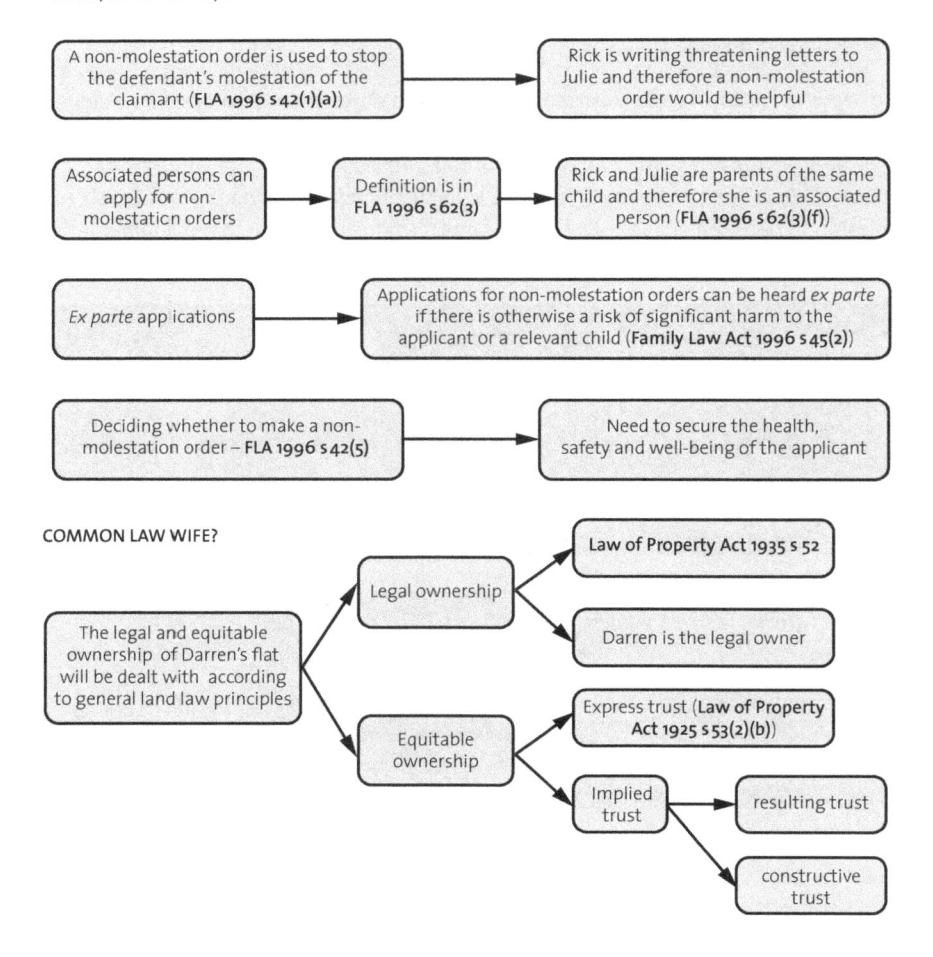

ANSWER

(a) In order to determine whether Julie can apply for a non-molestation order under **s 42** against Rick, it is necessary to consider whether Julie and Rick are associated persons within the definition in the **Family Law Act 1996 s 62**. Persons are associated if they are or have been married. There is no evidence of such a relationship here. They will also be associated if they are or were cohabitants; that is, lived together in the same household as husband and wife. This may have been the case here, or the couple may merely have lived in the same household, and be associated by virtue of this. Rick and Julie are not relatives, but they are the parents of the same child, and this would suffice to make them associated within the **Family Law Act 1996 s 62(3)(f)**.

Gemma is clearly a relevant child within **s 62(2)** as she is a child living with a party to the proceedings, as is Billy, even though he is not Rick's child. Consequently, Julie can seek a non-molestation order in respect of herself and both of her children. However, Darren cannot be protected by an order applied for by Julie, and would need to make his own application. He could face difficulty in doing this because there is no evidence that he and Rick are associated persons. They have never lived in the same household, and the only other possibility is that they both have or had parental responsibility in relation to the same child. If Julie and Rick were married then Rick would have had parental responsibility for Gemma, but if they were not married then only Julie would have parental responsibility for Gemma. There is no indication that Darren has parental responsibility for Gemma, and so no non-molestation order can be made under the Act in relation to Darren.[8]

Julie can seek a non-molestation order against Rick as a freestanding application; she does not need to be taking any other family proceedings. The court has a discretion whether or not to make the order and will look at all the circumstances of the case, including the need to secure the health, safety and well-being of the applicant and the two relevant children (**Family Law Act 1996 s 42(5)**). There is no requirement that the respondent has to have been violent; the order can be widely drafted to afford protection not just from violence but from pestering and harassment, and can specifically forbid letters and other attempts at communication. Clearly, Rick's violent past and present vindictive campaign would indicate a need for a non-molestation order to be made in order to safeguard Julie and the children. Furthermore under the **Family Law Act 1996 s 42A** if Rick were to breach the terms of the non-molestation order this would be a criminal offence.

Since Rick is still in jail and unable to actually harm Julie or the children until his release, it seems unlikely that an *ex parte* order will be necessary. If, however, Rick's release were imminent, and Julie needed immediate protection, an *ex parte* order could be obtained if it would be just and convenient to do so (**s 45**). It would be necessary to stress the threat of harm to Julie if the order were not made immediately, although a full hearing would be ordered later, at which point Rick could make representations.

---

8 As Darren's situation illustrates, although the definition of associated person is broad, it will not cover every individual who might be affected by domestic violence.

(b) Julie is mistaken. She currently has no rights to occupy Darren's flat. It seems on the facts that he is the sole legal owner and there is no evidence that Julie has obtained a beneficial interest, either expressly or via a resulting trust or constructive trust. She has only been living there for a year. There do not seem to have been any discussions about ownership and nothing on the facts suggests that she has either contributed to the purchase of the flat, or acted in some way to her detriment.

If Julie were to marry Darren she would acquire matrimonial home rights under the **Family Law Act 1996 s30**. These are defined in **s30(2)** as the right not to be evicted or excluded from the home unless by court order, and the right, if not in occupation, to enter and occupy with a court order. These rights exist in relation to any dwelling house that is or was intended to be the joint home of the parties. This means that Darren could not evict her unless he obtained a court order permitting him to do that, and it also means that Julie would be an entitled applicant in any proceedings she might bring to have Darren excluded from the home.

QUESTION 28

Amy married Ben two years ago after her marriage to Charles had ended in divorce. She did not obtain any substantial financial settlement as Charles was a penniless destitute. After their marriage, Amy and Ben lived together in the matrimonial home which Ben had bought in his name 10 years ago. Amy's two children, Diana and Edward, aged eight and six respectively, also lived with the couple.

As time has gone on, Amy has become increasingly bad-tempered with Ben and the children, although she has never actually been violent. She has joined a very extreme religious cult and, since Ben disapproves of it, she has become increasingly critical of his 'heathen influence' on the children. Amy has frequently criticised Ben in front of the children, becoming angry if he denies any of her suggestions. During one especially heated argument, Ben slapped Amy whilst she was hysterical. Ben is very fond of the children, who view him as their father, since they have had little or no contact with their birth father, Charles, since they were babies.

Five weeks ago, Amy told Ben during the course of a heated argument that she was no longer prepared to allow him to corrupt her children and, against Ben's wishes, she left, taking the children with her. They are all now staying with Amy's parents, Fred and Gertie, in their cramped council flat.

Amy has since confronted Ben, saying that their relationship is over, but that she will never divorce him for religious reasons. She told him to leave the matrimonial home so that she could return with the children, and she is adamant that he cannot remain. She has said that she will take legal action to enable her to return to the house.

▶ **Advise Ben on how the court would deal with the occupation of the family home.**

Domestic Violence and Occupation of the Home

How to Read this Question
This is another question on the court's powers under the **Family Law Act 1996 Part IV**. Unusually in this case you are advising the defendant, Ben.

Applying the Law

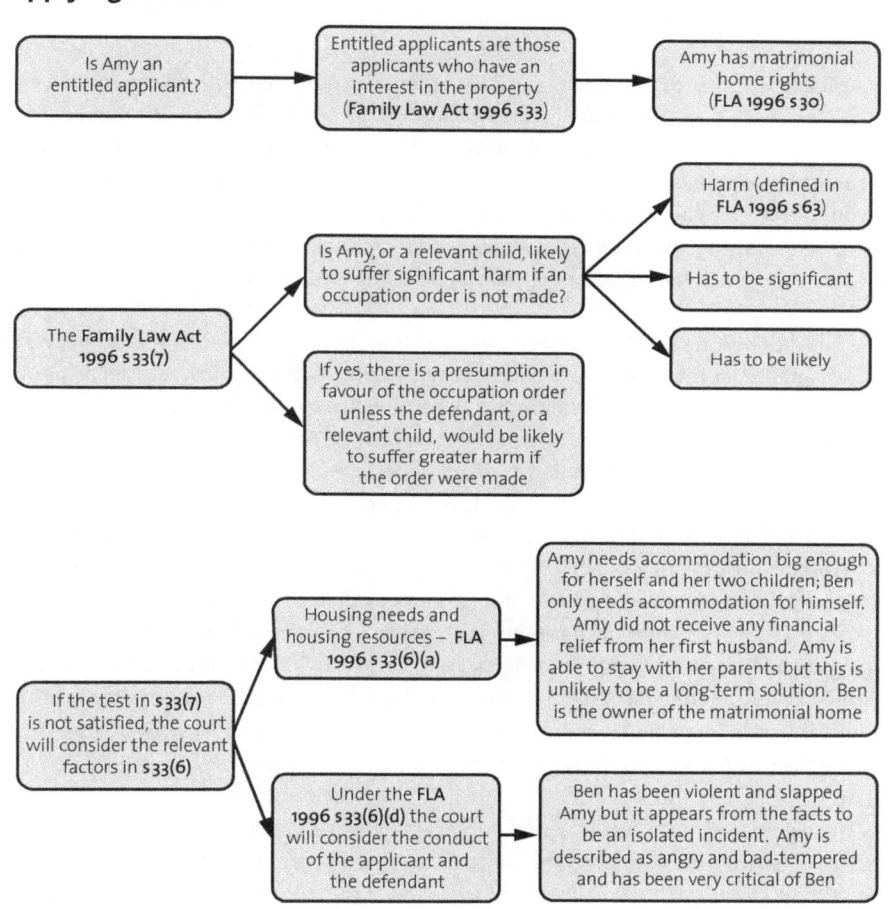

- Is Amy an entitled applicant? → Entitled applicants are those applicants who have an interest in the property (**Family Law Act 1996 s 33**) → Amy has matrimonial home rights (**FLA 1996 s 30**)

- The **Family Law Act 1996 s 33(7)**:
  - Is Amy, or a relevant child, likely to suffer significant harm if an occupation order is not made?
    - Harm (defined in FLA 1996 s 63)
    - Has to be significant
    - Has to be likely
  - If yes, there is a presumption in favour of the occupation order unless the defendant, or a relevant child, would be likely to suffer greater harm if the order were made

- If the test in s 33(7) is not satisfied, the court will consider the relevant factors in s 33(6):
  - Housing needs and housing resources – **FLA 1996 s 33(6)(a)** → Amy needs accommodation big enough for herself and her two children; Ben only needs accommodation for himself. Amy did not receive any financial relief from her first husband. Amy is able to stay with her parents but this is unlikely to be a long-term solution. Ben is the owner of the matrimonial home
  - Under the **FLA 1996 s 33(6)(d)** the court will consider the conduct of the applicant and the defendant → Ben has been violent and slapped Amy but it appears from the facts to be an isolated incident. Amy is described as angry and bad-tempered and has been very critical of Ben

ANSWER

Ben is the legal owner of the dwelling house, and since Amy has no legal or beneficial interest, she is given matrimonial home rights under the **Family Law Act 1996 s 30**. Amy is not occupying the home at present, but the dwelling house was at one stage the matrimonial home. Consequently, the issue of whether Amy can return and exclude Ben from the home will need to be resolved by the court under its powers in the **Family Law Act 1996 s 33** to make occupation orders.

The court can have jurisdiction to make a **s 33** occupation order if the dwelling house is, has been or was intended to be the home of the applicant and another person with whom the applicant is associated. The concept of associated person is defined in **s 62(3)**. Ben and Amy are clearly associated persons on the basis of their marriage. The court can, therefore, make an order regulating the occupation of the home. These orders can allow a person to remain in occupation, or to enter and occupy the home or part of it. It is also possible to prohibit the respondent from exercising his right to occupy, and require him to leave the home, or part of it, or the area in which it is situated.

In deciding whether to make an occupation order, the court will begin by considering the significant harm test in the **Family Law Act 1996 s 33(7)**. Under this provision, if it appears to the court that the applicant (here Amy) or a relevant child (here Diana and Edward) would suffer significant harm if the order were not made, this creates a presumption in favour of the occupation order being made which can only be rebutted by the defendant (here Ben) showing that if an order were made that would cause him greater harm than would be caused to Amy, Diana or Edward by an order not being made.

The question for the court therefore is whether Amy, Diana or Edward are likely to suffer significant ham if the order is not made. The facts clearly state that Ben has slapped Amy. Physical injury or hurt would be included as harm; however, it is questionable whether a slap would constitute significant harm. Moreover, unlike the criminal law, the provisions in the **Family Law Act 1996 Part IV** are aimed at protecting the applicant or relevant children and not at punishing the defendant. Whilst Ben's action in slapping Amy is bad, it does not seem to be part of a pattern of behaviour and therefore it is unlikely that the court would hold that it would mean that Amy would be at risk of significant harm unless the occupation order were made. Another argument that Amy might use is that her children are at risk of significant harm because of Ben's heathen influence. Although damaging a child's development, possibly by being a bad influence, would count as harm (**Family Law Act 1996 s 63**) there is nothing on the facts to suggest Ben is an especially immoral or dangerous influence. In short, it is unlikely that the court would decide that the **Family Law Act 1996 s 33(7)** were satisfied.

As the significant harm test in **s 33(7)** is not satisfied, the court will turn instead to the factors in **s 33(6)**. These require the court to take into account all the circumstances of the case, including the housing needs and resources of the parties and any relevant child, the financial resources of the parties, the likely effect of any order or non-exercise of powers by the court on the health, safety or well-being of the parties and any relevant child, and the conduct of the parties in relation to each other and otherwise.

Both parties need homes, Amy needs adequate accommodation for her and the children, and this need is not really being met by the cramped conditions at her parents'. Ben also needs somewhere to live, and if evicted he would not, as a single person, be a priority for local authority housing, although he may have more flexibility if he has income to pay rent in the short term. If the children were to live with Ben, this would increase his claim to remain in the home, but the presence of the children with Amy strengthens her claim to be able to enter and occupy. There is little evidence of detriment to Amy's health or that of the children if an order were not made, and although Ben has been violent once, his conduct has otherwise been good. Amy, on the other hand, has behaved in an extremely provocative manner and has contributed significantly to her own misfortunes. It may be that the court would be reluctant to exclude Ben without evidence that this is really essential. If an order were to be made, it can be for a specified time, or until an event takes place or until a further court order (**s 33(10)**). It remains to be seen whether the court will vary its practice under the old law of viewing exclusion of the spouse with the property interests as a short-term measure.

If an occupation order is made in relation to the dwelling house, either to let Amy occupy, or to exclude Ben or Amy, then the court has power to make ancillary orders under **s 40(1)** to order either party to pay the rent, mortgage, repairs or other outgoings on the property; or to pay the non-occupying party compensation for the loss of their right to occupy; or to make orders in respect of the furniture. The test as to whether such an order should be made is to consider all the circumstances of the case including the financial needs, resources and obligations of the parties (**s 40(2)**). There is no evidence regarding these matters in the present case, but if Amy has no resources it will not be possible to order her to make any such payments, although she can be required to take good care of the furniture.

In conclusion, Amy's arguments and claims against Ben seem somewhat flimsy and may not justify the making of an occupation order in her favour. If any order were to be made, given the circumstances, it is likely to be short term, to avoid the overcrowding until Amy can be rehoused.

7 Who is a Parent? Parental Responsibility and the Principles of the Children Act 1989

INTRODUCTION

In this chapter the focus switches to children. This chapter provides the background for subsequent chapters on private law orders, public law child protection orders and adoption.

Checklist

Students should understand and be able to apply the law relating to:

- who the law considers to be the child's mother and whether motherhood is dependent on a genetic link between the woman and the child (**Human Fertilisation and Embryology Act 2008 s 33(1)**);
- who the law considers to the child's father, including when assisted reproduction techniques are used (**Human Fertilisation and Embryology Act 2008 s 35**) and when the presumptions relating to paternity can be rebutted (**Family Law Reform Act 1969 s 25**);
- how the law treats female partners of mothers (**Human Fertilisation and Embryology Act s 42(1)**);
- the contents of parental responsibility;
- parental responsibility and changing the child's name: **Children Act 1989 s 13(1)(a)**;
- parental responsibility and removing the child from the jurisdiction: **Children Act 1989 s 13(1)(b)**;
- the contents of parental responsibility and the older child (*Gillick v West Norfolk and Wisbech AHA* (1986), *An NHS Trust v A, B and C and a Local Authority* (2014));
- caring for a child without parental responsibility: **Children Act 1989 s 3(5)**;
- who has parental responsibility if the parents are married: **Children Act 1989 s 2(1)**;
- who has parental responsibility if the parents are not married: **Children Act 1989 s 2(2)**;
- when an unmarried father has parental responsibility: when he is registered on the child's birth certificate (**Children Act 1989 s 4(1)(a)**), when he signs a parental responsibility agreement with the child's mother (**Children Act 1989 s 4(1)(b)**) or he is awarded parental responsibility after having applied to court for a parental responsibility order (**Children Act 1989 s 4(1)(c)**);
- how courts decide whether to make a parental responsibility order (**Children Act 1989 s 1(1)**) and in what circumstances the court will refuse or remove parental responsibility (*Re D* (2014), *Re T (A Minor: Parental Responsibility)* (1993));

- parental responsibility and female civil partners under the **Human Fertilsation and Embryology Act 2008** (**Children Act 1989 4ZA**);
- parental responsibility and step-parents: **Children Act 1989 s4A**. Step-parents can gain parental responsibility through parental responsibility agreements (**Children Act 1989 s4A(1)(a)**) or through parental responsibility orders (**Children Act 1989 s4A(1)(b)**);
- parental responsibility and child arrangement orders (**Children Act 1989 s8, s12**);
- parental responsibility and child protection orders – emergency protection orders (**Children Act 1989 s44(4)(c)**) and care orders (**Children Act 1989 s33(a)**);
- who has parental responsibility under a surrogacy agreement: what the effects of a parental order are and who can apply for a parental order (**Human Fertilisation and Embryology Act 2008 s54(2)**);
- the principle that the child's welfare is paramount (**Children Act 1989 s1(1)**);
- the use of the welfare checklist in the **Children Act 1989 s1(3)** to determine what is in the child's welfare in child protection cases and **s8** order cases;
- how courts interpret welfare;
- the no delay principle (**Children Act 1989 s1(2)**) and how this has been applied by the courts;
- the no order principle (**Children Act 1989 s1(5)**).

Up for Debate

- Should unmarried fathers automatically have parental responsibility for their children?
- How should the law respond to the increased autonomy of the older child?
- Should the law's response to children be paternalistic and protecting or should it promote independence?
- What is meant by the welfare of the child in a heterogeneous society?
- What should be the relationship between the welfare of the child and the human rights of adult members of the family?
- How important is the welfare principle?
- Should sperm or egg donors be anonymous?
- Is there a right to be a parent?

QUESTION 29

Nicola's daughter, Olivia, is 14. Olivia has never met her father, Peter. Peter and Nicola only had a very casual relationship and he left Nicola when she was five months pregnant. Ten years ago, Peter was sent to prison after he kidnapped and then violently attacked a research scientist who worked in a laboratory. The attack left the scientist blind. Peter was released from prison a year ago. Peter says that he is still opposed to animal experimentation but that he would no longer use violence as a way of stopping animal experiments. Olivia has a life-threatening heart condition for which she needs to take medication. She has now decided that she no longer wants to take her medication as it was developed

Who is a Parent? 123

following animal experimentation. Nicola knows that Peter has been writing to Olivia and she is very concerned that he has influenced Olivia to not want to take her medication. Peter has decided that he would like to develop his relationship with Olivia and as part of that he would like to gain parental responsibility for her. Nicola is opposed to this as she is worried about his influence on Olivia.

▶ Advise Nicola on:
   (a) Peter's application for parental responsibility for Olivia;
   (b) Olivia's refusal to take her medication.

How to Read this Question

There are two parts to this question and they should be dealt with separately. The first is how Peter could gain parental responsibility and the second is whether an older child, here Olivia, would be *Gillick* competent to refuse to take her medication.

Applying the Law

PETER'S APPLICATION FOR PARENTAL RESPONSIBILITY

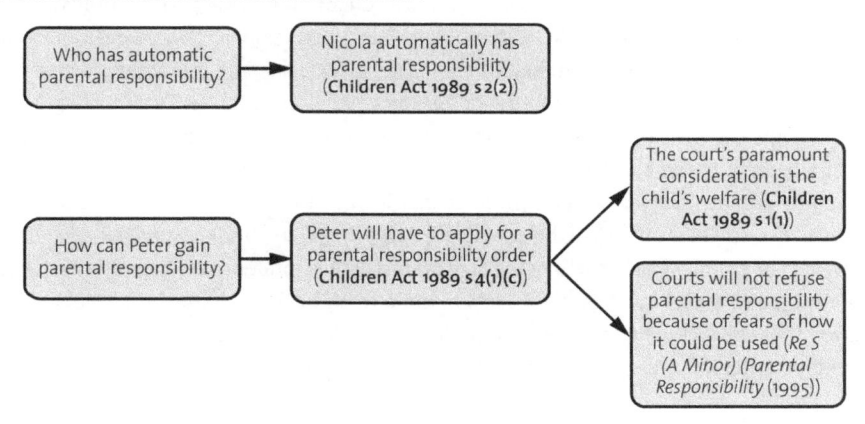

- Who has automatic parental responsibility? → Nicola automatically has parental responsibility (**Children Act 1989 s 2(2)**)

- How can Peter gain parental responsibility? → Peter will have to apply for a parental responsibility order (**Children Act 1989 s 4(1)(c)**)
  - → The court's paramount consideration is the child's welfare (**Children Act 1989 s 1(1)**)
  - → Courts will not refuse parental responsibility because of fears of how it could be used (*Re S (A Minor) (Parental Responsibility)* (1995))

OLIVIA'S REFUSAL TO TAKE HER MEDICATION

- Who can consent to Olivia taking her medication?
  - → Nicola → Consenting to medical treatment is one of the duties and rights of parental responsibility (**Children Act 1989 s 3(1)**)
  - → Olivia → *Gillick v West Norfolk and Wisbech AHA* (1985) – is Olivia *Gillick* competent?

- *Gillick* competence and refusal to take medication/have treatment
  - → Does the court view consenting to treatment and refusing treatment differently?
  - → Even if Olivia refuses, can Nicola consent on her behalf? *Re M (Medical Treatment: Consent)* (1999), *Re W (A Minor) (Medical Treatment)* (1993)

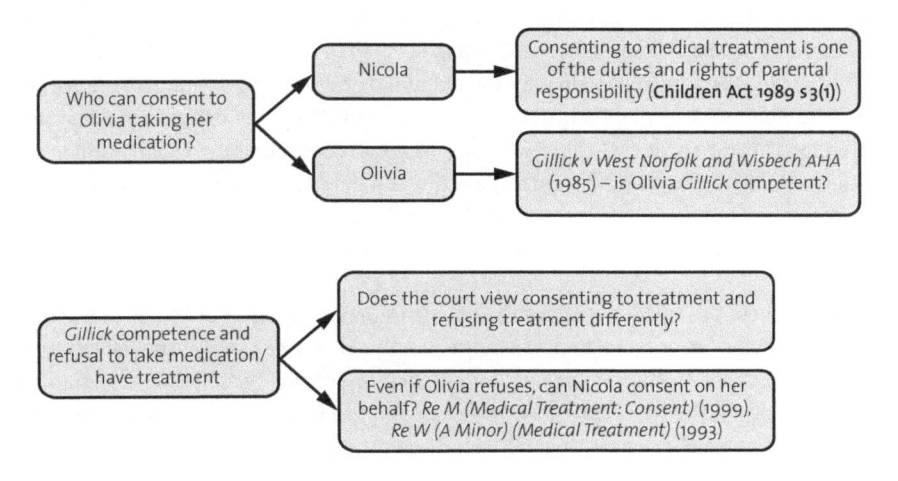

ANSWER

(a) Only Nicola has parental responsibility for Olivia. Nicola and Peter were not married and under the **Children Act 1989 s 2(2)** if parents are unmarried, only the child's mother automatically has parental responsibility. Furthermore, it does not seem that Peter has gained parental responsibility under the **Children Act 1989 s 4**. Olivia was born before the **Adoption and Children Act 2002** reformed the law so that if a father's name was on a birth certificate, he would have parental responsibility (**Children Act 1989 s 4(1)(a)**) and in any case given that he left Nicola during her pregnancy he would not have been around to have been registered on Olivia's birth certificate. The facts are clear that Nicola does not want Peter to have parental responsibility for Olivia and therefore a parental responsibility agreement is not an option (**Children Act 1989 s 4(1)(b)**). As a result, Peter will try to obtain parental responsibility through a parental responsibility order (**Children Act 1989 s 4(1)(c)**).

When deciding whether to award Peter parental responsibility for Olivia, the paramount consideration for the court is Olivia's welfare (**Children Act 1989 s 1(1)**). Whilst Nicola opposes Peter having parental responsibility, her opposition is only relevant if going against her wishes would harm her ability to look after Olivia and therefore ultimately be disadvantageous to Olivia's welfare. One reason why Nicola opposes Peter having parental responsibility is that she fears his influence on Olivia. It is arguable that this, by itself, will not prevent the court giving Peter parental responsibility. First, granting a father a parental responsibility order does not necessarily mean that other orders would also be made in his favour. It might be possible to give Peter parental responsibility but still restrict the contact that he has with Olivia to restrict his influence on her. Alternatively, it seems from the facts that Peter's beliefs might already have had some influence on Olivia given that she is hoping to refuse her medication. If this is the case then the link between whether Peter has parental responsibility and his ability to influence Olivia is weak.

Another argument against Peter having parental responsibility is that he has a conviction and has been in prison for a serious violent offence. On the other hand, Peter's offence was committed 10 years ago and he has completed his prison sentence, and Peter now says that he would not use violence. Olivia is 14. It is not clear on the facts what her view is, but if she was able to explain why she did or did not want her father to have parental responsibility this might influence the court. When considering whether to make a parental responsibility order the court will look at what commitment and attachment the father has shown towards his child (*Re H* (1993)). Peter disappeared when Nicola was pregnant and has spent the majority of Olivia's life in prison. He has not had the opportunity to spend time with Olivia and develop an attachment towards her.

Although there are many arguments against Peter having a parental responsibility order, it is nonetheless suggested that the court would make a parental responsibility order. Courts generally see a father applying for parental responsibility are positive and want to promote this. Furthermore, many of the reasons not to give Peter parental responsibility relate to his past behaviour – leaving Nicola during the pregnancy, criminal conviction.

(b) Olivia has an extremely serious heart condition for which she has been prescribed medication. Although the **Children Act 1989** does not detail the contents of parental responsibility, **s3(1)** states that parental responsibility is all the rights, duties, powers, responsibility and authority that a parent has in respect of a child. It is widely accepted that this includes the right to consent to the child receiving medical treatment. As has already been explained, Nicola has parental responsibility for Olivia (**Children Act 1989 s2(2)**), therefore Nicola is able to consent to Olivia receiving the medication for her heart condition.

Whether Olivia can be prescribed or made to take medication is, however, complicated by the leading case of *Gillick v West Norfolk and Wisbech AHA* (1985). In *Gillick*, the House of Lords determined that a teenage girl could receive contraceptive advice and be prescribed the contraceptive pill without her parents' approval if she was of sufficient maturity, understanding and intelligence to understand what was involved. In their discussions of the issues in *Gillick*, the House of Lords recognised that the nature of parental responsibility changed as the child grew and it was appropriate to afford the older child more autonomy and an increasing right to make the decisions associated with parental responsibility him or herself.

There is no set age at which a child will definitely be *Gillick* competent. It depends on the maturity and understanding of the individual. Olivia is 14. It is possible that some 14-year-olds would be *Gillick* competent; however, this does not mean that Olivia would be. *Gillick* competence requires maturity and understanding of all the issues from the teenager. Olivia seems to be refusing life-saving medication because of how it was developed. The court may be concerned that she does not seem to have considered what the impact of her refusal is likely to be. It is also probable that they would be cautious of declaring Olivia *Gillick* competent given that there is a strong chance that her views on animal testing are due to her father's influence rather than her own research and her own opinions. On balance, therefore, it is unlikely that the court would consider Olivia to be *Gillick* competent.

Even if Olivia were considered to be *Gillick* competent, it is possible that she might still be prescribed the medication. In contrast to *Gillick* itself, Olivia's case involves a refusal to take medication or use a treatment. Courts have decided that even if the older child has his own right to consent to medical treatment, the right of the parent with parental responsibility to consent because of parental responsibility remains and therefore treatment can carried out with the parent's permission notwithstanding the child's refusal (*Re M (Medical Treatment: Consent)* (1999), *Re W (A Minor)(Medical Treatment)* (1993)).

8 Private Law Disputes Relating to Children

INTRODUCTION

This chapter looks at **s 8** orders and how they can be used to manage a parent's relationship with his/her child and the parent's exercise of parental responsibility. This chapter will also look at how the court decides whether to make a **s 8** order and will therefore look at how welfare is interpreted.

Checklist

Students should understand and be able to apply the law relating to the following:

- the child arrangement order in **Children Act 1989** and how this has replaced the residence order (**Children and Families Act 2014 s 12**);
- is there a preference for children to live with their mothers? (*Brixley v Lynas* (1996));
- is there a preference for a child to live with birth parent(s)? (*Re M (Child's Upbringing)* (1996), *Re G (Children) (Residence: Same-Sex Partner)* (2006), *Re E-R (a child)* (2015), *Re B (A Child)* (2009));
- the use of shared residence by courts (*A v A (Minors) (Shared Residence Order)* (1994), *Re WB (Residence Orders)* (1994), *D v D* (2001), *F v F* (2003), *Re P (A Child)* (2005), *Re K (Shared Residence Order)* (2008));
- the child arrangement order and how this has replaced the contact order (**Children and Families Act 1989 s 12**);
- contact and domestic violence (*Re L (A Child) (contact: domestic violence)* (2000), *Re W (Children)* (2012));
- contact and implacable hostility (*Re O (Contact: Imposition of conditions)* (1995), *Re P (Contact Discretion)* (1998));
- enforcement of **s 8** orders: *CDM v CM, LM, DM (Children)* (2003), **Children and Adoption Act 2006 ss 3** and **4**, **Children Act 1989 ss 11A–11P**;
- contact between a parent and child is for the benefit of the child. Students should be aware of the different forms contact can take and be able to illustrate the courts' approach with examples of contact being allowed and being refused or restricted (*Re P (A child)* (2015));
- prohibited steps order (**Children Act 1989 s 8**). Students should understand that this order is used to stop a parent exercising his/her parental responsibility in a particular way (*Re A and B (prohibited steps order at dispute resolution appointment)* (2015));

- specific issue order (**Children Act 1989 s 8**);
- changing a child's name (**Children Act 1989 s 13(1)(a)**, *Dawson v Wearmouth* (1997));
- removing a child from the jurisdiction (**Children Act 1989 s 13(1)(b)**, *Payne v Payne* (2001));
- who is able to apply for any **s 8** order (**Children Act 1989 s 10(4)**) or for a child arrangement order (**Children Act 1989 s 10(5)**) without the leave of the court;
- getting leave to apply for a **s 8** order. For adults this is dealt with by the **Children Act 1989 s 10(9)**, for the child him or herself, the relevant provision is the **Children Act 1989 s 10(8)**;
- that when deciding whether to make a **s 8** order the child's welfare is paramount (**Children Act 1989 s 1(1)**) and the court will use the welfare checklist to determine what is in the child's welfare (**Children Act 1989 ss 1(3), 1(4)**); the use of welfare reports to determine what is in the child's welfare;
- the court will also consider the no delay principle (**Children Act 1989 s 1(2)**) and the no order principle (**Children Act 1989 s 1(5)**);
- the **Children and Families Act 2014 s 11** has introduced a presumption of parental involvement into the **Children Act 1989 s 1(2A), s 1(2B)**;
- the court can attach conditions to the **s 8** order (**Children Act 1989 s 11(7)**);
- what a family assistance order is and it when can be used (**Children Act 1989 s 16**);
- the use of the court's inherent jurisdiction and wardship: *London Borough of Tower Hamlets v M and Others* (2015).

Up for Debate

- Should shared residence be used unless it is impracticable or there is significant violence?
- How should the court approach implacable hostility and are the measures to enforce **s 8** orders effective?
- Does inherent jurisdiction still have a role?

QUESTION 30

Samantha, aged 14, lived with her parents, Janet and John, and her younger brother, Martin, aged nine, in the family home. For some time, Samantha has been arguing with John, primarily about her attitude to school and her relationship with her boyfriend, Zak, aged 17. Last month, after yet another argument with her parents, Samantha left home and went to stay with Zak at Zak's mother's home. Zak's mother is rarely at home and has no objection to Samantha staying there, but Janet and John want their daughter to come home.

Private Law Disputes Relating to Children | 129

Samantha has refused to return, and has threatened her parents that she will 'divorce' them, as she has read of similar cases in the newspapers. She also tells them she is going to the family planning clinic to obtain the contraceptive pill.

▸ Advise Janet and John as to whether Samantha can do this.

How to Read this Question
The question is about a child applying for a **s 8** order, so the issue of whether she would be given leave needs to be considered.

Applying the Law

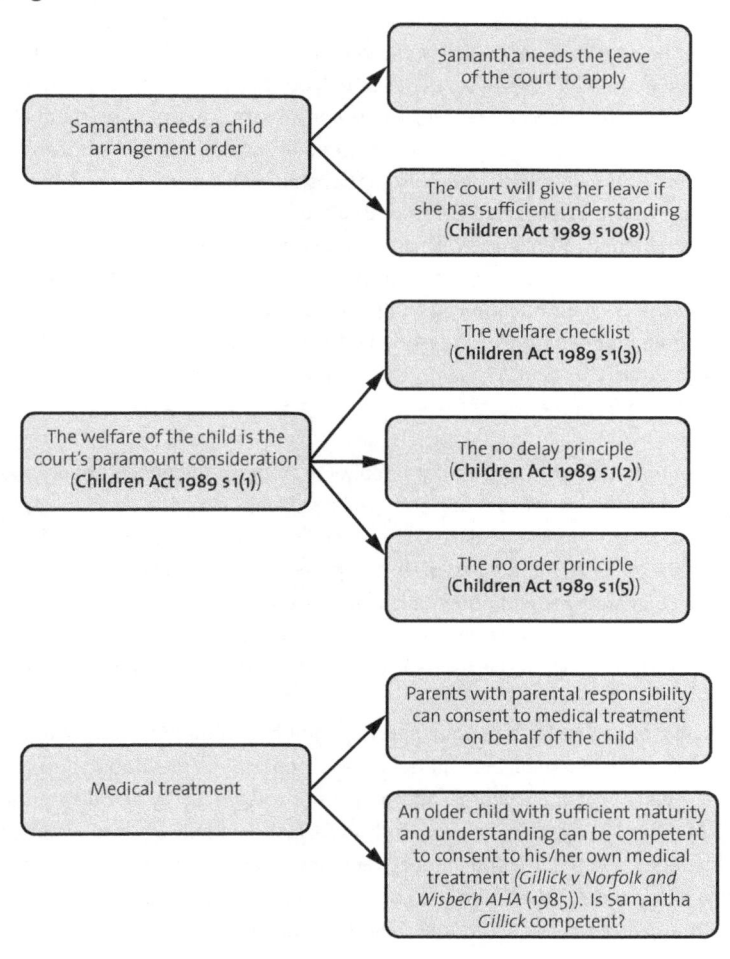

Samantha needs a child arrangement order
- Samantha needs the leave of the court to apply
- The court will give her leave if she has sufficient understanding (**Children Act 1989 s 10(8)**)

The welfare of the child is the court's paramount consideration (**Children Act 1989 s 1(1)**)
- The welfare checklist (**Children Act 1989 s 1(3)**)
- The no delay principle (**Children Act 1989 s 1(2)**)
- The no order principle (**Children Act 1989 s 1(5)**)

Medical treatment
- Parents with parental responsibility can consent to medical treatment on behalf of the child
- An older child with sufficient maturity and understanding can be competent to consent to his/her own medical treatment (*Gillick v Norfolk and Wisbech AHA* (1985)). Is Samantha *Gillick* competent?

ANSWER
Janet and John are Samantha's parents and as such one or both of them will have parental responsibility for Samantha. Parental responsibility is defined in the **Children Act 1989 s 3(1)** as 'all the rights, duties, powers and responsibilities and authority which by law a

parent of a child has in relation to the child and its property'. This concept is based on an obligation to nurture and care for a child, and replaces the somewhat possessory concept of parental rights, whereby some parents viewed their children as possessions to be controlled. There is, consequently, no automatic right for Janet and John to insist that their teenage daughter does as they say. Parental responsibility is borne by the natural mother of the child, and by the father if he was married to the mother at the time of the child's birth or conception: **s 2(1)**. Janet definitely has parental responsibility, and John may also have it automatically if he is married to Janet.

There is clearly a conflict here between the views of Janet and John as to what is best for their daughter, and Samantha's own views. As Samantha is a 14-year-old teenager, she can no longer be physically controlled in the way that a young child can, and parents have to accept that as their child grows older they will do less controlling and more advising: *Gillick v W Norfolk and Wisbech Area Health Authority* (1985).[1] In this case, there is genuine concern on the part of the parents about the suitability of their daughter's living arrangements and her relationship with Zak. This relationship would seem to be sexual, or about to become so, given Samantha's comments about contraception, and it is a criminal offence to have sexual intercourse with a girl under 16, even if she is a willing participant. Janet and John are also concerned about Samantha's education which they have a duty to ensure she receives: the **Education Act 1944**. They could attempt to remove Samantha from Zak's home, but can only use reasonable force; if excessive force is used then there may be an assault (*R v Smith* (1985)). Ultimately, this might provoke Samantha into seeking assistance from the courts.

There is no automatic right for a child to apply for an order under the **Children Act 1989**. **Section 10(8)** of the Act specifies that a child will need leave from the court to apply for one of the range of orders in **s 8**, and leave will only be granted if the court is satisfied that the child has sufficient understanding to make the proposed application. Samantha may wish to apply for a child arrangement order which would determine where she should live, a prohibited steps order to stop her parents removing her from Zak's home, and the issue of contraception could be raised as a specific issue order if still in dispute (**Children Act 1989 s 8**).

The court will look at Samantha's age, maturity and understanding before granting leave. A degree of conflict between teenagers and their parents is inevitable, and the courts have made it clear that the **Children Act 1989** is not to be used by any disgruntled teenager (*Re C (A Minor) (Leave to seek s 8 order)* (1994)). It should only be used where there is a genuine breakdown in the relationship between parent and child, and where there is such deep disharmony and mistrust that the court's intervention is necessary: *Re AD (A Minor)* (1993). Such applications are viewed as being serious and sensitive enough to warrant consideration by the High Court, and so Samantha's case, regardless of where it was commenced, would be determined by the High Court.

---

1 A child is '*Gillick* competent' to take decisions for themselves over things that are part of parental responsibility when the child is of sufficient understanding and maturity. It is judged on the individual child and whilst some will be *Gillick* competent at 14, others will not be.

In *Re C (Residence: Child's Application for Leave)* (1995) the court held that in deciding whether to give leave for a child to make a **s8** application, the child's interests are important, but are not the paramount consideration. The **s10** principles that apply when other people apply for leave do not apply to children where the consideration is whether the child has sufficient understanding. The court can also take into account the likelihood of the application succeeding. Here, the conflict is between Samantha and her parents, but the court cautioned in *Re C* about the detrimental effect of allowing a child to be a party to proceedings between arguing parents, where the child might hear evidence that could cause upset.[2]

Samantha is 14, and 14-year-old girls would normally have sufficient maturity to realise the long-term consequences of applying to live apart from their parents. The facts disclose that Samantha has not been doing well at school, but there is nothing to suggest that she is of below average intelligence. Her emotional maturity would need to be examined, but she seems to be exercising some degree of responsibility in seeking contraceptives, and it is likely that she is of sufficient maturity and understanding to be given leave to apply for a **s8** order. A 14-year-old's wishes were respected in a case involving education (*Re P (A Minor) (Education: Child's Wishes)* (1992)), and unless Samantha comes across in court as a petulant and stubborn child, it is likely she will be given leave to apply for a **s8** order.

In dealing with applications for **s8** orders, the court is required to take into account a number of important factors. The first of these is the non-interventionist policy (**s1(5)**), which requires the court to consider whether making an order is better than not making any order. This is in line with the philosophy of the **Children Act 1989** which is to encourage consensus, with the court's involvement seen as a last resort. It would seem that Samantha's relationship with her parents has probably deteriorated beyond the point where they are able to reach agreement; they seem to be opposed to each other, and so in a contested **s8** application the court's involvement seems inevitable.

Once the court becomes involved, it must have regard to the fact that 'delay in determining the question is likely to prejudice the welfare of the child': **s1(2)**. It will therefore be necessary to ensure that the dispute over Samantha's upbringing is resolved as quickly as possible, and to ensure that this happens the court will draw up a timetable for the proceedings (**s11**).

In a disputed **s8** application, the court must also have regard to the statutory checklist in **s1(3)**. The **Children Act 1989 s1(1)** makes the child's welfare the paramount consideration, and therefore this dispute will be resolved in the way in which Samantha's welfare is best served. The checklist in **s1(3)** lists a number of factors that should be considered, and these will be examined in turn.

First, the ascertainable wishes and feelings of the child concerned (in the light of her age and understanding) will be examined. As explained earlier, a mature 14-year-old will usually be able to express her wishes sensibly, and will be able to make decisions in her

---

2 Note that the test for leave to apply for a **s8** order is different if it is a child who is applying.

long-term interest: *Stewart v Stewart* (1973). However, the cases where greatest credence has been given to the wishes of the child have involved a child having to choose between two suitable parents or family members. In the instant case, Samantha is choosing to live away from her parents at Zak's house. It is not clear whether she has a positive relationship with Zak's mother, and it may be argued that it is not in Samantha's long-term interests to effectively live with her 17-year-old boyfriend whilst she is still only 14. If it appears that pressure has been put on her by Zak, then her views may be discounted (*Re S (Infants)* (1967)) if they are not in her long-term interests.

It will then be necessary to examine Samantha's physical, emotional and educational needs. She is still 14 years old, and has a need for a certain level of care and guidance. Zak's mother does not seem keen to play an active part in Samantha's upbringing, and she has a rather relaxed attitude that might not be in Samantha's best interests. The sexual nature of Samantha's relationship with Zak is something again that the court may be unwilling to condone positively by ordering that she, in effect, lives with him. Janet and John could also argue that they are able to provide a stable and caring home, and that Samantha has just been rebelling against their authority and trying to get her own way. By leaving to live with Zak, Samantha's relationship with her brother might suffer, and the courts take the view that siblings can offer each other support: *C v C* (1988). There is also genuine concern that Samantha's schooling will suffer if she lives with Zak since Zak's mother does not seem concerned to ensure Samantha goes to school. Education is viewed as important (*May v May* (1986)) and the court will be unlikely to make a child arrangement order if there will be a detrimental effect on Samantha's education.

The court will also look at the likely effect on Samantha of any change in her circumstances. It is considered undesirable to uproot children, since disrupting the status quo is often detrimental to the child's welfare: *J v C* (1970). However, Samantha has only been at Zak's for one month; it can hardly be said to be disruptive to return her to her parents. It would seem that her parents ought to be able to provide greater stability of care than Zak's mother, who does not seem very concerned for Samantha's welfare.

Looking at Samantha's age, sex, background and any characteristics of hers which the court considers relevant, it would seem that 14-year-old girls often have difficulty with their parents, yet are still in need of parental guidance. The next consideration is the harm that Samantha has suffered, or is at risk of suffering. There is no suggestion that Samantha has been harmed or abused by her parents, and this is to be contrasted with the evidence of the under-age intercourse she is having with Zak that a residence order would facilitate and condone.

The capacity of Samantha's parents and of any other relevant person to meet her needs would also be an important factor in determining where Samantha should live. Janet and John have discharged their parental responsibility towards Samantha in the past, and there is no evidence of any undesirable conduct or failings on their part. However, Samantha cannot be allowed to fend for herself; yet the consequences of allowing her to live at Zak's home would appear to be exactly that. Zak's mother is unconcerned about

Samantha's welfare, and seems unlikely to make the positive contribution of alternative care in other cases. Zak is only 17, and it seems unlikely that he could promote Samantha's welfare.

Therefore, despite her wishes to live with Zak, the illegal nature of the sexual relationship and the apparent lack of concern for her welfare exhibited by Zak's mother mean it is extremely unlikely that Samantha would be able to obtain a child arrangement order permitting her to live there.

However, the issue of contraception is likely to be resolved in Samantha's favour. In *Gillick v Norfolk and Wisbech AHA* (1985) the House of Lords recognised that whilst the law prohibited sexual intercourse with girls under 16, many such girls did engage in unlawful intercourse. A girl of sufficient maturity to have a sexual relationship and to seek contraceptive advice and services ought to be able to protect herself against pregnancy. It would not be in Samantha's best interests to prevent her from using contraception, as this would only lead to an unwanted pregnancy, which is hardly in the interests of the welfare of a girl of 14. This would give a competent child the right to consent to medical treatment against her parents' wishes; however, it seems that the *Gillick* decision has its limitations, and a *Gillick* competent child cannot refuse medical treatment that his or her parents consent to: *Re M (Medical Treatment: Consent)* (1999).

There is no point in trying to use the inherent jurisdiction of the High Court to make Samantha a ward of court. In *Re CT* (1993), it was stressed that wardship is exceptional and should only be used where the **s 8** orders do not adequately cover the problem being experienced in relation to the child. The only possible justification for Samantha being warded would be if her parents wanted to prevent her association with Zak. It would have to be shown that this was an extremely undesirable relationship, which could not be dealt with by making a **s 8** order. If Samantha were to become a ward of court, then the court would have responsibility for her welfare and could deal not only with where she lived, but also provide continuous control and supervision to prevent undesirable relationships. Samantha's welfare would be the only consideration, but this is an extreme measure to take.

Common Pitfalls

❖ Remember to check that leave would be given for Samantha to apply for a **s 8** order before considering the substantive merits of the application.
❖ Use the correct test for the application for leave.

Aim Higher

Apply the welfare checklist appropriately and make good critical use of the relevant case law.

/ 134 Q&A Family Law

QUESTION 31

Nina and Rob had an on-off relationship for several years, during which time their daughter, Tara, now aged five, was born. Rob often goes away travelling and whilst he has always seen Tara when he is in the UK, he can be away for months at a time without seeing her. Rob missed Tara's birth and did not see her until she was six months old. When Tara was three years old, Nina and Rob decided to split up for good. Rob continued to see Tara whenever he was at home and had her to stay at his flat. Three months after Rob and Nina split up, Nina began a relationship with Brad. Rob was very jealous of Brad's relationship with Nina, and one night, after drinking heavily, he went to Nina's house and stabbed Brad to death. He was tried for murder, but convicted of manslaughter and sentenced to seven years' imprisonment.

Whilst Rob was on remand, Nina allowed Tara to visit her father on three occasions. Rob wants to continue to have a relationship with Tara and wants to have contact with her. Nina wants nothing more to do with Rob, and does not want him to have anything to do with her. Nina has also had several letters from Jean, Rob's mother, asking to see Tara.

▶ Advise Nina.

How to Read this Question

Nina needs advice on potential applications for child arrangement orders from Rob and from Jean. Before looking at the substantive merits of these applications, answers should consider whether Rob or Jean would need the leave of the court to apply.

Applying the Law

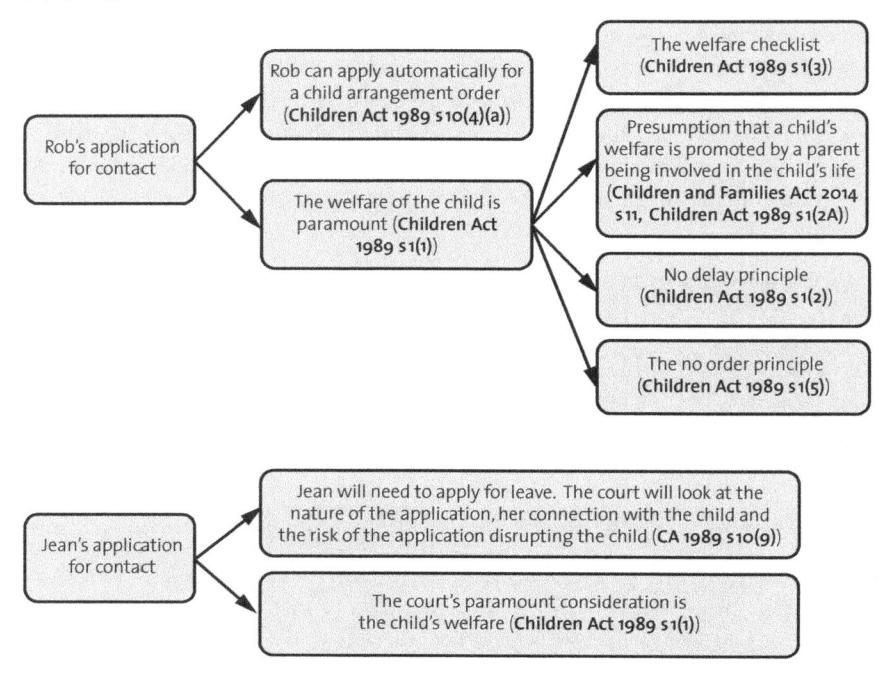

Rob's application for contact
- Rob can apply automatically for a child arrangement order (**Children Act 1989 s 10(4)(a)**)
- The welfare of the child is paramount (**Children Act 1989 s 1(1)**)
  - The welfare checklist (**Children Act 1989 s 1(3)**)
  - Presumption that a child's welfare is promoted by a parent being involved in the child's life (**Children and Families Act 2014 s 11, Children Act 1989 s 1(2A)**)
  - No delay principle (**Children Act 1989 s 1(2)**)
  - The no order principle (**Children Act 1989 s 1(5)**)

Jean's application for contact
- Jean will need to apply for leave. The court will look at the nature of the application, her connection with the child and the risk of the application disrupting the child (**CA 1989 s 10(9)**)
- The court's paramount consideration is the child's welfare (**Children Act 1989 s 1(1)**)

ANSWER

There are two issues for Nina – the relationship that Rob wishes to continue to have with his daughter and the contact that his mother, Jean, wishes to have with her grandchild. As both Rob and Jean want to have contact with Tara, the correct order for them to apply for is a child arrangement order (**Children Act 1989 s 8**), as this is the order that now controls where a child lives and with whom the child has contact (**Children and Families Act 2014 s 12, Children Act 1989 s 8**).

Rob, as the natural father of the child, can apply, as of right, for a **s 8** order including a child arrangement order (**s 10(4)**). When considering whether to grant an order, the court must bear in mind the non-interventionist policy: **s 1(5)**. This requires the court to make orders only where to do so is better than making no order at all. If no order is made in the present case, it is extremely unlikely that any agreement will be reached amicably between the parties. The circumstances of the breakdown in the relationship and subsequent homicide have ensured animosity and bitterness which are not conducive to the cooperation sought by the Act. There would obviously need to be a court-imposed settlement to this problem.

Clearly, any delay in resolving the problem would be prejudicial to the child's welfare, and the court is required to bear this in mind (**s 1(2)**), and draw up a timetable for the future conduct of the case to ensure that delay is kept to a minimum (**s 11**). This issue of contact between the child and her father concerns her upbringing and the **s 1(3)** checklist must be considered by the courts in making any contested **s 8** order. The paramount principle is that of the child's welfare (**s 1(1)**) but, in deciding how best to promote it, the court must have regard to the factors in **s 1(3)**.

Tara is aged five and will almost definitely remember her father, and may want to see him, since she will find it difficult to understand the enormity of what he did. As Rob has often been away, it may be, however, that Tara is used to not seeing her father and does not miss him or want to see him. Tara is considerably younger than the age at which the court tends to view the child's wishes as decisive; this is normally around the teenage years (*Stewart v Stewart* (1973)). She will have little awareness of the long-term consequences of her decisions, and so her views would be treated with caution. If she expressed a vehement opposition to visiting her father, the court would discount this if it were felt to be the result of pressure from Nina: *Re S (Infants)* (1967).

By examining the physical, emotional and educational needs of the children, the court usually recognises the desirability of maintaining or establishing contact with a natural parent: *Re H (Minors) (Access)* (1992). Rob is the natural parent of the child concerned, and in normal circumstances contact would be inevitable. There is, however, the difficulty caused by the crime he has committed. The courts are reluctant to expose children to persons of extreme depravity or criminality: *Scott v Scott* (1986). Rob has not been violent to Tara. It is arguable that the child's need for contact, especially Tara who had an established relationship with her father, outweighs any moral judgement on the behaviour of Rob. This is easier to sustain if Rob exhibits genuine remorse and regret for what has occurred. If, however, he is unrepentant, the court might be concerned that Tara will receive wrong messages about crime from her father, thereby doing her moral harm.

This issue of harm and the risk of it would count against Rob if there was any moral danger to Tara through contact, or any risk that she would be exposed to physical danger. Much will depend, therefore, on the attitude Rob has exhibited towards his crime, and possibly to Nina. It might not be in Tara's interests to have contact with her father if he is threatening and aggressive towards Nina. If Nina is deeply opposed to the idea of contact, and it can be shown that this causes her great distress, then the child's interest in seeing its natural parent may have to give way to its interests in maintaining a happy and healthy caring parent. Consequently, if contact is genuinely damaging to Nina's mental or physical health, then no order will be made: *Re B (A Minor) (Access)* (1992).

The **Children and Families Act 2014 s 11** has added a presumption of parental involvement to **s 1** of the **Children Act 1989**. Whilst Rob's parental involvement has not been steady or regular and he has committed a very violent offence, it is arguable that the benefits for Tara in maintaining some form of contact with her father outweigh the disadvantages. This is the case especially as that contact could take the form of indirect contact rather than specifying that Tara needs to visit her father in prison (**Children Act 1989 s 1(2B)**).

Regardless of the issue of contact with Rob, Nina must also deal with the issue of contact with Jean, Rob's mother and the child's grandmother. Jean is not entitled to apply for a **s 8** order as of right (**Children Act 1989 ss 10(4), 10(5)**); instead she must seek leave from the court (**s 10(9)**). In granting leave, the court will consider the factors in **s 10(9)**, namely the type of order being sought, the relationship between the applicant and child, and the risk of the application disrupting the child's life, thereby causing harm. Here, Jean would be seeking a child arrangement order which would enable her to have a relationship with her granddaughter. Whether leave would be granted would depend on the kind of relationship Jean had with Tara previously. If she had formed an integral part of her life, playing the role of grandmother, it is likely that she would be given leave. She would be seeking to reinforce an existing relationship and would not be seeking merely to interfere and disrupt.

If leave is granted, then the usual principles of non-intervention (**s 1(5)**), delay (**s 1(2)**) and welfare being paramount (**s 1(1)**) apply. The statutory checklist in **s 1(3)** would require the court to consider the child's wishes, but, as mentioned earlier, this will not carry much weight. The desirability of maintaining relationships with close blood relatives is an established principle, and it is difficult to see that it would be in the best interests of the child to be deprived of the love and affection of a grandmother because of the actions of her father. This assumes that Jean has played a part in Tara's life, and does not seek to disrupt or upset her. There does not seem to be risk of harm, and Jean's ability to care and cope with Tara might determine the kind of contact permitted. This could be by way of telephone calls, letters, visits or possibly even staying visits with her grandmother. Only if such contact could be demonstrated to be damaging to Nina's health, given the exceptional circumstances of the case, would contact be denied: *Re B (A Minor) (Access)* (1992).

QUESTION 32

Mike and Laura are getting divorced, but they are having difficulty making arrangements for their two children, Kate, aged 13, and Julia, aged six. Laura has set up home with Ian in his small house, which she admits will be cramped if both girls join her. Kate does not like Ian and is refusing to join her mother, complaining that Ian is bossy and makes her life a misery. Kate has a good relationship with Mike and wishes to stay with him. Mike is remaining in the former matrimonial home, having managed to raise enough cash by way of a mortgage to buy out Laura's share. Laura is unhappy with Kate being with Mike; she feels Kate is too young to make a decision and has been swayed by Mike's promises of a puppy if she stays with him.

Mike has agreed that Julia can live with Laura, as she is disabled and he would find it difficult to give her the care she needs. However, he is anxious to be able to see her each weekend and during the week if he can. Laura is opposed to this, claiming that it would be disruptive and she is keen that Julia looks on Ian as her new father. Mike has heard rumours that Laura is encouraging Julia to use Ian's surname instead of his.

▶ Advise Mike.

How to Read this Question

Mike wants advice on how to have Kate live with him and how to maintain contact with Julia. He also needs advice on Laura potentially changing Julia's name.

Applying the Law

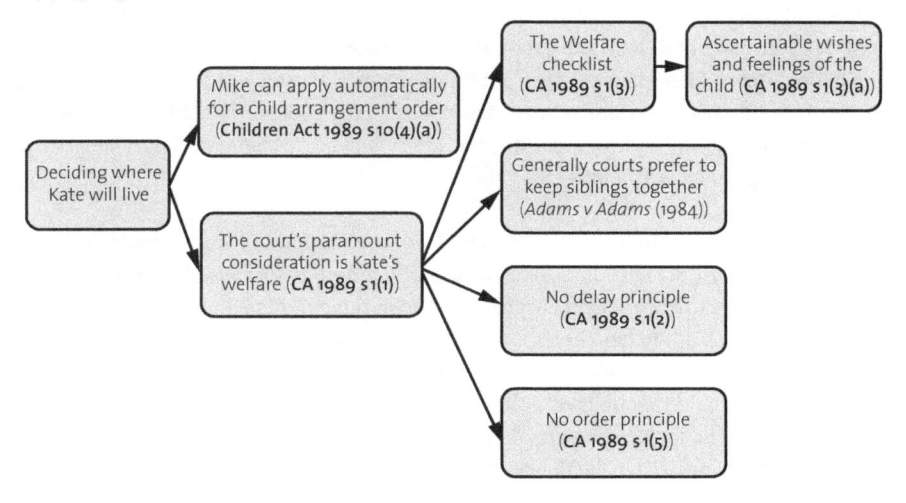

- Deciding where Kate will live
  - Mike can apply automatically for a child arrangement order (**Children Act 1989 s 10(4)(a)**)
    - The Welfare checklist (**CA 1989 s 1(3)**) → Ascertainable wishes and feelings of the child (**CA 1989 s 1(3)(a)**)
  - The court's paramount consideration is Kate's welfare (**CA 1989 s 1(1)**)
    - Generally courts prefer to keep siblings together (*Adams v Adams* (1984))
    - No delay principle (**CA 1989 s 1(2)**)
    - No order principle (**CA 1989 s 1(5)**)

Q&A Family Law

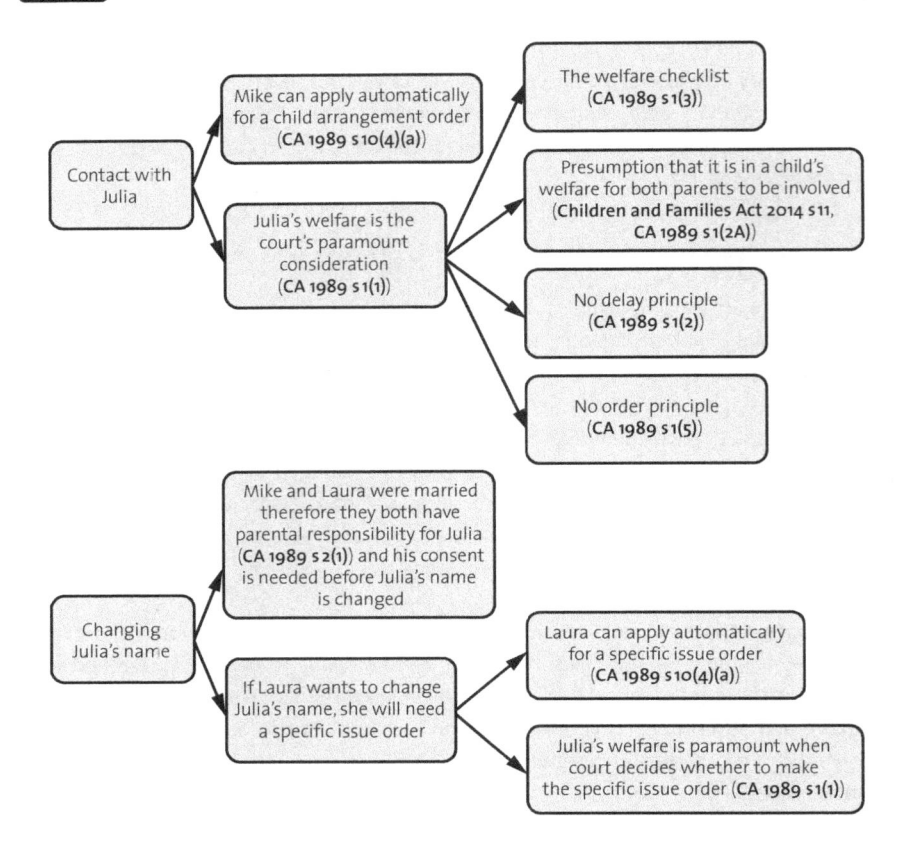

Contact with Julia
- Mike can apply automatically for a child arrangement order (CA 1989 s 10(4)(a))
- Julia's welfare is the court's paramount consideration (CA 1989 s 1(1))
  - The welfare checklist (CA 1989 s 1(3))
  - Presumption that it is in a child's welfare for both parents to be involved (Children and Families Act 2014 s 11, CA 1989 s 1(2A))
  - No delay principle (CA 1989 s 1(2))
  - No order principle (CA 1989 s 1(5))

Changing Julia's name
- Mike and Laura were married therefore they both have parental responsibility for Julia (CA 1989 s 2(1)) and his consent is needed before Julia's name is changed
- If Laura wants to change Julia's name, she will need a specific issue order
  - Laura can apply automatically for a specific issue order (CA 1989 s 10(4)(a))
  - Julia's welfare is paramount when court decides whether to make the specific issue order (CA 1989 s 1(1))

ANSWER

Since Mike and Laura were married, they both have parental responsibility for their children: **Children Act 1989 s 2(1)**. This is defined in **s 3(1)** as 'all the rights, duties, powers and responsibilities and authority which by law a parent of a child has in relation to the child and its property'. Both Mike and Laura will continue to have parental responsibility after divorce, as the **Children Act 1989** emphasises the continuity of parental care, and the emphasis is also on the obligation of the parent to meet the needs of the child, rather than the outdated concept of parental rights. Consequently, the important and paramount issue here is the welfare of the children (**s 1(1)**) rather than the wishes of the parties.

There are three issues that need to be resolved, namely, where Kate should live; the extent of Mike's contact with Julia; and the use of a different surname for Julia. The **Children Act 1989** tries to encourage consensus between the parents where possible, and the non-interventionist approach is enshrined in the Act: **s 1(5)**. On divorce, the parties are required to file a statement of arrangements for the children, detailing the measures that have been agreed and the areas of disagreement. If the parties have reached agreement there will be no need for the court to intervene, but if, as here, there are unresolved issues then the court will need to make the decision as to what is best for the children.

Private Law Disputes Relating to Children

The court has jurisdiction on divorce to make one or more of the **s 8** orders, namely a child arrangement; a prohibited steps order; and a specific issue order. The first issue concerns where Kate should live and this should be dealt with by way of a child arrangement order. Mike would be able to apply for a child arrangement order as of right as he is her father (**Children Act 1989 s 10(4)**). Delay is usually prejudicial to the welfare of the child (**s 1(2)**) and therefore it is necessary for the court to draw up a timetable for the conduct of the case (**s 11**) in order to minimise delay.

In determining where Kate should live, the court will have regard to the **s 1(3)** checklist, bearing in mind that Kate's welfare is the paramount consideration: **s 1(1)**. Kate's parents cannot agree where she should live and Kate herself has exhibited a preference for staying with her father, Mike. Kate is aged 13, an age at which her wishes are likely to be given weight by the courts: *Stewart v Stewart* (1973). Assuming Kate is reasonably intelligent and articulate, she is likely, at 13, to appreciate the long-term consequences of her decision. She has a good rapport with her father, but does not have a good relationship with Ian. There seems to be genuine difficulty, given Ian's forceful behaviour, and it may be argued that the attitude displayed by Ian and Laura in relation to Kate's sister, Julia, illustrates a somewhat heavy-handed attempt to replace Mike in the children's affections. This could be upsetting for Kate. Laura's view that Kate is too young to decide would probably not be shared by the court, and in *Marsh v Marsh* (1977) a child of 12 was able to state her preference.[3]

The only concern might be that Mike's promise of a puppy might be viewed as a bribe or pressure (*Re S (Infants)* (1967)), but given Kate's age and prior good relationship with her father, it is unlikely that this influenced her decision. Kate's physical, emotional and educational needs must be considered (**Children Act 1989 s 1(3)(b)**), and it is usual for teenage girls to live with their mother, who are often better equipped to deal with the problems of puberty: *Re W (A Minor)* (1983). On the other hand, in *Re H (A Minor)* (1980), this view was not given great weight by the Court of Appeal, who recognised that in many cases a father may be in a position to provide better care for a particular child than its mother. Kate has a better rapport with her father, and her relationship with her mother may be very strained if forced to live there. Both Mike and Laura can provide Kate with a home, although Mike's position is more comfortable than Laura's cramped house. Whilst material advantages get little weight (*Stephenson v Stephenson* (1985)), it does seem that the situation for Kate would be better if she lived with her father. The usual position of keeping siblings together for the mutual support they give each other (*Adams v Adams* (1984)) might not apply so strongly here, given the large age gap between the children, and the fact that Julia is disabled may mean that the needs of the individual girls should be considered separately (*B-T v B-T* (1990)).

At present, Kate has been staying with her father, and the court will consider the effect of changing this (**Children Act 1989 s 1(3)(c)**). There is generally a reluctance to disturb the established status quo (*J v C* (1970)) but, in this case, it would be difficult to argue that Kate's presence with Mike is so established that it cannot be varied (*Allington v Allington*

---

3 Applying the welfare checklist can be a delicate balancing exercise. Previous case law will give you some idea of how courts have interpreted and weighed the various factors in the past.

(1985)), especially since Laura has maintained contact. There is no suggestion that Kate would be at risk of harm with either parent (**Children Act 1989 s1(3)(e)**), and they both seem to have been loving and capable parents (**Children Act 1989 s1(3)(f)**). Nevertheless, Kate has a better relationship with her father, and her antagonism towards Ian may be difficult to overcome. It would seem, therefore, that Kate's welfare would best be served by making a child arrangement order that Kate should live with Mike and that she should have generous contact with Laura and Julia.

The situation concerning Julia raises two controversial issues, that of contact and change of surname. The parties are agreed that Julia should reside with Laura; however, the degree of contact is not agreed and so the court will need to consider making a child arrangement order under **s8**. Mike, as a parent, can apply as of right (**s10(4)**) and the problem will be resolved by the use of the **s1(3)** checklist to ascertain what is best for Julia since her welfare is paramount (**s1(1)**).

Julia is only six years old, and the nature and extent of her disability are unknown. Not a lot of weight would be attached to her wishes, as given her age she is unlikely to have the understanding of the long-term implications of a decision: *Stewart v Stewart* (1973). However, it is generally recognised that it is in the interests of her emotional needs to have contact with her natural parent: *Re H (Minors) (Access)* (1992) and parental involvement is presumed to be in a child's welfare (**Children and Families Act 2014 s11, Children Act 1989 s1(2A)**). Mike has been a good father to Julia and contact would only be denied if it were damaging to Julia. There is no suggestion that contact would be harmful to Julia (**Children Act 1989 s1(3)(e)**). The court would not be sympathetic to Laura's desire to replace Mike with Ian as Julia's father; this is generally viewed as being confusing and upsetting for a child. Julia has had a relationship with Mike for the past six years, and it would be in her interests for this to be maintained. Contact by telephone or letter may be difficult, and it seems likely that Mike will be allowed to visit Julia. Whether it will be practicable for him to take her out or have her stay with him will depend on the extent of her disability. It is desirable for there to be generous contact between parent and child but it may be necessary to restrict Mike's contact with Julia to certain periods. This provides a degree of certainty for Laura and Ian, who are trying to build a family life together, without being interrupted at unpredictable times by Mike wishing to see Julia. It would also enable Julia to be better prepared, and so some kind of formalised contact may be ordered.

The problem of Julia's surname has caused Mike some concern since Laura seems to want Julia to adopt Ian's surname. It is not possible to change a child's surname without permission from all those with parental responsibility or with leave from the court: **s13(1)(b)**. Mike has parental responsibility for Julia (**Children Act 1989 s2(1)**) and is refusing the name change, therefore Julia would need to apply for a specific issue order for the court to allow the name change (**Children Act 1989 s8**). Julia has a right to apply for a specific issue order (**Children Act 1989 s10(4)**) and the court will only allow the name change if it is in Julia's welfare (**Children Act 1989 s1(1)**). Courts recognise the significance of a child's name (*Dawson v Wearmouth* (1999)) and it is unlikely that the court would order a change of surname, as it usually is in the child's interests to preserve this link with her father: *W v A* (1981).

QUESTION 33

'Neither parent should be encouraged or permitted to think that the more intransigent, the more unreasonable, the more obdurate and the more uncooperative they are, the more likely they are to get their own way.' *Re O (Contact: Imposition of Conditions)* (1995) 2 FLR 124 at pp. 129–130.

▶ Discuss how successfully English courts have dealt with the difficulty of the obstructive parent.

How to Read this Question

The question is about whether and how parents seek to frustrate court orders and what measure English law has adapted to deal with this. It is also important to consider the effectiveness of these provisions.

Applying the Law

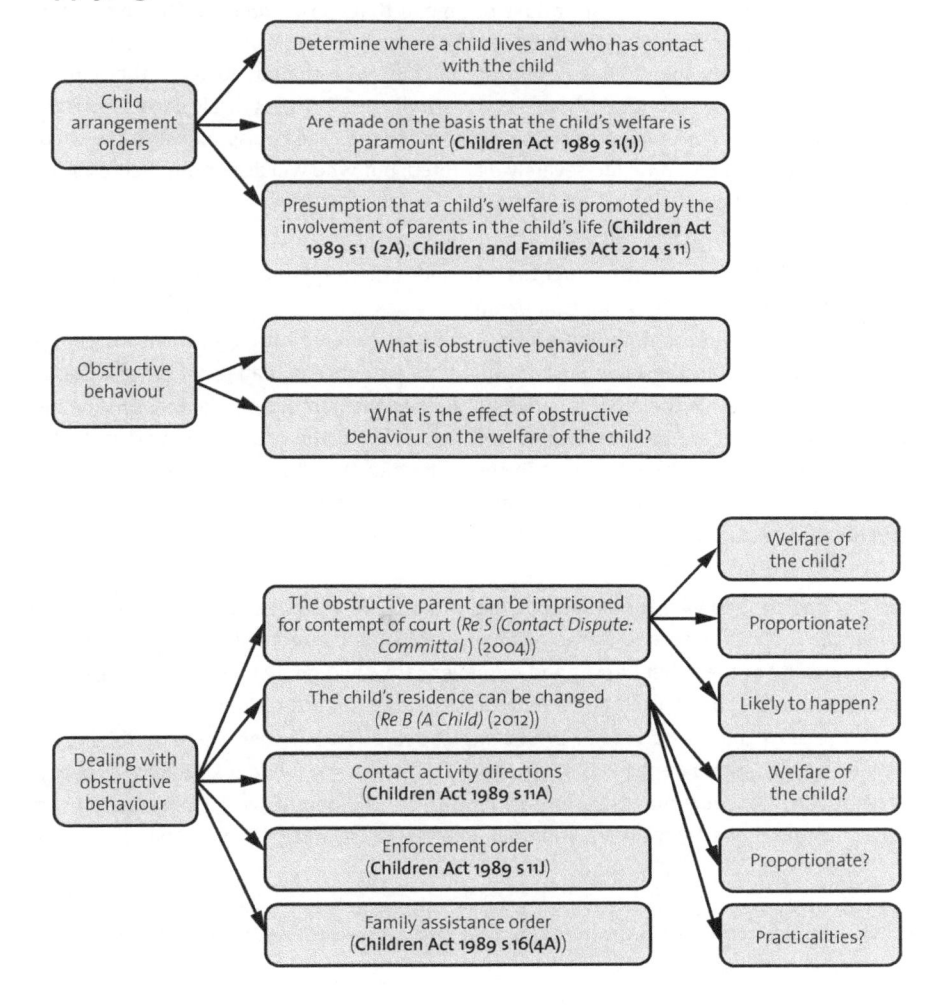

Child arrangement orders
- Determine where a child lives and who has contact with the child
- Are made on the basis that the child's welfare is paramount (**Children Act 1989 s1(1)**)
- Presumption that a child's welfare is promoted by the involvement of parents in the child's life (**Children Act 1989 s1 (2A), Children and Families Act 2014 s11**)

Obstructive behaviour
- What is obstructive behaviour?
- What is the effect of obstructive behaviour on the welfare of the child?

Dealing with obstructive behaviour
- The obstructive parent can be imprisoned for contempt of court (*Re S (Contact Dispute: Committal)* (2004)) → Welfare of the child? / Proportionate?
- The child's residence can be changed (*Re B (A Child)* (2012)) → Likely to happen?
- Contact activity directions (**Children Act 1989 s 11A**) → Welfare of the child?
- Enforcement order (**Children Act 1989 s 11J**) → Proportionate?
- Family assistance order (**Children Act 1989 s 16(4A)**) → Practicalities?

ANSWER

Private law child cases often take place against a background of family tensions and separations. It is perhaps unsurprising therefore that one of the main difficulties faced by the courts is that of the hostile and obstructive parent. **Section 8** orders are supposed to be based on the child's welfare (**Children Act 1989 s 1(1)**); nevertheless, the hostility of the resident parent to an order can sometimes be a factor. If a parent is very disturbed by the making of an order, this could affect their ability to care for the child and may be an argument against making the order. A parent may deliberately or subconsciously transmit their hostility to the child. If a child, especially an older child, is very reluctant to see the parent, the court may find it very difficult to order him or her to do so.[4]

Despite this, courts are clear that they will not allow the hostility of one parent to restrict the contact of another. This means that in some cases, **s 8** orders will be made despite the hostility of a parent; nevertheless, it does not mean that these orders will always be followed and this raises another issue: that of the enforcement of **s 8** orders. One option is to charge the obstructive parent with contempt of court with the possibility of that parent being imprisoned (*Re S (Contact Dispute: Committal)* (2004)). This is rarely used. Imprisoning the parent with care, whilst undoubtedly hard towards them, also punishes the child, who not only has their home life severely disrupted, but who will also often feel responsible for that punishment.

Another possibility is to vary the order to try to find something that the obstructive parent might find acceptable. For example, a parent may obstruct direct, unsupervised contact, but may be happy to promote indirect or supervised contact. Although this can seem a pragmatic way of reaching a compromise that both parents can manage, it is not without problems. Effectively, if the order is varied because of one parent's opposition, this means that the child's welfare has been subverted to pander to the obstructive parent. If the court decided that direct contact was in the welfare of the child, this is what should be promoted, not the compromise of indirect contact. Furthermore, this option in a way rewards the obstructive parent for their behaviour.

Another option is to vary the order, but this time to replace direct contact with shared residence. The idea here is to prevent one parent losing contact with the child because of the hostility of the other parent and to prevent the child being alienated against that parent. Although courts used to be reluctant to order shared residence, more recently they have seen them as a way of promoting cooperation between the parents and of preventing a hostile parent from obstructing contact (*A v A (Shared Residence)* (2004)). Alternatively, the court may transfer residence from the parent who is obstructing the contact to the other parent (*V v V (Contact: Implacable Hostility)* (2004)). The advantage

---

4   This question is about hostility and the making of **s 8** orders. It should focus on that rather than just discussing **s 8** orders in general.

of this approach is that it does potentially allow the child to maintain and develop a relationship with both parents. However, it cannot be an answer in every case. There may be situations where due to the distance that the parents live from each other, sharing or transferring residence is not an option because of the disruption that it will involve to the child. There may also be times where a parent desperately wants direct contact with a child but is not able or willing to have residence for the child and there may be situations where it is in the child's welfare to have contact with a parent, but not to live with that parent.

In recent years, fathers' rights groups have promoted the idea that mothers frequently obstruct contact and that the courts are ill-equipped or unwilling to deal with it. It is perhaps unsurprising therefore that the law in this area has recently been developed by the **Children and Adoption Act 2006**, which has introduced some measures into the **Children Act 1989** to promote and enforce contact. These include contact activity directions (**Children Act 1989 s11A**), checking that contract is followed through monitoring (**Children Act 1989 s11H**) and then in the case of non-compliance issuing warning notices (**Children Act 1989 s11I**) and then enforcement measures (**Children Act 1989 s11O**). The difficulty with these measures is that they are unlikely to please anyone. Parents denied access will likely prefer a more robust approach, whilst others will regret the punitive approach adopted by the Act and the fact that this reform has been based on the assumption that objection to contact and refusal to follow court orders are always motivated purely by hostility and never by the child's welfare.

QUESTION 34

Victoria and Albert are married and are both aged 45; they have three children, Edward, aged 14, Alice, aged 10, and Eugenie, aged two. The couple have recently separated, after Eugenie made certain remarks that Victoria construed as being allegations of sexual abuse against Albert. Albert has vigorously denied that anything improper occurred between himself and Eugenie, and states that Victoria was just looking for an excuse to leave him. Victoria has since moved into a large house owned by Alexandra, her lesbian lover, taking the children with her. Victoria wants the children to live with her, and does not want them to see Albert, whereas Albert is unhappy about the children being with Victoria and Alexandra.

▸ Advise Victoria on what approach the court would take concerning the children, if she were to divorce Albert.

How to Read this Question
The issues for Victoria are whether the court would agree to the children living with her and Alexandra and whether they would allow Albert to have contact with the children.

Applying the Law

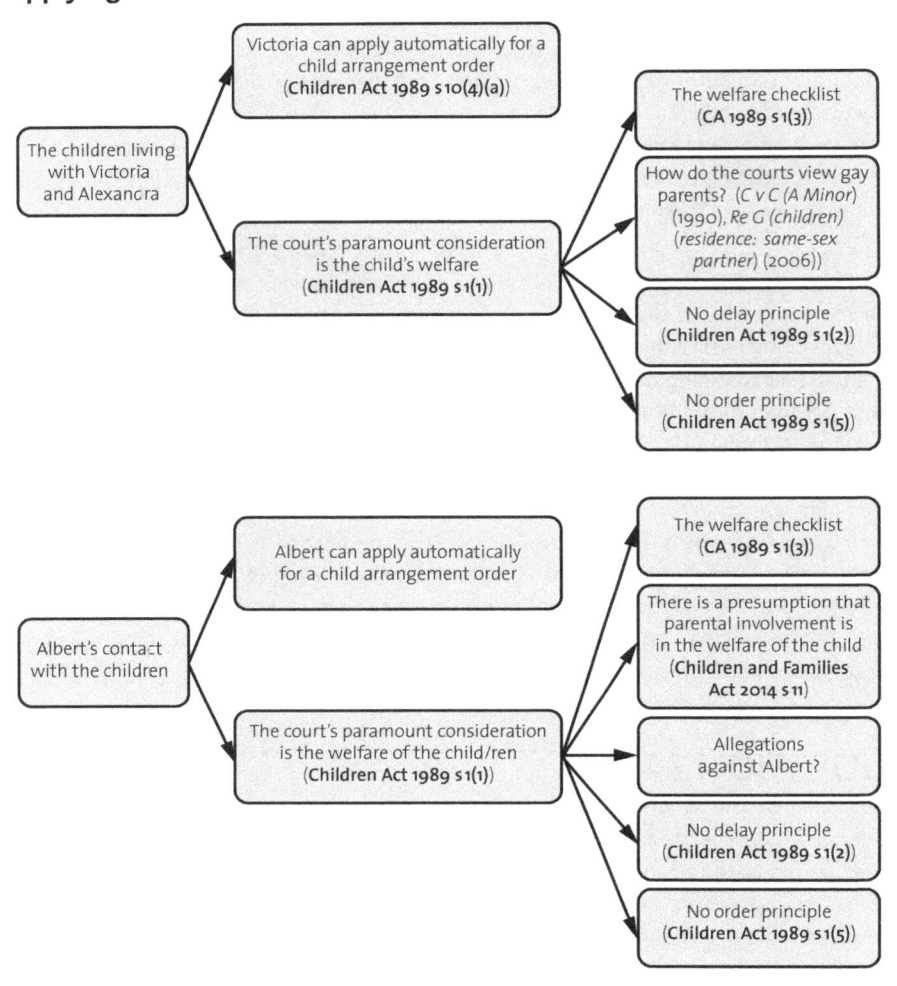

The children living with Victoria and Alexandra
- Victoria can apply automatically for a child arrangement order (**Children Act 1989 s 10(4)(a)**)
- The court's paramount consideration is the child's welfare (**Children Act 1989 s 1(1)**)
  - The welfare checklist (**CA 1989 s 1(3)**)
  - How do the courts view gay parents? (*C v C (A Minor)* (1990), *Re G (children) (residence: same-sex partner)* (2006))
  - No delay principle (**Children Act 1989 s 1(2)**)
  - No order principle (**Children Act 1989 s 1(5)**)

Albert's contact with the children
- Albert can apply automatically for a child arrangement order
- The court's paramount consideration is the welfare of the child/ren (**Children Act 1989 s 1(1)**)
  - The welfare checklist (**CA 1989 s 1(3)**)
  - There is a presumption that parental involvement is in the welfare of the child (**Children and Families Act 2014 s 11**)
  - Allegations against Albert?
  - No delay principle (**Children Act 1989 s 1(2)**)
  - No order principle (**Children Act 1989 s 1(5)**)

ANSWER

Victoria and Albert cannot agree where their children should live after their divorce. As Victoria wants the children to live with her she should apply for a child arrangement order. This **s 8** order controls where a child lives and who the child has contact with. As Victoria is the children's mother, she has an automatic right to apply under the **Children Act 1989 s 10(4)**. The court will decide whether to make a child arrangement order based on the children's welfare (**Children Act 1989 s 1(1)**) and will use the welfare checklist to decide what is in the children's welfare (**Children Act 1989 s 1(3)**).

The court will only intervene if absolutely necessary, and there is a non-interventionist policy (**s 1(5)**) of only making a **s 8** order if this would be better than not making one. Since Victoria and Albert are implacably opposed to each other's proposals, an order will be necessary. To avoid delay, which is viewed as prejudicial to the welfare of the child (**s1(2)**), once an application has been made for a **s8** order the court will lay down a timetable for the future stages of the case: **s11**.

In deciding whether to make a child arrangement order, paramount importance is given to the child's welfare (**s1(1)**), not the wishes of the parents, and the court will apply the statutory checklist in **s1(3)**. This contains various factors, namely, the ascertainable wishes and feelings of the child; its emotional, physical and educational needs; the likely effect of any change in circumstances; the age, sex, background and other relevant characteristics; the risk of harm; and the capability of the parents and any other relevant person to meet the child's needs.

In the present case, the two older children will be able to articulate their views, whereas Eugenie, at two, will have little or no understanding of what is happening. Edward, at 14, is of the age at which a great deal of weight would be attached to his views. He is likely to be '*Gillick* competent' in the sense that he has the intelligence and maturity to make decisions with an awareness of the long-term consequences: *Stewart v Stewart* (1973). Alice is 10 and, whilst her views will be considered, the weight accorded them will depend on her intelligence and maturity. In *Marsh v Marsh* (1977) the views of a 12-year-old and a nine-year-old were adhered to, and so Alice's views may well be taken into account. On the facts, nothing is mentioned as to the views of either child but, given the sensitive nature of Victoria's relationship with Alexandra, the ability of the children to accept this and not be unduly embarrassed by it will be important.

Looking at the physical, emotional and education needs of the children, together with their age, sex, background and other relevant characteristics, there are arguments both for and against Victoria. Eugenie is a young child, and there is a tendency to view young children as being better cared for by their mother: *Greer v Greer* (1974). Likewise, for older girls it might be argued that the problems of puberty are best dealt with by the mother: *Re W (A Minor)* (1983). Whereas for older boys, there is a somewhat weaker argument that they would be better served by being with their father, who can provide a role model for them in their adolescence: *W v W and C* (1968). However, these are now recognised as being generalisations, rather than presumptions, by the Court of Appeal in *Re H (A Minor)* (1990). The crucial question will be to look at the child's needs and see which parent can best meet those needs. There would need to be pressing arguments that Victoria's ability to provide care for her children should be overridden, and the main argument of Albert will be that Victoria's lesbianism prevents her from adequately caring for the children. In the past, this might have prevented the children from living with their mother, but now this is not necessarily so. However, if Albert was prepared to offer the children a home, then the court would look at the nature of the relationship. In *C v C (A Minor)* (1991), the court stressed that lesbianism was not an automatic disqualification of a mother from looking after her children. It is, however, an unusual background, but a sensitive, loving lesbian relationship can often be a more satisfactory environment for a child than a less sensitive or loving heterosexual relationship. More recently, the courts' view has changed and the fact that a parent is in a homosexual or lesbian relationship is not likely to count against them (*Re G (children) (residence: same-sex partner)* (2006).

There have been cases where mothers such as Victoria have been given residence, since they were in a better position to provide continuity of care for their children (*Re K* (1988)), whereas the father who had to work could not. The living conditions of both Albert and Victoria seem adequate, and the court is not overly concerned by material advantage: *Stephenson v Stephenson* (1985). However, it is usually desirable to keep brothers and sisters together (*Adams v Adams* (1984)) because of the mutual support they derive from each other. The two older children in the present case are reasonably close in age and their interests could better be served by being together.

The possible effect of change is unlikely to be influential here, as the current living arrangements are recently arrived at (*Allington v Allington* (1985)), so there is really no status quo to disrupt. It would be necessary to consider whether there is any risk of harm from Albert. There are the allegations supposedly made by Eugenie, which have been strongly denied. Allegations of child abuse are very easily made, and a chance remark by a child can easily be misconstrued. There does not seem to be any evidence to support Victoria's allegation, and it might be difficult to convince the court that Albert was a risk to the children. Even if there had been sexual abuse, there is no absolute rule prohibiting contact between a child and the abusing parent (*H v H* (1989)); much will depend on the circumstances of the case. Without wanting to trivialise sexual abuse of children, if the assault were not of the most serious nature and there was no lasting harm and genuine regret by the abuser, then the child may suffer more from a cessation of contact with the parent. Supervised contact may be in the child's best interests.

Looking at the ability of the parents to meet the children's needs, it seems that Victoria is more able to provide the day-to-day care that is usually desirable, and if Alexandra is a caring partner, this will improve her case, and consequently she may well obtain a residence order. It is nevertheless considered to be in a child's best interests to maintain contact with its father (*Re B (Minor) (Access)* (1984)), and there would need to be pressing reasons for terminating such contact. There is no evidence that Albert has harmed Alice or Edward and the evidence of harm to Eugenie is not strong. Consequently, there is likely to be a contact order enabling the children to see their father, unless they do not wish to do so. Even then, the court would be mindful of the possibility that they had been pressurised by Victoria.

QUESTION 35

Ellen and Faye moved in together in 2009. Later that year, Faye became pregnant. The child was conceived using sperm from a male friend, Graeme. In 2010, Faye gave birth to a son, Henry. Ellen and Faye decided that Henry would have Ellen's surname. Faye took a year off on maternity leave. After that she went back to work for three days a week. Ellen rearranged her work hours and looked after Henry for one day and the remaining day Henry went to a childminder.

Private Law Disputes Relating to Children

Last year the relationship between Ellen and Faye broke down and Ellen moved out. Ellen has moved one hour's drive away. She has secured a very good work promotion and financially is very stable. Since the split, Ellen has been travelling back to look after Henry during the week. She has also tried to visit Henry during the weekend, but Faye has made this difficult. Ellen often finds that Faye will not open the door when she arrives or that Faye and Henry will be out.

Ellen has now decided that she would like Henry to live with her. She feels that this is the only way that she can maintain a good relationship with Henry. She also feels that she will be better able to give Henry a good childhood. She has said that if Henry lives with her she will be able to send him to a local fee-paying school. Faye is clear that she wants Henry to stay living with her. She feels that the split between her and Ellen is too recent and too painful and at the moment it would be too upsetting for both her and Henry for him to go and stay with Ellen. She also wants to change Henry's surname so that he now has her surname.

- (a) Advise Faye on what will happen if Ellen applies to court for Henry to live with her.
- (b) Advise Faye on changing Henry's surname.

How to Read this Question

This question is about private law arrangements for a child after the relationship between his mother and her female partner break down.

Applying the Law

ELLEN APPLYING TO COURT FOR HENRY TO LIVE WITH HER

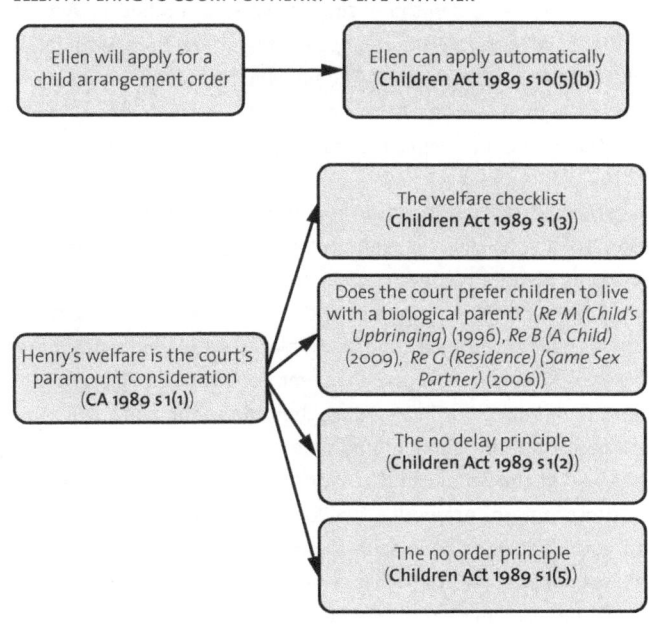

Ellen will apply for a child arrangement order → Ellen can apply automatically (**Children Act 1989 s 10(5)(b)**)

Henry's welfare is the court's paramount consideration (**CA 1989 s 1(1)**)
- The welfare checklist (**Children Act 1989 s 1(3)**)
- Does the court prefer children to live with a biological parent? (*Re M (Child's Upbringing)* (1996), *Re B (A Child)* (2009), *Re G (Residence) (Same Sex Partner)* (2006))
- The no delay principle (**Children Act 1989 s 1(2)**)
- The no order principle (**Children Act 1989 s 1(5)**)

CHANGING HENRY'S SURNAME

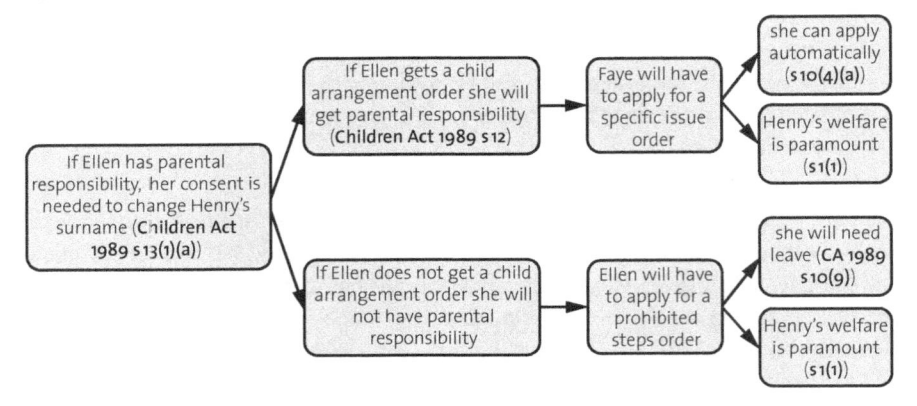

```
If Ellen has parental          If Ellen gets a child            Faye will have        she can apply
responsibility, her consent is arrangement order she will       to apply for a        automatically
needed to change Henry's       get parental responsibility      specific issue        (s 10(4)(a))
surname (Children Act          (Children Act 1989 s 12)         order
1989 s 13(1)(a))                                                                      Henry's welfare
                                                                                      is paramount
                                                                                      (s 1(1))

                               If Ellen does not get a child    Ellen will have       she will need
                               arrangement order she will       to apply for a        leave (CA 1989
                               not have parental                prohibited            s 10(9))
                               responsibility                   steps order
                                                                                      Henry's welfare
                                                                                      is paramount
                                                                                      (s 1(1))
```

ANSWER

Faye is Henry's mother and has parental responsibility for him (**Children Act 1989 s 2(2)**). Faye wants advice because her ex-partner, Ellen, wants to apply to have Henry live with her and because Faye wants to change Henry's name from Ellen's surname to her own surname. These two issues, where Henry should live and his surname, will be looked at in turn.

The child arrangement order (**Children Act 1989 s 8, Children and Families Act 2014 s 12**) can be used to determine where a child should live. Ellen will need to apply for a child arrangement order for Henry to live with her. Ellen has an automatic right to apply for a child arrangement order as Henry has lived with her since he was born (**Children Act 1989 s 10(5)**). The facts suggest that Faye is opposed to Henry spending much time with her and therefore it is very unlikely that Faye would agree to Ellen having Henry live with her, or to Ellen and Faye sharing residence; therefore this is a case where for Henry to live with Ellen a court order is needed and the no order principle is satisfied (**Children Act 1989 s 1(5)**).

The court will decide whether to make a child arrangement order based on Henry's welfare (**Children Act 1989 s 1(1)**) and will use the welfare checklist (**Children Act 1989 s 1(3)**) to determine what is in Henry's welfare. One issue in this case is that whilst Faye is Henry's biological mother, Ellen is not Henry's parent and does not have a biological link with him. Traditionally, courts have favoured a child being placed with a biological parent (*Re R (Child's Upbringing)* (1996)). The benefit to the child emotionally of being cared for by a birth parent and knowing their background, including their racial and cultural identity, outweighed other advantages that the child might gain through being cared for by someone other than a parent. On the other hand, it worth noting that the **Children Act 1989** does not contain a presumption in favour of children living with their biological parents, and more recent court decisions have seen a more nuanced approach. In *Re G (Children) (residence: same sex partner)* (2006) the House of Lords awarded residence to a child's biological mother over her lesbian ex-partner and stressed that it would usually be right for a child to be raised by a natural parent over a non-parent; however, the court in *Re G* did not find that there was a presumption in favour of natural parents. Furthermore, in *Re B (A child)* (2009) the Supreme Court awarded residence to a child's grandparents in preference to the child's father. The court in *Re B* were clear that there was no presumption in favour of natural parents and that it was the child's welfare that was crucial. This idea that a court would not necessarily favour a natural parent was also applied by the Court of Appeal in *Re E-R (A child)* (2015).

Looking then at Ellen's application, the fact that she is not the biological parent will not, by itself, prove fatal to her claim to have Henry live with her. More problematic for Ellen is the fact that Faye has been Henry's primary carer. A court is likely to be nervous of disrupting Henry by disturbing the status quo (**Children Act 1989 s1(3)(c)**) and there is nothing on the facts to suggest that Faye is not capable of responding to Henry's needs (**Children Act 1989 s1(3)(f)**) or that Henry is at risk of harm being cared for by Faye (**Children Act 1989 s1(3)(e)**).

On the other hand, Ellen has played an important role in Henry's life. Whilst not having a biological link to Henry, she has played a parental role, and she does look after him one day a week. It seems from the facts that his emotional and physical needs would also be supported with Ellen (**Children Act 1989 s1(3)(b)**) and that she too is capable of meeting his needs (**Children Act 1989 s1(3)(f)**). What is perhaps a little concerning in this scenario is that Faye is perhaps trying to limit Ellen's contact with Henry. It is possible for courts to change where a child lives if that is the only way in which the child is able to have contact. At the moment, there does not seem to be a need for this as Ellen is still seeing Henry once a week.

Financially Ellen is well off and she has said that if Henry were to live with her she would be able to educate him privately. Although the court will consider a child's material and educational needs (**Children Act 1989 s1(3)(b)**), the fact that Ellen has promised to educate Henry privately is unlikely to be significant.

On balance, it is unlikely that Ellen would succeed in getting a child arrangement order stating that Henry should live with her. Nevertheless, child arrangement orders can also be used to ensure that the child has contact with a named individual and it is possible that the court might make a child arrangement order to protect the contact between Henry and Ellen.

At the moment, Henry has Ellen's surname. Faye wants to change his surname so that Henry has Faye's surname. Under the **Children Act 1989 s13(1)(a)** everyone with parental responsibility needs to consent to a name change. As Faye is Henry's mother, she automatically has parental responsibility (**Children Act 1989 s2(2)**). Unless, Ellen has been able to obtain a child arrangement order stating that Henry is to live with her and therefore been give parental responsibility (**Children Act 1989 s12**), Ellen will not have parental responsibility. If, and it is unlikely, Ellen has parental responsibility, Faye will need a specific issue order to change Henry's surname. If Ellen does not have parental responsibility, she can only prevent Faye changing Henry's surname by obtaining a prohibited steps order.

Faye will be able to apply for a specific issue order automatically as she is Henry's mother (**Children Act 1989 s10(4)(a)**). Conversely, if Ellen applies for a prohibited steps order she will need the leave of the court; however, given her close connection with Henry, it is very probable that the test in the **Children Act 1989 s10(9)** will be satisfied and she will be given leave. The court will only allow Henry's name to be changed if it is in his welfare (**Children Act 1989 s1(1)**). It is recognised that a child's name is an important part of his identity (*Dawson v Wearmouth* (1999)). In Henry's case, it is unlikely that Faye would be able to change Henry's surname. Whilst Ellen is not Henry's biological mother, she has played an important parenting role and having her name recognises this and provides a link between Henry and Ellen. Furthermore, Henry was born in 2010. He will know his name and consider that to be who he is. Changing his name would perhaps be upsetting.

In conclusion, therefore, Ellen's application for a child arrangement order to have Henry live with her is likely to be unsuccessful. Faye, as the only person with parental responsibility, can change Henry's surname, but this can be prevented if Ellen obtains a prohibited steps order and it is probable that Ellen would be given leave to apply for a prohibited steps order and that the order would be made.

9 Children and the Local Authority

INTRODUCTION

Under the **Children Act 1989**, the local authority has duties to promote the welfare of children in their area. This may involve providing services for children in need or applying for compulsory court orders to protect these children from harm.

Checklist

Students need to understand and be able to apply the law on the following:

- the background to the **Children Act 1989** and how this has influenced the no order principle (**Children Act 1989 s 1(5)**);
- the idea of partnership and working together in the **Children Act 1989** and the **Children Act 2004**;
- the use of the welfare principle (**Children Act 1989 s 1(1)**) and welfare checklist in child protection (**Children Act 1989 s 1(5)**);
- voluntary accommodation under the **Children Act 1989 s 20**, *R (on the Application of G) v Southwark London Borough Council* (2009);
- the provision of services to children in need under the **Children Act 1989 Part III**. How is child in need defined? (**Children Act 1989 s 17(10)**);
- the duty to investigate a reasonable suspicion that a child currently suffering or is likely to suffer significant harm in the **Children Act 1989 s 47**;
- the duty to investigate child abuse in a private law case under the **Children Act 1989 s 37**;
- what the grounds are for obtaining a child assessment order (**Children Act 1989 s 43(1)**) and what effect that order has (**Children Act 1989 s 43(7)**);
- the grounds for applying for an emergency protection order, when any person can apply (**Children Act 1989 s 44(1)(a)**) and when the local authority can apply (**Children Act 1989 s 44(1)(b)**);
- the effects of the emergency protection order (**Children Act 1989 s 44(4)**), including parental responsibility (**Children Act 1989 s 44(4)(c)**) and the exclusion order under the **Children Act 1989 s 44A**;
- applying for an emergency protection order with and without notice;
- when a police protection order can be obtained and what effect it has (**Children Act 1989 s 46**);

- the effects of a care order (**Children Act 1989 s 33**) including parental responsibility (**Children Act 1989 s 33(3)**), the effects of a supervision order (**Children Act 1989 s 35**) and the choice between a care order or a supervision order (*Re O (Care or Supervision Order)* (1996), *Re V (Care Order or Supervision Order)* (1996));
- the threshold criteria in the **Children Act 1989 s 31**. What is meant by significant harm? (**Children Act 1989 s 31(9)**, *Humberside CC v B* (1993), *Re MA (Care Threshold)* (2009));
- when does the harm occur? (*Re M (A minor) (Care Order: Threshold Conditions)* (1994));
- what evidence is needed? (*Re H (Minors) (Sexual Abuse: Standard of Proof)* (1996), *Re B (Minors) (Sexual abuse: Standard of Proof)* (2008)). How is that evidence gathered? (*Z-O'C (children)* (2014));
- the harm has to be due to the care given or due to the child being beyond parental control (*Re L (Children)* (2006)). What if it is not clear who has harmed the child? (*Lancashire CC v B* (2000), *Re O and N (Children) (Non-accidental injury)* (2003), *Re S-B (Children)* (2009), *Re J (Care Proceedings: Past Possible Perpetrators in a New Family Unit)* (2013));
- when interim care orders are available and what the effects of an interim care order are (**Children Act 1989 s 38**). The use of an exclusion order under the **Children Act 1989 s 38A**;
- contact with a child in care (**Children Act 1989 s 34**) and when that contact can be refused (**Children Act 1989 s 34(6)**).

QUESTION 36

Harry and Isobel have two children, Jessica, aged 12, and Jack, aged 14. The local authority has received letters from the children's school, expressing concern over the wellbeing of the children. Jack is an unruly child and does not respond to discipline at school. He frequently does not attend school, and is making poor progress in his studies. The school is also concerned at reports that Jack spends time in the local shopping centre in the company of much older youths who have reputations for shoplifting and mugging.

Jessica has previously appeared to be a happy child but over the past few months she has become increasingly withdrawn and has occasionally been found weeping in the classroom. She refuses to talk to anyone about what is bothering her and will not undress for PE classes in front of anyone. Matters came to a head when Jessica fled in tears from a biology class on human reproduction. The school is concerned that Jessica may be suffering from sexual abuse.

The local authority's social worker has visited Harry and Isobel, who do not seem overly concerned, saying that 'boys will be boys, and Jessica's just moody'. Advise the local authority on the options open to it in respect of Jessica and Jack.

Table 9.1 Comparing Child Protection orders in the Children Act 1989.

	Child assessment order	Emergency protection order	Police protection order	Supervision order	Care order
Grounds	Reasonable cause to suspect child suffering or is likely to suffer significant harm. An assessment is necessary and an assessment will not take place without a CAO	Either reasonable cause to believe that child is suffering or is likely to suffer significant harm. Or that an investigation is being unreasonably obstructed	Reasonable cause to believe child will otherwise suffer significant harm	Court has to be satisfied child is suffering or is likely to suffer significant harm due to lack of parental care or is beyond parental control	Court has to be satisfied child is suffering or is likely to suffer significant harm due to lack of parental care/beyond parental control
Who applies	Local authority or authorised person	Any interested person if reasonable belief. Only the local authority can apply if investigation obstructed	Police constable	Local authority or authorised person	Local authority or authorised person
PR	No	Yes – **CA 1989 s 44(4)(c)**	No	No	Yes – **CA 1989 s 33(3)(a)**
Removal of child	No	Yes – **CA 1989 s 44(4)(b)**	Yes – **CA 1989 s 46(1)(a)**	No	Yes – **CA 1989 s 33(1)**
How long?	7 days – **CA 1989 s 43(5)(b)**	8 days – **CA 1989 s 45(1)**	72 hours – **CA 1989 s 46(6)**	Until the child is 18, or can be discharged if no longer necessary or not being complied with – **CA 1989 s 35(1)(b)**	Until the child is 18, or the order is discharged, or another order is made e.g. adoption

How to Read this Question

Students need to explain how the local authority can best use their powers and duties to protect Jack and Jessica.

Applying the Law

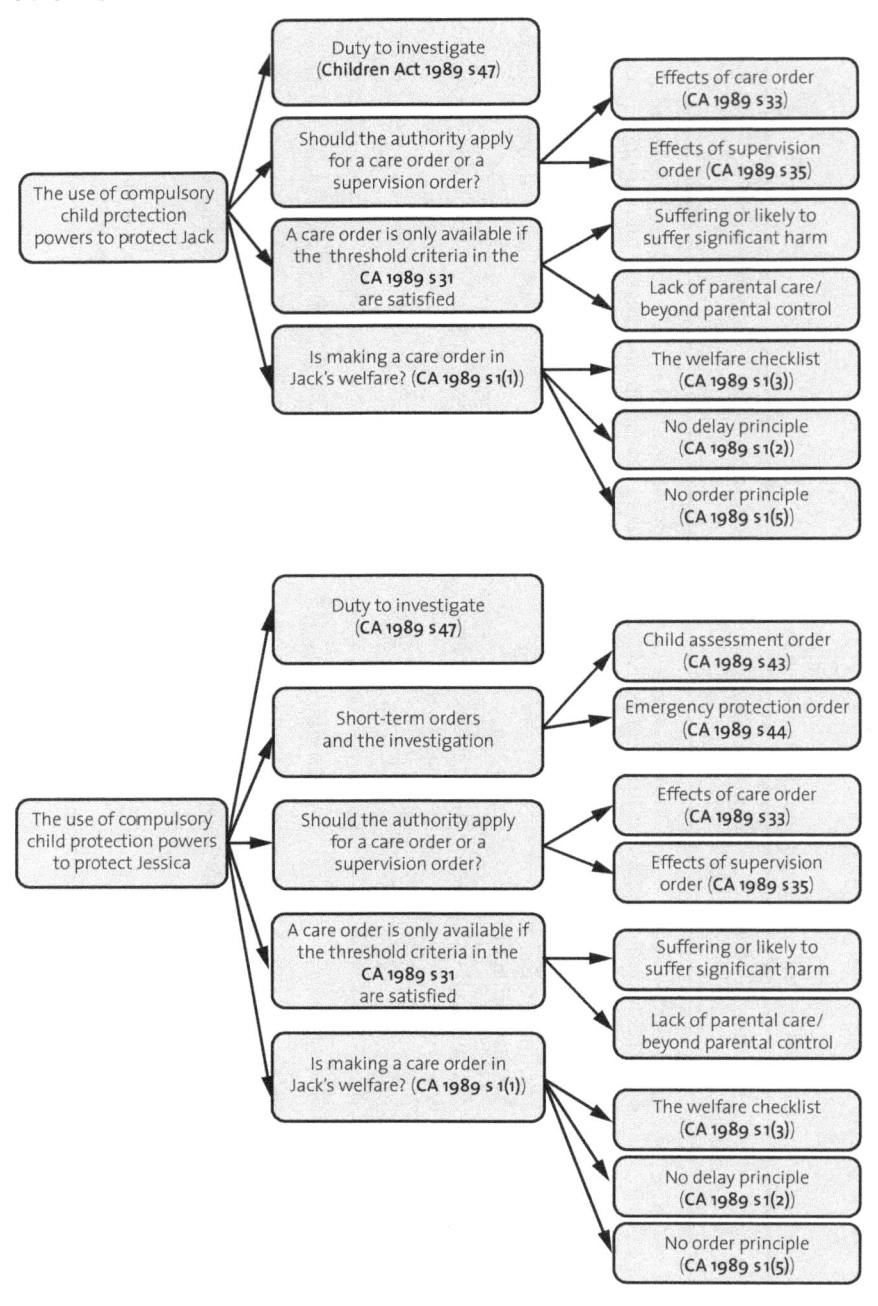

The use of compulsory child protection powers to protect Jack
- Duty to investigate (Children Act 1989 s 47)
- Should the authority apply for a care order or a supervision order?
  - Effects of care order (CA 1989 s 33)
  - Effects of supervision order (CA 1989 s 35)
- A care order is only available if the threshold criteria in the CA 1989 s 31 are satisfied
  - Suffering or likely to suffer significant harm
  - Lack of parental care/beyond parental control
- Is making a care order in Jack's welfare? (CA 1989 s 1(1))
  - The welfare checklist (CA 1989 s 1(3))
  - No delay principle (CA 1989 s 1(2))
  - No order principle (CA 1989 s 1(5))

The use of compulsory child protection powers to protect Jessica
- Duty to investigate (CA 1989 s 47)
- Short-term orders and the investigation
  - Child assessment order (CA 1989 s 43)
  - Emergency protection order (CA 1989 s 44)
- Should the authority apply for a care order or a supervision order?
  - Effects of care order (CA 1989 s 33)
  - Effects of supervision order (CA 1989 s 35)
- A care order is only available if the threshold criteria in the CA 1989 s 31 are satisfied
  - Suffering or likely to suffer significant harm
  - Lack of parental care/beyond parental control
- Is making a care order in Jack's welfare? (CA 1989 s 1(1))
  - The welfare checklist (CA 1989 s 1(3))
  - No delay principle (CA 1989 s 1(2))
  - No order principle (CA 1989 s 1(5))

ANSWER

Following a referral from the school, the local authority need to consider what harm Jessica and Jack are at risk of and what the appropriate solution is. The **Children Act 1989** prefers partnership and working with parents to coercive measures and help can be given to children in need to promote their welfare. Nevertheless, although both Jack and Jessica satisfy the test for children in need (**Children Act 1989 s17(10)(a)**), their parents appear uncooperative and uninterested and therefore this is not a case where services for children in need will be sufficient. It is important therefore to consider whether any of the child protection measures in the **Children Act 1989 Part IV** are available and how those measures might help Jack and Jessica.

Under the **Children Act 1989 s47** the local authority have a duty to investigate when it has reasonable cause to suspect that a child is suffering or is likely to suffer significant harm. This test is satisfied in Jack's case. The referral from school, the potentially dangerous friendship group and the persistent truancy will all lead to reasonable suspicion that Jack is at risk of harm.

The next issue is how to promote Jack's welfare long term. There are two long-term child protection measures in the **Children Act 1989**, the care order (**Children Act 1989 s33**) and the supervision order (**Children Act 1989 s35**). It is suggested that the care order is the more appropriate order. As Jack's parents are not cooperative, the more coercive powers of the care order, including the local authority gaining parental responsibility (**Children Act 1989 s33(3)**), are likely to be necessary.

In order to obtain a care order in respect of Jack, the local authority will first have to satisfy the threshold criteria in the **Children Act 1989 s31**. These are that they are satisfied that the child, here Jack, is suffering or is likely to suffer significant harm due to lack of parental care or to be being beyond parental control. This test does seem to be satisfied. Harm is defined in the **Children Act 1989 s31(9)** and it is clear from *Re O (A Minor) (Care Order: Education: Procedure)* (1992) that this can include truancy. Jack's friendship with older, badly behaved teenagers suggests future harm to him and it is very likely that without local authority intervention the truancy will continue. Furthermore, the harm suffered by Jack can said to be due to lack of parental care, or due to him being beyond parental control.

Once the threshold criteria is satisfied, the local authority would then need to convince the court that the principles of the **Children Act 1989** support the making of the care order. It is arguable that the welfare principle will be applied (**Children Act 1989 s1(1)**), notably because of Jack's emotional, physical and educational needs (**Children Act 1989 s1(3)(b)**), the harm Jack is at risk of suffering (**Children Act 1989 s1(3)(e)**) and Harriet and Ian's incapacity to respond to Jack's needs (**Children Act 1989 s1(3)(f)**). Moreover, this is a case where the parents are not willing to work with the local authority and the no order principle is satisfied (**Children Act 1989 s1(5)**).

Turning now to Jessica, following a referral from the school suggesting that Jessica has some issues with her body and has perhaps suffered sexual abuse, the duty to investigate under the **Children Act 1989 s 47** arises. This might reasonably include a physical examination of Jessica. Although Jessica's parents might cooperate with the investigation, if they do not it might be necessary to obtain a child assessment order (**Children Act 1989 s 43**) or, if they obstruct the investigation, an emergency protection order (**Children Act 1989 s 44(1)(b)**). The choice between the orders will depend on how much power the local authority need. The emergency protection order gives them parental responsibility (**Children Act 1989 s 44(4)(c)**) and enables the local authority to remove Jessica (**Children Act 1989 s 44(4)(b)**) or to exclude an alleged abuser (**Children Act 1989 s 44A**).

Jessica would also benefit from the local authority having parental responsibility (**Children Act 1989 s 33(3)**) and from perhaps being placed away from the family home, and therefore a care order seems to be an appropriate order to apply for. The questions therefore are whether the threshold criteria in the **Children Act 1989 s 31** are satisfied and whether the principles of the **Children Act 1989** support the making of a care order.

Sexual and physical abuse clearly comes within the definition of harm (**Children Act 1989 s 31(9)**). The issue is whether the report from the school detailing Jessica's reluctance to change for PE and her distress at a biology lesson is sufficient proof. In *Re B (Children) (Sexual Abuse: Standard of Proof)* (2008) the court decided that the standard of proof was balance of probabilities and there was not a rule that the more serious an allegation, the less likely it was to have occurred. In Jessica's case there may be an innocent explanation for her behaviour and much would depend on whether speaking to Jessica, a medical examination or any other investigations uncovered more evidence. If Jessica is suffering or at risk of harm the threshold criteria will be satisfied if that harm is due to lack of parental care or Jessica being beyond parental control.

If the threshold criteria are satisfied, the next issue is whether the welfare principle (**Children Act 1989 s 1(1)**) and the no order principle (**Children Act 1989 s 1(5)**) support the making of a care order. It is probable that they do because of Jessica's physical and emotional well-being (**Children Act 1989 s 1(3)(b)**) and the risk of her otherwise suffering harm (**Children Act 1989 s 1(3)(e)**).

In conclusion, therefore, it is suggested that the local authority should apply for a care order for Jack and Jessica. As part of the process, it is probable that the court would make an interim care order (**Children Act 1989 s 38**) providing Jack and Jessica with protection before the full order is made.

Common Pitfalls

- Be clear on how the threshold criteria are used.
- If the threshold criteria are not satisfied, then a care order or a supervision order will not be available.
- Even if the threshold criteria are satisfied, it is still necessary to explain whether the general principles of the **Children Act 1989** support the making of the care order.

Children and the Local Authority

Aim Higher

Understand the different effects of the care order and the supervision order and be able to explain which order is the most appropriate on the facts.

QUESTION 37

Molly has three illegitimate children by three different men, and has struggled to bring them up. Two years ago, Molly had a mental breakdown and was admitted to hospital. The two eldest children, Nathan and Oscar, were accommodated by the local authority with temporary foster parents, whilst the youngest child, Penny, was looked after by her paternal grandmother, Connie. When Molly was released from hospital, she demanded the return of her children, but was unable to cope with them, and severely neglected them. Again, the local authority and Connie stepped in to look after the children, at Molly's request, which they have done to date. Molly has recently begun to live with Frank, who has a criminal record of violence and sexual offences. Molly has indicated to the local authority that as soon as she feels up to it, she wants the children to live with her and Frank. Both the local authority and Connie are concerned about this, as Molly does not have a good record as a mother, and Frank's criminal record raises serious questions about his suitability as a substitute parent.

▶ Advise the local authority.

How to Read this Question

The issue here is that on the facts it would appear harmful to the children to live with Molly and Frank. Answers need to explain why it is harmful and what options are available to the local authority.

Applying the Law

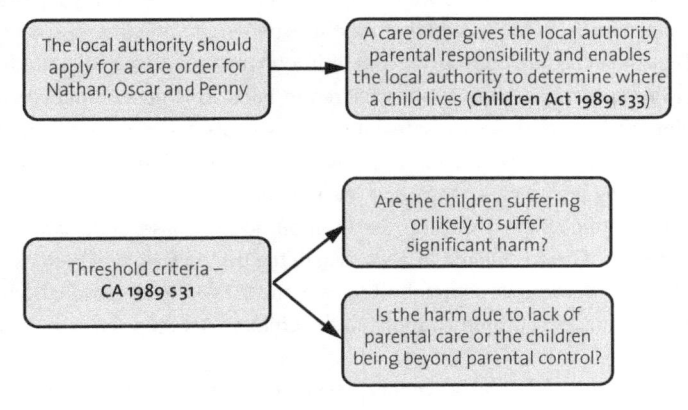

The local authority should apply for a care order for Nathan, Oscar and Penny → A care order gives the local authority parental responsibility and enables the local authority to determine where a child lives (**Children Act 1989 s 33**)

Threshold criteria – **CA 1989 s 31**
- Are the children suffering or likely to suffer significant harm?
- Is the harm due to lack of parental care or the children being beyond parental control?

Q&A Family Law

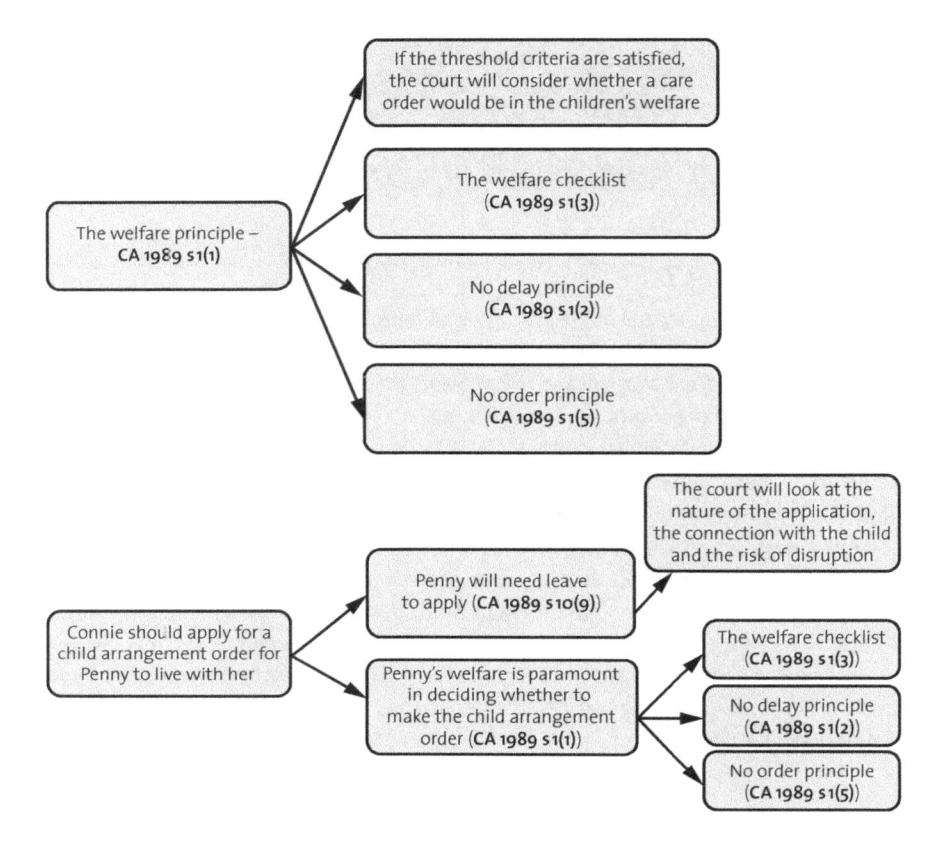

```
The welfare principle –
CA 1989 s1(1)
  ├── If the threshold criteria are satisfied, the court will consider whether a care order would be in the children's welfare
  ├── The welfare checklist (CA 1989 s1(3))
  ├── No delay principle (CA 1989 s1(2))
  └── No order principle (CA 1989 s1(5))

Connie should apply for a child arrangement order for Penny to live with her
  ├── Penny will need leave to apply (CA 1989 s10(9))
  │     └── The court will look at the nature of the application, the connection with the child and the risk of disruption
  └── Penny's welfare is paramount in deciding whether to make the child arrangement order (CA 1989 s1(1))
        ├── The welfare checklist (CA 1989 s1(3))
        ├── No delay principle (CA 1989 s1(2))
        └── No order principle (CA 1989 s1(5))
```

ANSWER

In this case the local authority requires advice on what steps, if any, it should take in relation to Molly's three children. It seems that Molly is the only person with parental responsibility over her children: **Children Act 1989 s2(2)**. This parental responsibility places an obligation on Molly to promote her children's welfare and to provide for their everyday needs. In the case of a person such as Molly, where a parent experiences difficulty in coping with the demands that their children impose, the local authority has a statutory duty under the **Children Act 1989 s17** to assist parents and children in need. This general duty to children in need requires the local authority to safeguard and promote the welfare of children within their area who are in need, and, so far as is possible, to promote the upbringing of children by their families by providing a range and level of services to assist with those children's needs: **s17(1)**. To supplement this duty the local authority is also under an obligation to provide accommodation to children in need, where the person who has been caring for the children is prevented, whether permanently or not and for whatever reason, from providing the children with suitable accommodation or care: **Children Act 1989 s20**.

In this case Molly's mental breakdown has prevented her from providing her children with the care that they require and so it is quite clear that the local authority has voluntarily entered into a relationship with Molly, whereby it has provided accommodation for the children. The essential nature of this relationship, though, is a voluntary one; a relationship has taken place through the consent of the parent, Molly. The local authority acquires no parental responsibility in the present situation and, instead, all the parental responsibility remains with Molly. The local authority has, by virtue of **s 22**, a duty to safeguard and promote the children's welfare and it is required to take into account the wishes and feelings of the children and the children's parents under **s 22(4)**. This requires the local authority, when making decisions, to consider those wishes and feelings and also the child's religious, racial and cultural background. In this case, little is known of the ages of the children and, as such, not much can be said about the impact of the children's views on how the local authority will proceed. However, the local authority has a duty to promote contact between the child and her parent and it is quite clear that until any compulsory powers are exercised, Molly has the right to contact with her children and she has the right to remove her children whenever she wishes without having to comply with any formal notice requirements. Thus, it would seem that Molly has the absolute right to remove her children from local authority care even though the local authority may be unhappy with her future living arrangements.[1]

The only option available to the local authority in relation to Nathan and Oscar who are voluntarily accommodated by the local authority is to take care proceedings under the **Children Act 1989 s 31**. The local authority could also apply for a care order for Penny; however, it is possible that Connie may want to continue to look after Penny and might try to apply for a child arrangement order with the effect that Penny lives with her (**Children Act 1989 s 8, Children and Families Act 2014 s 12**).

The local authority will only be granted a care order if the threshold criteria in the **Children Act 1989 s 31** are satisfied. The two boys are at present suffering no harm but there is the likelihood that they may suffer significant harm if they return to their mother's care. Harm is defined in the Act as meaning ill-treatment which can include sexual, physical and mental ill-treatment and impairment of health and development (**Children Act 1989 s 31(9)**). It does seem that if the children return to Molly, Frank's criminal record may pose a risk to them. Also, Molly's mental illness and her previous history indicate that the children's health and development may be impaired.

The second part of the statutory criteria is that the harm or likelihood of harm is attributable to the care being given to the child or likely to be given to him if the order is not made, not being what it would be reasonable to expect a parent to give him, or the child being beyond parental control. There is no evidence that Nathan and Oscar are beyond parental control, but the evidence does point to the level of care that the children might receive as not being at the level that it is reasonable to expect. If the statutory criteria are established, as in any **Children Act** order, the court must consider the child's welfare as its paramount consideration (**s 1(1)**), and in determining what is in the child's welfare the court will look at the **s 1(3)** checklist factors. The first of these factors is the ascertainable wishes of the children in the light of their age and understanding. As previously indicated, little is known of the age of

....
1   A care order would be a useful order for the local authority because it would give them parental responsibility, meaning they could direct how Molly exercised her parental responsibility.

these children, and if they are very young then the likelihood is that their wishes will not be given much weight. If the children are approaching teenage years then the court will give great credence to their wishes and to their fears about their future. If, as seems likely, the children are happy with the present arrangements and are concerned about returning to their mother, the court will be reluctant to allow this to occur. Clearly, the children's educational and physical and mental needs are being met in local authority care and there is serious doubt as to whether their mother would be able to meet such a need. There is also considerable benefit derived from keeping siblings together and it is not clear that Molly will be able to cope with both children. It is likely that both children have also had contact with their sister whilst she has been with her grandmother. Looking at the range of powers available to the court, the court is probably going to be mindful of the fact that a care order does give a certain degree of control over the children's well-being, whereas making no order at all would place the children at risk. This is not a case where the non-interventionist policy in **s 1(5)** would hold true.[2]

Care proceedings are usually taken after full notice is given to all the parties. This would require a children's guardian to be appointed in relation to the children and it would also require Molly to be given notice as a parent. This could alert Molly as to the steps the local authority is planning to take and may result in her demanding the immediate removal of the children from local authority accommodation. In the event of this occurring, the local authority may decide to apply for an emergency protection order under **s 44** of the Act. An emergency protection order may be applied for on the basis in **s 44(1)(a)** that there is reasonable cause to believe that the child is likely to suffer significant harm if he does not remain in the place where he is presently being accommodated. This order is a somewhat draconian measure and it can authorise the child to remain in the place where he is presently being accommodated immediately prior to the order (**s 44(4)(b)**). This order gives the local authority parental responsibility for the children for its duration (**s 44(4)(c)**). However, the order only lasts for eight days (**s 45(1)**) although it can be extended once for a further seven days if there is reasonable cause to believe that, if the order is not extended, the children are likely to suffer significant harm.

If an emergency protection order is made, the court will give directions as to whether Molly is to be allowed contact with the children. There is little in the facts to require contact to be forbidden as Molly has not physically ill-treated the children. However, it is quite clear that contact with Frank should be prohibited. The emergency protection order can be challenged by the children or by Molly, the parent, under **s 45(8)**, but this cannot be challenged until 72 hours have elapsed, and there will be no possibility of challenge if Molly was given notice of the hearing and was present at it (**s 45(11)**). This emergency protection order would give the local authority breathing space before a care order can be made. The care order under **s 31** would probably need to be an interim order until the full facts can be put to the courts. If a care order is made, the local authority acquires parental responsibility for the children. Molly

....

2 Applying for a care order or a supervision order is a two-stage process. First the threshold criteria must be satisfied, and then, if they are satisfied, the court will consider whether the principles of the **Children Act 1989** support the making of an order.

does not lose her parental responsibility but she will not be able to exercise it in a way that is inconsistent with the local authority's parental responsibility.

By having a care order in relation to the children, the local authority can decide where the children should reside. This may be in local authority care or with foster parents or it may be that the local authority will arrange for the children to live with members of their family; this may even include Molly, provided she agrees not to reside with Frank. The care order will remain in force until the children are 18 unless it is discharged earlier either on application by the parent or by the child or local authority (**s 39(1)**).

Turning to Penny, an alternative to a care order is for her grandmother, Connie, to apply for a child arrangement order for Penny to live with her (**Children Act 1989 s 8**). Connie does not come within the list of individuals who can apply automatically for a child arrangement order (**Children Act 1989 ss 10(4), 10(5)**) and therefore she would need the leave of the court to apply. Penny has lived with Connie for the last two years, there is a very close connection between Penny and her grandmother and an application for a child arrangement order would not be disruptive, therefore Connie would be granted leave to apply for a child arrangement order for Penny (**Children Act 1989 s 10(9)**).

If an application is made for a child arrangement order under **s 8**, the paramount consideration is the welfare of the child under **s 1(1)**. In determining what was in Penny's best interests, the court would have regard to the factors in the checklist (**s 1(3)**). This includes her ascertainable wishes and feelings, given her age and understanding; however, little is known of Penny's age and therefore little can be said about the weight that would be attached to her views. Her educational, emotional and other needs have been satisfactorily met by her grandmother over the past few years and it seems likely that the grandmother would be in a better position to meet those needs than the mother and her new partner. Indeed the mother has a poor history in relation to mothering skills, albeit not through her own fault, and it does not seem that the living conditions with Molly and Frank would be conducive to the child's best interest.

Although the court does like to keep brothers and sisters together because of the mutual support that they derive from one another (*Adams v Adams* (1984)), the children in this case have been used to living apart and therefore the mother's claim that she could accommodate them all together would have little weight. She has been unable to sustain in the past the obligation to care for all of her children together and it seems quite clear that the status quo would be disturbed if Penny were removed from her grandmother's care to be given to her mother. Although generally there is an advantage in care being provided by a parent, the parent's conduct in the past has not been such to inspire confidence. The parent's new partner does seem to pose a risk to the future well-being of the children in that he has a violent record and a record that involves sexual offences. In *Scott v Scott* (1986), the mother's partner had a history of violence and indecency and that offset any advantages that living with a mother would normally involve.

In conclusion, therefore, it would seem that this child's best interests might well be served by her remaining with her grandmother. In deciding whether to make a **s 8** order, the court will have in mind the need to avoid delay (**s(2)**) and the need to avoid unnecessary intervention (**s1(5)**). However, this is clearly a case where to allow the child to return to her mother may well wreak havoc with the child's welfare. Therefore the court will clearly have to consider whether to make a **s8** order in relation to the grandmother or whether to grant a care order in relation to the local authority. It seems clear that the local authority and grandmother are united in their concern about the well-being of the child and it seems possible that either course of action could be employed for the welfare of the youngest daughter. However, in an emergency it may be necessary to couple either the care order or the **s8** residence order with an emergency protection order. It is important to note that only the local authority can apply for the emergency protection order. Connie, as a grandparent, would have no *locus standi* to make such an application if her daughter were to demand the return of the child.

QUESTION 38

Sharon, aged 17, has one daughter, Jade, aged two. Sharon is unsure who Jade's father is. Sharon and Jade were living with Sharon's mother, Karen, but three months ago Sharon fell out with her stepfather, Liam, and since then Sharon and Jade have been renting a one-bedroomed flat. The health visitor has contacted the local authority to express her concern about Jade. Sharon had failed to keep a number of appointments at the clinic and when she had finally brought Jade, the child had a number of bruises and was wearing dirty clothes and a very wet and heavy nappy. Jade is a boisterous and unruly child, and Sharon admits to finding her hard to handle. When the health visitor asked Sharon about Jade's bruises, Sharon stormed out, telling the health visitor to mind her own business.
▶ Advise the local authority on what steps, if any, it should take.

How to Read this Question
The student needs to identify what issues on the facts are concerning the local authority and whether there is any appropriate action they can take.

Applying the Law

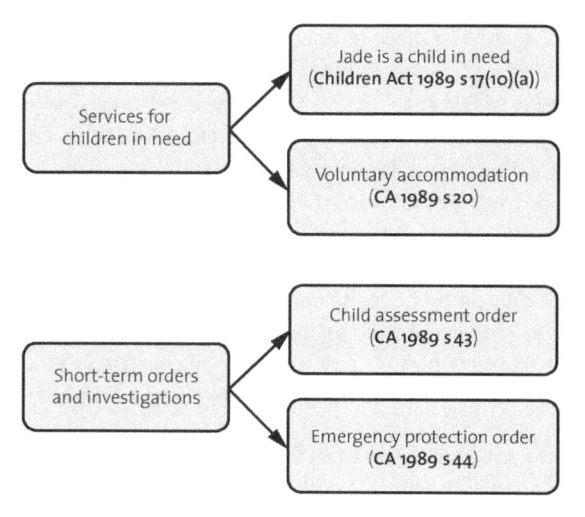

Services for children in need →
- Jade is a child in need (Children Act 1989 s 17(10)(a))
- Voluntary accommodation (CA 1989 s 20)

Short-term orders and investigations →
- Child assessment order (CA 1989 s 43)
- Emergency protection order (CA 1989 s 44)

Children and the Local Authority

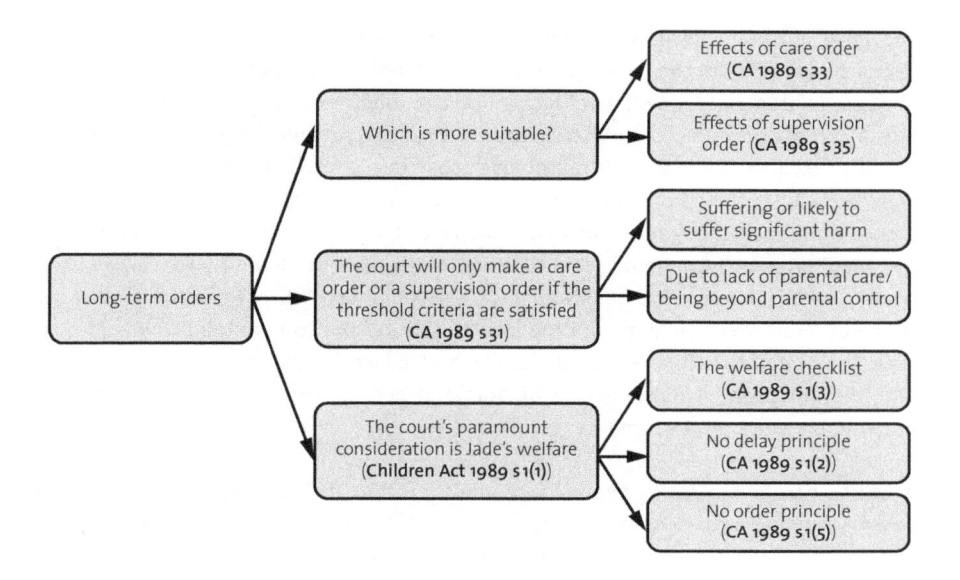

```
Long-term orders
├── Which is more suitable?
│   ├── Effects of care order (CA 1989 s 33)
│   └── Effects of supervision order (CA 1989 s 35)
├── The court will only make a care order or a supervision order if the threshold criteria are satisfied (CA 1989 s 31)
│   ├── Suffering or likely to suffer significant harm
│   └── Due to lack of parental care/being beyond parental control
└── The court's paramount consideration is Jade's welfare (Children Act 1989 s 1(1))
    ├── The welfare checklist (CA 1989 s 1(3))
    ├── No delay principle (CA 1989 s 1(2))
    └── No order principle (CA 1989 s 1(5))
```

ANSWER

Sharon is the one person who has parental responsibility for Jade (**Children Act 1989 s 2(2)**). Parental responsibility is defined as 'all the rights, duties, powers and responsibilities and authority which by law a parent of a child has in relation to the child and its property': **Children Act 1989 s 3(1)**. This stresses that Sharon has the obligation to care for her child, and to promote the child's welfare.

The health visitor's concern over Jade's welfare must be sensitively handled by the local authority; whilst they must obviously act swiftly to employ their statutory powers for a child at risk, they must also ensure that careful consideration is given as to whether any intervention is necessary.[3]

In Jade's case, it seems there are three issues that have concerned the health visitor: the bruises, the lack of explanation for the bruises and the dirty clothes and nappy. Many small children have bruises. Children are often very active, and can be clumsy and careless. It is submitted that it is not the bruises themselves that are the issue, but Sharon's reaction to being asked how those bruises occurred. Furthermore, whether bruising is significant depends on how extensive it is and where the bruises are sited. Moreover, even Sharon's reluctance to explain how the bruises occurred may be because she is afraid of the health visitor, or as a young, single mother fears being judged, rather than because she was responsible for them. The final issue that is likely to concern the health visitor is Jade's clothes. These were dirty and Jade's nappy was dirty too. Although this might suggest neglect or that Sharon is unable to cope, it could just be an unfortunate one-off.

---

3 If possible the local authority should try to work in partnership with the child's parent(s) and should prefer using services for children in need over coercive measures.

The local authority needs to determine whether Sharon is managing her parental responsibility without the need for interference, whether some action is required either to assist Sharon and Jade on a voluntary basis, or whether to protect Jade using compulsory orders from the court. The **Children Act 1989 s 47** requires the local authority to investigate cases where there is reasonable cause to suspect that the child is suffering, or is likely to suffer, significant harm. The concern of an experienced health visitor should not usually be ignored, and does indicate that some kind of investigation may be called for. Initially, it would seem that the local authority should try to work in partnership with Sharon. The philosophy of the **Children Act 1989** is to encourage cooperation between parents and the local authority, and to maintain, wherever possible, the care of the child within the family. A social worker should speak with Sharon, and relevant professionals, such as doctors and health visitors, can be consulted to obtain their views on the family.

It will be possible to gauge Sharon and Jade's position after talking with Sharon, and possibly holding a case conference. If, as seems likely, Sharon is experiencing difficulty coping with the demands of bringing up a two-year-old child, then the local authority may be able to provide assistance. There is a general duty on a local authority to safeguard and promote the welfare of a child in need, and to do this by promoting Jade's upbringing within the family by providing services to help meet the child's needs: **Children Act 1989 s 17(1)**. Jade will qualify as a child in need if she is unlikely to achieve, or maintain, or have the opportunity of achieving or maintaining, a reasonable standard of health and development (**s 17(10)**) unless the local authority provides services to facilitate this. Health includes both mental and physical health (**s 17(11)**), and development includes the child's physical, intellectual, emotional, social or behavioural development.

Little is known about Sharon's socio-economic background, but it is likely that as a young single parent she is socially disadvantaged and not economically well-off. Her living conditions may be such that Jade is frustrated and bored, and might well qualify as a child in need. The local authority, in partnership with Sharon, could provide a range of services, including such things as nursery provision, clubs, etc. to provide Jade with stimulation, and Sharon with some relief from the pressures of continuous child care.

The local authority could offer to accommodate Jade voluntarily under **s 20** if Sharon is prevented (whether or not permanently and/or for whatever reason) from providing Jade with suitable accommodation or care. At the moment, Sharon is living in a one-bedroom flat, having left her mother's home. Without further information it is impossible to state how suitable this flat is. Voluntary accommodation can only take place if Sharon requests the local authority to assist her, and could be used to provide short-term care for Jade whilst Sharon sorts out other aspects of her life. Since this arrangement would be entirely voluntary, Sharon could remove Jade from the local authority's care at any time without having to comply with any formal requirements: **s 20(8)**. Before the local authority provides accommodation for such a child, it must ascertain the wishes of the child (**s 20(6)**) but, as Jade is only two, this will not be possible. Whilst Jade is being accommodated by the local authority, it has a duty to safeguard and promote her welfare (**s 22(3)**) and to consult Sharon and take into account Sharon's wishes and the religious, racial, cultural and linguistic characteristics of the child (**s 22(5)**). Sharon would be encouraged to keep close contact with Jade and to remain involved with her, so that when Sharon's position has stabilised, she and her child can be reunited. The local authority does not acquire parental responsibility for a child voluntarily accommodated with it, and these measures are useful to help a family through difficult times.

It may be that, if Sharon persists in being evasive and abusive when asked about Jade, the local authority will need to satisfy itself that Jade is not suffering harm due to abuse or neglect. One option here would seem to be an application to the Family Proceedings Court for a child assessment order: **Children Act 1989 s 43**. This is the usual means of discovering what is happening to the child in circumstances where parental cooperation has not been forthcoming. The local authority must give notice of its application to Sharon, and the court will only grant an order if the applicant has reasonable cause to suspect that the child is suffering, or is likely to suffer, significant harm. Jade's bruising and Sharon's reluctance to take her to the clinic, and her aggressive reaction to the health visitor, might suffice to establish this. In addition, it is necessary to show that an assessment of the child is necessary to establish whether she is suffering, or is likely to suffer, significant harm, and that it is unlikely that any satisfactory assessment will be made without a child assessment order. Sharon's uncooperative stance makes it likely that the grounds for an order have been established. However, as with all orders under the **Children Act 1989**, the child's welfare is the paramount consideration (**s1**), and the court will wish to ensure that there is as little delay as possible (**s1(2)**) once it determines that making an order is better than not making an order (**s1(5)**).

An assessment order lasts for a maximum of seven days, and Sharon will be ordered to ensure that Jade turns up at the appropriate time and place for assessment. Jade would normally remain at home, unless the order specifies that she remain in another place, for example, a hospital (**s 43(9)**). The local authority does not acquire parental responsibility.

If Sharon refused to comply with the child assessment order, or the local authority formed the view that Jade was in immediate danger, then an application could be made for an emergency protection order. This is a more serious measure, and should only be taken in cases where there is a clear, pressing need to protect a child at risk. The basis for granting an order under **s 44** to the local authority is that there is reasonable cause to believe that the child is likely to suffer significant harm if she remains where she is and is not removed to local authority accommodation. The alternative is to show that enquiries are being made in respect of the child, and that those enquiries are being frustrated by Sharon unreasonably refusing access to Jade. There is then the need to show that access to the child is required as a matter of urgency. The emergency protection order lasts for eight days, although it may be extended for a further seven days: **s 45(6)**. The order can authorise the removal of Jade from her home, and gives the local authority parental responsibility for the limited time the order is in force. The court will decide whether Sharon should have contact with Jade during this time, and the order can only be challenged by Sharon, or Jade (s45(8)), once it has been in force for 72 hours, provided they had no notice of the original hearing (s45(11)).[4]

If, after examining Jade, the local authority is still concerned about her well-being, then there are two further options available: the care order or supervision order (s31). The option of wardship is no longer available for local authorities. The local authority must apply to the Family Proceedings Court, or County Court and High Court in complex cases, making Sharon, the parent, and Jade, the child, respondents in the case.

The basis for a care or supervision order may be found in s31, and the court must be satisfied that the child is suffering, or is likely to suffer, significant harm, and this is attributable to the care being given to the child not being what it would be reasonable to expect a parent to give him, or the child is beyond parental control. There would be a need to establish significant harm which means ill-treatment, physical, sexual or mental abuse, or impairment of health and development. This must go beyond an occasional bruise, and it must be shown that the care being provided by Sharon falls short of what care can reasonably be expected.

QUESTION 39

Andrew and Beth have a son, Charlie, who is nine months old. Throughout Beth's pregnancy, Andrew had been having a relationship with Dawn, and when Charlie was six weeks old Andrew left Beth and moved in with Dawn. Dawn has an 18-month-old daughter, Ella. Charlie lives with his mother, but stays with Andrew, Dawn and Ella once a week. Andrew also had his son for a weekend two months ago so that Charlie and he could attend a family celebration together.

Last month, Beth took Charlie to hospital as he was not well. As part of the doctor's investigations, the doctor discovered several internal injuries. Further investigation shows that these injuries are non-accidental and have been sustained over a considerable period of time. It is not possible to determine whether the injuries occurred whilst Charlie was in Andrew's care, or whilst he was in Beth's care. Both Beth and Andrew deny hurting Charlie.

▶ **Advise the local authority on what measures should be taken in respect of Charlie and whether anything should be done to protect Ella.**

How to Read this Question

Here there are two children who need protection from the local authority. In respect of Charlie, the problem is that it is not clear who is responsible for harming him. As for Ella, she is not yet suffering any harm, but she may be at risk of harm if Andrew was responsible for hurting Charlie.

---

4 The emergency protection order is a more serious order than the child assessment order. The EPO gives the local authority parental responsibility whereas the CAO does not and can lead to the child being removed. It is not surprising therefore that the grounds for obtaining the EPO are more serious than the grounds for obtaining the CAO – belief of abuse in the case of the EPO rather than suspicion in the case of the CAO.

Applying the Law

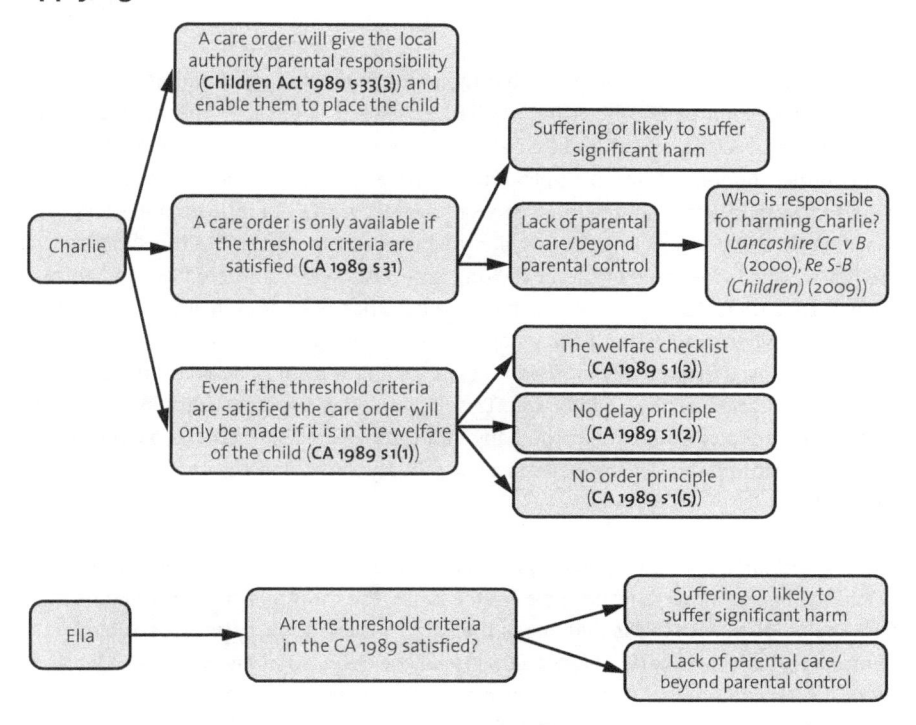

```
Charlie ──┬──▶ A care order will give the local
          │    authority parental responsibility
          │    (Children Act 1989 s 33(3)) and
          │    enable them to place the child
          │
          ├──▶ A care order is only available if ──┬──▶ Suffering or likely to suffer
          │    the threshold criteria are          │    significant harm
          │    satisfied (CA 1989 s 31)            │
          │                                        ├──▶ Lack of parental ──▶ Who is responsible
          │                                        │    care/beyond           for harming Charlie?
          │                                        │    parental control      (Lancashire CC v B
          │                                                                   (2000), Re S-B
          │                                                                   (Children) (2009))
          │
          └──▶ Even if the threshold criteria  ──┬──▶ The welfare checklist
               are satisfied the care order will  │    (CA 1989 s 1(3))
               only be made if it is in the welfare
               of the child (CA 1989 s 1(1))     ├──▶ No delay principle
                                                  │    (CA 1989 s 1(2))
                                                  │
                                                  └──▶ No order principle
                                                       (CA 1989 s 1(5))

Ella ──▶ Are the threshold criteria ──┬──▶ Suffering or likely to
         in the CA 1989 satisfied?    │    suffer significant harm
                                      │
                                      └──▶ Lack of parental care/
                                           beyond parental control
```

ANSWER

The purpose of care orders is to provide long-term protection to children who are otherwise at risk of significant harm. In this question, the local authority are faced with two children, Charlie and Ella, and the issue is whether a care order would be available in respect of either of those children and whether it would be an appropriate measure to take.

The care order gives the local authority parental responsibility (**Children Act 1989 s 33(3)**). This would enable them to have some control over important decisions relating to the child. The care order also places the child in local authority care and makes the local authority responsible for determining where the child is placed. Whilst a care order can be made and the child remains placed in the family home, it is fairly usual for a care order to result in the child being removed from the family home where the child is at risk and placed somewhere else.

A care order can only be made if the threshold criteria are satisfied (**Children Act 1989 s 31**). The question therefore is: is Charlie suffering or likely to suffer significant harm and is the harm due to either lack of parental care or being beyond parental control? Medical evidence has established that Charlie has sustained non-accidental injuries. Physical injury comes within the definition of harm (**Children Act 1989 s 31(9)**) and given the repeated nature of the physical harm and the fact that it has required hospital treatment, it would be fair to say that it is significant.

More problematic is the requirement that the harm be due to lack of parental care or the child being beyond parental control. In Charlie's case, it is unclear whether his injuries were sustained whilst he was in the care of this mother, Beth, or whilst he was in the care of his father, Andrew. If, for example, Andrew were responsible for the harm and Beth were to refuse to allow Andrew unsupervised contact with Charlie, it becomes less likely that Charlie will be likely to suffer significant harm and therefore the threshold criteria are not satisfied. The issue of the unknown perpetrator was considered by the House of Lords in *Lancashire CC v B* (2000). In that case, a baby had been shaken. It was not possible to establish when exactly the shaking had occurred and it could have been when the child was being looked after by his mother, it could also have been done when the child was being looked after by the childminder. Despite this, the House of Lords held that the threshold criteria were satisfied. The baby had clearly been harmed and as long as the harm was attributable to the parents or a primary carer, the threshold criteria were satisfied.

Looking at Charlie's situation, this would mean that even though it is unclear whether his mother or his father were responsible for the harm, the threshold criteria would be satisfied. The problem with this is that one of the parents is not going to be responsible for the harm and a blameless parent is going to possibly be deprived of his or her child. Furthermore, it is recognised that it is generally in a child's welfare to have a relationship with his or her parents and the **Children Act 1989** supports the idea of children being raised by their parents; despite this Charlie is going to be taken away from this parents, at least one of whom will be blameless. Nevertheless, the decision in *Lancashire CC v B*, and therefore the approach in Charlie's case, is not really surprising. The alternative is that Charlie be left in the care of a parent who has been responsible for causing him significant physical harm.

Even if the threshold criteria are satisfied, a care order would only be made if it is in Charlie's welfare (**Children Act 1989 s1(1)**). The court will use the welfare checklist (**Children Act 1989 s1(3)**) to determine what is in Charlie's welfare. Under the **Children Act 1989 s1(3)(b)** the court will consider a child's physical, emotional and educational well-being. Charlie is currently suffering significant physical harm, therefore it would seem that his physical well-being supports a care order. On the other hand, he might perhaps suffer some emotional harm from being removed from his parents and therefore his emotional well-being might argue against a care order. Similarly, when looking at the harm that Charlie is at risk of (**Children Act 1989 s1(3)(e)**) physical harm argues in favour of a care order whilst potentially emotional harm argues against it. Under the **Children Act 1989 s1(3)(c)** the court will consider the effect of the child of a change of circumstances. Whilst there would be a disruption to Charlie if a care order were made, this would be justifiable if it were to remove him from a dangerous situation. Finally, the court might look at how capable Andrew and Beth are at meeting Charlie's needs (**Children Act 1989 s1(3)(f)**) and given that one of them is responsible for causing Charlie physical harm, this again would be an argument in favour of a care order. In another unknown perpetrator case, *Re O and N (Children) (non-accidental injury)* (2003), the House of Lords decided that if the threshold criteria were satisfied, the child's welfare would support the making of a care order.

In conclusion, therefore, a care order would be available in respect of Charlie and it would be an effective way for the local authority to protect Charlie. The next question is whether a care order or a supervision order would be available for Ella. Ella's situation is different. Unlike Charlie, there is no evidence of abuse. The concern in Ella's case is that Andrew is potentially responsible for the physical harm of Charlie and he is now living with Ella.

Although the threshold criteria (**Children Act 1989 s 31**) have to be satisfied to get a care order and to get a supervision order, the effects of the care order and the supervision order are different. Whilst a care order enables the local authority to place the child and gives the local authority parental responsibility (**Children Act 1989 s 33**), the supervision order gives the local authority the power to advise, assist and befriend (**Children Act 1989 s 35**). Given the fact that Ella is not currently suffering harm and there is no suggestion that her mother is a danger to her, the supervision order might seem the more appropriate order, although it would depend on how cooperative Dawn is.

The local authority would only be able to obtain a supervision order if the court is satisfied that Ella is currently suffering or is likely to suffer significant harm. There is no evidence that Ella is currently suffering significant harm, the idea that she is at risk of suffering harm in the future is based on the chance that Andrew is responsible for harming Charlie and might therefore be likely to harm Ella. Nevertheless, it is not clear that Andrew is responsible for harming Charlie, and even if he is, that does not necessarily mean that he will also harm Ella. In *Lancashire CC v B* (2000) the court also had to consider the position of the childminder's child. The childminder could have been responsible for shaking the baby and therefore there was an argument that her own child was also at risk and the threshold criteria were satisfied in respect of her own child. The court rejected this. The childminder's child was not currently suffering harm and as it could not be established that the childminder was responsible for harming the baby, the court could not be satisfied that it was likely that the childminder's child was at risk of harm in the future. Applying this to Ella's case, it seems that the threshold criteria are not satisfied and therefore a supervision order would not be available.

10 Adoption

INTRODUCTION

Many family law syllabuses will conclude by looking at long-term arrangements for looking after children, namely adoption orders or special guardianship orders. This topic often follows conveniently from child protection as one of the outcomes for a child who is removed from their parents and placed in care might be an adoptive placement.

Checklist

Students should know and understand the following:

- the age limits on being an adopter (**Adoption and Children Act 2002 ss 50, 51**);
- the age limits on who can be adopted (**Adoption and Children Act 2002 s 47(9)**);
- how the **Adoption and Children Act 2002** developed the law on which couples can adopt (**Adoption and Children Act 2002 s 144(4)**, *Re S and J* (2004), *Re S and J* (2014));
- placing a child with consent in an agency adoption (**Adoption and Children Act 2002 s 19**);
- when a placement order is available: **Adoption and Children Act 2002 s 21**;
- the duty to inform the local authority in a non-agency placement: **Adoption and Children Act 2002 s 44**;
- how long the placement is for: **Adoption and Children Act 2002 s 42**;
- the effect of placement on parental responsibility (**Adoption and Children Act 2002 s 25**), contact (**Adoption and Children Act 2002 s 26**), removal (**Adoption and Children Act 2002 s 30**);
- ending a placement order (**Adoption and Children Act 2002 s 24**, *DL and ML v Newham LBC and the Secretary of State for Education* (2011));
- the child's welfare is paramount in the decision on whether the child should be adopted by the prospective adopters (**Adoption and Children Act 2002 s 1(2)**). The court will use a welfare checklist to determine what is in the child's welfare (**Adoption and Children Act 2002 s 1(4)**);
- the welfare checklist in the **Children Act 1989 s 1(3)** and the welfare checklist in the **Adoption and Children Act 2002 s 1(4)**;
- the importance of a child's biological relations (**Adoption and Children Act 2002 s 1(4)(f)**, *Re C (Family Placement)* (2009));
- the significance of a child's race – the **Adoption and Children Act 2002 s 1(5)** has been repealed by the **Children and Families Act 2014 s 3**;

Q&A Family Law

- whose consent is needed for the adoptive order? **Adoption and Children Act 2002 s 52(1)**;
- dispensing with parental consent: **Adoption and Children Act 2002 s 52**, *Borough of Poole v Mrs W and Mr W* (2014), *Re P (Placement Orders: Parental Consent)* (2008);
- the effects of adoption order (*Webster v Nolfolk County Council* (2009));
- post-adoption contact – **Children and Families Act 2014 s 9, Adoption and Children Act 2002 ss 51A, 51B**, *Re R (adoption: contact)* (2005), *Re J (a child: adopted child: contact)* (2010), *MF v LB of Brent and Others* (2013);
- who can apply for a special guardianship order: **Children Act 1989 s 14A(5)**;
- the effects of a special guardianship order: **Children Act 1989 s 14C**;
- the choice between an adoption order and a special guardianship order (*Re N (adoption order)* (2014)).

QUESTION 40

Anna and Bertie were married five years ago, and had a daughter, Carrie, who is now two. Bertie was a famous footballer, but the marriage encountered difficulties when he began to experiment with drugs. One night, whilst under the influence of drugs, Bertie became violent and assaulted Anna, breaking her nose. Bertie was horrified by what he had done and voluntarily entered a rehabilitation centre, but Anna divorced him on the basis of his behaviour. Anna subsequently married David, and Carrie lives with them. David adores Carrie and would like to adopt her. Bertie has tried to maintain contact with Carrie.

▶ Advise Anna and David whether they will be able to adopt Carrie.

Table 10.1 Parental responsibility in adoption order, special guardianship and child assessment order compared.

	Adoption order	Special guardianship order	Child arrangement order
Does it give PR?	Yes (**Adoption and Children Act 2002 s 46(1)**)	Yes (**Children Act 1989 s 14C(1)(a)**)	Yes (**Children Act 1989 s 12**)
Is PR shared?	No	Only in a couple of exceptional cases (**Children Act 1989 s 14C(1)(b)**)	Yes. More than one person can have PR (**CA 1989 s 2(5)**). Generally, can act without consulting (**CA 1989 s 2(7)**)
Name change?	Yes, adopters can change the child's name	Need consent of everyone with PR (**CA 1989 s 14C(3)(a)**)	Need consent of everyone with PR (**CA 1989 s 13(1)(a)**)
Removal from the jurisdiction	Yes, adopters can remove the child from the jurisdiction	Need consent of everyone with PR (**CA 1989 s 14C (3)(b)**)	Need consent of everyone with PR (**CA 1989 s 13(1)(b)**)

Adoption

How to Read this Question
Although the question states that Anna and David want to adopt Carrie, answers should explore other ways of caring for her too.

Applying the Law

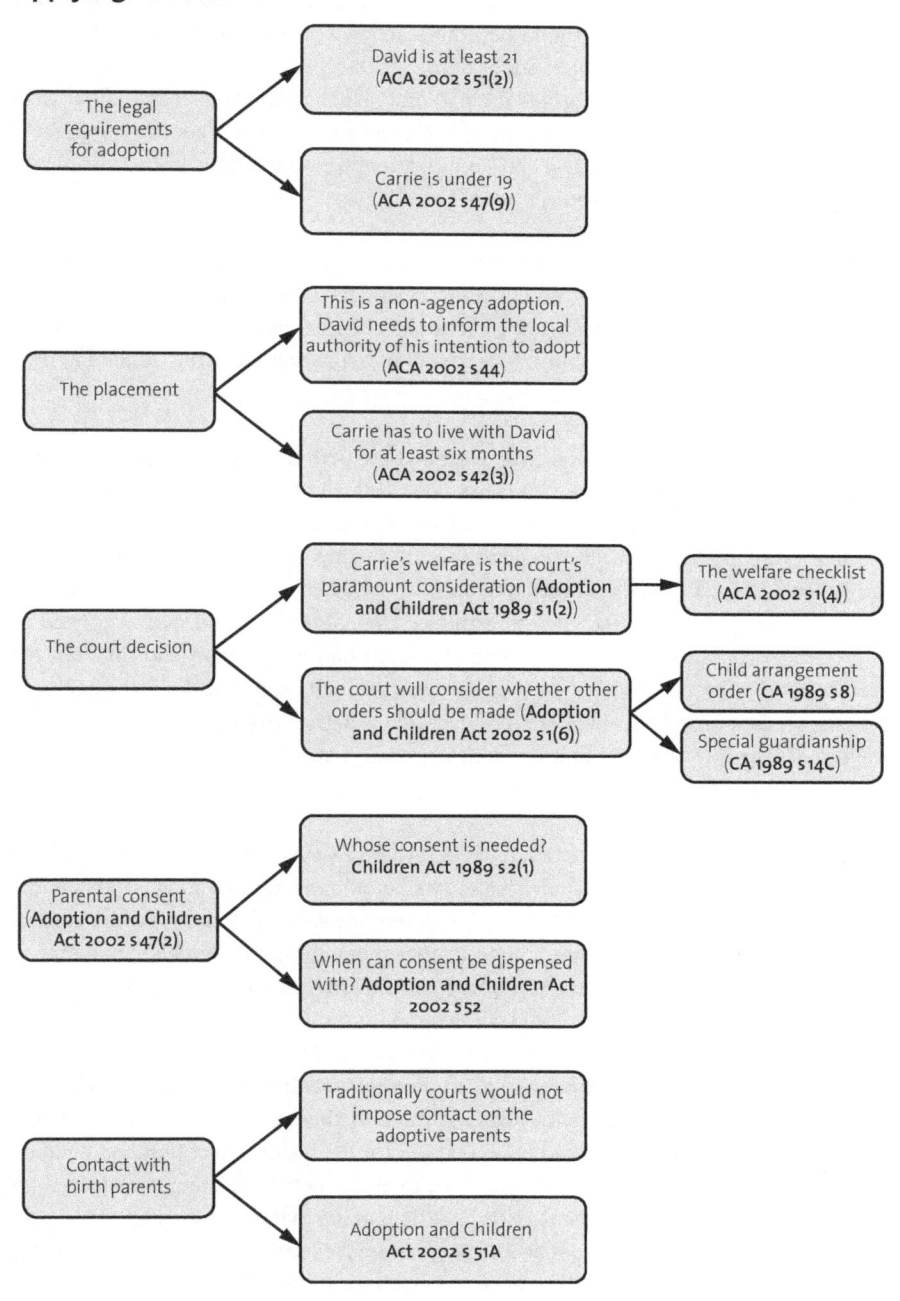

- **The legal requirements for adoption**
  - David is at least 21 (ACA 2002 s 51(2))
  - Carrie is under 19 (ACA 2002 s 47(9))

- **The placement**
  - This is a non-agency adoption. David needs to inform the local authority of his intention to adopt (ACA 2002 s 44)
  - Carrie has to live with David for at least six months (ACA 2002 s 42(3))

- **The court decision**
  - Carrie's welfare is the court's paramount consideration (**Adoption and Children Act 1989 s 1(2)**)
    - The welfare checklist (ACA 2002 s 1(4))
  - The court will consider whether other orders should be made (**Adoption and Children Act 2002 s 1(6)**)
    - Child arrangement order (CA 1989 s 8)
    - Special guardianship (CA 1989 s 14C)

- **Parental consent (Adoption and Children Act 2002 s 47(2))**
  - Whose consent is needed? **Children Act 1989 s 2(1)**
  - When can consent be dispensed with? **Adoption and Children Act 2002 s 52**

- **Contact with birth parents**
  - Traditionally courts would not impose contact on the adoptive parents
  - Adoption and Children Act 2002 s 51A

ANSWER

Anna and David want David to adopt Anna's daughter, Carrie. Adoption would mean that Carrie would remain living with Anna and David and would give David parental responsibility. Moreover, if the adoption is allowed this would mean that Carrie's birth father, Bertie, would be legally classed as a stranger to Carrie (**Adoption and Children Act 2002 s 46(2)(a)**). As David is Carrie's stepfather, there are two possibilities for David to adopt Carrie: David and Anna could both adopt Carrie, or David could adopt his stepdaughter. Whilst adoption usually extinguishes the parental responsibility of everyone other than the adoptive parent(s), if the second option is chosen and just David adopts Carrie, Anna will still be Carrie's mother and will retain her parental responsibility. In the rest of this question it is assumed that David will adopt Carrie.

In order for David to adopt Carrie, he has to be at least 21 years old (**Adoption and Children Act 2002 s 51**). Although the facts do not state David's age, it is probable that he is at least 21 so this requirement is satisfied. Carrie cannot be adopted unless she is under 19 (**Adoption and Children Act 2002 s 47(9)**). She is only two and therefore this requirement is clearly satisfied.

Before a child can be adopted, that child must first live with the potential adopters (**Adoption and Children Act 2002 s 42**). There are two ways a child can come to live with the adopters, either by being placed with the adopters by an adoption agency, in which case the agency adoption procedure is followed, or by already living as part of the adopter's family, in which case the non-agency procedure is followed. In David's case, Carrie is already living with David and therefore this is a non-agency case. David will need to inform the local authority that he intends to adopt Carrie (**Adoption and Children Act 2002 s 44**). The reason for this is so that the local authority can visit the placement and prepare welfare reports to help the court decide whether the adoption is in Carrie's welfare. Under the **Adoption and Children Act 2002 s 42**, Carrie has to be placed with David for six months before he can apply to adopt her.

The court will only make an adoption order in favour of David if it is in Carrie's welfare to do so. The welfare of the child is now the court's paramount consideration (**s 1(2)**) and the court will use the welfare checklist in **s 1(4)** to determine what is in Carrie's welfare. From the facts, it seems that David has a good relationship with Carrie and would be able to care for her and meet her needs (**Adoption and Children Act 2002 s 1(4)(b)**). The main problem for the court is the fact that an adoption order would terminate the parental responsibility of Bertie and make him a legal stranger to his daughter. Although the facts state that Bertie has been violent in the past (**Adoption and Children Act 2002 s 1(4)(e)**), he has tried to maintain contact with his daughter and the court might well feel that it would not be in Carrie's interest to erase Bertie from her history (**Adoption and Children Act 2002 s 1(4)(c)**). Furthermore, Bertie has tried to obtain help for his problem and it is far from clear that he would be violent again. One advantage that adoption might have over alternatives is that it is permanent and because it removes Bertie's parental responsibility there would be no danger of Bertie interfering in how Anna and David were raising Carrie.

It is submitted, however, that this reasoning is less pertinent on these facts as Bertie does not seem to have undermined David and Anna's raising of Carrie.[1]

Furthermore, it should be noted that under the **Adoption and Children Act 2002 s1(6)** the court does have to consider whether any alternatives to adoption could better promote the welfare of the child. It is unclear why David wishes to adopt Carrie but if it is because he wishes to strengthen his rights in relation to Carrie, this could also be done through a child arrangement order or a special guardianship order, both of which would give David parental responsibility. If a child arrangement order is made then this would determine that Carrie lives (**Children Act 1989 s 8**) with David and Anna and would give David parental responsibility (**Children Act 1989 s 12**). Bertie would remain Carrie's father. He would retain parental responsibility and his right to apply for **s 8** orders to, for instance, secure his contact with his daughter would remain (**Children Act 1989 s 10(4)**). If David becomes Carrie's special guardian, the parental responsibility of Bertie is significantly curtailed, whilst not being extinguished completely (**Children Act 1989 s 14C**).

It is unlikely that the court would make an adoption order in this case. Carrie still has a relationship with her birth father and although Bertie has a violent and drug-using past, it seems that he has acknowledged that and has taken steps to deal with his issues. It is arguable that it is to Carrie's benefit to know both her birth parents as well as to have a good loving relationship with her stepfather. There is nothing on the facts that suggest that Bertie has undermined Anna or David and therefore there does not seem to be any reason to shut him out of Carrie's life by making the adoption order. Instead this seems that it may be a case where a child arrangement order setting out that Carrie lives with David and Anna and as a consequence giving David parental responsibility is the most appropriate order.

If the court had decided that adoption would be in Carrie's welfare, then the adoption order could only be made if Bertie consented to the adoption, or if his consent was dispensed with. It is unlikely that Bertie would consent. His consent could, however, be dispensed with if Carrie's welfare required it (**Adoption and Children Act 2002 s 52**). Although on the facts given, Carrie's welfare does not seem to require Bertie's consent to be dispensed with, if it were decided that her welfare did support adoption then arguably her welfare would require Bertie's consent to be dispensed with. In other words, it is difficult to think of a situation where the court decides that it is in a child's welfare to be adopted, but their welfare does not require a parent's consent to be dispensed with.

QUESTION 41

Tamsin is five. Tamsin's mother, Sarah, is an alcoholic and Tamsin is usually cared for by her maternal grandparents, Ruth and Peter. Although Tamsin usually lives with Ruth and Peter, occasionally Sarah demands that Tamsin leave her grandparents and come and live

---

1 Under the **Adoption Act 1976**, which was the previous adoption law, the child's welfare was the first consideration. The **Adoption and Children Act 2002 s 1(1)** changed this so that the child's welfare was the paramount consideration. This means that not only does the child's welfare outweigh all other considerations, it outweighs all other considerations put together.

with her. Ruth and Peter feel that this is very disruptive and upsetting for Tamsin and they also feel that Sarah's lifestyle means that she is not properly meeting Tamsin's needs. They would like to be able to keep Tamsin with them, but they do not feel that they can refuse Sarah's demands to return Tamsin to them. Ruth and Peter would like to become Tamsin's permanent legal carers and are considering adoption as a way of achieving this.

▶ **Advise Ruth and Peter.**

How to Read this Question

Although answers to this question need to explain adoption procedure and whether adoption would be allowed in this case, it is important to also discuss other ways in which Ruth and Peter can have permanent care for Tamsin and whether they might be more suitable.

Applying the Law

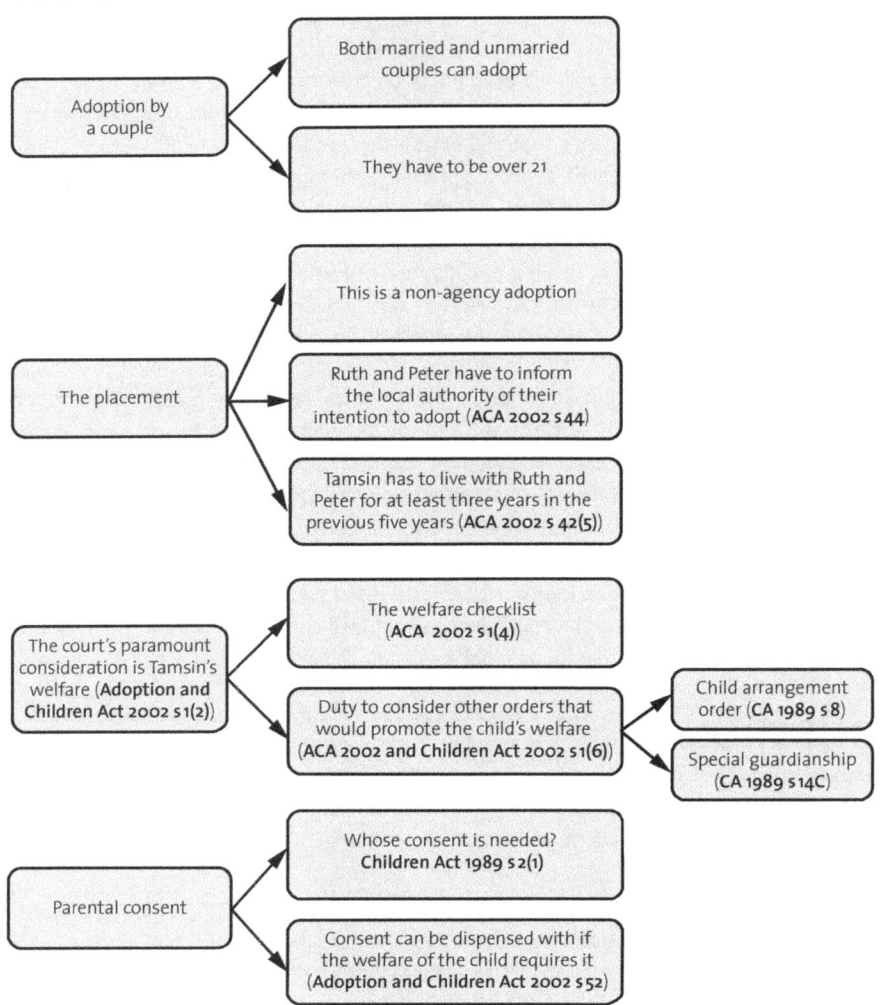

Adoption by a couple
- Both married and unmarried couples can adopt
- They have to be over 21

The placement
- This is a non-agency adoption
- Ruth and Peter have to inform the local authority of their intention to adopt (**ACA 2002 s 44**)
- Tamsin has to live with Ruth and Peter for at least three years in the previous five years (**ACA 2002 s 42(5)**)

The court's paramount consideration is Tamsin's welfare (Adoption and Children Act 2002 s 1(2))
- The welfare checklist (**ACA 2002 s 1(4)**)
- Duty to consider other orders that would promote the child's welfare (**ACA 2002 and Children Act 2002 s 1(6)**)
  - Child arrangement order (**CA 1989 s 8**)
  - Special guardianship (**CA 1989 s 14C**)

Parental consent
- Whose consent is needed? **Children Act 1989 s 2(1)**
- Consent can be dispensed with if the welfare of the child requires it (**Adoption and Children Act 2002 s 52**)

ANSWER

Ruth and Peter want to become their granddaughter Tamsin's permanent carers. They are considering adoption but it may be that other options, a child arrangement order or a special guardianship order, are more appropriate and more likely to be awarded by the courts.

Under the **Adoption and Children Act 2002** there are two main types of adoption – an agency adoption and a non-agency adoption. Under an agency adoption, the child is placed with the adoptive parents by the adoption agency. Under a non-agency adoption, the child does not need to be placed by the adoption agency because the child is already living with the prospective adopters. In this case, Tamsin is already living with Ruth and Peter so this is likely to be a non-agency adoption and they will have to give the adoption agency notice of their intention to adopt Tamsin under the **Adoption and Children Act 2002 s 44**. The purpose of giving this notice is to enable the local authority to support the family and so that the local authority is able to report to the court on whether adoption advances the child's welfare.

In order to adopt, Ruth and Peter both have to be over 21 (**Adoption and Children Act 2002 s 50**). Given that Ruth and Peter are grandparents, this requirement is clearly satisfied. They are entitled to adopt as a couple, and since the **Adoption and Children Act 2002** they will be able to adopt as a couple whether they are married or not, provided that their relationship is stable. Tamsin satisfies the requirements to be adopted in that she is not yet 19 or married (**Adoption and Children Act 2002 s 47(9)**). Finally, before Ruth and Peter can apply to court for an adoption order, Tamsin must have been living with them for a certain amount of time; in the case of Ruth and Peter, this is three years, whether or not continuous, in the preceding five years (**Adoption and Children Act 2002 s 42(5)**).

Tamsin's welfare is the court's paramount consideration in deciding whether to make the adoption order (**Adoption and Children Act 2002 s 1(2)**) and the court will use the welfare checklist to determine what is in Tamsin's welfare (**Adoption and Children Act 2002 s 1(4)**) as well as considering whether there are any other orders which might promote Tamsin's welfare. On the facts, Tamsin is well cared for by Ruth and Peter. They seem able to respond to her physical and emotional needs (**Adoption and Children Act 2002 s 1(4)(b), s 1(4)(f)**). In contrast, Tamsin risks harm with her mother, who is alcoholic and unable to properly care for Tamsin. Furthermore, the fact of being taken away from her established home with her grandparents by her mother is in itself a harm and one which adoption would prevent (**Adoption and Children Act 2002 s 1(4)(e)**).

On the other hand, there are problems with adoption. If Ruth and Peter adopt Tamsin, it would mean that her grandparents would become her parents and her birth mother would be her sister. This would be difficult and confusing for Tamsin. Moreover, at present, Sarah is an alcoholic; if she were ever able to recover from this, she may be able to resume care of her daughter and therefore adoption, which permanently removes her parental responsibility, may not be the best option for Tamsin's welfare.

The court also have to consider whether there are any other orders which would promote Tamsin's welfare and which might be preferable to adoption. Adoption does not just determine where a child lives and give the adopters parental responsibility, it removes the birth parent, and in the case of interfamily adoption it distorts the family relationship. If the aim is to give Ruth and Peter parental responsibility and to enable them to care for Tamsin, there are other, less extreme orders that would achieve this. A child arrangement order (**Children Act 1989 s 8**) determines where a child lives, and gives the person(s) with whom the child is living parental responsibility (**Children Act 1989 s 12**). A special guardianship order gives the special guardians parental responsibility (**Children Act 1989 s 14C**). For most decisions, the special guardians have exclusive parental responsibility and therefore Ruth and Peter would be able to prevent Sarah from removing Tamsin and be able to decide how to raise Tamsin; however, there are a couple of extremely significant decisions where Sarah's consent would still be needed.

One crucial difference between adoption and child arrangement orders or special guardianship orders is that in the former the birth parent is no longer classed as a parent and therefore loses the right to apply for **s 8** orders. In contrast, under a child arrangement order, or special guardianship order, the **Children Act 1989 s 10(4)** still applies and the birth parent can apply for **s 8** orders without the leave of the court. Potentially this could be disruptive and given that Sarah has a history of removing Tamsin from Ruth and Peter it is not too far-fetched to suggest that Sarah might use **s 8** applications to upset and disrupt Ruth and Peter looking after Tamsin.

On the facts, it is suggested that the choice is probably between an adoption order and a special guardianship order. The child arrangement order does not adequately protect Ruth, Peter and Tamsin from interference from Sarah. As for the choice between adoption order and special guardianship order, it is difficult to determine on the few facts which is the more suitable. In adoption's favour is the fact that it does give the greatest security and it is a lifetime order. On the other hand, this comes at the price of distorting the family tree.

If the court decide that adoption is in Tamsin's welfare then an adoption order can only be made if Sarah consents or if her consent is dispensed with (**Adoption and Children Act 2002 s 47(2)**). Sarah's consent is needed as she has parental responsibility for Tamsin (**Children Act 1989 s 2(2)**). It is unlikely that Sarah would consent, and therefore the court needs to consider whether Sarah's consent can be dispensed with. Although Sarah is an alcoholic, it is unlikely that she would be deemed incapable of giving consent, and therefore the question is whether Tamsin's welfare requires Sarah's consent to be dispensed with. Whilst the word requires does indicate that it is necessary for Tamsin's welfare for Sarah's consent to be dispensed with rather than merely preferable (*Re Q* (2011)), it is unlikely that a court would decide that adoption was in a child's welfare and then decline to make the order because of a parent's refusal.

Another possibility is that Ruth and Peter themselves decide not to apply for an adoption order, but instead to seek a child arrangement order or a special guardianship order. Ruth and Peter can apply automatically for a child arrangement order (**Children Act 1989 s 10(5)(b)**). The court would decide whether to make the child arrangement order on the basis of the welfare principle (**Children Act 1989 s 1(1)**) and the welfare checklist (**Children Act 1989 s 1(4)**). Given that Ruth and Peter are already caring for Tamsin and making the order would provide continuity of care rather than disruption, the order would be made. Ruth and Peter can also apply for a special guardianship order (**Children Act 1989 s 14A(2)(a)**, **Children Act 1989 s 14A(5)(c)**, **Children Act 1989 s 14A (5)(e)**). The court would decide that a special guardianship order was in Tamsin's welfare (**Children Act 1989 s 1(1)**). In both the child arrangement order and the special guardianship order the no order principle is satisfied (**Children Act 1989 s 1(5)**) as without the orders, Sarah is able to remove Tamsin.

Common Pitfalls

It is important not just to discuss adoption in general, but to explain what the adoption procedure is in this case and whether the child's welfare supports adoption in this case.

Aim Higher

- Be clear on how adoption, special guardianship and child arrangement orders differ and how each can be used to support the child's welfare.
- Be balanced and be able to explain any weaknesses with the different orders as well as their strengths.

QUESTION 42

To what extent does the special guardianship order offer a useful alternative to the adoption order?

How to Read this Question

Answers need to explain what the effects of the special guardianship order are and how these differ from those of an adoption order. Answers should explore whether the special guardianship order offers a useful alternative long-term measure to adoption.

Answer Plan

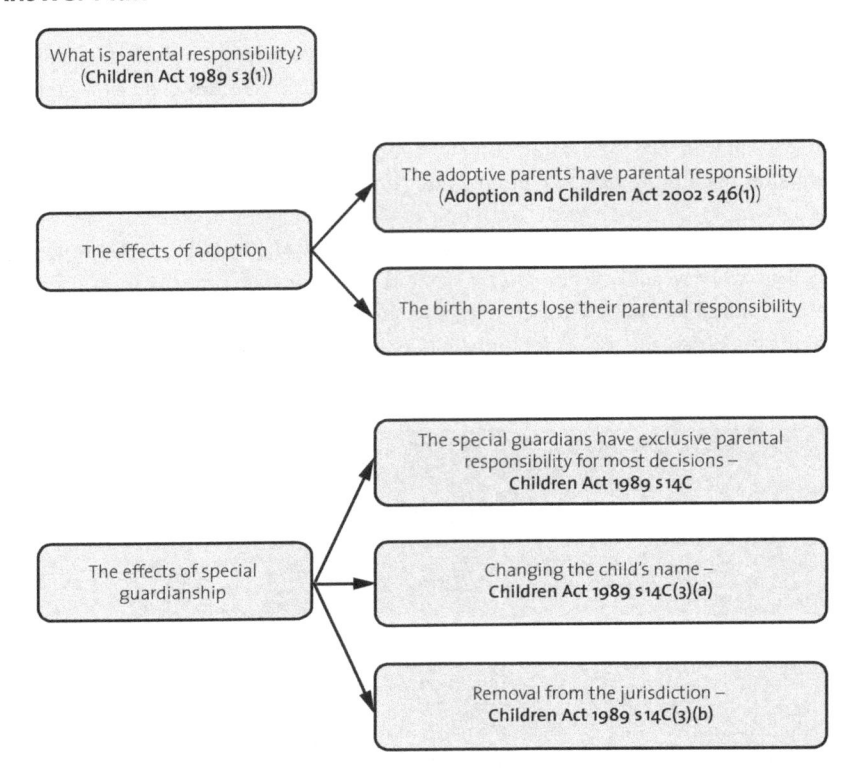

- What is parental responsibility? (**Children Act 1989 s 3(1)**)

- The effects of adoption
  - The adoptive parents have parental responsibility (**Adoption and Children Act 2002 s 46(1)**)
  - The birth parents lose their parental responsibility

- The effects of special guardianship
  - The special guardians have exclusive parental responsibility for most decisions – **Children Act 1989 s 14C**
  - Changing the child's name – **Children Act 1989 s 14C(3)(a)**
  - Removal from the jurisdiction – **Children Act 1989 s 14C(3)(b)**

ANSWER

When an adoption order is made, parental responsibility belongs exclusively to the adoptive parents. The parental responsibility of the birth parents comes to an end and legally they become strangers to the child (**Adoption and Children Act 2002 s 46(1)**). As well as reforming adoption law, the **Adoption and Children Act 2002** introduced special guardianship orders. Like adoption orders these are intended to offer a stable way of caring for and having responsibility for a child, but unlike adoption orders, the special guardianship order does not completely remove the parental responsibility of the birth parents. Under a special guardianship order, the special guardian will have exclusive parental responsibility for most decisions (**Children Act 1989 s 14C(1)(b)**); however, there is a core of especially significant decisions where the agreement of the birth parents, who have parental responsibility, is also required. This includes changing the child's surname (**Children Act 1989 s 14C(3)(a)**), removing the child from the jurisdiction for more than three months (**Children Act 1989 ss 14C(3)(b), 14C(4)**) and agreeing to the adoption of the child (**Children Act 1989 s 14C(20(b))**).

The idea behind special guardianship is that it offers a stable alternative to adoption in situations where adoption might not be appropriate. These situations are ones where, whilst the child may need a person to take on the responsibility of caring for them, they may not need or want a new parent and therefore adoption may not be suitable. The three situations that are most often thought to fulfil this are, first, the situation where a member of the child's family wants to adopt them (kinship adoption); second, adoption of an older child; and third, adoption within a particular racial context. With an older child, he or she will often have formed a close bond with a birth parent that may make adoption and the legal extinguishing of that bond inappropriate. Special guardianship may be an appropriate way of responding to the child's need for care whilst recognising the reality of the relationship between the child and his birth family. On the other hand, it is important to note that the nature and reality of adoption has also developed and it is possible for an adoption order to be made that does allow for continued contact, indirect or direct, to be allowed after the order. As for the racial dimension, some groups do not adopt for religious or cultural reasons. Special guardianship orders allow these individuals to undertake the long-term care of children. This may well be a particular advantage to children who also come from those racial groups.

One situation where special guardianship might be more appropriate than adoption is where a member of the child's family, for example a grandparent, wants to adopt the child (*Re S (Adoption Order or Special Guardianship Order)* (2007)). One difficulty with adoption in this situation is that it distorts family relationships. The child's grandparent becomes their parent, their parent is now a sibling, and so on. Nevertheless, when a court has to determine whether to make an adoption order or a special guardianship order, it has to do so on the basis of the child's welfare (**Adoption and Children Act 2002 s 1(2)**) and although the potential distorting of family relationships may be an important factor in this, it will not be the only consideration and there may be situations where adoption is preferred even in the kinship adoption context.

One advantage which adoption has over special guardianship is that it is arguably more secure. When an adoption order is made, the birth parent becomes a legal stranger. One effect of this is that they no longer have a right to apply for any **s 8** orders in respect of the child and therefore the child's new family life cannot be disrupted by spurious **s 8** applications. In contrast, with a special guardianship order, the birth parent remains the child's parent and therefore the order always risks being disrupted by applications for contact or residence or the special guardian's exercise of parental responsibility being curtailed under **s 8** of the **Children Act 1989**.

Along with adoption and child arrangement order, the special guardianship order offers another means by which a person can have parental responsibility for a child and be responsible for their care. As it offers something between those two orders there will be situations where it will be the most appropriate way of promoting the child's welfare.

QUESTION 43

Dawn is 25. She suffers from borderline personality disorder which is exacerbated by alcohol or drugs. Two years ago Dawn gave birth to a daughter, Evie. Evie was the result of a one night stand and neither she, nor Dawn, has seen Evie's father since. When Evie was about seven months old, a neighbour called the police after Evie was left alone whilst Dawn went out one night. This led to a police protection order and then to Evie being voluntarily accommodated under the **Children Act 1989 s 20**. Attempts were made to rehabilitate Evie with her mother, but sadly these always broke down, either as a result of Dawn's mental health, or because of her drinking and drug use. The local authority now believes that the best option for Evie is for her to be adopted and they have identified a couple they believe to be suitable, Fiona and Gary. Dawn has said that she is very unhappy at the proposed adoption and that she will not let Evie stay with Fiona and Gary. Dawn also has evidence that her own mental condition will worsen if the adoption is successful.

▶ Advise Fiona and Gary on the procedure to adopt Evie and discuss whether the adoption would be successful.

How to Read this Question

Answers need to be able to identify and explain the relevant adopton procedure and discuss whether adoption would be in Evie's welfare.

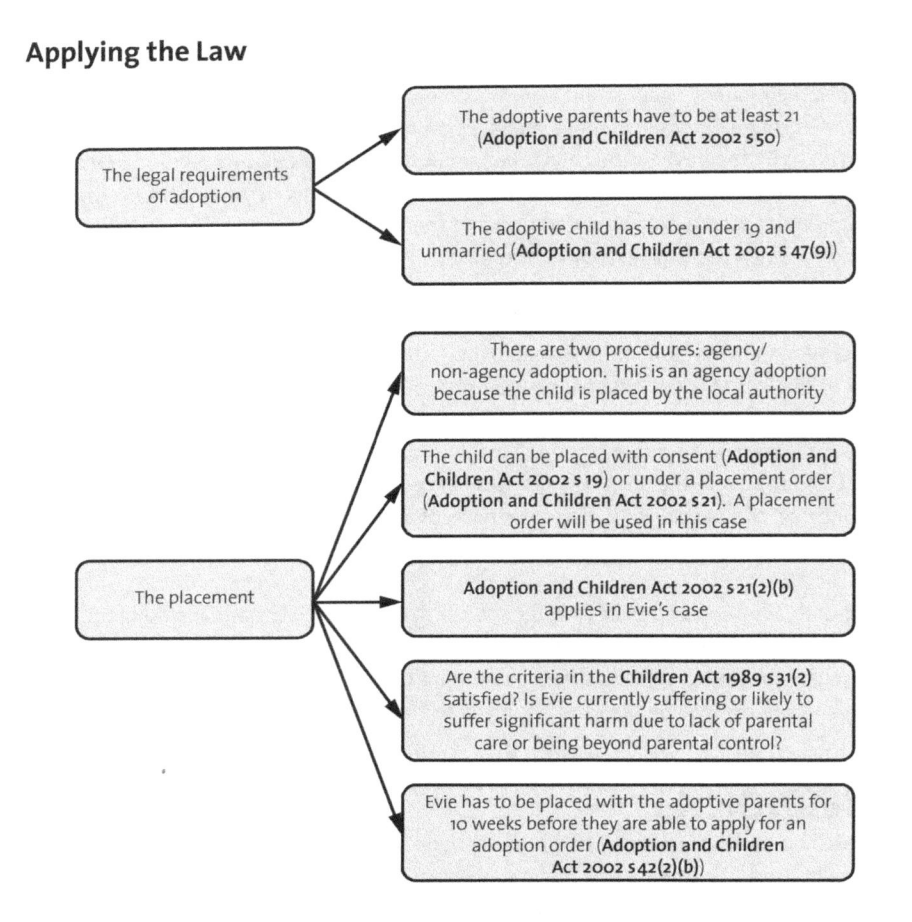

Applying the Law

The legal requirements of adoption
- The adoptive parents have to be at least 21 (**Adoption and Children Act 2002 s 50**)
- The adoptive child has to be under 19 and unmarried (**Adoption and Children Act 2002 s 47(9)**)

The placement
- There are two procedures: agency/non-agency adoption. This is an agency adoption because the child is placed by the local authority
- The child can be placed with consent (**Adoption and Children Act 2002 s 19**) or under a placement order (**Adoption and Children Act 2002 s 21**). A placement order will be used in this case
- **Adoption and Children Act 2002 s 21(2)(b)** applies in Evie's case
- Are the criteria in the **Children Act 1989 s 31(2)** satisfied? Is Evie currently suffering or likely to suffer significant harm due to lack of parental care or being beyond parental control?
- Evie has to be placed with the adoptive parents for 10 weeks before they are able to apply for an adoption order (**Adoption and Children Act 2002 s 42(2)(b)**)

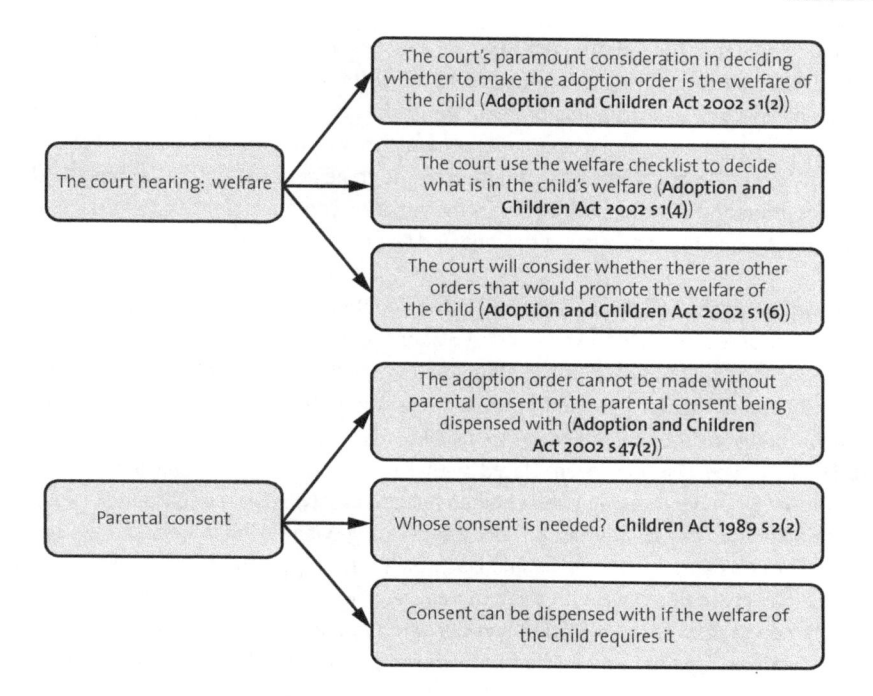

```
                    ┌──────────────────────────────────────────────┐
                    │ The court's paramount consideration in deciding │
                    │ whether to make the adoption order is the welfare │
                    │ of the child (Adoption and Children Act 2002 s1(2)) │
                    └──────────────────────────────────────────────┘
                    ┌──────────────────────────────────────────────┐
┌───────────────────┤ The court use the welfare checklist to decide │
│ The court hearing:├→ what is in the child's welfare (Adoption and │
│ welfare           │ Children Act 2002 s1(4))                      │
└───────────────────┤                                               │
                    └──────────────────────────────────────────────┘
                    ┌──────────────────────────────────────────────┐
                    │ The court will consider whether there are other │
                    │ orders that would promote the welfare of      │
                    │ the child (Adoption and Children Act 2002 s1(6)) │
                    └──────────────────────────────────────────────┘

                    ┌──────────────────────────────────────────────┐
                    │ The adoption order cannot be made without     │
                    │ parental consent or the parental consent being │
                    │ dispensed with (Adoption and Children         │
                    │ Act 2002 s47(2))                              │
                    └──────────────────────────────────────────────┘
┌───────────────────┐┌──────────────────────────────────────────────┐
│ Parental consent  ├→ Whose consent is needed? Children Act 1989 s2(2) │
└───────────────────┘└──────────────────────────────────────────────┘
                    ┌──────────────────────────────────────────────┐
                    │ Consent can be dispensed with if the welfare of │
                    │ the child requires it                         │
                    └──────────────────────────────────────────────┘
```

ANSWER

Having tried to rehabilitate Evie with her mother, Dawn, the local authority has now decided that Evie's needs will be served best by being adopted and have identified a suitable couple. As this is a case where the local authority would be placing the child for adoption, it would be an agency adoption. Agencies can place children either with parental consent (**Adoption and Children Act 2002 s 19**) – meaning with the consent of parents with parental responsibility – or through a placement order (**Adoption and Children Act 2002 s 21**). In this case, Dawn will have parental responsibility as she is Evie's birth mother (**Children Act 1989 s 2(2)**). As Evie was the result of a one night stand, and the father has not been seen since, she is likely to be the only parent with parental responsibility for Evie. On the facts, Dawn is opposed to the adoption and therefore the local authority will only be able to place Evie for adoption if they are able to obtain a placement order.[2]

The grounds for obtaining a placement order are set out in the **Adoption and Children Act 2002 s 21(2)**. **Subsection 21(2)(a)** does not apply here, because although there has been local authority involvement, it does not seem, on the facts, that Evie has actually been made subject to a care order. Similarly, **subs 21(2)(c)** is not relevant as Evie does have a parent, namely Dawn. Consequently, whether a placement order would be available depends on whether **subs 21(2)(b)** is applicable. **Subsection (b)** refers to cases where the

---

2 The first stage in the adoption process is the placement of the child with the prospective adoptive parents.

criteria in **s 31(2)** of the **Children Act 1989** are satisfied. In other words, it refers to children who are currently suffering, or who are at risk of suffering, significant harm. On the facts, Dawn has a drink and drug use problem which has made her incapable of meeting her daughter's needs; therefore a case could be made that were Evie to be returned to Dawn's care she would be at risk of significant harm through neglect. On this basis **subs 21(2)(b)** of the **Adoption and Children Act 2002** is satisfied, a placement order can be obtained and Evie can be placed for adoption with Fiona and Gary.

The purpose of the placement is to enable the adopters and the child to know each other and for social workers to check whether the adoptive placement does support the needs of the child. According to **s 42(2)** of the **Adoption and Children Act 2002**, Evie has to be placed with Fiona and Gary for a minimum of 10 weeks. When the placement order is made, the local authority will obtain parental responsibility for Evie (**Adoption and Children Act 2002 s 25(2)**) and once Evie has been placed with Fiona and Gary, they will obtain parental responsibility for her (**Adoption and Children Act 2002 s 25(3)**). This is important because one of the attributes of parental responsibility is deciding where a child lives, and as Dawn is opposed to Evie staying with Fiona and Gary, their having parental responsibility strengthens their ability to have Evie with them during the placement without Dawn removing her. Furthermore, **s 30(2)** of the **Adoption and Children Act 2002** makes it clear that Dawn does not have a legal right to remove Evie from Fiona and Gary's care during the placement order. Dawn could apply for the placement order to be revoked. To be successful in doing this, she would have to show that there has been a change in circumstances since the placement order was made, and on the facts, this does not appear to be the case.[3]

After placement, the next stage is for Fiona and Gary to apply to the court to adopt Evie. The court will have to check that the legal requirements for adoption are satisfied. Both Fiona and Gary must be over 21 (**Adoption and Children Act 2002 s 50**), which, although the facts are not explicit, it will be assumed that they are. The court will also need to check that Evie has been placed with them for long enough. Even if these legal requirements are satisfied, the court will only make an adoption order if it is in Evie's welfare so to do (**Adoption and Children Act 2002 s 1(2)**). The court will use the welfare checklist to determine whether Evie's welfare supports an adoption order being granted (**Adoption and Children Act 2002 s 1(4)**). Furthermore, because adoption determines not only where a child lives and who raises that child, but also the child's family status, it would not be enough for Fiona and Gary to show that they are suitable carers for Evie; they would also have to show that adoption is the best way of meeting her needs and the court will consider whether there are any, more suitable, orders that should be made (**Adoption and Children Act 2002 s 1(6)**).

Although there is not much information in the facts, it is arguable that Fiona and Gary would be able to convince the court that adoption would be in Evie's welfare. It does seem that Dawn is not able to provide a stable environment for Evie, and adoption does offer

3   Under the previous adoption law (**Adoption Act 1976**) the adoptive parents did not gain parental responsibility until the adoption order was made. This left the adoptive parents in a vulnerable position during the placement as they would not have parental responsibility but the birth parents still would.

Adoption | 185

the child long-term stability, therefore it could be argued that adoption is better for Evie's needs and protects her from harm which she might otherwise suffer through Dawn's neglect (**Adoption and Children Act 2002 s1(4)(b), s1(4)(e)**). Moreover, as Evie has spent most of her life in voluntary accommodation, there is not the concern that adoption would be taking her away from the family home and disrupting her life. One issue is Dawn's health. She claims that were Evie to be adopted, her health would deteriorate. Sadly for Dawn, this is irrelevant for the court. It is Evie's welfare that is paramount (**Adoption and Children Act 2002 s1(1)**), which means that it outweighs all other considerations.

Adoption is not the only way for Fiona and Gary to gain parental responsibility and have Evie living with them. The court could make a child arrangement order (**Children Act 1989 s8**) which determines where the child lives and gives the person with whom the child lives parental responsibility (**Children Act 1989 s12**). Alternatively, the court could make Fiona and Gary special guardians of Evie. This would give Fiona and Gary exclusive parental responsibility for most decisions affecting Evie (**Children Act 1989 s14C**). The problem with both the child arrangement order and special guardianship is that Dawn would remain Evie's mother and would retain her right to apply for **s8** orders without the leave of the court (**Children Act 1989 s10(4)**). Put simply, there is a greater risk of Dawn disrupting Evie's life with a child arrangement order or a special guardianship order and adoption offers more security.

For these reasons it is likely that the court would decide that adoption is in Evie's welfare. The next stage is to check whether Dawn is consenting. The consent of every parent with parental responsibility is needed before an adoption order can be made (**Adoption and Children Act 2002 s46**). As has already been explained, Dawn would have parental responsibility for Evie (**Children Act 1989 s2(2)**) so therefore her consent would be needed. As Dawn is likely to refuse her consent, the court would only be able to make the adoption order if her consent can be dispensed with under the **Adoption and Children Act 2002 s52**. Under this provision, the court can dispense with a parent's consent if the welfare of the child requires it. This means that it has to be necessary, rather than merely preferable, for the child's welfare that the adoption go ahead and the parent's refusal to consent be overruled (*Re Q* (2011)). The problem is that once the court has decided that it is in a child's welfare to be adopted, it is going to be exceptionally rare that the court will not decide that the child's welfare means that a parental refusal to consent should be overruled.

In conclusion, this is a case where an agency adoption of Evie by Fiona and Gary would be allowed.

QUESTION 44

Emily is five and has cerebral palsy. When Emily was six months old her mother, Debra, decided that she did not want to look after Emily and she was voluntarily placed in local accommodation under the **Children Act 1989 s20**. Since that time Emily has been looked after by foster carers and she has been with her latest carers, Clare and Brenda, for three years. Clare and Brenda have decided to apply to adopt Emily. Andrew is Emily's father.

Andrew did not have much of a relationship with Debra and only found out about Emily when she was three months old. He visited Emily a couple of times a year and has sent her birthday and Christmas cards. Six months ago, Andrew married Zoe. Andrew and Zoe have decided that they would like to have Emily live with them, or at least be more involved.

▶ Advise Andrew and Zoe on whether Brenda and Clare would be able to adopt Emily.

How to Read this Question

Andrew and Zoe want advice. As Brenda and Clare hope to adopt Emily, they need advice on what the procedure for this adoption is and whether they would be successful in opposing the adoption. The facts also state that Andrew and Zoe want to be more involved in Emily's life, including perhaps having Emily live with them. Answers should also explore how they could have Emily placed with them and whether such actions would be successful.

Applying the Law

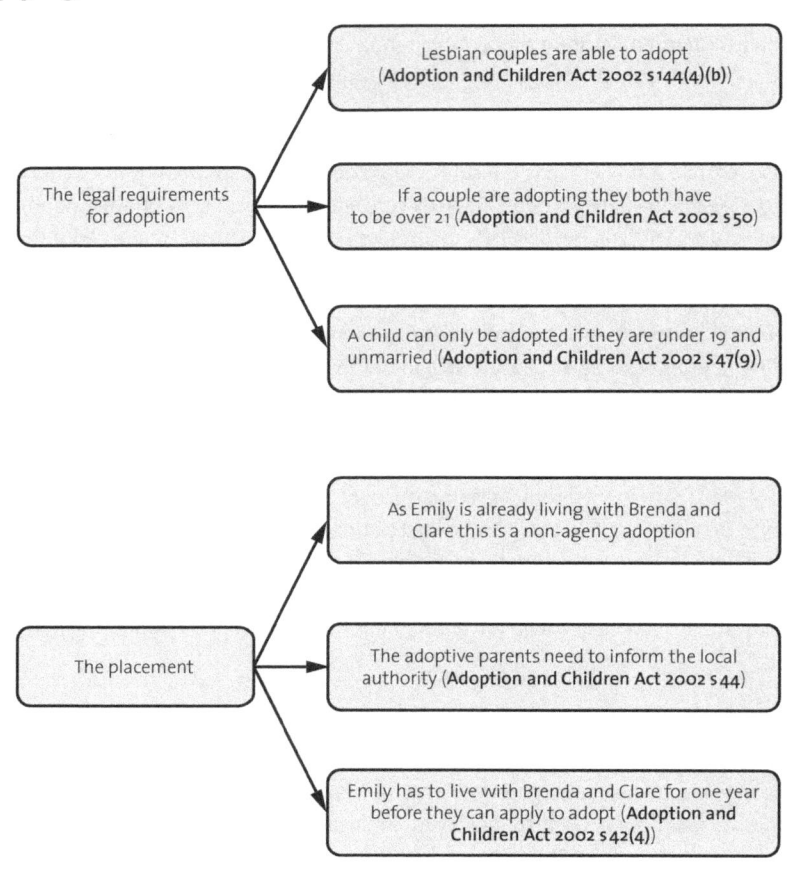

The legal requirements for adoption:
- Lesbian couples are able to adopt (**Adoption and Children Act 2002 s 144(4)(b)**)
- If a couple are adopting they both have to be over 21 (**Adoption and Children Act 2002 s 50**)
- A child can only be adopted if they are under 19 and unmarried (**Adoption and Children Act 2002 s 47(9)**)

The placement:
- As Emily is already living with Brenda and Clare this is a non-agency adoption
- The adoptive parents need to inform the local authority (**Adoption and Children Act 2002 s 44**)
- Emily has to live with Brenda and Clare for one year before they can apply to adopt (**Adoption and Children Act 2002 s 42(4)**)

Adoption 187

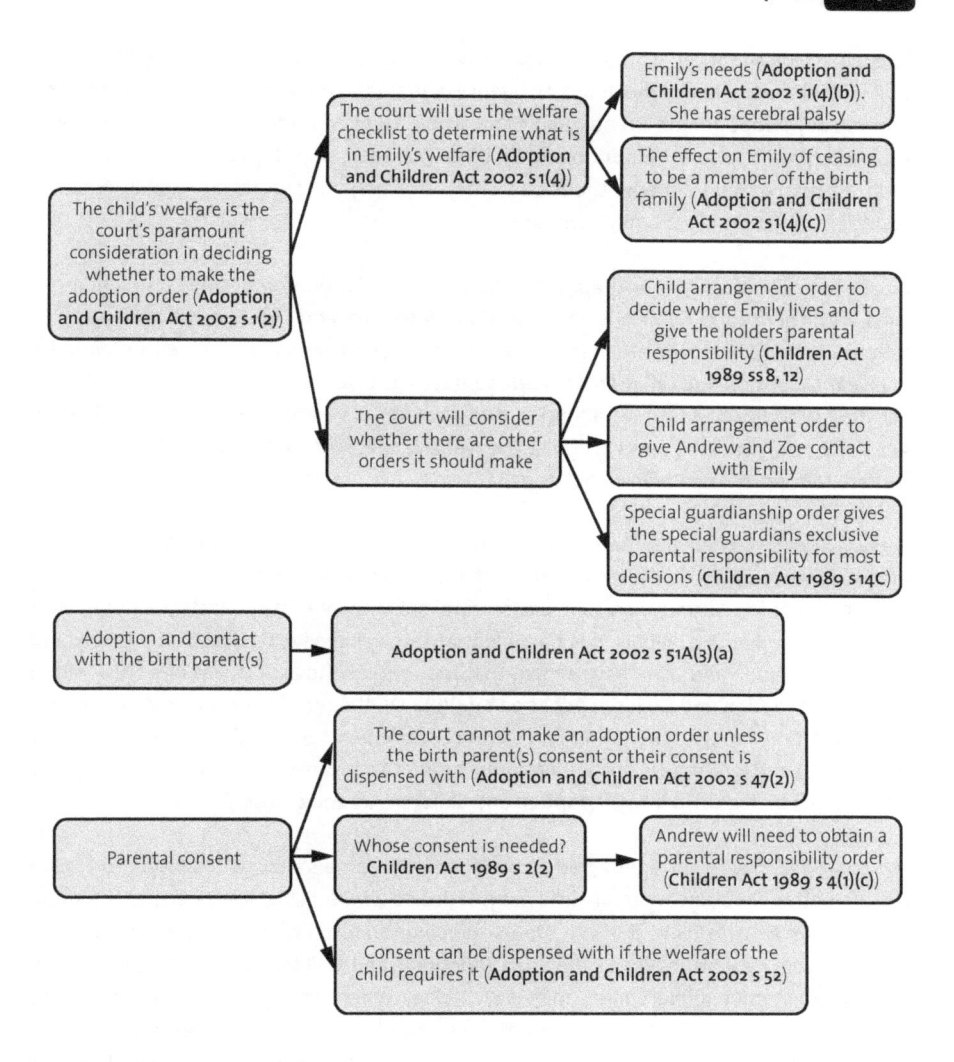

```
                                                                    ┌─────────────────────────────┐
                                                                    │ Emily's needs (Adoption and │
                                                                    │ Children Act 2002 s1(4)(b)).│
                                              ┌──────────────────┐  │ She has cerebral palsy      │
                                              │ The court will use│  └─────────────────────────────┘
                                              │ the welfare       │  ┌─────────────────────────────┐
                                              │ checklist to      │  │ The effect on Emily of      │
                                              │ determine what is │  │ ceasing to be a member of   │
                                              │ in Emily's welfare│  │ the birth family (Adoption  │
                                              │ (Adoption and     │  │ and Children Act 2002       │
                                              │ Children Act 2002 │  │ s1(4)(c))                   │
                                              │ s1(4))            │  └─────────────────────────────┘
┌──────────────────────┐                      └──────────────────┘
│ The child's welfare  │                                             ┌─────────────────────────────┐
│ is the court's       │                                             │ Child arrangement order to  │
│ paramount            │                                             │ decide where Emily lives    │
│ consideration in     │                                             │ and to give the holders     │
│ deciding whether     │                                             │ parental responsibility     │
│ to make the adoption │                                             │ (Children Act 1989 ss 8, 12)│
│ order (Adoption and  │                                             └─────────────────────────────┘
│ Children Act 2002    │                      ┌──────────────────┐   ┌─────────────────────────────┐
│ s1(2))               │                      │ The court will   │   │ Child arrangement order to  │
└──────────────────────┘                      │ consider whether │   │ give Andrew and Zoe contact │
                                              │ there are other  │   │ with Emily                  │
                                              │ orders it should │   └─────────────────────────────┘
                                              │ make             │   ┌─────────────────────────────┐
                                              └──────────────────┘   │ Special guardianship order  │
                                                                    │ gives the special guardians │
                                                                    │ exclusive parental          │
                                                                    │ responsibility for most     │
                                                                    │ decisions (Children Act     │
                                                                    │ 1989 s 14C)                 │
                                                                    └─────────────────────────────┘
```

```
┌──────────────────┐        ┌──────────────────────────────────────────┐
│ Adoption and     │   →    │ Adoption and Children Act 2002 s 51A(3)(a)│
│ contact with the │        └──────────────────────────────────────────┘
│ birth parent(s)  │
└──────────────────┘

                             ┌──────────────────────────────────────────┐
                             │ The court cannot make an adoption order  │
                             │ unless the birth parent(s) consent or    │
                             │ their consent is dispensed with          │
                             │ (Adoption and Children Act 2002 s 47(2)) │
                             └──────────────────────────────────────────┘
┌──────────────────┐         ┌──────────────────────┐   ┌──────────────────────────────┐
│ Parental consent │   →     │ Whose consent is     │ → │ Andrew will need to obtain a │
│                  │         │ needed? Children Act │   │ parental responsibility order│
│                  │         │ 1989 s 2(2)          │   │ (Children Act 1989 s 4(1)(c))│
└──────────────────┘         └──────────────────────┘   └──────────────────────────────┘
                             ┌──────────────────────────────────────────┐
                             │ Consent can be dispensed with if the     │
                             │ welfare of the child requires it         │
                             │ (Adoption and Children Act 2002 s 52)    │
                             └──────────────────────────────────────────┘
```

ANSWER

Andrew is Emily's birth father. Emily is currently living with her foster carers, Brenda and Clare, who plan to adopt Emily. Andrew will be opposed to this. He wants Emily to live with him and his wife Zoe. It is important therefore to consider what the adoption procedure would be for Brenda and Clare and whether they would be likely to be successful.

Brenda and Clare would be able to adopt as a couple. Given that Emily has already been living with the two of them for three years, it appears that their relationship is stable, and the law no longer distinguishes between married and unmarried couples and gay and straight couples (**Adoption and Children Act 2002 s 144(3)**). Furthermore, it is very probable that they are both over 21 (**Adoption and Children Act 2002 s 50**) and Emily is under 19 and not married (**Adoption and Children Act 2002 s 47(9)**), therefore the age requirements for both adopters and adoptive child are satisfied.

There are two adoption procedures: agency adoption where the child is placed for adoption with the adopters by the adoption agency, and non-agency adoption. This would be a non-agency adoption and Brenda and Clare would need to inform the local authority of their intention to adopt (**Adoption and Children Act 2002 s 44**). This would be so that the local authority could support them and Emily and prepare reports to explain whether adoption would promote Emily's welfare.

Prospective adopters can only apply to court for an adoption order when the child has lived with them for a sufficient period of time (**Adoption and Children Act 2002 s 42**). As they are foster carers who are planning to adopt, in Brenda and Clare's case that period is one year (**Adoption and Children Act 2002 s 42(4)**). The court's paramount consideration in deciding whether to make an adoption order is Emily's welfare (**Adoption and Children Act 2002 s 1(2)**) and the court will use the welfare checklist to decide what is in Emily's welfare (**Adoption and Children Act 2002**).

Emily is already settled with Brenda and Clare. After the disruption of being taken from her mother and being looked after by different foster carers, there now seems to be some stability in her life. Furthermore, she has cerebral palsy and whilst the facts are not explicit on how severe her disability is, it is possible that she will need extensive care possibly into adulthood. Brenda and Clare have shown that they are meeting the needs of a child with a disability (**Adoption and Children Act 2002 s 1(4)(b)**). On the other hand, against adoption is Emily's relationship with her father and stepmother. Andrew visits his daughter a couple of times a year and whilst he is not a main carer, it might be in Emily's welfare to maintain that link with her biological identity (**Adoption and Children Act 2002 s 1(4)(f)**).

The court also has to consider whether there are other orders that would promote Emily's welfare better. Crucially, adoption does not just decide where a child lives and give the adopters parental responsibility, it also removes the parental responsibility of the birth parents. They become legal strangers to the child (**Adoption and Children Act 2002 s 46**). A child arrangement order (**Children Act 1989 s 8**) decides where the child lives and gives the person(s) with whom the child lives parental responsibility (**Children Act 1989 s 12**). A special guardianship order gives the special guardian(s) exclusive parental responsibility for most decisions, but there remain a core of especially crucial decisions where the consent of the birth parents with parental responsibility is still needed (**Children Act 1989 s 14C**).

In Emily's case, it is submitted that the adoption order better provides security and permanence and better promotes her welfare. If a child arrangement order or a special guardianship order is made, the birth parent remains entitled to apply for s 8 orders automatically (**Children Act 1989 s 10(4)**) with the potential disruption this could cause. Furthermore, adoption is a lifetime order. In contrast, a child arrangement order only lasts at most until the child is 18, as does the special guardianship order. Given Emily's special needs, this is arguably important.

Although the court would likely decide that adoption is in Emily's welfare, it does not necessarily mean that Andrew's involvement with Emily would end completely. The idea of open adoption, where the child retains some contact with the birth family, is more accepted. Furthermore, under the **Adoption and Children Act 2002 s 51A** the court can make an order requiring the adopters to allow contact between the child and other significant individuals. As Andrew is her father and Zoe his wife, they would come within the list of people in whose favour such an order could be made (**Adoption and Children Act s 51A(3)(a)**). It is not clear on the facts how Brenda and Clare would view this contact, and traditionally courts have been reluctant to impose contact on unwilling adopters (*Re R (adoption: contact)* (2005)), but it is possible that contact would be seen as supporting Emily's welfare and therefore an order made.

Having decided that adoption is in Emily's welfare, the court can only make the adoption order if the parents with parental responsibility consent, or their consent is dispensed with (**Adoption and Children Act 2002 s 47(2)**). As Debra was not married when she had Emily, only Debra will automatically have parental responsibility for Emily (**Children Act 1989 s 2(2)**). Moreover, on the facts, it is extremely unlikely that Andrew will have parental responsibility through being on Emily's birth certificate (**Children Act 1989 s 4(1)(a)**) or through a parental responsibility agreement with Debra (**Children Act 1989 s 4(1)(b)**), therefore Andrew would need to apply to court for a parental responsibility order (**Children Act 1989 s 4(1)(c)**). The court's paramount consideration in deciding whether to make the parental responsibility order would be Emily's welfare (**Children Act 1989 s 1(1)**). It is probable that the court would make the order seeing it as important for Emily's welfare that Andrew's fatherhood is acknowledged and that he is allowed to be involved in the adoption process.

On the facts it is likely that Andrew would refuse to consent to the adoption. If this were to happen, the adoption could only go ahead if his consent could be dispensed with. Under the **Adoption and Children Act 2002 s 52** parental consent can be dispensed with if the welfare of the child requires it. Although the word 'requires' suggests that it has to be necessary rather than merely preferable to dispense with parental consent due to the welfare of the child, it is unlikely in reality that a court would decide that it was in a child's welfare to be adopted and then allow the adoption to fail purely because of the birth parent's refusal to consent. As a result, it is probable that Andrew's (and Debra's, if relevant) consent would be dispensed with under the **Adoption and Children Act 2002 s 52**.

In conclusion, Brenda and Clare would be able to adopt Emily, but Andrew would still be able to have contact and in time this may become staying contact.

QUESTION 45

Hayley is 25. Hayley's third child, Katy, is two months old. Hayley's first child, Isobel, is eight. She was removed from Hayley's care when she was 18 months old after serious physical abuse and neglect and was later adopted. Hayley's son, Josh, is four. He was taken into care because of neglect when he was six months old and has also been adopted. The local authority is concerned about Hayley's ability to care for her new child. At the moment Hayley has agreed to Katy being voluntarily accommodated under the

Children Act 1989 s 20 but Hayley has said that she hopes eventually to get Katy back and have her living at home. The local authority would like to place Katy for adoption. Hayley is strongly opposed to this. She argues that because she is now older she will be able to care for Katy. She also argues that Katy has a different father than her older children and that some of the abuse and neglect of the older children was due to their father. Katy's father left Hayley not long after she discovered she was pregnant and does not want to be involved with Katy's future. Hayley admits that she has significant mental health issues which can make it difficult for her to care for her children but she believes that now she is no longer pregnant and is able to take all her medication again she will be more stable and be able to look after Katy.

▶ Advise the local authority on the adoption procedure in this case and whether an adoption order would be likely to be made.

How to Read this Question

You need to advise the local authority on what the adoption procedure would be and whether an adoption order would be made in this case.

Applying the Law

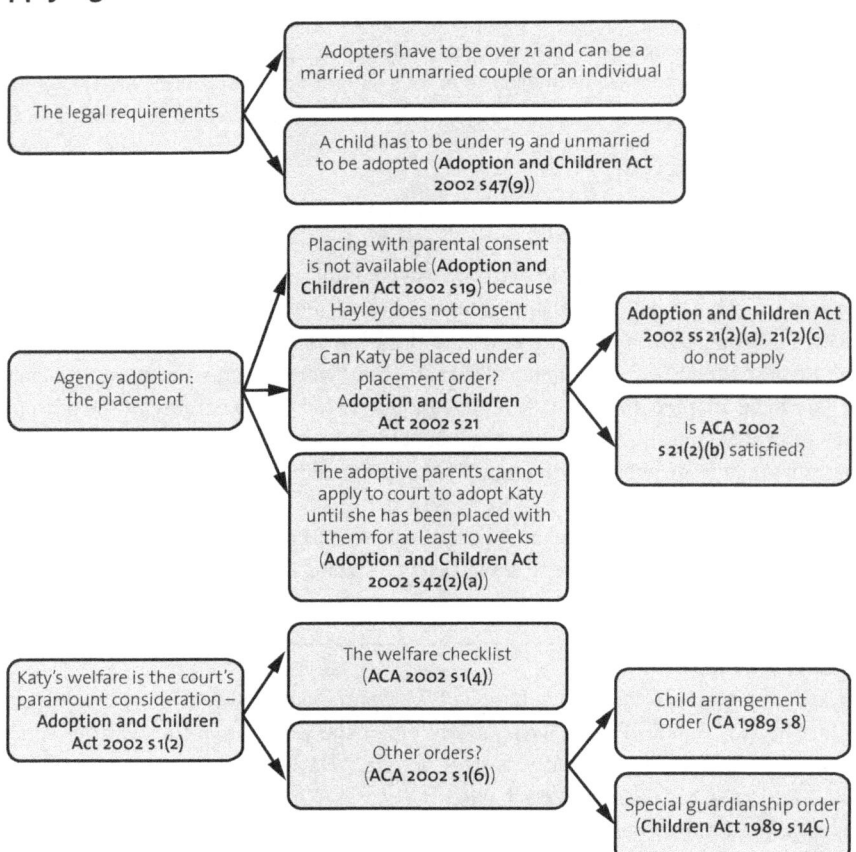

The legal requirements
- Adopters have to be over 21 and can be a married or unmarried couple or an individual
- A child has to be under 19 and unmarried to be adopted (**Adoption and Children Act 2002 s 47(9)**)

Agency adoption: the placement
- Placing with parental consent is not available (**Adoption and Children Act 2002 s 19**) because Hayley does not consent
- Can Katy be placed under a placement order? **Adoption and Children Act 2002 s 21**
  - **Adoption and Children Act 2002 ss 21(2)(a), 21(2)(c)** do not apply
  - Is ACA 2002 s 21(2)(b) satisfied?
- The adoptive parents cannot apply to court to adopt Katy until she has been placed with them for at least 10 weeks (**Adoption and Children Act 2002 s 42(2)(a)**)

Katy's welfare is the court's paramount consideration – Adoption and Children Act 2002 s 1(2)
- The welfare checklist (**ACA 2002 s 1(4)**)
- Other orders? (**ACA 2002 s 1(6)**)
  - Child arrangement order (**CA 1989 s 8**)
  - Special guardianship order (**Children Act 1989 s 14C**)

Adoption

```
┌─────────────────┐      ┌──────────────────────────┐
│                 │─────▶│ The court cannot make    │
│                 │      │ the adoption order without│
│                 │      │ the birth parent(s)      │
│                 │      │ consenting or consent    │
│                 │      │ being dispensed with     │
│                 │      │ (Adoption and Children   │
│                 │      │ Act 2002 s 47(2))        │
│                 │      └──────────────────────────┘
│ Parental consent│      ┌──────────────────────────┐
│                 │─────▶│ Whose consent is needed? │
│                 │      │ (Children Act 1989 s 2(2))│
│                 │      └──────────────────────────┘
│                 │      ┌──────────────────────────┐
│                 │─────▶│ Parental consent can     │
│                 │      │ be dispensed with if     │
│                 │      │ the welfare of the       │
└─────────────────┘      │ child requires it        │
                         │ (Adoption and Children   │
                         │ Act 2002 s 52)           │
                         └──────────────────────────┘
```

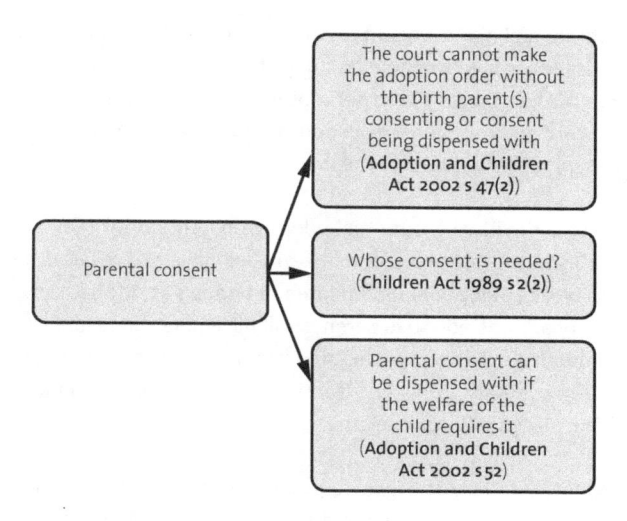

ANSWER

Katy is currently being voluntarily accommodated. The local authority plan for her is for her to be adopted. There are two adoption procedures: agency adoption where the child is placed for adoption by the adoption agency and non-agency adoption where the child is already living with the adopters. In this case, the local authority, as an adoption agency, would be placing Katy for adoption and therefore this is an agency adoption. The local authority will need to identify suitable adopters for Katy. Both couples and individuals are able to adopt, the only requirement is that they are over 21 (**Adoption and Children Act 2002 ss 50, 51**). Apart from that the adoption agency is bound by the principle that the welfare of the child is paramount (**Adoption and Children Act 2002 s 1(2)**) and will try to match Katy with adopters who are able to promote her welfare.

In an agency adoption, it is possible for the child to be placed with parental consent (**Adoption and Children Act 2002 s 19**), or under a placement order (**Adoption and Children Act 2002 s 21**). As she has parental responsibility for Katy (**Children Act 1989 s 2(2)**), Hayley would be able to consent to Katy's placement, but on the facts it is clear that she will oppose the adoption and therefore would not consent to the placement. Consequently, the only way that Katy can be placed for adoption is under a placement order. As Hayley can be found, and a care order is not currently in place for Katy, neither **subs 21(2)(a)** or **21(2)(c)** apply, therefore a placement order will only be available if **subs 21(2)(b)** is satisfied; namely if the conditions in the **Children Act 1989 s 31(2)** are satisfied in relation to Katy.

The conditions in the **Children Act 1989 s 31(2)** are that the child is suffering or is likely to suffer significant harm due to lack of parental care or the child being beyond parental control. Hayley's older children, Isobel and Josh, were removed from her care and adopted because of physical abuse and neglect. Physical abuse and neglect come within the definition of harm (**Children Act 1989 s 31(9)**). Whether Katy would be likely to suffer significant harm would be judged on the balance of probabilities (*Re B (Sexual Abuse: Standard of*

Proof) (2008)). Given that both her siblings have suffered harm and neglect and Hayley has continuing mental health issues, it is reasonable to suggest that Katy would also be at risk of significant harm were she to be returned to her mother's care. Furthermore, this harm is due to lack of parental care and therefore the conditions in the **Children Act 1989 s 31(2)** are satisfied and a placement order would be available.

During the placement, Katy will live with the potential adoptive parents until they are able to apply to adopt her. As this is an agency placement, Katy will have to live with the adoptive parents for at least 10 weeks (**Adoption and Children Act 2002 s 42(2)(a)**). During the placement, the local authority and the adoptive parents will have parental responsibility for Katy (**Adoption and Children Act 2002 s 25**), this, and the fact that only the adoption agency would be able to remove Katy from the adoptive placement (**Adoption and Children Act 2002 s 30**), make the placement more secure.

The court will only make the adoption order if the legal requirements for adoption are satisfied and if adoption promotes Katy's welfare (**Adoption and Children Act 2002 s 1(2)**). It is Katy's welfare which is paramount. Hayley's welfare and her mental health would be relevant only insofar as it impacts on Katy's welfare. The court will use the welfare checklist in **subs 1(4)** to determine what is in Katy's welfare. The court will consider the extent to which Katy is at risk of harm (**Adoption and Children Act 2002 s 1(4)(e)**): Katy's older siblings suffered physical harm and neglect whilst in Hayley's care and Katy herself has been placed in voluntary accommodation. Hayley suffers from mental illness which has impaired her ability to recognise or meet her children's needs. Moreover, Katy's father has left and is therefore not around to help Hayley or care for Katy. Hayley does claim that her situation now is distinguishable from how it was with her older children. Katy has a different father and therefore Isobel and Josh's abusive father is not involved. Hayley is older and, she claims, more mature, and able to control her mental health with appropriate medication. Nevertheless, despite Hayley's claim that Katy's situation is different from that of her older children, it is very likely that a court would consider the risk of harm to Katy to be significant (*Borough of Poole v Mr and Mrs W* (2014)).

The court has to consider whether there are other orders which would better support Katy's welfare (**Adoption and Children Act 2002 s 1(6)**). The child arrangement order (**Children Act 1989 s 8**) can be used to determine where a child lives and gives the person with whom the child lives parental responsibility (**Children Act 1989 s 12**). Special guardianship gives the special guardians exclusive parental responsibility for most decisions (**Children Act 1989 s 14C**). Nevertheless, in Katy's case, an adoption order is preferable. Unlike the child arrangement order or special guardianship it lasts for Katy's life. Furthermore, under an adoption order, in contrast to the child arrangement order or a special guardianship order, legally Hayley becomes a stranger to Katy and loses her right to apply for **s 8** orders.

Having decided that adoption would be in Katy's welfare, the next issue is whether Hayley would consent to the adoption or whether her consent can be dispensed with (**Adoption and Children Act 2002 s 47(2)**). Hayley's consent is needed because she has parental responsibility for Katy (**Children Act 1989 s 2(2)**). On the facts, it is most probable that Hayley would refuse consent to the adoption. If this were to happen, the adoption could only proceed if Hayley's consent were dispensed with (**Adoption and Children Act 2002 s 52**). The grounds for dispensing with consent are that Hayley is incapable of giving consent, or that Katy's welfare requires that Hayley's consent is dispensed with.

Although Hayley clearly has mental health issues requiring medication, it is not clear that these would make her incapable of consenting to adoption. Instead it is more likely that Hayley's consent will be dispensed with on the grounds that Katy's welfare requires it. The word 'requires' suggests that it must be necessary for Katy's welfare to dispense with Hayley's consent rather than merely preferable. It is, however, difficult to imagine that a court would decide that a child's welfare supported adoption but allowed itself to be prevented from making an adoption order by the parent's refusal to consent. In other words, if it is in a child's welfare to be adopted, then it will usually also be the case that the child's welfare will require parental consent to be dispensed with. For these reasons, it is probable that Hayley's consent would be dispensed with and the adoption order made.

Index

Page numbers in *italics* denote tables.

abuse of children **155–6, 159, 167–8, 191**
adoption **171–93**; adoption orders **172, 174, 175, 177, 178, 182, 184, 188, 189, 190, 192**; age requirements, adopter and adoptee **171, 173, 174, 176, 177, 182, 184, 186, 187, 190**; agency adoption **171, 174, 177, 182, 183, 186, 187, 191**; child arrangement order as alternative to *172, 173,* **175, 176, 177, 178, 179, 185, 187, 188, 190, 192**; and contact with birth parents **171, 172, 173, 174, 187, 188–9**; by homosexual/lesbian couples **186**; kinship **175–9, 181**; and local authorities **174, 176, 182, 183, 186, 187, 191**; by married couples **176**; non-agency **171, 173, 174, 176, 177, 182, 186, 187, 191**; open **188**; parental consent **172, 173, 175, 176, 178, 183, 185, 186, 189, 190, 191, 192–3**; and parental responsibility **171,** *172,* **174, 180, 188**; placement orders *see* placement orders; and race **171**; special guardianship order as alternative to *172, 173,* **175, 176, 177, 178, 179–81, 187, 188, 190, 192**; by unmarried couples **176**; and welfare of the child **171, 173, 174, 176, 177, 183, 184, 185, 187, 188, 190, 191, 192, 193**
adultery **14, 19, 21, 25, 34, 36, 37, 62, 74, 77**
arranged marriages **13**
arrest, power of **104, 111–12**
assisted reproduction **121**
associated persons **99, 102–3**; non-molestation orders **101, 103, 108, 111, 112, 113, 114, 115**; occupation orders **105, 118**

bankruptcy **90**
behaviour: and divorce **19, 21–2, 25, 29, 30, 37**
bigamous marriage **5**

Booth Committee on Matrimonial Causes Procedures **37–8**
capacity to marry **5–6, 9**
care orders **122, 152,** *152, 153,* **154, 155, 157, 159–61, 166, 167–9**; interim **152, 156**; threshold criteria **152, 154, 156, 157, 159, 163, 167, 168, 169**; welfare checklist **154, 158, 159, 163, 167, 168**; welfare principle **156, 158**
child arrangement orders **127, 134–7, 147, 158, 161–2**; as alternative to adoption *172, 173,* **175, 176, 177, 178, 179, 185, 187, 188, 190, 192**; and contact **135–7, 138, 140, 144, 146**; and parental responsibility **122, 127, 148,** *172,* **178, 185, 188, 192**; and welfare of the child **129, 134, 135, 137, 138, 139–40, 141, 144–5, 148, 161, 179**
child assessment orders **151,** *153,* **154, 156, 162, 165**
child maintenance **67–80**; assessment **67**; biological/adoptive children **67, 73, 74, 78**; child/children of the family **68, 73, 74–5, 76, 78, 79**; collection **68**; and consent orders **78, 79**; and earning capacity **76**; formulae for calculating **67**; and income **76**; lump sum orders **73, 75, 78**; non-payment **68**; non-resident parent **67, 68, 72, 78, 79**; periodical payments **73, 75, 76, 78, 79**; and presumption of legitimacy **74**; private ordering **67**; property adjustment orders **73, 79**; and standard of living **76–7**; and State benefits **76**; step-parent liability **78**; unmarried adult partners **68, 97**
child protection: and local authorities **151–69**; and welfare of the child **122, 151**; *see also* child protection orders

Index

child protection orders 122; care orders *see* care orders; child assessment orders 151, *153*, 154, 156, 162, 165; emergency protection orders 151, 153, 154, 156, 160, 162, 165–6; police protection orders 151, *153*; supervision orders 152, *153*, 154, 155, 163, 166, 169

children: abuse of *see* abuse of children; adoption of *see* adoption; beyond parental control 152, 154, 155, 156, 157, 159, 163, 167, 168, 182, 191; and clean break divorce 47, 76; contact with *see* contact; contraception for 130, 133; and domestic violence 99, 103, 104, 105, 108, 110, 111, 112, 113, 115, 118; education 130, 132, 149; *Gillick* competent 123, 125, 129, 130n1, 145; harm 151, 152, 154, 155, 156, 157, 159, 165, 166, 167–8, 182, 184, 191, 192; of homosexual/lesbian partners 143–6, 146–50; lack of parental care 154, 155, 156, 157, 159, 163, 167, 168, 182, 191; legitimacy, presumption of 74; and the local authority *see* local authorities; medical treatment, consent to 123, 125, 129; in need 151, 155, 158, 162 (accommodation for 158, 162, 164–5); relevant child concept 99, 103, 104, 105, 106, 108, 110, 111, 112, 113, 115, 118; removal from the jurisdiction 128, 180; residence, shared or transferred 141, 142–3; special guardianship *see* special guardianship; surname, change of 137, 138, 140, 146, 148, 149–50, 180; welfare of *see* welfare of the child

civil partnership 11–14; dissolution of 11, 12, 14; nullity of 11, 12; and parental responsibility 122; void 3, 12; voidable 3, 12, 13

clean break divorce 41, 45–8, 51, 61, 73, 79; and children 47, 76; pension splitting 48

cohabitants: beneficial interest in property 94–7, 99; with children 97; and domestic violence 100, 102, 103, 106; non-molestation orders 113, 115; occupation orders 100, 106, 107, 112–13

cohabitation: and child maintenance 72; long-term 97

common law marriage 9, 10

compensation 41, 51, 53, 61

consent: adoption *see* adoption; separation with 21, 29, 36, 37;
separation without 21, 24, 29, 36, 37, 50; to medical treatment 123, 125, 129

consent orders 78, 79

constructive trusts 81, 84, 85, 86, 87, 88, 91, 92, 94, 95, 96, 116

consummation of marriage 13; and transsexuality 16; *see also* non-consummation

contact: and child arrangement orders 135–7, 138, 140, 144, 146; with a child in care 152; and domestic violence 127; enforcement measures 141, 143; implacable hostility to 127; post-adoption 171, 172, 173, 174, 187, 188–9

contact activity directions 141, 143

contact orders 127, 146; *see also* child arrangement orders

contempt of court: obstructive parents 141, 142

contraception for children 130, 133

Criminal Injuries Compensation Scheme 61

death, presumption of 8, 9, 32, 33, 35

desertion 19, 25, 26, 27n5, 30–1, 37

detrimental reliance 81, 83, 87, 91, 94, 96

disability 50, 59, 61, 62

dissolution of civil partnership 11, 12, 14

dissolution of marriage 33, 35

divorce 19–40; and adultery 19, 21, 25, 36, 37; availability of 20–3, 29–32; and behaviour 19, 21–2, 25, 29, 30, 37; clean break in *see* clean break divorce; consent to 23, 27; and desertion 19, 25, 26, 27n5, 30–1, 37; fault-based facts 36, 37–8, 46; financial provision following *see* financial provision; five facts 20, 21, 24, 25, 29, 36; and hardship 19, 23, 27, 28, 31, 38; information meetings 39; intolerability 21; irretrievable breakdown 19, 21, 24–5, 29, 36, 38, 46, 50; legal aid 38; living apart 19, 22, 23, 26–7, 31, 36; mediation 19, 38–9, 55; no-fault 36, 37, 38, 39, 40; procedure 19, 35–40; reconciliation 25, 26, 39, 40; and religion 28, 31, 32, 50; separate households 27, 31; separation 23, 25 (with consent 21, 26, 29, 36, 37; without consent 21, 24, 29, 36, 37, 50); special procedure 22, 36, 37

DNA testing 74

domestic violence 55, 99–119; associated persons 99, 101, 102–3, 105, 108, 111, 112;

and cohabitants 100, 102, 103, 106; harassment 103; harm (balance of 105, 108, 110; significant 99, 105, 107, 108, 110, 118); and homosexual relationships 103; molestation 99, 103, 104; non-molestation orders *see* non-molestation orders; occupation orders *see* occupation orders; and relevant child concept 99, 103, 104, 105, 106, 108, 110, 111, 112, 113, 115, 118
domicile: and marriage 5–6, 9–10
duress: civil partnership voidable because of 13; marriage voidable because of 3, 13, 34

education 130, 132, 149
emergency protection orders 151, *153*, 154, 156, 160, 162, 165–6
enforcement orders: contact 141, 143
exclusion orders 151, 152
express trusts 81, 91, 94, 116

family assistance orders 141
financial hardship: divorce 23, 27, 28, 31, 38
financial provision for adult partners 31–2, 41–66, 69–72, 73, 74; and behaviour 70; and children's welfare 47, 48, 50, 56, 57, 58, 59, 60, 61; clean break 41, 45–8, 51, 73; compensation 41, 51, 53, 61; and conduct 44, 52, 57, 60, 62, 71; County Court applications 43, 45, 69, 71–2; during marriage 41, 42–5, 69–72; and earning capacity 44, 47, 51, 53, 60, 61, 70; equal division of property 41, 53, 57–9; failure to maintain ground 43, 45, 70, 72; and financial resources 44; and income 44, 61; lump sum awards 43, 44, 45, 65, 70, 72; Magistrates' Court applications 43–5, 69–70; pensions 27–8, 31, 41; periodical payment orders 41, 43, 44, 45, 63, 64–6, 70, 71, 72; post-marriage agreement 55, 59; pre-nuptial agreements *see* pre-nuptial agreements; and self-sufficiency promotion 44, 46, 61; and State benefits 61–2, 70
financial provision for children *see* child maintenance

gifts 88; between engaged couples 82, 83–4

Gillick competence 123, 125, 129, 130n1, 145
grandparents: adoption by 175–9, 181; application for child arrangement order 135, 136–7, 158, 161–2

harassment 103
hardship: and divorce 19, 23, 27, 28, 31, 38
harm: balance of harm test 105, 108, 110; definition of 110, 156, 159; unknown perpetrator of 152, 166, 167, 168, 169; *see also* significant harm
homosexual and lesbian relationships: and adoption 186; and child care 143–6, 146–50; civil partnership 3, 11–14; and domestic violence 103

implied trusts 81, 84, 85, 88, 91, 92, 94
inheritance: failure to provide reasonable financial provision 93
injunctions 100
interim care orders 152, 156
intolerability 21, 34–5

joint bank accounts 82, 83, 84, 88
judicial separation 32, 33, 34–5
'jury test' 30

land ownership 81
Law Commission: on divorce 38, 39, 46; on domestic violence 10, 102–3, 104; on matrimonial home rights 105; on non-molestation orders 104; on occupation of the home 105; on pre-nuptial agreements 57
legal aid 43; divorce 38
legitimacy, presumption of 74
lesbian relationships *see* homosexual and lesbian relationships
lex loci 9, 10
local authorities: and adoption 174, 176, 183, 186, 187, 191; and child protection *see* child protection; duty to investigate 154, 155–6, 164; parental responsibility 155, 156, 157, 160–1, 165, 167, 184, 192; partnership with parents 151, 164

maintenance *see* child maintenance; financial provision
marriage: arranged 13; bigamous 5; capacity 5–6, 9; common law 9, 10; consummation of 13; couples'

marriage *continued*
  contributions to 44, 50, 57, 60, 62, 92–3, 94; dissolution of 33, 35; and domicile 5–6, 9–10; and *lex loci* 9, 10; non-consummation of *see* non-consummation of marriage; nullity of *see* nullity of marriage; polygamous 5, 6, 10; sham 3; step-relatives 6–7; and transsexuality 3, 14–17; void 3, 5, 8, 10, 11, 15, 17, 33; voidable *see* voidable marriage
Martin order 48
matrimonial home 84–6, 87–94
matrimonial home rights 99, 101, 104–5, 107, 109, 111, 112, 116, 117
matrimonial property 53, 57, 58–9
mediation: divorce 19, 38–9, 55
medical treatment: consent to 123, 125, 129; refusal of 123
mental illness 25, 26, 34, 71, 159, 192
Mesher order 48, 63, 64, 65, 66
mistake, marriage voidable for 32, 34
molestation 99, 103, 104, 111; *see also* non-molestation orders

name *see* surname
no delay principle 122, 129, 134, 137, 138, 144, 147, 154, 158, 163, 167
no order principle 122, 129, 134, 137, 138, 144, 147, 151, 154, 155, 158, 163, 167, 179
non-consummation of marriage 5, 13, 34; incapacity 7, 8, 13, 33; just cause for 33n10; wilful refusal 7, 8, 10, 13, 32, 33, 34
non-molestation orders 99, 103–4, 107, 109n5, 111–12, 114, 115; arrest, power of 104, 111–12; associated persons 101, 103, 108, 111, 112, 113, 114, 115; cohabitants 113, 115; *ex parte* applications 100, 114, 115; length of 104; and relevant child concept 103, 104, 111, 113
nullity of civil partnership 11, 12
nullity of marriage 3, 4–11, 32, 33–4; duress 3, 13; non-consummation *see* non-consummation; and transsexuality 15–17; void marriage 3, 5, 8, 10, 11; voidable marriage 3, 5, 8, 10, 11, 13

obstructive parents 141–3
occupation of the home 104–5; *see also* matrimonial home rights; occupation orders

occupation orders 105–7, 108–11, 117–19; ancillary orders 108, 111, 119; arrest, power of 104, 112; associated persons 105, 118; balance of harm test 105, 108, 110; and children 99; cohabitants 100, 106, 107, 112–13; entitled applicants 99–100, 101, 105, 106, 107, 108, 109, 112, 117; *ex parte* applications 100; length of 100, 106, 113; and matrimonial home rights 99, 101, 105, 107, 109, 111; non-entitled applicants 99–100, 101, 105, 106, 107, 109; and relevant child concept 105, 106, 110, 112; significant harm cases 99, 105, 107, 108, 110, 118

parental care, lack of 154, 155, 156, 157, 159, 163, 167, 168, 182, 191
parental control, children beyond 152, 154, 155, 156, 157, 159, 163, 167, 168, 182, 191
parental responsibility 121–5, 158, 159; and adoption 171, 172, 174, 180, 188; and child arrangement orders 122, 127, 148, 172, 178, 185, 188, 192; and child protection orders 122; and child's medical treatment 123, 125, 129; and child's name change 121, 180; definition of 129–30, 163; fathers 121, 124, 130; and female civil partners 122; local authorities 155, 156, 157, 160–1, 165, 167, 184, 192; married parents 121, 130; mothers 121, 124, 130; and the older child 121, 125, 130–3; presumption of parental involvement 128, 136, 140; and removing child from the jurisdiction 121; and special guardianship orders 172, 175, 178, 180, 185, 188, 192; step-parents 122; and surrogacy agreements 122; unmarried parents 121, 124; and welfare of the child 122, 123, 124, 138
parental responsibility orders 121, 122, 124, 186, 189
parents: biological 147, 148–9; local authority partnership with 151, 164; married 121, 130; obstructive 141–3; unmarried 121, 124; *see also* parental care; parental control; parental responsibility; step-parents
partnership with parents: local authorities 151, 164
pensions: and divorce 27–8, 31, 41, 48; splitting 48

placement orders 171, 182, 183–4, 190, 191–2; ending of 171; length of 171
police protection orders 151, *153*
polygamous marriage 5, 6, 10
pre-nuptial agreements 41, 52–7, 59, 63; and autonomy 56; children's welfare and enforceability of 56, 57, 59; as immoral and contrary to public policy 55, 59; independent legal advice and enforceability of 54, 56, 57, 59; refusal to apply 54, 55, 59
pregnancy 8; *per alium* 10, 34
prohibited steps orders 127, 130, 148, 149, 150
property 81–97; beneficial interest against third parties 87–90; beneficial interest or entitlement 81, 82, 83, 84–6, 90–7, 105, 109, 116; beneficial ownership 81, 83, 91, 95, 97; cohabitee beneficial interest 94–7, 99; common intention to share 81, 83, 86, 87, 88, 91, 92, 93, 96; contribution to improvement of 91, 92–3; detrimental reliance 81, 83, 87, 91, 94, 96; equal division of 41, 53, 57–9; gifts 88; gifts between engaged couples 82, 83–4; joint bank accounts 82, 83, 84; land ownership 81; matrimonial 53, 57, 58–9; matrimonial home 84–6, 87–94; matrimonial home rights 99, 101, 104–5, 107, 109, 112, 116, 117; occupation 89; orders for sale of 89–90, 93; property adjustment orders 73, 79; settlement of property order (Mesher order) 48, 63, 64, 65, 66; share ownership 83, 84; trusts 81, 83, 84, 85, 86, 87, 88, 91, 94, 96, 116
proprietary estoppel 81, 94, 95, 96

race: and adoption 171
religion: and divorce 28, 31, 32, 50
removal of a child from the jurisdiction 128, 180
residence: shared or transfer of 141, 142–3
residence orders 127, 130, 162; *see also* child arrangement orders
resulting trusts 81, 83, 87, 88, 92, 94, 95, 116

s8 orders 127, 129–33, 135, 175, 178, 181, 188, 192; prohibited steps orders 127, 130, 148, 149, 150; residence orders 127, 130, 162; specific issue orders 128, 130, 138, 140, 149, 150; *see also* child arrangement orders
same sex couples *see* homosexual and lesbian relationships
separation 23, 25; with consent 21, 29, 36, 37; judicial 32, 33, 34–5; without consent 21, 24, 29, 36, 37, 50
sexual abuse of children 143, 146, 155–6, 166, 191
sham marriage 3
share ownership 83, 84
shared residence 142–3
significant harm 151, 152; adoption orders 192; care orders 154, 155, 157, 159, 166, 167–8; child assessment orders 165; occupation orders 99, 105, 107, 108, 110, 118; placement orders 182, 184, 191; supervision orders 166; *see also* abuse of children
special guardianship orders: as alternative to adoption 172, 173, 175, 176, 177, 178, 179–81, 185, 187, 188, 190, 192; and child's name change 180; and parental responsibility 172, 175, 176, 178, 180, 185, 188, 192; and removal from the jurisdiction 180
specific issue orders 128, 130, 138, 140, 149, 150
State benefits 61–2, 70, 76
step-parents: and child maintenance 78; parental responsibility 122; and step-child relationships 5, 6–7
supervision orders 152, *153*, 154, 163, 166, 169
surname, child's change of 137, 138, 140, 146, 148, 149–50, 180
surrogacy agreements 122

threshold criteria: care orders 152, 154, 156, 157, 159, 167, 168, 169; supervision orders 163, 169
transsexuality: and marriage 3, 14–17
trusts: constructive 81, 84, 85, 86, 87, 88, 91, 92, 94, 95, 96, 116; express 81, 91, 94, 116; implied 81, 84, 85, 88, 91, 92, 94; resulting 81, 83, 87, 88, 92, 94, 95, 116

unsoundness of mind, voidable marriage 32, 34

venereal disease 34
void civil partnership 3, 12
void marriage 3, 5, 8, 10, 11, 15, 17, 33
voidable civil partnership 3, 12, 13

Index

voidable marriage 3, 5, 8, 10, 11, 13, 15–16, 32, 33; duress 3, 13, 34; lack of consent through mistake 32, 34; non-consummation 32, 33, 34; unsoundness of mind 32, 34

wardship 133, 166
welfare checklist: adoption 171, 173, 174, 176, 177, 183, 184, 187, 188, 190, 192; care orders 154, 158, 159, 163, 167, 168; child arrangement orders 129, 134, 137, 138, 139, 140, 144–5, 148, 161, 179; child protection 122, 151; s8 applications 128, 131; supervision orders 163

welfare of the child: and financial provision for adult partners 47, 48, 50, 56, 57, 58, 59, 60, 61; no delay principle 122, 129, 134, 137, 138, 144, 147, 154, 158, 163, 167; no order principle 122, 129, 134, 137, 138, 144, 147, 151, 154, 155, 158, 163, 167; and parental responsibility 122, 123, 124, 138; and special guardianship arrangements 179
welfare principle 151, 155; adoption 185, 191, 193; care orders 156, 158; child arrangement orders 135, 179; child protection 151